DATE DUE

HENRY MCBRIDE
SERIES IN
MODERNISM AND
MODERNITY

Eugene Jolas

Man from
Babel

**EDITED, ANNOTATED
AND INTRODUCED BY
ANDREAS KRAMER AND
RAINER RUMOLD**

Yale University Press

New Haven & London

This book has been published with assistance
from the fund for the Henry McBride Series in
Modernism and Modernity established by
Maximilian Miltzlaff.

07
by
n

by Tseng Information Systems, Inc., Durham,
North Carolina.
Printed in the United States of America
by Vail-Ballou Press, Binghamton, New York.
Library of Congress Cataloging-in-Publication
Data
Jolas, Eugene, 1894–1952.
Man from Babel / Eugene Jolas ; edited,
annotated, and introduced by Andreas Kramer
and Rainer Rumold.
    p.   cm. — (Henry McBride series in
modernism and modernity)
Includes index.
IBSN 0-300-07536-7
1. Jolas, Eugene, 1894–1952 — Biography.
2. Poets, American — 20th century — Biography.
3. Modernism (Literature) — United States.
4. Journalists — United States — Biography.
5. Translators — United States — Biography.
6. Editors — United States — Biography.
I. Kramer, Andreas.   II. Rumold, Rainer.
III. Title.   IV. Series.
PS3519.O33Z468   1998
811'.52 — dc21
[B]   98-6674
                 CIP
A catalogue record for this book is available
from the British Library.
The paper in this book meets the guidelines for
permanence and durability of the Committee on
Production Guidelines for Book Longevity of the
Council on Library Resources.

10 9 8 7 6 5 4 3 2 1

THE

HENRY McBRIDE

SERIES IN

MODERNISM AND

MODERNITY

The artistic movement known as modernism, which includes the historical avant-garde, produced the most radical and comprehensive change in
Western culture since Romanticism. Its effects reverberated through all
the arts, permanently altering their formal repertories and their relations
with society at large, and its products still surround us in our workplaces
and homes. Although modernism produced a pervasive cultural upheaval,
it can never be assessed as an artistic movement alone: its contours took
shape against the background of social, political, and intellectual change,
and it was always bound up with larger questions of modernity and mod-
ernization and with the intellectual challenge of sifting their meanings.

Henry McBride (1867-1962), who wrote weekly reviews of contemporary art for the New York *Sun* (1913–1950) and monthly essays for the *Dial*
(1920–1929), became perhaps the leading American critic to write percep-
tively and winningly on modern art. He discussed difficult artistic issues in
a relaxed, engaging, yet informed style, one that is still a model of clarity,
grace, and critical responsiveness. The Henry McBride Series in Modernism and Modernity, which focuses on modernism and the arts in their
many contexts, is respectfully dedicated to his memory.

CONTENTS

ILLUSTRATIONS

*We went to the Shakespeare Bookshop in the Rue de l'Odéon and asked
Sylvia Beach to speak in our favor to James Joyce. This she very kindly
did and within a few days, overjoyed, we held in our hands a bulky
manuscript bearing the title "Work in Progress."*

*One Sunday afternoon, at the end of 1926, Joyce invited Miss Beach,
Mlle. Monnier, Paul, Maria and myself to his home in the Square Robiac,
to listen to him read from the opening pages of his manuscript, which was
subsequently to appear in the first issue of transition.*

It might be said that Eugene Jolas owed much to the matchmaking skills of
Sylvia Beach: the association with Joyce, a recluse who admitted few into
his inner circle, helped launch *transition* and later establish it as an important, even legendary, publication. At his first meeting with James Joyce in
1924, Jolas had committed the faux pas of asking the author for a newspaper
interview (which was never granted); Sylvia Beach, meanwhile, was mo-
tioning covertly to her imprudent guest to desist. As a reporter, Jolas would,
in fact, never succeed in interviewing the author of *Finnegans Wake*, yet the
literary man Jolas, along with his wife, Maria, would become the closest
of friends with Joyce. Until now, literary posterity has hardly registered
Eugene Jolas's remarkable accomplishments. Apart from his action-packed
life as a journalist, he was a contemplative poet and a man of letters. The
events of his life made his writing of *Man from Babel,* from the 1940s until
his untimely death in 1952, a matter of personal urgency. The extremely belated initial publication of the work now, more than forty-five years after it
was written, may leave readers wondering why the solitary Joyce formed so
close an intellectual and personal bond with Jolas. Many will connect his
name with Joyce's, yet not realize that Jolas was an extraordinary talent in
his own right. He was the most successful editor of the international avant-
garde, a political journalist whose activities in post-war Germany led to the

establishment of a free democratic press there, a poet, and a critic of his time.

Eugene (or Eugène) Jolas was born in Union City, New Jersey, in 1894, the son of immigrant parents. His father, Pierre Eugène Jolas, was French; his mother, Christine Ambach, was born in the Rhineland; and the conflict between their languages and cultures would shape their son's life. When Eugene was two, the family returned to the town of Forbach in Lorraine, an area populated chiefly by native speakers of French, even though it had become a part of the German state in 1871 when Otto von Bismarck defeated Napoléon III. There, in a region characterized by two competing languages, French and German (or actually three, counting the regional patois), Eugene received his early education. Instruction at the local Catholic grammar school and, from 1906 to 1909, at the Catholic seminary in Montigny-Metz, was conducted in German. His Catholicism remained with him throughout his life, alternately sustaining and haunting him at critical junctures.

Amid growing political tensions between the French and German components of Alsace-Lorraine, young Jolas decided to return to America in 1909, not least because he wanted to avoid being drafted into the detested German army. His baggage was light — just a few belongings, topped off by the family violin. Substantial, though, was the cultural and political heritage he was to bring to America: his hatred of German authoritarianism and militarism on the one hand, and his veneration for German Romantic poetry (particularly that of Novalis) on the other. Jolas, an autodidact, had learned of Novalis's work from Ricarda Huch's influential *Die Romantik* (first published in 1899), which inaugurated a neo-Romantic fashion in German writing. When the European dreamer encountered the "American dream" as an adult, he awoke to more modernity than he had envisioned. Jolas's childhood daydreams of a primitive life remote from the decadence of Europe had been inspired by James Fenimore Cooper's Leatherstocking tales. At "home" again in the land of his birth, Jolas found the American social reality harsh but inspiring. In New York he witnessed a dynamic democracy at work, to which the most diverse ethnic groups had pledged allegiance. His was, after all, the typical ordeal of the immigrant. In the beginning he comfortably lodged with family, Uncle John and Aunt Theresa, but he quickly tired of their tutelage. His first job was as a delivery boy for "a surly North-German with a harsh accent" who owned a grocery store on Columbus Avenue. Young Jolas became streetwise, fighting it out with "a polyglot amalgam of pinched youngsters" for a wage of five dollars a week (Chapter 2). By comparison, his brother Jacques, who had followed him to New York, was already an accomplished pianist who easily found employment in the music scene of Manhattan and Brooklyn. Eugene began to acquire English informally on the streets, and soon, from 1910 to 1912, formally, at De Witt Clinton Evening High School (where he also learned Spanish). Yet the language of the spirit was still German for him; he continued to write neo-Romantic poems in German, with occasional lyrical forays into English. Simultaneously, he rigorously pursued the dream he had long harbored of becoming a journalist—the success story of Joseph Pulitzer had fired his imagination.

He managed to find his first job in Pittsburgh with a German-American daily, the *Volksblatt,* but soon grew aggressively discontented at being consigned to the backward-looking ethnic environment that he had hoped to leave behind. His transfer to the local *Post* as an "automobile reporter" meant that he had to move toward "belated Americanization of an American." In 1917, Jolas was drafted into the U.S. Army Medical Corps; he was stationed at Camp Lee, Virginia, and, after the armistice, at Fort Sheridan, Illinois, where he continued to work as a journalist, reporting for hospital and camp newspapers. These activities prepared him for tasks on a much larger scale during and after World War II: from 1942 to 1950, he would work for the U.S. Office of War Information and the Information Control Division in occupied Germany.

Jolas's encounters as a poet with American urban modernity produced a curious effect. He had to acquire a third language, in the beginning reminiscent of his parents' imperfect English. It is noteworthy that he learned English and the language of American poetry simultaneously yet separately from New York street slang. By contrast, multicultural conditions in the present-day United States allow the integration of major aspects of American experience into ethnic communal life and, conversely, admit some aspects of the ethnic experience into the American way of life. (Contrary to the former notion of a "melting pot," diversity is now in favor.) The "Spanglish" of the streets and of Latino or Chicano poetry, for example, is rooted in the speakers' language and culture of origin, as preserved within Latino ethnic communities in the United States. Jolas's later multilingual poetry, in which words from three languages were combined and fused in a single text (his Eur-American philology, as he called it in *Man from Babel*), was, however, a speculative, idealistic form of expression, a means of anticipating a transnational, transatlantic culture in the image of America.

As a young poet, Jolas perhaps saw New York City (the epitome of metropolitan modernity) through the eyes of the futurists, that is, in European aesthetic terms. The adolescent Jolas marveled at modern skyscrapers, at the "vertical reality" that he regarded as a mark of modern Romanticism. He admired the speed of cars, and movement, as a symbol of America's dynamism and forward-looking attitude. Always hungering for new words that would break through stereotypes, he developed a creative prose style—the hallmark of his autobiography—that somehow manages to uncover the present moment embedded in the past and recapture immediacy through retrospection.

Gradually, Jolas would become accepted as an American journalist. In fast-paced urban America, he began to consider himself part of the "advance-guard of a future journalism" (Chapter 3). He never really achieved the status as an American poet to which he had aspired from the time his first book of poetry, *Ink,* was published by Rhythmus Press in 1924. He received support and guidance from Louis Untermeyer and Frank Harris, among others (they themselves kept up with European culture and actively translated from European languages). A colleague of Jolas's at the *Chicago Tribune,* in reviewing his first collection of verse, described him as "a pioneer of American poetry": "If America is to have any poetry at all, it must grow on her own soil, and she must look for it from poets like Eugene Jolas, who have divined the secret of the 'true romance' hidden beneath the materialistic mask of American life."[1]

Jolas's pioneering role was, however, fraught with contradictions, as Sherwood Anderson would point out, more or less overtly, in his introduction to Jolas's next collection, *Cinema:* "Jolas is a poet feeling his way. The energy of America, the fast pace here, the growth and development of our industrial life, Pittsburgh, Chicago, the Kentucky Derby, the bootlegger, our skyscrapers, our great mills, the Ford. All these things excite and fascinate the man. He wants to be thought of as an American himself. Well, his heart is here."[2] And how could he have become an American poet, given that he considered poetic language to be not only a superior medium to everyday communication but the vessel for metaphysical experience?[3] Such views also estranged him from his fellow reporters, who quoted Walt Whitman's poetry to Jolas, while pointing to the American "bard's" poetic use of everyday words. Later, as editor of *transition,* Jolas could never attune himself to Gertrude Stein's "little household words" either (nor to her personality), though she, too, was experimenting with language and though in his journal he promoted her work as no other at the time did. Only occasionally would Jolas admit to himself the instability of his identity, which he nevertheless pronounced to be representative of the "post-Whitmanesque American":[4] "I was a Neo-American poet," he writes in *Man from Babel* (Chapter 8). Throughout his life, Jolas attempted to synthesize and unite experiences that, because they were essentially fragmented, were a source of conflict and suffering for him.

Even though *Man from Babel* apparently represents a link between his dual careers as a journalist and as a poet, Jolas was unable to resolve other fundamental dichotomies: he could never limit himself to a single language or country. Having successfully turned his back on German-language papers in America, he worked in the city-room or on the police beat for American papers such as the Savannah *Morning News,* the Waterbury *Republican,* and the New York *Daily News.* But his visits to Paris in 1923 and 1924 persuaded him to take a position with the Paris office of the *Chicago Tribune.* He started out as city-editor, applying American tabloid techniques. When Ford Madox Ford relinquished his literary column on the Parisian cultural scene, Jolas saw his chance. In 1924, he started his "Rambles Through Literary Paris," a column that brought him into close contact with the literary and artistic avant-garde community there. The "Rambles" were a truly astounding achievement for a self-taught literary critic: the blend of vivid, close-up, on-the-scene reporting of the "culture beat," Jolas's sure instinct for which of the many new movements and personalities were of lasting value, and his refined grasp of the artistic and intellectual issues were unparalleled.

After fifteen years of searching, Jolas had come into his own. Yet his *Wanderjahre* (educational travels) were not yet at an end. On 12 January 1926 he returned to New York City and married Maria McDonald. Born in Louisville, Kentucky, in 1893, she was a woman of considerable creative talent, a singer who had been trained in pre-war Berlin, New York, and Paris—the city where they met and "decided to get married almost immediately" (Chapter 5). Betsy, the first daughter, was born in 1926; a second daughter, Marie Christina (Tina), in 1929. Both daughters would have distinguished intellectual and artistic careers: Betsy became a composer of modernist music, Tina a translator of poetry.

Back in Paris, Jolas put the know-how gained through his "Rambles" to use in launching the greatest literary project and most enduring achievement of his life: the "little magazine" *transition.* His wife, too, has to be given credit for his success. Maria had developed her skills as a translator of the work of André Breton, Philippe Soupault, and many others. She also had a pragmatic turn of mind, as is attested by her contribution as secretary and chief correspondent in the conduct of the journal's affairs. *Transition* became a unique meeting ground for the most prominent members of the international avant-garde, among them James Joyce, Gertrude Stein, Samuel Beckett, Hans (Jean) Arp, André Breton, Carl Einstein (who served as liaison with other German Expressionists), and Gottfried Benn. Twenty-seven issues of the journal were published in Paris between 1927 and 1938; issues 24–26 were edited from New York in 1936–37. In addition to being a multilingual poet, critic, and editor, Jolas was also a pioneering translator: his and Maria's translations of Kafka's *The Judgment,* which they called *The Sentence* (1928), and *Metamorphosis* (1936–38) were the first in English; Jolas's powerful translation of Alfred Döblin's *Berlin Alexanderplatz* (1931) the first and only.[5] The purpose of the journal was primarily to introduce the Anglo-American world to European intellectual and artistic endeavors (to "bait the Babbitt with monstrous paradoxes" — Chapter 6) and to familiarize European readers with the work of American writers. Among his many achievements in that context, the serial publication of Joyce's *Finnegans Wake* constitutes a highlight.

Beyond that, *Man from Babel* will call renewed attention to the unique, although now of course dated, avant-garde project for modernity that informed all of Jolas's activities. In the course of his transatlantic travels during the period between the wars, Jolas became increasingly cognizant of the modern "malady of language" that had haunted Nietzsche and earlier the Romantics. He himself, in reflective moments, experienced it in quite a tangible way as a journalist.[6] He was beginning to believe in the supranational mission of the language of poetry; but his faith would be severely tested by the political upheaval of the times.

In the following pages we draw the reader's attention to four factors that were particularly important in the development of Jolas's thought and activities. First, of crucial significance for an understanding of the motivations underlying *transition* are Jolas's experiences in the conflict-ridden bi- or trilingual region of Alsace-Lorraine, where the struggle for political dominance expressed itself through the struggle for linguistic dominance. Second, Jolas's relationship with the Surrealists in Paris laid the groundwork for *transition*'s "Revolution of the Word." Third, a closer view of Jolas's relationship with Joyce will sharpen the intellectual profile he sketches in the autobiography. Fourth, we shall focus on Jolas's activities in post-war Germany, which were a significant contribution to the American denazification of the German press and intelligentsia.

Jolas and the Rise of the Avant-Garde: From Region to Metropolis

To fully understand Jolas's motivations in launching *transition* as a bridge for and bridgehead of the international avant-garde, we need to return to Jolas's account of his experiences in Alsace-Lorraine, a region dominated by linguistic conflict. Jolas's "father-tongue" was French, and his mother spoke to him in the "peculiar amalgam of the speech of her Rhineland youth and Lorraine and Alsatian locutions intertwisted with American phrases," [7] yet Jolas wrote his poems in High German, even those published in magazines and newspapers in Lorraine. [8]

His experience in the borderland of Alsace-Lorraine made Jolas realize that the god of modernity, nationalism, was inadequate for people wishing to make sense of everyday life. [9] As a consequence, he came to favor a nonideological regionalism. The problem, however, is that Jolas's regional loyalties were split between a sympathy for the French political cause and an affinity for German culture. Unambiguous, however, is his negative reaction in *Man from Babel* to the vast political power and military uniformity of the German bureaucracy in the border area after 1870, as well as to the German attempt to impose a monolingual culture on the multilingual region, a "veritable linguistic melting-pot" (Chapter 1).

In addition, Jolas, whose Catholicism had been reinforced at home and in school, was bound to oppose Prussian Protestantism. But he tended, as did Catholic France as a whole at that time, to regard regional customs as a viable form of opposition to rising French secular centralism. Thus, Jolas's regionalism corresponds to and yet distinguishes itself from such provincial French cultural movements as the aggressive Alsace-Lorraine nationalism of Maurice Barrès and his *confrères* (who resented the German military success) or the Breton or Provençal revivals around 1900 (which in turn were a reaction to the drastic expansion of French culture after 1870). Jolas admired Barrès's novels "with their moving, romantic evocations of the Metz of another epoch" [10] and apparently accepted the ideology expressed in these books, according to which some form of evil modernity—a centralized bureaucratic state, the exploitative capitalist economy, or decadent metropolitan life—would inevitably uproot regional cultures and destroy the good old-fashioned values connected with the "earth." The autobiography makes no mention of Barrès's longstanding involvement in a brand of right-wing politics that blended authoritarianism, republicanism, anti-Semitism, and anticapitalism.

Jolas's romantic regionalism was compatible with the universalist conception of modernity that he had begun to develop in the early 1920s, after his return to Lorraine. In Strasbourg he witnessed and participated in efforts to create a supranational artistic community in a climate of international reconciliation. His experience with the group l'Arc (the Bridge), led by Henri Solveen, was crucial: Jolas, who contributed to the circle's publications in German, French, and English, felt at home there as a poet and a journalist, and the experience set him to thinking about founding a magazine of his own, which was to become *transition*. In *Man from Babel* he presents *transition* as having grown directly out of his involvement with Henri Solveen's "Bridgemen," who sought to reconcile regional linguistic differences and achieve artistic unity. *Transition* was to become another "bridge" on a global scale, in a world where regions had become continents. Its aim was to present "the spirit of various continents to the English-speaking world"[11] and to foster an "esthetic synthetism" to which not only Europe and Asia but also the Americas would bring their vision (*transition* 9 [1927], 191). In his later trilingual and multilingual poetry Jolas would include esoteric linguistic elements, in a (not always successful) effort to construct such a "synthetist" language, of which Joyce's *Finnegans Wake* would become the most memorable modernist example.

Jolas's aesthetic utopianism, like that of all avant-gardists, is never really apolitical. His notion of modernity seeks to correct the flaws of the two master narratives of modernity—nationalism and capitalism, which lead to centralization, standardization, and the leveling of differences. The man from Lorraine insists on "a supra-national conception which reveres and protects the indigenous and the individual, which welcomes the vigor of the primitive and appreciates the refinement of high civilization."[12] Hence *transition*'s political mission: "We consider the increasing tendency toward centralisation, both in the economic and political sphere, dangerous, unless curbed by a regional consciousness." In short, the sense of the indigenous remains a "catapulting force." With regard to America, he regretted seeing "how the regional particularities are being destroyed," feared mass consciousness, and worried that life in general would become gray, monotonous, and uniform.[13]

For a brief time only, Jolas was expressly receptive to leftist ideas. Writing passionately about the "lot of the worker" in America and Europe, he envisaged the possibility of a kinder, gentler capitalism that would work for the masses, or even a mass-based "communistic capitalism"—a merging of capitalism and communism. Jolas saw some benefit in the experiments of Soviet literature as the "first definite attempt to create a collective expression."[14] Subsequently, inspired by the avant-garde's ethnological turn, Jolas was to put the emphasis on the idea of a prerational, mythical collective. The Revolution of the Word announced in *transition* 16–17 (June 1929) was meant as a "complete metamorphosis of the world" that is an act of aesthetic autonomy which derives from the individual's creativity and therefore transcends any political or religious dogmatism.

Jolas's Revolution of the Word and Surrealism

Jolas first heard about Surrealism in Strasbourg in 1923 through his friend Marcel Noll, later director of the Galérie Surréaliste, and Noll's friends Breton and Eluard, who "frequently visited Strasbourg during that period, because the city seemed to them a symbol of the romantic outlook they were then seeking."[15] Later still, Jolas described Surrealism as a phenomenon "that seemed to me more Celtic than Latin" — in other words, more Romantic than classical, more German than French. It was the heir of Novalis, Jean Paul, and Achim von Arnim, "who gave the surrealists of the early period their direction."[16] What interested Jolas about Surrealism was its exploration of the collective unconscious.

Initially, his sympathies lay with the (short-lived) form of Surrealism propounded by his Alsatian friend, Yvan Goll, for Jolas saw it as a constructive approach to found an international movement that might be aligned with a global revolution in literature and the arts. Only in early 1925 did Jolas come to appreciate Breton's brand of Surrealism. His interview with Breton, published in the "Rambles" of 5 July 1925, is proof that he gained access to the Surrealists' inner circle.[17] Jolas's autobiography leaves no doubt that he admired Breton's creativity, intellectual abilities, leadership, and provocative élan. It is believable that one day he announced to Maria that he had "almost signed up,"[18] "swept into the Surrealist avalanche" (Chapter 6); yet his editorials and articles show that he maintained his intellectual independence from the main Surrealist camp.

Of course, *transition* did publish important Surrealist work, so much, indeed, that it was known as the American Surrealist Review.[19] The apolitical, purely aesthetic *Commerce,* however, was to become more important to Jolas than *La Révolution Surréaliste* ("the world's most scandalous review" — see Chapter 5) and its political agenda: "The *early* surrealists and ourselves [at *transition*] were undoubtedly fellow-travellers."[20] Characteristically, Jolas would emphasize the anti-ideological primacy of poetry: "Poetry in itself is a revolt."[21] Hence his preference for Surrealist poets such as Paul Eluard (who was to become his friend and introduce him to Surrealist circles), Robert Desnos, Philippe Soupault, and Léon-Paul Fargue, all of whom he translated into English. Unlike many of the Surrealists, Jolas was not interested in Breton's antiliterary posturing; rather, he was interested in creative writing as an art form. That is why he grew more and more unsympathetic to Breton's fascination with automatic writing, which Jolas, Noll, and Schickele had tried out in Strasbourg in 1923, writing trilingual *poèmes en commun,*[22] and which Jolas had for a while appreciated as "a method worthy of the age of psychoanalysis" (Chapter 6).

Although he continued to frequent Surrealist circles until 1930, he broke with the ideology of the movement "when Breton and Eluard abandoned their high idealist conception for a communist interpretation of life."[23] Jolas remains silent on that score in *Man from Babel*, but his Surrealist sympathies and the Surrealist flirtation with communism gave *transition*'s critics plenty of opportunity to attack Jolas's politics. To Michael Gold on the left, political principle was being dominated by a playful aestheticism that smacked of bourgeois decadence.[24] And Malcolm Cowley as well as Matthew Josephson (who had translated much post-Dadaist French writing into English in the early 1920s) abandoned their Surrealist sympathies in favor of the proletarian realism that Jolas hated so much. To the British writer Wyndham Lewis on the right, *transition* was avant-gardistic in intent but blind to Surrealism's communist leanings, as "The Enemy" made more than clear in his books *Time and Western Man* and *The Diabolical Principle*.

Jolas objected to any totalitarian implications that might attach to his fascination with "mythos," and like many intellectuals of his day, he strove to re-evaluate collective experience as that of "a community of spirits who aim at the construction of a new mythological reality."[25] Under the increasing pressure of the "mythological realities" of communism and fascism, however, Jolas sought refuge in a philosophy of language ultimately rooted in a vatic, quasi-religious view. Hence he grew "tired of playing with anarchic words that brought only the incantatory sterility of estheticism"; he discovered "verticalism" under the inspiration of his reading of the mystic St. John of the Cross.[26]

The growing distance from Breton is also exemplified by Jolas's choice of a "white" romanticism inspired by Novalis and centering on the idea of verticalism. He charged the Surrealists with promoting a "black" romanticism, which to him meant more than an interest in the Gothic writing of historical Romantics: it included, first, the strong religious indictment "that Surrealism was a doctrine of satanic inspiration"[27] and, second, the charge that the Surrealists' attitude toward fascism was inspired by pure demonology rather than active resistance.[28]

Jolas's was a unique contribution to the ongoing, intense debate between Marxists and modernists, at the heart of which lay divergent ideas about language and writing. Beyond historical interest, little about the Revolution of the Word could stir us any more. But it is this very historical interest that makes us aware of how distanced we are from Jolas's project and the emotions and visions of his day, and how seriously the poetic attack on representation was taken by all involved, friend or foe. It is easy to see why the modernist position irritated avowed Marxists, and perhaps not surprising that Jolas's excursion into the "collective" mind was condemned by many, among them a British commentator who detected "a strong near-fascist flavour about Jolas'[s] julep" and argued that Jolas wanted to "chuck reason and intellect overboard and line up with the very discreditable emotion-mongers of Nazi 'paganism.' "[29]

The "Joyous Click"

The story of Jolas's friendship with James Joyce is told with warmth and affection, beginning with Joyce's reading from "Work in Progress" in December 1926 and ending with the drama of 1940, when Maria Jolas helped the Joyce family flee from Paris to Vichy and eventually to Switzerland. But the story transcends the friendship; Jolas's personal linguistic quest enables him to emphasize, and empathize with, Joyce's reactions to leftist attacks on his work, particularly on *Finnegans Wake*.

Joyce welcomed both the support and encouragement of "his editors," Eugene and Maria Jolas and Elliot Paul, the "joyous click" — whose enthusiasm withstood even his endless additions to the "final" proofs — and the defense that the work received in the pages of *transition*. Jolas's keen sense for verbal experimentation led him to see Joyce's "Work in Progress" as a landmark document in his Revolution of the Word and in the agenda for *transition*.[30] In praising Joyce, this astute exponent of the avant-garde recognizes that the radical disintegration of the normative word and its meaning are central to "Work in Progress," and he further accepts that the word itself was the real "metaphysical problem of the day."[31] Indeed, Jolas celebrates Joyce's text as "the most important contribution to modern mythology and philology in our time."[32] For the man from Babel, "Work in Progress" was the principal text of the avant-garde, the unsurpassed exemplar of the "Language of the Night" whose mingling of archaic and modern, individual and universal experience was central to the mythological preoccupation of Jolas's own poetics. As Joyce would say about his own writing: "It is not I who am writing this crazy book. It is you and you and you and that girl over there and that man in the corner" (Chapter 9).

After his public rejection of the Surrealists, Jolas was able to devote his full critical attention to the aesthetic attempt to define modernity — and to Joyce. In his article about Joyce the "myth-maker" in *transition* 27, Jolas's attempts to ethnologize the "mythos" come to fruition. In Jung's writings Jolas found the metaphysics he had sought in vain in Freud's work. Through the notion of archetypes, Jung had found a way to link individual images, symbols, and myths with the universal. The approach made it possible to shift the attention from the personal to the collective unconscious, assumed to be common to all cultures and capable of revitalizing both the individual and the collective.

Jolas found such collective images already inscribed in Joyce's text, that is, in its style *and* subject matter, in its language. In so doing, Jolas may have been "out-Junging" Joyce, who did not think much of the Swiss "Reverend." But on these grounds Jolas managed to develop a reading of "Work in Progress" that fit the author's method of writing.[33] Joyce always maintained that *Finnegans Wake* was a book primarily about the night, "a nocturnal state, lunar,"[34] and stressed his intention "to reconstruct the nocturnal life."[35] The subject, as Jolas read the work, required the systematic "darkening" of each and every term.

After Joyce's death in 1941, Jolas reinforced the pan-romantic view that caused him to draw a more or less straight line from Novalis to the Irish writer: "Joyce was consciously searching for the language of the night. While Novalis, in his Romantic-Symbolist novel *Heinrich von Ofterdingen*, which begins with a dream and ends in the unconscious, writes in the language of the day, Joyce, whose universal conception manifests certain similarities with the mythological tale of the Romantic writer, wants to find a new medium for the dynamic of the irrational."[36]

In other words, Jolas's key witness remains Novalis, the poet dedicated "to the resurrection of the golden age that existed before Babel" through the conscious cultivation and heightening of interiority that would make it possible to penetrate, illuminate, and integrate the irrational nocturnal world of the dream and the unconscious.[37] So grand a vision of the redemption of modernity determines Jolas's outlook that the very title of his journal, *transition,* reflects the Romantic "notion of transition from one plane of human evolution to another."[38]

His faith in the power of the word and in the creative spirit of the international avant-garde, which Joyce's work exemplified, made Jolas the movement's most effective editor. In the "heroic" phases of Expressionism, Italian futurism, and Surrealism, adherents shared a faith in the power of their subversive discourses to realize the goals of universal, collective experience. Rather than break with the Romantic tradition, however, as Dada and futurism stipulated, Jolas resolutely advocated retaining idealism as an essential element of the modern experience.[39] As if oblivious to the realities of the war, he steadfastly asserted, as late as 1941: "I wanted to make *transition* an organ for a modern pan-romantic revolution."[40] He clearly regards twentieth-century avant-garde movements first and foremost as efforts to establish a new mythology for the modern world. Jolas's understanding of the avant-garde thus runs counter to the Dadaists and Surrealists' own professed antipathy to idealism and to art, as it does to Walter Benjamin's contemporaneous embrace of Surrealism and condemnation of Expressionist idealism. Jolas's aggressive rejection of Marxist thinking sprang from two widely divergent sources: first, his spiritual affinity with German idealism, and second, his experience of modern capitalist Fordist America. Both helped shape Jolas's adamant personal commitment to fight against Nazism and his condemnation of Soviet totalitarianism in the last two decades of his life.

The "Culture-Bearer" of Democracy in Post-War Germany

Jolas wrote, in "To My Mother Engulfed in the War" (Chapter 10):

Hitler is Daniel's beast with the iron teeth
He is the raucous voice smattering lies
But do not be afraid in the panting nocturne
The evangel of the angels wakes and is ready to strike

Among the Jolas papers in the Beinecke Library at Yale one can find a bizarre, even surrealistic, montage in the form of a greatly oversized greeting card. On it, Jolas is pictured as a white knight charging the dragons and demons of the evil realm that separated the German people from the rest of the world. It was signed and presented to him by his staff in 1946 when he left his post as editor-in-chief at the Deutsche Allgemeine Nachrichten-Agentur (DANA) in Bad Nauheim.[41]

In the ferocious battle against Nazism, Jolas was able to unite his vision of the liberating artistic revolt of the international avant-garde with the pragmatic ethos of the American journalist. The member of the Psychological Warfare Division landed at Utah Beach behind the invading troops and arrived, a militant moral force, in defeated Germany, by way of France and Luxembourg. Having long regarded political conflict as linguistic war, Jolas views himself as a reporter-warrior in a "savage war of words": "In the war's inferno these words crashed, blasted, strafed, pounded, shelled, roared, wept and shrieked in my inner ear, now in French, now in English, now in German"; his task is to make words "explosive as rockets against the Axis war machine" (Chapter 10). His self-avowed mission is to eradicate the Nazi phrases and slogans, so representative of that warped mentality, as a cancerous outgrowth of the modern "malady of language." Clearly, even this press officer in action had not freed himself from his Romantic legacy—hence a certain self-aggrandizement reminiscent of the avant-garde's self-centered posturing. In a draft version of a prologue to his autobiography Jolas would write: "Yes, I am an American press officer. I think and write in German like a mythical 'culture-bearer' to a people who have just passed through the Hitlerian night and who are still sick in heart and mind. I am engaged in a supreme adventure, in a Gutenbergian rite, that is rooted in the magical forces of language."

At this point in his career Jolas saw himself as a culture-bearer (*Kulturträger*) charged with the task of defending the Occident. "Whatever holocaust may be in store for us, in this era of hydrogenic tremors and panic, we newsmen must go on, reporting the Kinesis of life, feeling our way through the dark labyrinth, always a pilgrim to the sacred logos."

With regard to the practical side of his assignment in Germany, Jolas sought out anti-Nazi printers and editorial assistants from the population, or trained very young Germans from scratch, when the *Aachener Nachrichten* was revamped in January 1945 as the first democratic paper in postwar Germany. Jolas struggled to replace the traditional German commentary style and *feuilletons* ("journalistic poison"), massively abused under the Nazis, with American-style reporting of objective facts. Only Theodor Heuss, then co-editor of the *Rhein-Neckar Zeitung* in Heidelberg (and later the first president of the West German Federal Republic), seems to have supported Jolas's point of view at the first German journalistic congress in Marburg. Jolas's activities led to the establishment of the Deutsche Allgemeine Nachrichten-Agentur (DANA) in Bad Nauheim in September 1945 and to the founding of a school of journalism there. DANA was later to become the dpa (Deutsche Presse-Agentur), synonymous with the German press. In April 1946 Jolas received the Medal of Freedom from the Military Government for Germany in recognition of his war-time and post-war services.

His varied and extremely effectual efforts to build a new democratic press and foster democratic awareness in post-war Germany included the creation of a "think paper," *Die Wandlung* (transformation), its title recalling a key tenet of the Expressionist movement in the teens. The journal produced thirty-seven issues between October 1945 and December 1949 and had a circulation of forty thousand. The autobiography compresses the several years of denazification efforts, whose complexity is documented in the archival material. In particular, the archives contain Jolas's extensive correspondence. His letters to the U.S. Military Government regarding the establishment of a school of journalism and of a high-caliber journal discuss the aim of promoting the re-education of German intellectuals. His minutes of interviews with prospective contributors and DANA journalists probe deeply into the candidates' intellectual and political past.

In letters to Dolf Sternberger, who was his first choice for editor-in-chief of *Die Wandlung*, Jolas sets forth the goals of the publication. He recommends the organized debunking of Nazi terms such as *Führer, Einsatz* (the unquestioning accomplishment of a mission), *Betreuung* (taking care of, which became a perverse euphemism for "finishing off," in the case of Jews and communists, for example). Sternberger instituted a column in *Die Wandlung* exposing the sordid reality behind such euphemisms and later collected the individual glosses in a *Wörterbuch des Unmenschen* (Dictionary of the monster).[42]

For Jolas, there was only one question: whether a society allows both the individual and the collective the free use of language, and access to its boundless creativity. At the same time, his four-page biweekly *Mitteilungen* from Heidelberg provided concrete accounts, together with photographic documents from the concentration camps, of the suffering of the German Jews. Jolas had also two large wall posters printed, with texts and photographs assigning guilt to the German nation, forty thousand copies of which were distributed throughout the country. He writes in *Man from Babel* in connection with the German people's very mixed reaction to the revelation of their crimes, "I felt ashamed of the German blood in my veins" (Chapter 11). The themes and topics of *Die Wandlung* were selected with the closest attention to important events such as the Nuremberg war crimes trials. Jolas attended the trials every other week as part of his duties at DANA, in order to furnish Sternberger with first-hand documentation for *Die Wandlung*. In addition to supplying timely, concrete details about current events and the immediate past, the think paper delved into the question of individual and collective German guilt, in more abstract discussions (on the model of Karl Jaspers's *Die Schuldfrage*, 1946) by such leading intellectuals as Sternberger, Hannah Arendt, and Marie Luise Kaschnitz.

Bringing the philosopher Karl Jaspers onto the editorial board of *Die Wandlung* was a major coup for Jolas. Jolas, whose previous interest in Heidegger had soured,[43] was apparently attempting to forge an elitist common front between a moral existentialist mentality, modernism, and democratic thought. The publication of Sternberger's translation of T. S. Eliot's *East Coker* and Wilhelm Hausenstein's translation of Arthur Rimbaud's *Bateau ivre* attest to this aim; other articles established a transatlantic connection with the American democratic experience.[44]

The autobiography also traces another story, that of the historical and problematic link between Romanticism and German politics. Jolas had not considered their interrelatedness until his return to Germany in 1945, but once given responsibility for the denazification and re-education of the German intelligentsia, he began to review the work of his favorite

Romantics, including the "gentle Novalis." He soon discerned in their proclamations of a German national identity and of Germany's superiority over its neighbors a clue to the sources of Nazi ideology. An unpublished essay, "Romanticism and Metapolitics," amplifies one theme of the autobiography:

> When, at the close of World War II, members of the Allied Psychological Warfare Division undertook to denazify and democratize German intellectual life, they were obliged to face the fact that certain elements of Nazi "ideology" had undoubtedly been rooted in romanticist currents of over 150 years before. Many of the Nazi documents found revealed a parallelism between the murderous tenets of the Hitlerian usurpers and those professed by the poets and philosophers of what had been one of the richest periods in any modern literature. Liberation of the concentration camps was to uncover further horrible evidence of what long fermentation of the seemingly innocuous utterances of that time had done to the German spirit. The fates of millions of human beings tortured and massacred in the name of Teutonic supremacy were shown to have been linked to that older epoch when, traditionally, an elegiac idealism was to have prevailed.[45]

Jolas's metaphysical temperament had long precluded any critical insight into the relation between culture and politics. He experienced "a sense of betrayal" when he realized how "those . . . who loved poetry and the manifestations of a star-hungry humanism" had failed to react to "the collective sadism which the descendants of the Romantics had demonstrated with such unbelievable violence." In the light of recent events, he now becomes aware that "biological racism, anti-Semitism, aggressive nationalism were all detectable to a greater or lesser degree" in the works of many Romantic writers such as Arnim and Görres, or of thinkers such as Herder and Fichte.[46] Even in the shock of that recognition, though, Jolas maintained his quasi-religious belief in "white" romanticism and modernism.

His enthusiasms had also blinded him to the "dark" side of modernism. In particular, he had a weakness for Gottfried Benn's pseudo-anthropological valorization of the archaic elements of creativity. In fact, at the expense of achieving a balanced critical approach to the age of technology, Jolas was never to renounce his infatuation with the archaic.[47] In the final issues of *transition*, he omitted any reference to Benn, who in his 1933–34 essays on art and culture (though not in his poetry) had unreservedly embraced the ideology of National Socialism. Jolas's admiration for him had been kindled by Benn's "The Island" and "The Birthday" (which Jolas translated in *transition* 2 and 5 [1927] respectively). They were part of a cycle of short experimental prose written in 1914–17, which in many ways anticipated Surrealist writing techniques. Jolas's translations were accompanied by a short essay, "Gottfried Benn" (*transition* 5). In "A Review" (*transition* 12, 1928, p. 142), reflecting on the achievements and direction of the first year of the journal, Jolas referred and deferred to Benn's influence: "With Dr. Benn, we persist in asking for the metaphysical man"; and as late as 1935, Jolas had made contact with the German poet in order to glean his views for "Inquiry into the Malady of Language." [48] Retrospectively in the autobiography, however, Jolas recasts his personal encounter with Benn during a visit to Berlin during the winter of 1929–30 in a much more critical tone. His friend Carl Einstein had urged him to visit the German capital: it might be his last chance to meet the Expressionists he had translated, among them Döblin and the playwright Carl Sternheim. On that occasion Jolas, though he could not suppress his fascination with the poet, was dismayed by Benn's barely concealed fascist convictions.

The man from Lorraine fought the enslavement of language by nationalism once again in post-war Germany. He continued to see conflicts between human beings primarily as linguistic conflicts and misunderstandings. His call to engage in the "war of words" goes beyond mere propaganda and has a deeply felt metaphysical basis. The themes of battle and conflict inform *Man from Babel* from beginning to end. In this spirit Jolas speculates in the epilogue to *Man from Babel*: "Why should language not be channeled into a universal idiom? Seven years ago I called this potential tongue Atlantica, because I felt that it might bridge the continents and neutralize the curse of Babel." This "atlantic" language, reminiscent of the utopias of Plato, Bacon, Novalis, and Hoffmann, would be the medium for the realization of a universal democratic potential.[49] In that spirit, Jolas advocated a "modern revaluation of Novalis's magic idealism." [50]

Strangely enough, only in post-war Germany was Jolas everything he had ever been, rolled into one. He was the man from "America Mystica" of his multilingual poetry; he was the transatlantic liberator, come to expose the evil of German totalitarianism, which has once more suppressed and divided his "borderland" Lorraine; and he was the speculative romantic attempting to synthesize the fragments of modernity into a higher universal language grounded in aesthetic as well as moral commitment.

All things considered, the account of Jolas's life retains throughout a unique, if problematic, blend of German romanticism and American optimism. For the Anglo-American audience, *Man from Babel* will contribute to the ongoing reappraisal of the era of the international avant-garde. Just as *transition* was a "kind of higher journalism" for its editor, his auto-biography constitutes a rare hybrid between the Surrealist vision and the reporter's working perspective on the often sensationalized activities of American exiles in Paris. As far as Jolas's personal outlook and work are concerned, the negative myth of loss (the "lost generation," in Gertrude Stein's words to Hemingway) is transformed into one of the search for renewal and redemption. For historians and literary scholars, the memoir offers a plethora of authentic details about Joyce's work, Surrealism and its reception before it became fashionable in New York, and the relations between the Expressionists and Jolas's circle. Beyond that, the timeliness of *Man from Babel* lies in its contribution to our understanding of the historical avant-garde. In the metamorphosis of the movement from the counter-culture of the interwar period to the quasi-official culture of a free world engaged in the confrontational politics of the Cold War, Jolas was an active, if somewhat naive, player. This critical chapter in the rise of the avant-garde is still little known by comparison with the legendary decades of the teens and 1920s.

For German readers, Jolas's autobiography will point up the complications and pitfalls of a metaphysical Weltanschauung, even as it bears witness to the promises and achievements of a belief in *Geist* and *Kultur*. Of particular significance are the chapters on post-war Germany. Jolas understood the concentration camps and the Holocaust to be the consequence of an authoritarian nationalist and racist mentality that compelled the populace either to participate with conviction in genocide or to endorse it passively, rather than to offer collective resistance to it. His analysis is especially timely in view of the current debate over the findings and assessments of historians such as Christopher Browning and Daniel Goldhagen. Those who would insist on the conditions exculpating the German people under the Nazi dictatorship will be put to shame by the "apolitical" Joyce's humble assessment of his own situation and conduct in occupied France: "What can an individual do in times like these? I think he can only help personally those who are threatened" (Chapter 9).

Voices like Jolas's may indeed be crucial to our reassessment of the moral, intellectual, and political climate of post-war Germany. His appraisal differs markedly from the convenient image many German intellectuals have advanced of post-war German writers' critical incisiveness. A case in point, often cited, is Gruppe 47, convened under the leadership of Hans Werner Richter to protest U.S. Cold War intervention in 1947 into the leftist editorial views expressed in the Munich-based journal *Der Ruf*. By contrast,

Jolas writes about the equivocal stance taken by German intellectuals and writers during a congress at Point Zero, in the first hour of post-war German literature: "With a few notable exceptions, their utterances were pompous, hollow and full of resentment against the occupational powers. I heard not a single admission of Germany's guilt. In the verbose and often puerile discourses there was no intercontinental perspective, only a narrow Teutonic self-sufficiency and insistence on a resurgent nationalism."[51]

Jolas takes to task such conservative writers as Rudolf Alexander Schröder and Ernst Jünger, the "arch-militarist" subsequently awarded the Goethe Prize and officially honored on his centenary in March 1995. By contrast, Jolas holds up as an example Fritz von Unruh, the playwright who returned to Germany after the war from exile in America. Quite typically, he singles out as Unruh's heritage "the international humanism which marked the Expressionist era" and praises his speech at a writers' congress in 1948 as having evoked "a democratic consciousness" that "shook his listeners with a masterful exposé of Hitler's crimes against the spirit."[52]

It is no accident, then, that Jolas mistrusted the "strongly anti-romantic" and "bloody realism" of Hans Werner Richter and his group. Predictably, his sympathies lay with the "spiritual" writers who practiced "a synthesis of Expressionism and Surrealism, and emphasized the metamorphosis of the narratives into fables and magic tales of terror."[53] Except for those, however, he finds the "ferment and audacity" of French, English, or American writing to be lacking in German literature. In his view, a tired "classicism, neo-Romanticism and apocalyptism" dominate the work of writers such as Werner Bergengruen or Hans Carossa.[54] Although we may no longer share Jolas's spiritual criteria, we can recognize his keen sense for real deficiencies. He points out the tendency of West German writers to dwell more on the individual victim or outsider, the individual "good" German, than on the losses of other people or ethnic groups, and he remarks on the absence in post-war German literature of the theme of freedom: "We know that during the war there was hardly any literature of resistance inside Germany against Hitler and that, with the exception of Munich, there was no intellectual underground that expressed itself in creative work against Nazi sadism. Is it therefore to be wondered that the theme of the age-old struggle for freedom is hardly noticeable in contemporary German letters? In talking to German writers one found a pathological self-pity" (Chapter 12).

The primary significance of Jolas's account of the interwar avant-garde for our current debates about the function of art and literature may be the necessity for a re-evaluation of the moral dimension of modernism, which has long been sidetracked in favor of aesthetic and formal concerns. The Surrealist Philippe Soupault, Jolas's friend since the early 1920s, hinted at that necessity in a 1958 eulogy of Jolas. As a poet and critic of his times, said Soupault, Jolas possessed a moral imagination that identified aesthetics with ethics—a positive legacy of German Romanticism. Soupault went on to describe him as

> the most honest—I would say, the most hopelessly honest—human being who has lived in our age. If one recalls his nature, it is not surprising that the predominant memory of Eugene is that of a man full of wrath. His revolt was pure and genuine. He did not tolerate any compromise. . . . He was the contrary of a cheater. Even the cheaters he did not cheat. . . . Like Arthur Rimbaud, he viewed his poetry as a derailment of the senses, but also as his refuge. With constancy he searched to give the poet new powers. Now, in 1958, can we assess what a gigantic role he gave himself: he wanted to be the liberator of language.[55]

Jolas's insight into the avant-garde still represents a timely contribution to the contemporary debate. Most accounts stress the cosmopolitanism and internationalism of the modernist movement and present the metropolis as the key factor in avant-garde culture. *Man from Babel* offers a reminder that aspects of modernism were in fact fueled by popular and provincial energies. Many, if not most, of the modernists came from the outskirts of metropolitan culture. The well-documented modernist interest in primitivism and the repeated calls for a new barbarism should be reconsidered in the context of that provincialism.[56]

Jolas's personal hinterland was also the point of contact between two or more languages. Our conceptions are reshaped by writers with an acutely developed awareness of language and languages—Eugene Jolas, René Schickele, Jean Arp, and Yvan and Claire Goll among them: in the modern world, monolingualism and monoculturalism are the exception rather than the rule. Regionalism was more to Jolas than an individual influence. Much of what he had to say about local "mythologies" now forms part, in the modern literary disciplines, of the great post-colonial effort to correct the shortcomings of the Western nationalist conception of modernism.

Jolas's self-image as a man from Babel is both a sincere perception and the product of a unifying stylization. *Man from Babel*, whose author "seeks through linguistic, psychological and philosophical struggles an Occidental unity in himself and the world around him; who believes that the Occident is One, and that America represents the hope for a synthesis of races and languages," may indeed be telling us as much about the contradictory nature of modernist and avant-garde writing, its visions and hopes in an era of world wars, revolutions, and totalitarianism, as it does about its author.[57]

ACKNOWLEDGMENTS

The editors would like to express their gratitude to friends and colleagues for their interest in and support of this project. Our first acknowledgment is to Maria Jolas, who initially brought the existence of her husband's unpublished autobiographical writings to Rainer Rumold's attention while he was doing research in Paris in the early 1980s. Their daughters, Betsy and Tina Jolas, have supplied us with numerous materials, including alternative drafts and most of the photos reprinted here, and last but not least with valuable information concerning Eugene Jolas and his innumerable acquaintances in France and the United States. Christine Froula and Marcia Gealy of Northwestern University, Reinhold Grimm of the University of California at Riverside, Klaus Kiefer of Bayreuth University, John McCarron of the *Chicago Tribune,* Gerald Mead of Northwestern University, and Marjorie Perloff of Stanford University have given us valued opinions about one or another aspect of the edition. Special thanks go to Lawrence Rainey of the University of York, whose expertise in avant-garde and modernist studies has greatly contributed to the progress of the project. Thanks go also to Vincent Giroud, curator at Yale University's Beinecke Rare Book and Manuscript Library, and the members of his staff. Our research was supported by an ACLS–DAAD stipend (1993–94), one of the first transatlantic Collaborative Research Grants, and by the College of Arts and Sciences, Northwestern University.

NOTE ON THE TEXT

Maria Jolas, who collaborated with Eugene Jolas in writing his autobiography, noted that the work was "started in German — dictated to me — in late 1941."[1] In fact, however, Jolas had begun work on an autobiography sometime in the 1930s, for already in 1939 an American critic quoted from an "as yet unfinished" manuscript entitled "Frontier-Man."[2] One excerpt from the manuscript, "Surrealism: Ave atque Vale," was published as an article in the little magazine *Fantasy* in January 1941. In a note, the editor, Stanley Dehler Mayer, announced "an autobiography which is to be not a mere anecdotal narrative, but a panorama of an often amazing period in its intellectual and spiritual quests."[3] Another excerpt appeared as "My Friend James Joyce" in the *Partisan Review* in March 1941. The dictation sessions of "late 1941," in other words, were a resumption of work that had been suspended only briefly. From then on, Jolas worked at his autobiography incessantly. In 1942, Jolas joined the Office of War Information. Despite a demanding job that from 1944 to 1950 required extended stays in England, France, and Germany, he continued to work on the manuscript, updating the story of his life to include the most recent events and experiences and often drawing on the diaries he had begun to keep in 1942. He would dictate new episodes to an army stenographer and send the shorthand manuscript to his wife to be typed out and returned to him for revision.

Jolas came to feel that the events of the war required a dramatic reconceptualizing of the book. In spring 1940, he wrote to his wife that he had completed the first chapters of a revised version that he hoped to submit to a suitable publisher. But his conception of the book still wavered: in June 1944, just after D Day, he called it "my novel — autobiography — my fact and fiction book."[4] The description suggests that he added fictional elements to the story of his life. He sometimes disguised names of persons and places for reasons of security, as in the case of the Lorraine town of Forbach, which he called Liring in his manuscript.

Undoubtedly his participation in the war effort in Europe made Jolas feel "that the autobiography was still incomplete the way it was finally done in New York" — that is, the version he had completed before leaving for London in March 1944.[5] In October 1944, Jolas was still uncertain about the exact shape the book should take. On the one hand, after devising a proper ending that brought together the many threads of the narrative, he wrote to Maria that "Man from Babel" (the title was mentioned for the first time) would appear in 1945, to allow him time for other projects.[6] On the other hand, only one day later, he considered rewriting it completely and publishing the autobiography "in the form of three separate books: the news story including the present experience; the frontier story and then the language story with Paris and New York."[7] Negative replies from publishers who had been approached by his wife and by a literary agent prompted Jolas to change his mind yet again. On 1 January 1945, he was determined to publish his autobiography in two books, one dealing "with the frontier town" and the other with "the migration of language." Some time later, he proposed to write "a continuous series of autobiographical narratives or novels," which were again to include the themes of the frontier, migration, and language.[8] And later in 1945, the autobiography was said to incorporate a reportorial book provisionally called "News for the Germans."[9]

During the mid- and late 1940s, the manuscript was sent to publishers who, as surviving letters indicate, expressed genuine interest in it but made acceptance conditional on completion of the manuscript. Though Jolas and his wife continued to work on the manuscript after he left the army in April 1950, his premature death in May 1952 prevented him from completing a definitive version of the autobiography. Perhaps during one of these final moments of renewed revision, Jolas wrote: "I spent half the night reading my Babel manuscript. What interesting material and what *bad* writing! The next six months will be devoted to a stylistic reformation! . . . I am recasting the whole book. There will be a Paris book, an Immigrant book etc. Anti-biography as creation!"[10]

As a result of his inability to complete the autobiography, Jolas left behind a number of versions and synopses that fill nine boxes and comprise well over a hundred folders in the Jolas collection at the Beinecke Rare Book and Manuscript Library at Yale University. These versions were left at different stages of the editing process by Jolas and his wife. There are long versions of about seven hundred pages (Drafts B, C, and E) and later, abridged versions of roughly four hundred pages (Drafts A and D). The present text is based on the corrected carbon of Draft D (folders 183–89), which represents Jolas's own selection from the hundreds of pages of drafts and contains his handwritten amendments and corrections. This excerpted version appears to be the latest, and thus presumably the one that Jolas intended for publication. Maria herself apparently did not learn of its existence until after her husband's death.[11] But the fact that she supplied occasional re-phrasings and proposed certain stylistic improvements to the manuscript suggests that she accepted the relatively final character of this particular version. Our edition of *Man from Babel* incorporates all her changes.

What is presented here is not a critical edition, however, but a reader's edition. Jolas's autobiography resists the editorial ideal of the single, uni-fied, and accurate text, and we have considered the version used here to be a text that allows a number of further changes. The changes we have made fall into three categories: 1) the omission of passages, particularly in the first four chapters; a good number of Jolas's poems have been omitted, too; 2) the addition from other draft fragments of passages that were omit-ted from Draft D, most notably Chapter 9, "Ananke Strikes the Poet"; and 3) the replacement of text and minor alterations in wording (we have drawn on other drafts by Jolas for the new phrasings). In the notes we account for each change and generally state or imply the rationale for the alteration.

To give the reader an idea of the principles guiding such editorial inter-ventions, we now propose to give one example from each of the three cate-gories. The first omission from Jolas's account is on page 6. After the words "the débâcle of 1870," two paragraphs have been deleted. The first of the paragraphs reads:

> My father made constant trips to the villages to visit his clerical *clientèle* and would often do odd jobs for them, for he was an able artisan. This gave him opportunities for conversation with *MM. les Curés,* who were fond of him and encouraged his story-telling interludes about the mys-terious and fabulous America of his youth. Sometimes we children were allowed to go along, and we pulled a two-wheeled wagon piled high with hammers, saws, paint-boxes, brushes and plaster statues of saints over hills and through forests and villages. While father tinkered away at his work, we usually play-acted liturgical ceremonies in the church, or climbed to the organ-loft with other children from the villages visited. The task finished, father and the curé never failed to sample the parish-house "mirabelle," while Jacques, who early showed marked musical gifts, set the organ roaring into the empty nave.

The ensuing paragraph described in more than 150 words the location of the Jolas family home in Forbach and contrasted the busy little town with the surrounding forests and ancient buildings. Lorraine is depicted as a country of coal mines, blast furnaces, medieval ruins and battlefields — all ideas that have already been touched on or will be mentioned later, in Chapter 1. Cutting the two paragraphs not only eliminates repetitious information but brings into clearer focus the chapter's thematic unity.

Following this description of Forbach's situation in Lorraine, which we excised, is a paragraph on the "sharp cleavage" in Forbach between pro-French and pro-German sentiments, which we have retained. It echoes the concluding sentence of the paragraph in which Jolas described his father's customers as Frenchmen at heart. The political situation, in other words, is merely a way for Jolas to restage the conflict between languages. The interplay of language and politics will be decisive for Jolas's entire career, including his modernist program for the "Revolution of the Word."

Throughout this edition of *Man from Babel,* insertions have been made from earlier drafts by Jolas. The prologue, the epilogue, and Chapter 9 have been taken from earlier versions, and excerpts from them have also been integrated into existing chapters. Twelve paragraphs from Draft E and draft fragments have been incorporated into Chapter 12, for instance. Those passages show Jolas as an extremely well-informed and discerning observer of German post-war literature. On the one hand, they show that Jolas the journalist and editor, in part through his assessments of Germany literary activity and its political implications, continued his literary interests after 1945. On the other hand, the supplementary passages present a distinctive assessment of German post-war writing by a contemporary critic — an assessment notable for its indictment of the "Realism" that has come to be associated with the Gruppe 47. Jolas's perceptive description of the beginnings of that influential group of progressive and democratic writers rounds out the German theme which runs through the entire autobiography. Similar considerations stand behind the other additions.

The third category of changes is more modest in scope and effect. Sometimes text has been replaced by phrases, or in a few cases paragraphs, from other drafts. Spelling of names has been corrected, as has the occasional grammatical lapse. We clarify issues that are merely alluded to in Draft D to provide further context for the reader. An example occurs in Chapter 7. Two paragraphs from Draft D (pp. 209–10) have been replaced with five paragraphs from Draft E. The replacement paragraphs give a fuller account of Jolas's friendship with and indebtedness to the German-Jewish writer Carl Einstein, who encouraged Jolas to visit his friends Benn, Döblin, and Grosz in Berlin. Arp (who is not mentioned in the relevant passage in Draft D), Einstein, and Jolas planned to edit from their base in Paris a German poetry series that was to be Expressionistic, Romantic, and internationalist in spirit. Once again, this information was not to be found in Draft D.

The rationale behind these editorial interventions has been simple: to produce a readable autobiography. We have cut down on at least some of the author's prolixity and have added significant episodes from the story of his life. The present text highlights Jolas's rootedness in the pre-1914 culture of the "borderland"; his return to Lorraine in 1922 and involvement in the Strasbourg avant-garde at a time when several crosscurrents—the Romantic heritage, Expressionism, Surrealism, and the Alsatian vernacular—briefly resurfaced there to produce an exciting regional and international artistic phenomenon; his critical stance on the emerging autonomist movement in Alsace in the late 1920s; his commentaries on the work of James Joyce, particularly *Finnegans Wake;* and finally his commentaries on and involvement in the literary and intellectual scene in post-war Germany.

The current edition of *Man from Babel,* we believe, serves two further purposes. First, it throws into relief Jolas's optimistic attempt to unite the extraordinarily diverse representatives of the avant-garde in a Revolution of the Word, as a response to the conflicts and chaos of the interwar era. Second, it opens the way for a reassessment of Jolas's autobiography, particularly in the light of the contemporary discussion of modernism and the avant-garde.

All my life has been dominated by the romantic emotion, by a tendency to transform the existing reality, by placing the accent on the dream rather than on the objective awareness of living. There was a kind of recklessness in this, a taking of risks, even a certain psychic violence which propelled my imagination into far-off regions in a miraculous exploration.

As a boy in a European frontier-land I daydreamed America. It became to me a paradisal continent where tropical and the arctic exoticism reigned supreme. Early in my German reading, I learned to know of a time when poets and fabulists created magical word-conjunctions, when they sought the Gothic wonders of the Christian Middle Ages, when they chanted the night and the evocation of ghosts and sidereal ecstasies. I read Novalis, Brentano, Tieck, Wackenroder, Görres, Hoffmann, Grimm, Goethe and Schiller in a mood of intoxication during my early years in the melancholy land of Lorraine, and my first attempts at verse were all dictated by these writers. In the aura of their words I discovered a wild, rhapsodic liberation from the burden of European history, and I sought in rhymes, like "Nacht" and "Pracht," "Leid" and "Freud," "lind" and "Wind," a musical experience that may seem infantile today, but constituted for the young, dream-haunted phantast the true sigils of his creative life.

I emigrated to America and tried to adjust myself to the metallic quality of New York; it was a difficult process of education, but gradually I saw in the vertical reality of the sky-towering landscape of Manhattan a new dimension, a modern romanticism of aspirations that led me to a luminous universe of americanesques. I became a newspaperman and the life of the reporter assumed a liturgy of quivering sacrifices. Life to me suddenly had planetary illuminations, and there was nothing more oneiromantic to me than the noisy atmosphere of the city-room.

The migratory instinct, the melody of *Fernweh,* of "far-aching" nostalgias, possessed me always. In New York I projected myself into Western regions; the names of California, Oregon, Mississippi had occult evocations.

Then came the hunger for Europe again, the urge to walk down the naves of age-old Gothic cathedrals, the longing to tramp over tree-bordered country roads through France and Germany, or to roam through mystery-laden, crooked streets of the little frontier-towns of my childhood. Wandering became a myth and music.

Romanticism accompanied me through the years after World War I, and nothing prevailed against this veritable pathology of the spirit. Often I felt I was isolated in the world, friendless and the aim of sneers and mockery on the part of my contemporaries. Some vestigial element gave me strength; some atavistic memory of countless European generations kept working in me; the forests of my ancestral land roared still in my unconscious. Back and forth across the Atlantic went the restless road. I was always pendulating between the two continents. I had an affection for America, where I was born, but I also felt the emotional pull of the European world. I was an intercontinental amalgam.

Paris lured me, but New York always remained the real city of my dreams. My children were born in France, they were American citizens, but they were also European the way their father was. I threw myself into the European maelstrom, as I had once done in America, and my aesthetic enjoyment was heightened. I belonged everywhere and nowhere and I was forever homesick for other shores, for other river-banks, for other chimerical cities of my fancy.

Language became a neurosis. I used three of the basic world languages in conversation, in poetry and in my newspaper work. I was never able to decide which of them I preferred. An almost inextricable chaos ensued, and sometimes I sought a facile escape by intermingling all three. I dreamed a new language, a super-tongue for intercontinental expression, but it did not solve my problem. I felt that the great Atlantic community to which I belonged demanded an Atlantic language. Yet I was alone, quite alone, and I found no understanding comrades who might have helped me in my linguistic jungle.

I tried to combine the Cartesian mode of thinking with my idealistic philosophy, and it seemed to work for a while. But something in me drew me back again and again into the wilderness of the irrational, and I sought my salvation in the ambiance of the cosmological irreality. I hammered at the gates of the numinous, and looked for a synthesis of time and space in the depths of my own being. The pilgrimage for the absolute haunted me, and I wandered to the hieratic mountains of liturgy and prayer. I was looking for divine irruption into the sad, sick world of the quotidian.

I am a man of the West, and my migration will always go towards the sunset. But I also know that the Occident is one. I am still a romantic, a dreamer, a man from Babel. Open-eyed I walk into the byss of the Night, and I seek the marvelous of the star-flooded skies.

1

EUROPEAN FRONTIER WORLD

When I arrived in New York four decades ago, as an immigrant from Europe, I was really coming home to my native land; for I was born in one of the ramshackle farmhouses that used to dot the Palisades, near the New Jersey town of Union City, on the west bank of the Hudson river. There it was that, hardly four weeks old, I was baptized according to the rite of the Roman Catholic faith, to which I have adhered—with rebellious interruptions—throughout my life. Despite this act of faith on the part of my parents, I have also come to believe that there must be some accuracy in the auguries of the astrologers. For I came into the world under the zodiacal sign of the scorpion, and I do not remember that this symbol of restless migrations, with its contradictions of geographical, linguistic and psychic change, has ever ceased to make itself felt in my life.

When I was two, and Jacques, my American-born brother, was one year old, my parents left for what was to have been a brief visit to their native Europe, from where, after a brief visit to the ancestral country, they planned to return to New York and settle there. They were armed for this journey with a passport signed by the then secretary of state, T. Willard Straight, requesting "all whom it may concern" to permit the citizen Eugene Jolas, accompanied by his wife and two babies, "safely and freely to pass and in case of need to give them all lawful Aid and Protection." But although they reached their destination without incident, fate intervened against their return to the New World. A third brother arrived a few months after they landed in Europe, and soon there was no longer sufficient cash to pay for another transatlantic voyage. Again and again the journey was envisaged, then reluctantly postponed, as the family continued to increase with almost rhythmic regularity. Finally the project became merely a dolorous fiction in the minds of our progenitors, although during my entire Lorraine boyhood I remember hearing my parents speak with deep nostalgia of their immigrant years in the New Jersey diaspora, where in retrospect they had been hopeful and lighthearted. Thus, although I was a native-born American, I became, paradoxically, a European, and it was not until adolescence that, like any other immigrant, I set out towards realization of the Columbian dream.

I grew up, an American in exile, in the hybrid world of the Franco-German frontier, in a transitional region where people swayed to and fro in cultural and political oscillation, in the twilight zone of the German and French languages. We lived in Forbach, a small provincial town much like hundreds of others scattered throughout the eastern part of France, not far from the Luxembourg and Saar borders. In July 1870 a bloody battle was fought on the hills outside our town, and after having been a French community for over two hundred years, Forbach became German, as a result of the Treaty of Frankfurt. An integral part of Lorraine, it has changed political allegiance three times since then and is today once more part of the French nation and of the department of the Moselle. Four brothers and a sister were born in this anomalous and unstable orbit and have participated in its vertiginously changeful destiny. Despite strong family ties, there was already in our childhood an antithesis between the European and American members of the family, and sadly, unavoidably, this has grown with the years, history abetting. From the first, Jacques and I were aggressively conscious of our Atlantic heritage, and never wanted to be known as Europeans, but as Americans. Later, when the economic struggle threatened to overwhelm our little tribe, it was natural that our thoughts should turn hopefully toward the liberating vision of the overseas continent with the magic name.

Although my father's maternal family had lived in Forbach for many centuries, he was actually born in nearby French Lorraine, not far from Verdun. As a youngster hardly out of his teens, he emigrated alone to America, worked as a machinist and in other capacities in and around Manhattan, and soon acquired a romantic love for his adopted land. He met my Rhenish mother, who had also emigrated as a young girl, at the home of American relatives of hers, and they were married a few years later. She was a woman both gay and deeply religious, typical of the people of her native province, and she raised her ever-growing family in the strict orthodox tenets of continental Catholicism. At home, we heard her speak her Rhenish German, and in the streets we learned a Franconian *patois*. Father preferred his native French. In addition, my parents often conversed in English, using probably a crude, immigrant speech, but which had a special sound that impinged happily on our ears, evoking as it did the far-off birthland of Jacques and myself. There was never any doubt about it: my parents had left their hearts in America. In Forbach father was known as "the American." From his years in the United States he retained a sense of democratic liberty, and his passion for individual freedom often led to clashes with the local authorities, who were saturated with Prussian nationalism.

After his return to Europe, he worked for a number of years as foreman in one of the local coal mines, and I remember him coming home from work, his face smeared with coal dust, carrying a rude, pointed stick that echoed rhythmically on the hard macadam. After the death of his grandmother, who had reared him, he lost no time in establishing his independence. When he came into his inheritance, which consisted of a small sum of money, a house, a garden and a few acres of meadowland and grainfields, he became half farmer, half shopkeeper. He opened a general store to which he soon added a little book and stationery department, with a sideline of Catholic devotional articles, such as statues, prayer-books and rosaries. His customers were mostly peasants from the nearby villages, as well as priests and teachers, many of whom were at heart still Frenchmen and had not forgotten the débâcle of 1870.

In the town there was a sharp cleavage between the pro-French and pro-German elements of the population, a cleavage that expressed itself not only in the linguistic sphere, but also in the opposed national sympathies. The old Lorrainers were, for the most part, inclined to think mournfully of the broken nexus with the history of France, and did not hide their dislike of the "Prussiens." They had a cult for Napoléon I, were Catholic and conservative, and remained strictly aloof. A few, however, were liberal republicans and read anti-clerical Paris newspapers. Others accepted the consequences of the Frankfurt Treaty and rallied to the Kaiser's regime. These were German patriots who voted centrist or conservative during the Reichstag elections. The German newcomers, who for the most part were bureaucrats and administrative officers from the other side of the Rhine, kept to themselves, and there was only an official contact between them and the local population. They were violently anti-French in spirit and utterance, and regarded the French language as a canker and a nuisance.

The Lorraine-Saar region, being rich in iron and coal mines, attracted workers from every part of Europe, and already in my childhood Italian, Polish, Serbian, Austrian and German laborers had founded families and intermingled with the native population. It was a veritable linguistic

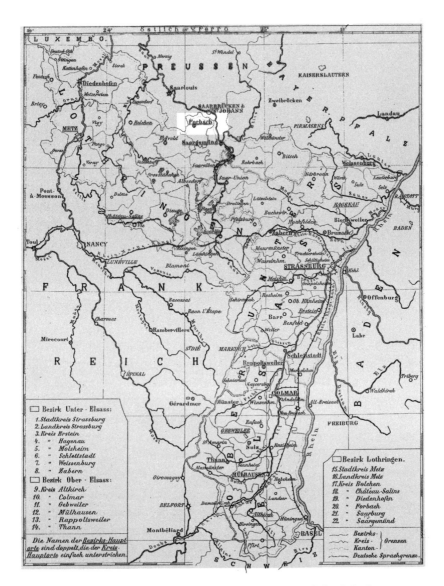

1. Map of Alsace-Lorraine (around 1910), from Max Rehm, *Reichsland Elsaß-Lothringen: Regierung und Verwaltung, 1871–1918* (Bad Neustadt, Germany: Pfaehler, 1991). Copyright 1991 Verlag Dietrich Pfaehler, Bad Neustadt. Used by permission.

melting-pot, like the one I was to know in America years later, with the difference, however, that in this chaotic frontier-land the problem of a crucible language apparently has yet to be solved.

Thus, I was early made aware of the primordial importance of language and its flux, and this had already become something of an obsession when,

2. The Jolas shop in Forbach. Pierre Eugène Jolas is on the left. Used by permission.

in school, I experienced the antithesis of our patois and "High" German. Later, when French words entered my vocabulary, the bilingual conflict was a daily one. For we saw France and Germany confronting each other, tunneling each other's crypts, parrying each other's blows in the continuation of age-old paradoxes. We watched the hopeless attempts by first one, then the other of the two antagonistic cultures to create a living amalgam in the souls of the people. In this nerve-tremulous landscape between the Moselle and the Saar Rivers, hemmed in by languages and dialects ready to spring at each other's throats; in this area where two nations combated each other in a subtle conspiracy of vocabularies and grammars, I grew up in the medley of Europe's decadence. Here I saw life across the spite-fences of history, fences that were linguistic and religious as well as political. As a child I watched the drama of misunderstanding through the confusion that hovered over inimical words. Around me I heard the clash between the Latin and Teutonic vocables. I witnessed, at first hand, the impact of two tongues in daily life. I saw how they changed inwardly, how they fled each other, how they went through alternations of love and hate.

Historically, the problem of the two languages has long been a thorny one. The conflict has persisted in fact for more than two centuries, fanned now by one, now by the other neighbor. And since all discussion as to the origin and psyche of the people in the frontier provinces is inevitably related to the question of language, interest in this internecine phenomenon has been pronounced, the more so because the linguistic and political frontiers have hardly ever coincided. For this reason, the nation in the saddle has usually tried to merge them: the French attempted to push the enemy speech beyond the Moselle, Nied and Saar rivers, while the Germans tried to maintain their language in the Vosges, and even to extend it west of the three rivers. When the war of 1870 broke out, the French language had made considerable progress in Lorraine. It was spoken throughout the province, both officially and privately, and was also taught in the schools. But after 1872, the Germans did not encourage the use of French by native Lorrainers, and rammed, instead, a bureaucratic German idiom down their throats.

As little children we prattled in a dialect related to that of Luxembourg and the Flemish countries. Things and persons invented in infant musing were not real to us, until we had found names for them in this frontier patois. We listened to the legend-words of old women who knew countless incantatory rhymes. All the ABC inventions which every child makes in his early life were cast by us in the well-pitched vocables of our home idiom, in the jarring and discordant words of Forbach. "Voulez-vous vous weg-schere', petits voyous," shouted Madame Frank when we made too much noise near her house.

French, my father's native tongue, remained pure sound for many years. It thrust itself into my consciousness by slow degrees, opened up gleaming horizons, floated about me like an occult aura. For many Lorrainers before 1914, it had the timbre of a lost cause wafted tenderly from across the nearby frontier. It brought vibrations of a romantic past, memories of shared experiences, evocations of a collective nostalgia. My father spoke it with the village teachers and priests, and with visiting relatives from over the border, especially with his own father, or with friends who had not lived down the rankle of the Franco-Prussian cataclysm. We heard it, too, scattered in shreds and fragments through the speech of the people. It went its stubborn way, nurtured by local irredentists, seductively invading both the dialect and the High German vocabulary.

But the German language remained the dominating medium of communication. We heard it in school, we heard it from the arrogant officials who had invaded the land from "inner Germany." The yawping commands of the military brought it to our attention when the border garrison practiced the goose-step on the parade-ground. The German soldiers stationed in our town were usually from North Germany, and their grunting speech was a constant source of resentment to many of us; they, in turn, did not like the French words and phrases with which the local speech was dotted. The older people of the town, most of whom still remembered the easy French regime before 1870, displayed sullen irritation at the raucous dialogues of the outsiders.

For me, German was my mother tongue and French my father tongue, and from infancy I had to face the problem of sound-shifting in the two languages. In addition, many phonetic shades occurred from village to village, from town to town, and there were a number of communities where one section spoke a French patois, while the other used a German dialect. I might, however, have eventually liberated myself from the European burden and made a choice between French and German had not the American language joined the fray in my adolescent years. But emigration only brought further disorder, a sort of glotto-pathology for which there has seemed to be no permanent remedy.

My first schooling was in a *salle d'asile* run by Sisters of the Divine Providence. It was a Catholic kindergarten where we were taught communal prayers, relieved by children's songs and games in both German and French. Here I seem to have given early manifestation of certain heretical tendencies, and there was a school incident that became legendary in the family. I was little more than four years old, so the story went, when one day I was reproved by the nun in charge for some minor transgression. She grew, in fact, so irritated at my mutinous behavior that she punished me by making me stand in a corner. Suddenly I turned on her, tore the large black cross from her white plastron, and screamed my displeasure in no uncertain terms. There was an uproar in the classroom and the Superior had to be called in to restore order. That night the nun told my mother gravely: "That child needs watching; he has the devil in him."

Grammar school remains a nightmare in my memory. Our teachers were for the most part *immigrés* from Prussia—"Preyss," as they were called by the Lorrainers—Teutons of the military type, gruff, pedantic, ponderous, tyrannical, who sought to instill into our young minds their conviction of German superiority. The school was just opposite our house, and from the window of our living room we could look directly into the spacious classroom where the three Rs were taught in the snarling idiom of the German barracks, and the bamboo cane was used with considerable frequency and savagery. Group singing of patriotic German songs was an important part of the curriculum, and often we were made to march through the streets in military formation—always in military rhythm—singing marching songs in German.

After attending elementary school, I was transferred to the *collège,* where the Imperial German educational system was in full sway. Except for a very few native Alsatians or Lorrainers, all the teachers were from northern Germany. They brought with them a harsh, guttural speech and abrupt, staccato gestures, well suited to the apodictic phrases they hurled at us. I recall one of these men, our history professor — known out of school as a secret tippler and *coureur de femmes* — who taught us fantastically spurious versions of events since the time of Charlemagne, in a continuous distortion of history. Indeed it was not until a number of years later, in America, that I was able to check his statements and satisfy myself that his interpretation — which was the official German one — was a form of national lying. The revival of antique Germanism was the constant mot d'ordre, and denigration of France — the *Erbfeind* or "hereditary enemy" — became a militant slogan, presented with grossly simplified accounts of victories in the latest war. Our school-books fairly ranted about Germany's might and the greatness of the Hohenzollern leadership. Our teacher quoted the historian Treitschke as saying: "A state that renounces war and submits to the demands of an international tribunal renounces thereby its sovereign power, that is, itself. . . . The most terrible weapons are absolutely legitimate."

Education under the Prussian regime continued to be strict, even puritanical. Nineteenth-century conventions were still adhered to, and faith in the omniscience of a supreme state authority was fostered with iron determination. Men wore grotesque beards and mustaches above ludicrously high wing collars, and their role in family life was feudal and dictatorial. Women wore cumbersome corsets stiffened with whalebone, and spent their lives in a position of accepted inferiority. Sex was never discussed openly, a veil of hypocrisy covering all erotic manifestations. Class consciousness was marked, and professors cultivated a pretentious social hierarchy, frequently resulting in life-long enmities among their dull, stodgy wives. The idea of European concord was throttled by the slave-theory of a militaristic hegemony.

The great military and civilian event of the year was the Kaiser's birthday, for which preparations were made many weeks ahead. In school, at a gathering of all the classes assembled for the event, there were recitations by the pupils and stiff patriotic speeches by the teachers. There was also on that day — January 27th, usually marked by heavy snow — a big military parade. On this occasion soldiers marched in goose-step down the street to the market-place, where a celebration was held outdoors, however bitter the weather. The Governor of Metz was present, and after officially acknowledging the honors, he made a brief speech. Then the commanding officer, in a peremptory Prussian tone, barked his eulogy of the *Oberste Kriegsherr*—the Supreme Warlord.

I saw the Kaiser several times in those early years. One occasion was when he was on his way to spend a holiday at the Château d'Urville, near Metz. His snow-white train stopped at our station, where all the schoolchildren were lined up well before the appointed hour. He appeared at the window and looked down on us as we fluttered our little flags. *"Hoch! Hoch! Hoch!"* we shouted. He never smiled. On another occasion we were taken to the town of Morhange—the scene of one of the first frontier battles of the early months of 1914—where we had to wait for many hours in the blazing heat for him to pass by. It was a pompous affair. Gold-braided generals on horseback clattered down the beflagged street while hundreds of soldiers goose-stepped behind. The Kaiser finally appeared, mounted on a white horse, his withered right arm hanging limply, his uniform a cameo of glittering medals. Once more I was struck by the condescending dullness of his gaze.

As I muse over those years, in the European ambiance of pre-1914, I remember many books that were given me for Christmas or on other feastdays, and over which linger a glamour, a golden haze that I like to recapture in moments when time is abolished and I am catapulted again into the vanished era of childhood and the discovery of the world. I recall particularly certain romantic books; the *Märchen* or magic tales of Brentano, Bechstein, Grimm and Andersen, as well as lyrical poems, among which Tieck's lines: "Wunderbare Mondennacht. / Steig empor mit alter Pracht!" impressed themselves upon my mind with incantatory force. But I also devoured other books of a more robustly magical nature, such as *Robinson Crusoe*, Fenimore Cooper's *Leatherstocking Tales*, Gerstäcker's *The River Pirates*, Karl May's *Winnetou*, Beecher Stowe's *Uncle Tom's Cabin*. Those were the days when an Ameromantic vocabulary excited my youthful dreams, when I began to use such words as "savannah," "prairie," "lasso," "tomahawk," "paleface," "Indian," "calumet," "trapper," "coureur des bois," "medicine man," and other exotic terms that evoked a distant Wonderland. Then there were the fantastic tales of the *pays messin*—known then as Lothringen, with Metz as its capital—in which the Grauli dragon on the Gothic cathedral of Metz played an outstanding part. Among the many books I read in my early years, I believe, however, that Adalbert Stifter's *Studien, Nachsommer* and *Witiko* made the deepest impression upon me; this prose writer of genius knew how to describe landscapes and the season's changes in a way that I, as a youngster, had experienced them.

In a style modeled on that of Tieck, I soon began to evoke in sophomoric verse the medieval background of the *Schloßberg,* the macabre solitude of cemeteries, the first girl's "mystery-smoldering" eyes, far-off landscapes:

Ich sehne mich nach blauen Weiten,
Nach Inseln, wo die Palmen weh'n,
Wo schöne Frauen träumend geh'n
In schmelzend weichen Sommerzeiten.

Later, I devoured not only poetry but certain popularized treatises on the new evolutionary doctrines of Darwin, which Ernst Haeckel presented in a series entitled "Riddles of the World." German and French books by Barrès, Hauptmann, Holz, Liliencron were also favorites, and I gradually drifted into the individualistic exaggerations that dominated the writing of that period. There were a few German boys in school who shared my literary enthusiasms, and like myself refused to join in with those students who roared "gaudeamus igitur" in the local taverns in order to demonstrate their solidarity with academic customs from the other side of the Rhine.

More and more fascinated by the printed word, I began to write little lyrical sketches for the local newspaper, *Der Grenzbote,* or *Frontier Messenger,* which was edited by a friend of my family, Heinrich Neumann. Neumann had a keen intelligence and a newspaperman's temperament, both of which impressed me. To be sure, the paper was somewhat parochial, but in his perceptive editorials Neumann undoubtedly did seek to build a bridge with the western neighbor, much to the disgust of the Germanophiles. I don't recall reading any real news in the little sheet, but that was true of most European newspapers of the time. (Many years later, in occupied Germany, I was to combat this shortcoming, although unsuccessfully.) Neumann worked in a dust-flecked little *Redaktion* on the main street, where I often tarried in order to watch the proceedings. The musty, spider-web-hung composing-room with its two linotype machines was the place in which I liked most to loiter, captivated as I was by the mysteries of journalistic technique. For already I knew that one day I would become a newspaperman, that I would be a worker in this word-factory in which, as Neumann warned me, "nerves of steel" were required.

Our teacher talked to us of the inner tensions in Alsatian intellectual life. A magazine called *La Revue Alsacienne,* edited by Dr. Bucher, encouraged a regional culture in the French idiom, while such younger men as René Schickele and Ernst Stadler used German as their instrument of expression. A third group, composed of French idealists, tried to construct a spiritual bridge over the Rhine, in the face of strong opposition. But a horde of fatuous pan-German professors—pilloried later by the local cari-caturist, Hansi—covered the land with arrogant assertions which had the authority of official sanction.

It was at this same period that I passed through the religious crisis that decided my parents, at the suggestion of a clerical friend, to have me study for the priesthood. In a way it was a relief to be sent to the Catholic seminary at Montigny, near Metz, where the French language and French civilization dominated, and where I was conscious of absorbing a more humanistic culture. Yet even in these sheltered surroundings I could not but notice that the political horizon in Europe had become gusty with fore-bodings. In the schoolyard, conversation often turned to the subject of the next war. Memories of the 1871 siege persisted in the talk of our elders, and occasionally, during our communal walks in the Val de Metz, we students visited the battlefields of Mars-la-Tour, St.-Hubert or St.-Privat, where we were plunged into the temper of the 1870 conflagrations. When the first Zeppelin passed over Metz, the silver flash and the machine's rumble were like a sibylline omen to the frontier-people, and there was a real interna-tional incident when the airship flew over the nearby French border. Even the youngest of us sensed a smell of powder in the air.

There was something about the long summer vacations of those years that still lives in my memory: the scent of fresh hay, dreamy, lazy meander-ings through valleys and forests, geographical daydreams and, more than all else, the discovery of history. The European's love of the past is a form of fetishism that contrasts with the American's more realistic attitude. Henry Ford's famous dictum—"history is bunk"—expresses well the American pioneer's contempt for European commemorations of dynastic wars, reli-gious discords, frontier transformations; a contempt that has its roots in a dynamic acceptance of the time and in the devaluation of inherited tradi-tions. But we who grew up in the heart of the continent where evolution was measured in terms of thousands of years had a reverence for dates and relics, and we learned to distinguish the great epochs of national change by remembering place-names associated with war, slaughter and torture. Dur-ing our *grandes vacances,* we were shown battlefields and ruined castles, Gallo-Roman museums, the scarred remains of *Burgen* once occupied by robber barons, the remnants of villages and towns annihilated during the Thirty Years' War. The dusty vaults of Gothic cathedrals and the local relics of the *limes,* the ancient Roman border fortresses along the Rhine, all these were presented to us with reverence, and left us awed by their great age.

As economic conditions at home worsened, it became necessary to with-draw me from the Metz seminary. On my return to Forbach, what was my joy to find that plans for sending me to America were under discussion. Germany's aggressive attitude towards France and England seemed to foreshadow war. In three years I would be of military age. The American saga soon became for me a feverish, almost hysterical fiction, nurtured by my father's stories, by my own reading about Columbus and Pizarro, and by my Atlantic-hungry imagination. In the attic I unearthed all the dust-covered English books, magazines and newspapers that Father had brought back from America, and, with the help of a dictionary, laboriously studied their contents. Thus began a journey into language that was to last many years. Slowly I picked my way through the syntactical puzzle of the new tongue, which captivated me with its humor and precision. I learned about the New England Pilgrims, about Washington, Jefferson and Lincoln, as well as about Columbus, whose heroic myth fascinated me. I learned about the great achievements of the pioneers who had pushed back the frontier ever further towards the West, and gradually the European frontier began to recede in my mind. I read about the modern builders of skyscrapers, the constructors of railroads and bridges, the inventor of the telephone. Soon I had created a Super-America of my own, fable-clothed and wonderful.

But increasingly hard times made my trip to America impossible of realization for the moment. Then, one day, a letter arrived from my mother's sister in New York. Aunt Theresa related the latest family events and distributed transatlantically God's blessing over our home. She enclosed several family photographs: snapshots of the fourteen-story building on Central Park West in which they were living, of Uncle John and of Cousin Madeleine. Her letter gave me an idea. I wrote her immediately, proposing that she send me a steamship ticket, which I promised to repay as soon as I should have found work. Although I had hardly expected it, a reply containing a second-class ticket and innumerable exhortations arrived in due course. My father expressed pleased surprise, in which relief that there would now be one less mouth to feed seemed to predominate. Mother wept at the thought of our separation. I was happy and eager to go.

The date of departure was set for November. With it I experienced my first sensations of adult liberty. As I watched the soldiers on the *Exerzierplatz* going through their mechanical drill, I felt jubilant at the thought that I would never be pressed into the service of their loathsome machine. When the annual October *Kermesse* came round, I participated in its ritual with a mingled sense of ecstasy and sadness, convinced that it was for the last time.

I was attracted as never before by the colored booths with toys and *nougat*, the Ferris Wheel, or *lindau*, the merry-go-round, the man with the blood-curdling posters describing fearful events in far-away countries, the enchanting *images d'Epinal*. All the *marchands forains* were French, from Nancy, and their attempts to speak the local patois produced guffaws of laughter from the listeners. Here we saw our first *cinématographe*. The films shown were rudimentary, but to us they were nothing short of magical, and I still recall the sharp smell of steam issuing from the long, low tent, the interior of which seemed mysterious and exotic. Usually Far-Western pictures were shown, horribly blurred, yet they found an echo in our Indian romancing.

We were only five years from the First World War, and the mood of the festivity seemed to be fraught with a desperate joyousness. It was as though the people of Forbach knew what lay in store for them. A few more weeks and all this would be for me the European past. Occasionally I left the whirligig of the market-place and wandered alone through the fields and nearby forests, from where I could still hear the distant sounds of the merry-go-round organ playing its melancholy airs. Suddenly I felt a deep love for the Lorraine landscape; never had the sunsets seemed more beautiful to me.

One day Father took me to the attic, selected a large oblong trunk from a heap of dusty boxes and knick-knacks, and opened it almost ritualistically. I knew it well: the lock was rusty and creaked, a colored photograph of the Statue of Liberty was pasted on the inside.

"I guess it'll do for another trip," he said. We brought the trunk down and Mother began to pack my few belongings. On the top she placed my violin, a prayer book, a rosary, and some blessed images of Our Lady of Perpetual Succor. A few days before my departure, I made farewell calls on relatives and friends. I was a hero for a day.

In the evening before the impatiently awaited day, I roamed the streets in our neighborhood for the last time. My town was drinking in the blue vapors of late autumn as the inhabitants sat gossiping on the low stoops of the houses. A woman was singing to a child. From time to time a locomotive puffed over the bridge that formed the horizon of our street. A drunken soldier reeled out of a tavern. When the Angelus tinkled over the gables, old women stiffened under their white bonnets and prayed rapidly: Ave Maria. Children shouted in the alleyways, their games tumbled through the courtyards.

Before dawn Father and I had left the little frontier-town for Antwerp. Mother was in tears, my brothers and sister stood in the window, watching. It was still quite dark and rain was falling. Only a few coal miners were tramping through the street. The bell in the church tower rang for matins. Through the early morning gloom I saw my family for the last time, dimly.

A neighbor called from a window. Then the gables of the houses disappeared. Woods and fields and all the familiar landscapes vanished in the morning mist. I said good-bye to my childhood.

The train passed through Luxembourg, then Belgium. In Antwerp, having two days before us, Father and I visited the museums and churches, or simply wandered along the quays watching the harbor life. A thick fog lay over the Scheldt, where we saw freight being loaded for the Congo. Father and I exchanged few words, for there was a silent embarrassment between us. But I felt free, immensely so; free of paternal authority, of ecclesiastical tutelage, of political and military serfdom; free to go towards a new world, towards the distant horizons of my aerial imagination. I was carrying out the first and most important decision of my life. I had consciously chosen freedom, and now I was leaving parents and family in order to realize that choice.

At dusk on the second day we said good-bye. I heard my father's last words with a slight quiver. His face looked pale. A brass band was playing. Handkerchiefs waved. Standing on the deck of the *S.S. Finland,* I watched the stooped figure of my father vanish into the Flemish fog.

2

IMMIGRANT INTO NEO-AMERICAN

As the liner neared New York on an afternoon in late autumn, my first sensation was one of almost religious awe. The many-towered city of my dreams stood sky-storming before me, crowded ferry-boats crossed and re-crossed the harbor, the sky was mottled with ruddy clouds. The very air had a winey, invigorating tang, a curiously electric quality that, ever since, I have associated with Manhattan. I invaded this brawling stone-world with exhilaration, my eyes fixed ecstatically on the titanic proportions of the cosmopolis. The thought came to me with explosive force that I was returning to my native land, a land whose language I did not know, a land whose customs were alien to me, but whose wonders I was eager to explore. However much of a greenhorn I might seem, paradoxically, I was coming home.

My immigrant relatives were at the pier, and we greeted one another with a certain embarrassment, for, in reality, we were strangers. Hardly a half-hour later, the elevated railroad had brought us to their fourteenth-story apartment in the Lorington, on Central Park West, where Uncle John was employed as superintendent. That night I saw New York from the roof of the skyscraper, and I reacted to its modernistic beauty with romantic emotion. My first poems in the New World were written in German in this urban aura that contrasted so sharply with the European landscape I had left only a short time before:

Ich steh' auf himmelragendem Gemäuer,
Allein im Schmelz vom letzten Abendschein;
Die wilde Stadt umbraust mich ungeheuer —
Mein Herz schlägt traumgebannt in Stahl und Stein.

Uncle John, who had left Forbach when he was seven years old, just after the Franco-Prussian war, astonished me by speaking the dialect of that region, despite almost half a century spent in New York. He liked to evoke the battle that had taken place near our town, after which he and a band of urchins had accompanied the French troops of Gen. Frossard across the hills. He had, in fact, quite a store of anecdotes of that period, which he told humorously, commingling Franco-German with American words, which made us laugh a good deal.

Aunt Theresa and their daughter Madeleine made me feel immediately at home in the skyscraper Tusculum, and I listened eagerly to their talk. My aunt had emigrated from the Rhineland in the eighties and had practically forgotten her native speech, using only the somewhat barbarous immigrant English that often characterizes the first generation. My cousin, however, a pretty, grave-eyed girl of my own age, spoke only English, and at first I had great difficulty in communicating with her. I learned with regret that she was planning to begin her novitiate in the French Catholic convent of Notre Dame de Lourdes as soon as she graduated from high school.

Almost immediately I began to meet other immigrant relatives from the Alsace-Lorraine diaspora, scattered about in Manhattan, Brooklyn and the little towns on the New Jersey Palisades. They had built a kind of family state of their own in which the "official" language was a jargon that unfortunately retarded my acquisition of English. On Sunday afternoons I was taken to their family gatherings, many of which were held in Brooklyn where Uncle John's sister and her Alsatian husband were living in parochial quietude.

Occasionally the older members of the tribe, most of whom hailed from the Moselle and Rhine countries, would talk about President Taft's conflict with Teddy Roosevelt's Bull Moose Party, which had just made its appearance, and I was immediately attracted by Teddy's dramatically presented doctrines. More often, however, they talked nostalgically about the old country, or expressed their naive cult for the great Napoléon; and whenever they warmed up under the influence of home-made *quetsch* or apricot wines, they inevitably sang old French war songs that pilloried the *Prussiens* as topers and dullards.

Although my relatives continued to be extremely kind to me, they had little understanding for the iconoclastic elements of my temperament. This fact, added to my own youthful impetuosity, not to say intellectual intolerance, gradually created psychic tensions, and after a few months I noticed, or thought I noticed, that the family's attitude towards me had begun to chill. I decided to move and with the little cash I had brought with me rented a furnished room in a tenement-house on 100th Street, between Columbus and Amsterdam Avenues. Before leaving the skyscraper home, I promised my relatives to repay the money they had advanced for my passage, as soon as I should find work. Now that I was free of their tutelage, I redoubled my efforts to find a job, and finally found one as a delivery boy in a grocery store on Columbus Avenue.

Here I checked in at six in the morning, and usually worked without interruption until eight in the evening. It was still dark when I arrived at the store, and the first milk wagons were just beginning to rumble along the avenue. The elevated trains, filled with workers and white-collar slaves, crashed their noisy steel-echoes against the adjacent walls. A lot of snow fell that first winter, and I recall slopping through the slush with my milk bottles and packages, feeling forsaken and homesick. This was particularly so when I had to enter certain rat-infested basements reeking with the stench of garbage and urine, in order to place the orders on the different dumb-waiters. I felt nervously irritated when shrill, ill-humored voices bellowed down from above, with rarely a word of thanks. At that hour the janitors were just getting up in their tepid cubbyholes, babies were howling, the day was beginning with its preludes of wretchedness.

The boss, a surly North German with a harsh accent and a penchant for obscene talk, arrived at seven o'clock. The first regular orders having already been filled, now began the busy routine of the day. For me this involved pushing a handcart filled with heavy baskets through the streets, going from basement to brownstone house or apartment building, then returning for further orders. The glacial air of the streets stung my face, and I shivered in the thin clothes I had brought from Europe.

Around me I saw treacly bourgeois comfort. The blocks between Columbus Avenue and Central Park West contained mostly private houses, standing side by side in monotonous rows. The men were downtown, making money, the women lazing at home, waited on by immigrant servants. I, however, saw only the kitchens and the basements. I was earning five dollars a week, out of which I put aside one dollar in order to repay my relatives, and I was hungry most of the time. Often I played with the idea of looking for something better. But the thought of being out of work, even for a few days, frightened me. In the early morning hours I had seen scavengers, ragged men and women, treasure-picking in the garbage cans that stood before the houses. This sight had filled me with sinister forebodings.

One day some neighborhood children began to taunt me with derisive shouts of "dirty foreigner." When I left the house a few hours later, I found that they had dragged my cart a good block away from where I had put it. I saw them tittering joyously at my discomfiture, pointing at me and yelling their childish objurgations. I had been working since dawn in these spidery basements and was in a state of neurotic fidgets. "Dirty foreigner" — I heard it plainly now. Something in me whirled and pounded. Setting my basket down, I raced towards them and pummeled the ones I caught with all my might. Back in the store, the boss grunted and shouted: "A bit faster, God damn it! Get going."

Quite naturally I became a recognized member of an unorganized guild of delivery boys who worked in the same blocks between Central Park West and Columbus Avenue that I did. For they too were foreigners, who spoke every European tongue, poor, dirty aliens, a polyglot amalgam of pinched youngsters from Ireland, Italy, France, Germany, Hungary. We had a strong sense of solidarity and comradeship, exchanged confidences about the "old country," shared one another's family news received in letters from abroad. Most of these boys were sons of worker or lower-middle-class families who like me had been sent over to escape military service. Their ambition seemed to be limited to one day becoming "bosses" themselves in the new country. At the same time they were in league against their "bosses" and they counseled one another as to the best methods of obtaining a raise or gaining other rights. Generally their wages ranged between five and seven dollars a week.

Many of our problems were discussed in the little basement restaurant on Columbus Avenue where we took our meager meals. The proprietor was an elderly, greasy Hungarian, an ex-butcher, whom we called Hans. He did the cooking himself and for a few dimes gave us a little meat, potatoes and bread. Here we aired our grievances, cursed, gossiped about the girls of the neighborhood, told jokes. What a *baragouin* we spoke! If I recall rightly, we used a grotesque alloyage of primitive English and illiterate German, mingled with accents and sonorities from Balkan and Latin tongues. We even developed a sort of universal medium of our own, based on deformations of certain stock English phrases picked up at random during our trips through the neighborhood. Our basement "club-room" had the atmosphere of a den peopled by international conspirators, if rather innocent ones.

On Sundays an elegiac calm settled over the city. Although I had to work at the grocery store in the morning I was free in the afternoon, and usually spent my time scanning the *Sunday World,* the *New Yorker Staatszeitung* and the *Courrier des Etats-Unis.* I studied them most carefully in fact, for my ultimate aim was to find a job as a reporter, although that seemed a very remote possibility. I read German and American books, poems by Bryant, Lowell and Longfellow, stories by Poe and Hawthorne, anything I could lay my hands on, in order to learn English. On this Sabbath day it was quiet in the tenement-house, and from time to time I could even hear the silvery clang of the bells in the Methodist church on nearby Amsterdam Avenue.

A new chapter in my immigrant life was soon to begin. It began, in fact, at the moment the boss sent me to his bank to deposit a hundred dollars. As I walked along, a terrible temptation came to me. Why should I not keep the money and simply disappear in some Western city? For my imagination was haunted by a Western dream, realization of which seemed to promise escape from the tortuous reality of my Manhattan existence. I remember walking like a somnambulist through the Broadway crowds till I found myself on the river-bank, staring at the New Jersey coast opposite. In my revery I saw myself starting all over again in some mythical town outside the diaspora, beyond Chicago, where I might work in happy, human sur-roundings. Fortunately, my mother's teaching prevailed and I hurried to the bank and got rid of the money. With my heart pounding, I rushed back to the store and plunked the bank-book on the counter. The boss looked at me angrily: "You been gone a long time, you son of a bitch. Where wuz ye?"

"I'm not a son of a bitch," I shouted back.

"Well, you're fired anyway," he snarled. "You kin take your money next Sunday and git the hell out of here."

Now began a period of utter wretchedness. I had not been able to save anything, and I found it very difficult to get a new job. In the end I found myself working as a delivery boy again, this time with a wholesale grocer on Broadway where I received room and board for a nine-hour day, with Sundays free. Finally a fortunate break came when I was accepted for a "white-collar job" as clerk in the international bookshop of G. E. Stechert. Here I felt truly happy, in an atmosphere of German, French and English books, for the most part textbooks for American universities.

It was at this point that my brother Jacques came to join me in our native land. He had more luck than I, for he managed to find work almost im-mediately, as a stock boy in the music publishing house of Witmarck & Sons, in Tin Pan Alley. Then, after a few weeks, when they learned that he was an accomplished pianist, he began to "plug" their song hits, such as Ernst Ball's *Love Me and the World Is Mine* and *Mother Machree*. I used to accompany him and the singer on their nightly invasion of the "nickelode-ons" which were beginning to spring up all over New York and Brooklyn, and I enjoyed immensely these incursions into "Little Bohemia."

Together we gradually began to feel that we were on our way to a better comprehension of America. Human relations were more pleasant, and we came to know many new people, among whom were some authentic Americans. We also got to know some young girls, with whom we promptly fell in love, even to the point of quarreling over them. Meanwhile Jacques continued his musical studies and we played violin sonatas together on our day off. Somehow we felt optimistic about the future, without concern for what might be our struggles later on. Our weekly earnings increased, and we were able to put small sums aside in a postal savings account, which gave us confidence.

During this pleasant if rather anarchic period I remember dreaming a lot. My dreams were usually based on subjective experiences, and most of them were tinged with melancholy recollections of my childhood in a lost Europe. I recall, in particular, one dream which recurred a number of times in ever-new form, in ever-new transformations. It seemed to me that I was walking through my home-town. On a street corner I met an old school-mate dressed in a multicolored suit and wearing a shining high hat. We greeted each other coldly, almost as though we had never met before. Rain fell monotonously on the slate roofs of the low houses, which were shut-tered tight. I asked him, "What is going on behind those shutters?"

"The dance of the hours," he said.

In another dream I was in the Forbach railroad station watching a train arriving from Metz. A large crowd milled about the depot, and I found it strange that nobody spoke English. Yet it was a very international crowd: French, German and Flemish were being spoken, and I listened with great curiosity. I was suddenly hailed by my father, who appeared carrying a large box on his shoulders. After a long silence he said, "Let's take that car-riage over there."

An old coach drawn by two horses wearing black and silver funeral trap-pings stopped at the curb. It was raining heavily now, and the empty streets were suddenly enlivened by youngsters who shouted patois words with mysterious incantations.

Then I found myself alone in the cemetery, by my mother's grave. When I woke, I was weeping bitterly.

At this period I spoke English with awkward hesitation, for the inner mechanism of its grammar still escaped me, and after many months I was still translating from one language to the other. It was not a pretty speech, this Manhattan patter I heard about me, with its gross phonetic distor-tions and its frequently vulgar obscenities, and I regard it today as almost a philological miracle that I did not retain its baser characteristics. When I finally heard about the possibility of having free lessons in New York's night schools, I decided to make a systematic study of English, and enrolled at the DeWitt Clinton Night High School, then situated at Fifty-ninth Street and Tenth Avenue. With a number of other foreigners and a few native New

Yorkers, I was initiated into the secrets of English composition. Professor Thomas Sullivan, an Anglo-Irish-American instructor with a magnetic personality and poetic awareness, introduced us to Poe, Bryant, Emerson. I threw myself into the new grammatical world, and made exciting discoveries. A new measure for feeling things came to me, a new means for absorbing the living elements of being, for enlarging my conscious and unconscious sensations. Reading English poetry, particularly, gave me a blinding revelation of new values, and when we were introduced to Milton and Shelley, I realized that my preconceived notion that English lacked melodiousness was entirely false.

As I continued to read, I began to write down *in English* the images that were forming in my mind. I was inclined towards a bizarre, fantastic style and took an almost mad pleasure in certain recondite words encountered during my reading. Here, in the new vocabulary, was an answer to my need for exaggerating every experience, for evading the realities of everyday life, for living in a *camera obscura* world of my own invention. Everything that was inexplicable, abnormal, romantic, attracted me, whereas what existed in fact usually left me indifferent. I liked to evoke daydreaming tales in which magicians, spooks, Indian sorceresses and winged animals mingled in glamorous confusion. An inexplicable apprehension led me to veil the outside world which was proving so disappointing, while I reproduced my inner images with phantasmatic words.

In class, contact with native Americans gave me a glimpse of an America I had had little opportunity to know thus far, and I began to feel a sense of democratic comradeship, something I had missed heretofore.

One evening as I was walking home alone beneath the high, swinging arc-lamps of Broadway, English words heard at school continued to sing in my ears. Quite spontaneously a phrase welled up in me that seemed to have rhythm and cadence. I was in a night-mood, and the words "I am the blazing torch of night" chanted in my mind. The shimmering wonder of the light-flooded asphalt had entered my spirit, and I began to add to the line. Somehow, the rhymes came with ease, and soon whole stanzas were forming in my brain. I was discovering a poetic world of my own in English, a world related not to archaic romanticism, but rather to the metallic wonder of the big modern city. That night I wrote my first poem in English, and it was an unforgettable experience to read it in print some time later in the school magazine, *Chronicle*. To be sure, I continued to write in German, but English sounds slowly began to force themselves to the surface. I mingled free verse and traditional stanza forms. One of my early lyrical attempts in English was the following:

I stand desolate before the funeral pyre of my youth.
Out is the dance and the magic of blessed dreams;
And through the world goes a wind of despair.

Oh my soul, sing your pain-rhythmed song
Through the night-dark desert of your exile;
O weary soul, pray before the fire
Of a repentance seeking the litany of a devotion.

Your days were hung with mourning wreaths and lonely;
Your nights were distorted in a madness of longing;
Autumn was above your hut like a rain
That cries through pine-woods at dusk.

Now winter comes and plays its sneering preludes;
And wanderers stride patiently through agonies;
And my youth lies dead in the asylum of illusions;
And morning stares through the windows of sadness.

But I also felt that this immigrant existence could not go on, and I was ready to do anything that would enable me to emerge from the foreign diaspora. I haunted the Carnegie libraries throughout the city and read all the books I could find, especially works on sociology and general literature. By way of preparing myself for the ardently desired newspaper position, I absorbed everything that fell into my hands concerning this profession. I read technical books on reporting and the editorial branches, made myself familiar with the mechanics of a composing-room, and devoured biographical sketches of American newspapermen. One day, in a saloon on Eighth Avenue, I made the acquaintance of an elderly gentleman named Ralph Lind who said he was a newspaperman. This was my first direct contact with an American journalist.

Lind was himself "out of a job" and so for a while I saw a good deal of him. He told me he had worked for years as a reporter on the *New York World,* after coming to New York from Boston. I listened eagerly to his stories. He talked about the inner workings of his reportorial activity and regaled me with many anecdotes. He was a great admirer of Joseph Pulitzer, owner and editor of the *World,* and I was fascinated by his intimate biographical sketches of the Hungarian immigrant who had become a newspaper magnate. More and more the story of Pulitzer's life thrilled me, for unconsciously I saw in it a pattern for my own; I sensed certain analogies between his struggles and mine. Lind recalled that Pulitzer had landed in Boston at the age of seventeen, enrolled in the Union Army and fought in the Civil War. After Appomattox, he set out for St. Louis, which he succeeded in reaching by stoking coal on a ferry-boat on the Mississippi. Once there, he found work with a German-American daily, the *St. Louiser Abendblatt,* and soon discovered his real field of action. He first became a German reporter and then, after he had learned English, joined the *St. Louis Post-Dispatch,* which he later bought and built into a powerful organ of Mid-western public opinion. I listened, fascinated, to his story.

Lind drifted out of my life, and I continued earning my ten dollars a week in the warehouse. But somehow the dream of becoming a newspaperman had taken root, and Pulitzer remained my model. I asked myself if I should not follow his example and try to find work on a foreign-language daily; for my English was still shaky, and I did not trust my ability to write it quickly and fluently. At Lind's suggestion, I had already visited city-editors in Park Row, but the heterodoxy of my diction and my timidity undoubtedly militated against me. Meanwhile, that famous street remained the fiction of my waking and my dreaming hours. I roamed about the neighborhood, frequented the saloons where newsmen gathered, talked to them of my ambitions. They seemed to find these somewhat exaggerated and comical, and one, in fact, advised me frankly to improve my English before trying to realize such a goal. Undaunted, I continued to regard the *New York World* building, with its golden cupolas, as the symbol of a fabulous temple that I felt I would one day enter.

Finally I took my courage in hand and paid a visit to the editorial rooms of the German-language *New Yorker Staatszeitung.* There was no vacancy, but someone suggested that there might be one on an immigrant paper in Pittsburgh. I wired immediately, and the next day received an affirmative reply. Not entirely disinterestedly, I went to see my relatives to say good-bye, for I found myself obliged to ask them for a loan in order to make the journey. Uncle hemmed and hawed, upbraided me for my shiftlessness, said I was still a "greenhorn," but let me have ten dollars. I took the train for Pennsylvania Station with a certain sadness at leaving New York, whose cosmopolitan movement I had grown to like in spite of the difficulties of my existence there, but elated at the prospect before me. This was my first real journey outside the Hudson city. As the train raced through New Jersey and I listened to the wail of the locomotive's whistle, I thought ironically that, although I was passing through the state where I was born, I was still a "foreigner" in my native land.

I arrived in Pittsburgh on a cold, snowy February evening. The tall chimneys of the steel mills and glass factories pierced the sky. Blast furnaces belched soot and smoke. I felt exhilarated by the lurid cosmos, the cloudy world of industry, grandiose and Dantesque.

As I entered this new phase of my American life, I thought again of Pulitzer. Now, I too, had come west groping towards adventure. I knew, however, that this was to be only an interlude; I was still skirmishing in the arena of the immigrant, I had not yet reached the mystical heart of American assimilation. In the kinetic industrial world into which I was now catapulted, I was to feel for a long time that I was struggling in a prison cell. I passed through warring idioms and Old-World attitudes, but somewhere I felt a metamorphosis awaited me, even though the road should prove a rugged one.

As soon as possible, I presented myself at the office of the *Volksblatt,* a German-American daily, printed on the presses of the *Gazette Times,* the oldest English-language newspaper west of the Alleghenies. At first, I felt happy in the anarchic climate of the editorial room, with its smell of ink and noise of the linotype machines cascading from next door. In fact, all my life seemed to have been a preparation for this moment, and I began with enthusiasm my job of translator and rewrite man. I soon learned the technique of the American news-story transmuted into German. The local news, forwarded hourly by the Tri-State News Bureau, was "packaged" by the city-editor, a German-speaking Pole, who sent us out into German-, Austrian-, or Swiss-American circles to check on details and obtain interviews. The *Vereine,* or club activities, had also to be covered.

The atmosphere of the city-room was forbidding and one sensed there a psychic tension; it was as though the editors were not quite sure of themselves, or as if they felt they were living outside the common life of the American city. There were about a dozen of us, mostly elderly men, with a few youngsters, among whom I was the Benjamin. They were of Austrian, Czech, Hungarian, Polish, German and Swiss origin, and although many of them had been in the United States for years, few spoke English fluently, or even correctly. There were no typewriters in the office, and our pens scratched all evening over the yellow sheets, trying to mold into German the news distributed by the American agencies. We had to write our own headlines, which I found a challenging task. Clustered about large desk-tables, we toiled in glum silence.

In the evening there was a pause of half an hour, usually spent in a nearby saloon kept by two brothers, natives of Luxembourg. Here much boozing went on; whiskey was cheap then, and the regular tippling made it possible to strangle a growing nihilism. The older men exchanged reminiscences about their immigrant years and criticized American customs. As far as I could judge, they had all gone through almost identical experiences in New York, before joining the local writing fraternity. But their inner lives were variously mutilated and cramped. Each one seemed to have a secret hidden away, and it was difficult to find out the original motive for emigrating. In any case, no passionate desire to exchange autocracy for democracy was ever expressed by any of them.

As I gained familiarity with the subtleties of the English language, I began to realize with near astonishment that mine was a different philological outlook. Their narrow assumption that their Teutonic tongue was the "greatest in the world" irked me. At first I tried to argue with them. I tried to persuade them, with the superior knowledge of my young years, that English was infinitely richer in actual words than German. This they rejected as nonsense, with smiling contempt—although they knew literally nothing about either English or American literature, both of which were simply nonexistent for them. They cited in high-flown terms mediocre examples of their own nationalistic culture, and often I had to listen to their smug asseverations, while they pounded the table with Prussian arrogance and shouted their burgher dicta of supremacy! However, if they irritated me I was also fast becoming their *bête noire*.

"You're talking to older men, who have been here longer than you have, you little greenhorn," a Bavarian shouted, his face livid with fury.

"Well," I insisted, "I do know something about the English language, which is more than you do . . ."

"He's just bluffing," a Saxon yelled. "He'll never learn that language."

Even the German linguistic traditions of the newspaper were decidedly archaic. Such ludicrous medieval terms as *sintemalen* and *alldieweil* for *weil* (because), *ansonsten* for *sonst* (otherwise), etc., were often used—and I could not help smiling at certain awkward turns of speech that paralleled the inelegant barbarisms of Pennsylvania Dutch. The diction of these exiles was untouched by the modern currents that had set in with Nietzsche. One day a particularly crass provincialism of style caused me to burst out laughing in the midst of work. Schlueter, the assistant telegraph editor, an oldster with a goatee, who hailed from somewhere in Prussia, jumped up and roared that he would not stand for my presence any longer. The editor-in-chief, Sommer, a Sudeten German with a sense of humor and inexhaustible patience, mediated between us.

I got along better with the younger immigrants, who drifted in and out, usually remaining no longer than five or six months. They were a little older than I, for the most part in their early twenties, and had only recently left the Kaiser's Germany, either to escape service in the imperial army, or urged on by a powerful American romanticism. They seemed to have a more natural affinity with the climate of liberty than their middle-aged colleagues, were avid to learn English, and speedily adopted the American attitude towards life. I became friendly with some of them, and since their desire to Americanize themselves harmonized with my own, we always spoke English together — haltingly, to be sure, yet with a constant effort towards grammatical precision. They introduced modern terms into the newspaper style and we became allies in the fight against the obsolete phraseology of the older, moth-eaten immigrant generation.

At the same time I was reading more and more English poetry in a state of near wild drunkenness, uncritically, haphazardly — everything that fell into my hands, from William Ernest Henley to Walt Whitman. Poetry was an emotion that lifted me into moods of other-worldliness, a metaphysical liberation in a musical rhythm. Henley's *Margaritae Sorori,* for instance, left emotional prolongations of sadness long after I had read it, and the lines "Night with her train of stars / And her great gift of sleep" could bring tears to my eyes. Some of my own English efforts were in that spirit, or else under the stylistic influence of Francis Thompson, whose *Hound of Heaven,* "The Poppy" and *Sister Songs* became great favorites of mine.

The more I lived in the marginal world of phonetics, to which I was attracted, the more the new words impinged on the old ones. Then, gradually, I came to a point where I no longer translated from German into English, but slipped almost imperceptibly into the new rhythm. Creatively, German had not been killed in me — it could never be killed — but it was fast being pushed deep down into the lowest stratum of my unconscious. As I look at some of the poems I wrote in that period, I find a tortured element in them; they were still European in their lyrical depths, but something more crystalline about them foreshadowed, even then, an Anglo-Saxon tonality. I was beginning to write humanistic, expressionistic lyrics in which I gave free rein to my attitude towards the great industrial Nineveh, generally under the influence of Whitman and Sandburg. Having noticed that the *Pittsburgh Gazette Times* printed a poem every day on its editorial page, I decided to try my luck. I submitted a number of these poems to the editor-in-chief, and to my delight he published several of them during the following weeks. He also asked me to his office and encouraged me to write more. Here is one of these poems, written under Whitman's influence:

You who are imprisoned
In the cosmos of your longings
Hammering forever your fists
Against the iron bars of a madness
I salute you.

Dust-sprinkled wanderers in the forests of tears,
You enter the ecstatic evening,
Drinking the ultimate sunbeam
With the trembling cups of your hands,
Awaiting the fulfillment of dreams
Darkling from out the brain of your wishes.

Lonely poets in city-rooms,
Watching the stars through dusty windows,
I greet you.
I send the flame of my spirit
To aliens groping in mill-towns,
To young girls seeking blossoms of love,
To deserted young mothers in hall-rooms,
To the suffering ones moaning in hospitals,
To the disinherited in asylums,
To children cheated out of laughter,
To all the troubled ones who lost their faith,
To all those who hunger for a Savior . . .

Somewhere you will find the summer-gardens
In a valley of visionary dreams;
Your spirits will float
Above cities of miasma,
And smile in a litany of peace.

Soon I began to feel that the time was ripe for me to make a clean break with alien journalism. I had conquered the English language (or so I thought), and I wanted to work in an American city-room. I wrote numerous letters of application for work to the city-editors of the *Gazette Times,* the *Pittsburgh Sun,* the *Pittsburgh Post,* the *Pittsburgh Press.* Several times I was summoned for interviews, but my nervousness probably increased my foreign accent, and nothing came of them. One night, when I was feeling pretty desperate, a telephone call came for me at the *Volksblatt* from a Mr. Merchant, editor of the *Post*. "Can you come around to see me tomorrow?" "Yes, Sir," I fairly shouted into the receiver, and I was there bright and early the following morning. He offered me the job of "automobile-reporter" and although I knew nothing about automobiles, I blithely accepted.

I left the German-language world with no regrets, although I was warned by my chief that I need not come back if the "English job" did not turn out as I hoped. But this did not affect me. I felt confident that I could do the work. I realized, too, that this was the turning-point in my pilgrimage towards Americanization — towards the belated Americanization of an American. The night, as I boarded the street-car for the suburbs to announce the stupendous news to my American landlord's family, I knew that I was leaving the immigrant atmosphere forever, and that I would never return to it.

While the new job did not make great demands on invention, fancy or imagination, it tended to give me a sense of the dynamics of life. The people I had to interview, and with whom I was in constant contact, were the automobile dealers, drivers and mechanics of "Automobile Row." They were men from the farms and small towns, men from the workers' circles, the American people *in nuce*. They had dauntless faith in the possibilities of the motor industry, and not only did they romanticize the machine, they idealized it, worshipped it. I learned the intricate mechanical vocabulary without, however, understanding much about the subject. I used it almost rhapsodically, in fact, in news stories about endurance runs. Movement became a drug. I had to attend state fairs with representatives of Maxwell, Packard, Roamer, Hupmobile and other makes of cars. I wrote flashy advertisements for local dealers, talked with the owners, described their satisfaction in eulogistic word-pictures. I was happy; for was I not, even now, and however remotely, in the linguistic universe of Shakespeare's tongue?

Into this period of mechanistic euphoria crashed the echo of the shot fired at Sarajevo, and I suddenly felt very lonely. I meditated bitterly on the dementia that struck men periodically with its plague of hate and sadism and destructiveness. Across the world there spread an odor of death that reached even the shores of America. From the steel city I watched the antipodal sentiments confronting each other. I saw the conflict in terms of a millennial war, in terms of my Franco-German frontier tragedy. After work I wandered gypsy-like through the nocturnal streets, and my eyes pierced neurotically into the murk of the river-banks along which sprawled the

3. Jacques Jolas, cousin Madeleine, and Eugene, New York, 1912. Used by permission.

busy munitions mills. Often I was drunk and lay with *filles de joie*. Against the savagery of the day's impressions I set the assiduity of a macabre imagination.

For a time I felt, with certain of my contemporaries, that pacifism was the only answer to violence. I believed in the eventual victory of humanitarian socialism; I was deeply imbued with Tolstoy's ideas; I shared Christ's admonition that "ye resist not evil" (Matt. 5:39). As the war continued in violence, however, I understood more and more clearly that I should have to take my place in the ranks — that whatever our sentiments, we were all to be swept into the cauldron. Most of the young men of my generation were hurled willy-nilly into the abyss, and soon masses of them began to march to a new continent, to adventures in combat, to mutilation, or to death. All were marked by the terrible experience, either spiritually or physically. In the First World War, the American soldier felt that he was a crusader, warring against the autocratic egotism of feudalists and militarists. For me, the experience was a bitterly personal one. But it also undoubtedly spelled the completion of my Americanization. As a result of it I became a part of American life, I shared the common existence of the American people. My apprenticeship was to be finally completed through the momentum of the national army.

I was drafted in 1917 and sent to a Southern military cantonment. It was a rain-gray evening as we draftees marched towards the B & O Railroad

4. Visiting father and son, Pittsburgh, 1914. Used by permission.

station, while crowds lined the streets to cheer the departing rookies. I felt forsaken, for there was nobody to see me off. Already during the long train trip, however, I had my first glimpses of that marvelous comradeship which was to be so characteristic of army life. There was a rare good nature among these hundreds of lads from every profession and calling, en route for a life they had never anticipated. Very soon I realized that American humor was a thing apart.

But what interested me most was the variety of American speech that I

5. Eugene Jolas (photographed sometime during World War I). Used by permission.

heard about me: new words that surprised me—words from the workers' universe or from that of small towns; words that were signs for precise objects, words that came from ancient English traditions. They were profane words, crude words, voluptuous words, occult words, concrete words. There were turns of speech I had not heard before, a scintillating assemblage of phonetic novelties that enlarged my vision. At the camp we lived in barracks, and I heard my buddies use the fermenting American speech devoid of literary ornamentation. I heard the vocabulary of the bunkhouse, the steamer, the construction camp, the brothel, the machine shop, the steel mill. I heard the lexicon of the farmhouse and the mountain cabin. I heard the words of sissies, fairies, homos, pretty boys, pimps. I heard the clerical vocables of the religious-minded. I heard the talk of salesmen, newspapermen, photographers, railroad clerks, truck drivers, saloon keepers, postal clerks, detectives, working stiffs. I listened to the different shadings in the speech of soldiers from the Southwest, the deep South, the industrial cities of Pennsylvania, the East.

Living among these young men who came from every part of America, I felt a spiritual community, and my neo-American consciousness was vivified thanks to the conditions of close fraternization that obtained in the barracks. Here was truly a melting-pot, Franco-Belgian-Serbian-German-Austrian-Bohemian-Americans in our outfit mingled with native-born Americans with Anglo-Saxon names, and our conversations were often filled with picturesquely distorted English and foreign words that quickened my Babel fantasies. The lexical and grammatical deviations from the norm in which the aliens indulged amused me at first, but they also gradually came to irritate me, for I was engaged in a pilgrimage to the precisions of American grammar and syntax, and these foreign aberrations disturbed me. I had gone beyond this rudimentary phase of my linguistic Americanization, and the half-American, half-European periphery on which my friends were still content to live seemed to me to be a sign of mental inferiority.

After a few months I was named secretary to the chief psychiatrist at the base hospital. The spectacle of human malady which I watched at close range in Ward 33 was an overwhelming experience. Here both Negroes and whites from Southern and Northern states passed through the ward for mental examination, and cases of schizophrenia, alcoholism, dope addiction, psychopathic conditions of all kinds came to our attention. Sometimes the patients were kept under observation for a long period, at the end of which they were either discharged as incurable or returned to their regiments with specific recommendations. My duty consisted in typing their case histories. I had to listen to fantasies and hallucinations, to frantic screams, to incessant weeping. I heard paranoiacs crying out against a hostile world.

The experience was a searing one and I wrote a number of poems about the neuropathic ward, which I sent to Louis Untermeyer for appraisal. At his suggestion I made efforts to have the collection printed, but the interested publishers only asked for a guarantee; one, a Boston firm, even asked for $400. I was poor and could not consider such an outlay, so the poems did not appear until years later, when the poet Oscar Williams published them in his magazine, *Rhythmus*.

After working for a while as hospital reporter, gathering material for the history of the institution, I was detached to the divisional camp newspaper, *The Bayonet*. We were a group of reporters, under Lt. Seikel, who covered happenings in the camp, sought interviews with officers and enlisted men, and in general presented the picture of a busy military station. Working with us was Lee Pape, whose exquisite short story "Little Girl" I remembered having read in the *Smart Set* some years before. Pape and I became good friends.

It was in this Virginia camp that I got my first glimpse of Southern living, which still presented many features of colonial days. The forests nearby seemed to have remained untouched by man and, in autumn, offered a magic spectacle of rutilant color. We visited the trenches of the Civil War and were told stories of that conflict by veterans of the Confederacy. We listened to Negro farmhands singing their work-songs in the fields. We were invited for meals in pleasant Southern homes, where we heard the gracious Southern speech. All of us had love affairs with pretty Southern girls.

In due course I was made a sergeant. But by that time I had grown irked by the security of my war job, and I wrote to the War Department, asking to go overseas as an interpreter. At one moment I was even ordered to be ready to leave. The armistice intervened, however, and I was sent instead to the Surgeon General's office in Washington, on special duty. There I was told that my services would be required for the launching of a newspaper at Fort Sheridan, Illinois, where a reconstruction hospital had been installed. I arrived in Chicago on a snow-whirling day and began work as a reporter on the *Recall*.

A Mergenthaler and a rotary press were set up at the camp, and our chief, Lt. Wright, manipulated the machines. Sgts. Larry Smith and Jake Constantine, our pretty nurse-reporter, "Jerry" Lorentz, and I kept the columns filled with first-hand news of the many wounded soldiers in the various wards and accounts of their heroic attempts to learn new trades. I also ran a column to which I gave the mildly nostalgic title of *Recalletto*. We all lived together in a spacious house in nearby Highland Park, from where we occasionally went to Chicago to take in a theater or a lecture. In summer there arrived three charming new lodgers who were members of the Chicago Opera Company. We immediately became devotees of the open-air performances of "La Bohème," "Rigoletto" and the other popular operas performed at Ravinia Park, where the three girls were working.

Meanwhile I was also writing a series of poems, "Reconstruction Days," and sent a group of them to Harriet Monroe, editor of *Poetry, a Magazine of Verse,* published in Chicago. She did not like them, and returned them with a rather deprecatory note. I next despatched them to a Greenwich Village magazine in New York, *The Pagan.* Much to my satisfaction, the editor, Joseph Kling, printed them in an issue that also contained the first published pages of Hart Crane, whom I was to meet and publish myself many years later, in Paris.

Then came the post-war years; the gray and feverish years of readjustment, the years of the speak-easy, of new slang, of never-ending travels. I felt decades removed from the claustral nightmare of the immigrant, for somehow, as a result of my period in the U.S. Army, I seemed to have crossed the boundary line: the war of languages was over for me, and the tumult of the interlocking words was beginning to abate.

A year after the armistice, I was discharged from the army and returned to New York. I had no friends there, and no funds other than the discharge money given me by the army. So once more I haunted the employment agencies and public libraries. Those were bleak days and nights. My first job was that of delivery boy in a steel shop on Desbrosses Street. Finally, I became a proof-reader on the newspaper *Women's Wear,* in whose Fourteenth Street office I worked at night with a crowd of somewhat cynical newsmen who took neither the vocabulary nor the subject of feminine fashions too seriously. In the early morning, after work, we used to gather in a Third Avenue speak-easy for drinks and talk. Unfortunately, however, even this far from brilliant existence proved short-lived, and I soon became a victim of the first depression.

When at last I was offered a job as reporter on the Savannah *Morning News,* I again had to ask my relatives to pay my fare there. I left for the deep South during an icy gale, and the following day found myself transplanted into an Elysian landscape of palmettos and sunshine. Roaming through the Southern town before starting work, I delighted in the light-glinting mood of the wide streets and grassy parks, the colonial architecture, the Spanish moss draperies on live oaks, the many varieties of exotic trees. I heard again the speech of the South, the slur words of the Negroes, soft laughter in little alleys; I listened to street meetings at dusk: an itinerant colored preacher shouting a strange mixture of Biblical imagery, Kraal rhythms mingling with Baptist hymns, the lilt of unreal vocables.

For the first time I was now a full-fledged reporter in an American city. The secrets of prisons and courts were mine, the darkling enigmas of human conflicts and transgressions. During the afternoon I watched legal casuistry at work in the federal, police and municipal courts. I listened to a case of peonage being tried before a federal judge. I watched the under-dog in fetters, the wriggling of the criminal psychopath. My newspaper companions were for the most part native Georgians. In the days following pay-day, we occasionally hired a sleepy-looking horse and buggy that stood at the corner of Main and Oglethorpe Streets and told the old driver nod-ding on the coachman's seat to take us to a house on the outskirts of town. Here, in the plush-covered parlor, we raised a lot of "ruckus," danced with the girls to the tawdry tunes of an old-fashioned gramophone, drank awful "hootch" served by colored waitresses. The presence of sailors of various nationalities gave this harbor bordel an international character. Our visits usually lasted well into dawn.

Humorous as well as tragic cases were tried in the different courts, and stories of human guilt became almost a commonplace. Certain of them emerged, however, from the general welter of misery and crime.

"He put the herbs on me, Jedge," said a young Negro woman in the mu-nicipal courts, when her case came up before the magistrate. It was a morn-ing in early spring; the sun shone through the open window of the court-room, which was almost empty. "What do you mean by 'herbs'?" asked the judge impatiently. "Well, Jedge," replied the black girl, "M' husban' was runnin' aroun' with another girl and he said to me one day: 'Git out quick, I got another sweetheart.' And I says, 'I won't git out.' And he says, 'You won't? We'll see.' And then one morning I wakes up and there he was in the kitchen fiddlin' around wid some pots and pans and I says, "Whadcha doin' there?' And he says, 'Gittin' the coffee ready.' And then he left. And then I tasted the coffee, Jedge, and what do I fin'? There was some funny leaves swimmin' around there and when I tasted it I felt kinda dizzy . . ."

The coal-black defendant was put on the stand. He fumbled with his collar: "Ain't no truth to all that, Jedge. Ain't done nothin' to this woman. She's nagging me all the time and I wanna git a divorce." "Case dismissed," said the judge.

Other cases came up: theft and burglary and rape and mayhem, and lesser evils. Whites and blacks followed one another on the stand in motley sequence. Human passion was dramatized here in legalistic terms. As hate, misunderstanding and conflicts were presented before the Law, the life of the port unfolded in all its ugliness.

I remember another story: The courtroom was crowded when the Negro's case came up. He was a young chap named Joe Jackson, and the charge was rape and murder. Witnesses had given an account of his actions near the scene of the brutal murder of a white woman, on a farm just outside Savannah. He admitted the first charge, but denied having killed the woman. The jury filed out and soon returned with a verdict of guilty. The judge put on his little black cap and sentenced Jackson to "be hanged by the neck until death occurs."

The condemned man was put in a cell at the county prison, where I visited him several times. Once I accompanied a local women's group called the Helping Hand, whose members visited the prison on Sunday afternoons, held religious services and sought to comfort the inmates. Jackson, whose execution was to take place in a few weeks, joined the converts and sang hymns with them in a warm bass voice.

With the sheriff's permission I talked to him through the door of his cell. He was singing softly hymns he had known as a child or which he had heard recently. "How're you feeling, Joe?" I asked. "Tolerable, boss, tolerable," he said. He started to walk up and down slowly, mumbling his favorite hymns, which he punctuated with occasional strange, almost primitive stammerings.

"Joe," I said one evening, "have you made your peace with the Lord?"

"Sure have, boss," he said.

Suddenly he turned and whispered through the bars: "You know, boss, I ain't done this thing nohow." Yet I knew he had admitted it.

I watched the gallows being built at the other end of the prison yard. All the cells were quiet except for an occasional moan. When they took Joe out the next morning at eleven o'clock, he was singing a hymn at the top of his voice, and the singing did not stop until the trap was sprung.

The numerous court cases I reported in this Southern town gradually wearied me by their sordidness, and although I was unable to save much from my skimpy salary, as the year came to a close, I began to envision flight again. Flight meant taking a train for the unknown, it meant geographical dislocations, it meant miraculous possibilities. I lived with Freudian "imago" fantasies, especially after re-opening a correspondence with the French girl of my immigrant days, who was now working in New York. In the liquescent twilights of the Southern port I saw the cubes of Manhattan's sky-piercing buildings in grandiose silhouette, and before me scintillated the phantasms of a modern Byzantine existence. I left my work on a day when "the ghost was walking," and entrained for the North.

I knew I should have to organize my life more economically, but nevertheless I enjoyed this nomadism, this freedom of movement which was like a heady draught. My mental development needed tempering, for I was lured by many beckoning alternatives. In the train I thought of the fellow workers I had left behind in the South, and recalled their city-room stories, their iterant amatory dramas set in the most unexpected circumstances. They were a merry lot, those hitch-hikers and gypsies. I felt at one with these condottieri of the road.

3

ROVING REPORTER

I reached New York in a practically penniless state, and started to look for a job right away. Once more I became a familiar figure in Park Row, where I approached tough city-editors in a monotonous daily routine, but without success. At night I slept with other tramps on the Central Park meadow behind the Maine monument, to be wakened at dawn by the tap of a policeman's stick on my feet. Somehow I managed to scrape along on quarters and dimes borrowed haphazardly from newspapermen encountered during these disheartening visits.

One day, in desperation, I entered the office of the German-American daily the *Staatszeitung* and, to my surprise, was immediately offered a job. I felt relieved. But as I walked towards Chambers Street and saw the sign of the AP office there, I began to muse over the problem. In a flash I saw that I would actually be regressing in my Americanization, if I were to accept the offer of the German-Americans. Had I not left that world forever some years before, in a desperate attempt to escape from the melting-pot? Had I not made a solemn vow in Pittsburgh that I would take my place in the ranks of the Americans among whom I belonged by right of birth? Had I not relinquished the German language forever in those days of my emigration, when the vision of Shakespeare's tongue had shone like a blessed light before me? Now that I came to think about it, I hadn't liked the editor's phiz either when we were speaking German just now, and besides I had been away from the Teutonic language for so long that I felt re-adaptation would be a difficult task. It didn't take long to convince myself that I would be betraying my American conscience if I returned to the foreign-language press, and I finally decided to drop the whole matter. It was a sacrifice, for I had a ravening, raging desire to have a job again.

A short time after, as wrapped in my American pride, I strolled disconsolately down Eighth Avenue, I ran into an old army buddy who was working with the New York City News Association. When I said I was looking for work, he told me that a new and revolutionary type of daily had just been launched by Capt. Joseph Patterson, of the *Chicago Tribune* dynasty, and that this "tabloid" was looking for reporters. I "hit" my friend for carfare and was soon in the office of the *Daily News,* on Park Place. As Phil Payne, the city-editor, inspected me through his gold-rimmed glasses, I felt ashamed of my shabby clothes. Finally he said: "I'll give you a chance. Just wait until I call you."

While waiting, I read copies of the paper that were lying about on the desks, and talked with some of the reporters, young fellows like myself, who gave me an idea of what would be expected of me. The aim was to go out on stories, get facts and pictures, and then return as quickly as possible to write the yarn in brief flashes. The "pix," I was told, were the prime requisite, and no story was worth much without them. I learned among other things that the "tab" had had a hard struggle, and that until quite recently the new formula had not seemed to strike fire. Often even there had been rumors among the staff members that it was about to fold. It had managed to keep afloat, however, for the simple reason that millions of dollars were being poured into it, and some of the reporters had defiantly bought stock in the venture at a low price. For several months it had been laboring against public indifference, as well as against the resistance of traditional journalism in New York. The boys on the other papers had sneered at its "tawdriness" and predicted its early demise. Then there had occurred a psychological miracle, and the indefinable thing called success had come almost overnight: in the subways and elevators and street-cars the despised picture-paper had now blossomed forth and a new journalistic chapter had begun in America. I listened with great interest to these background notes, although I was beginning to feel that my chances of entering this charmed circle were probably few.

Finally, however, Payne called me and handed me a slip of paper on which was scribbled the name of a French woman and an address in Jersey City. "Her husband is scheduled to be executed in Trenton prison," he said casually, "and she might have something to say." With my heart beating hard, I took the ferry to New Jersey and called on the woman. She spoke hardly any English and we began to talk in French. Other reporters who were there did not seem to think much of the story and most of them left, while I continued to ask her for details of the evidence she possessed of her husband's alleged innocence. He had been convicted of robbing a bank and shooting the cashier. She was a rather handsome woman and at my request gave me a snapshot. Although her story was not very convincing, she wept as she spoke of her husband, and I felt there were some good human interest elements in the yarn. When I returned to the office, I reported my findings and was told to write the story. To my surprise and relief, it was given a two-column head and Phil Payne put me on the pay-roll. He also gave me an advance on my salary, with the advice to buy a clean shirt and get a shoe-shine.

At the *News* we were pioneering in a new journalistic dimension. We "tab" reporters wanted to witness all the hidden life of the city: births and deaths, accidents, surgical operations, copulations, dramas of love and hate. We had the pathological desire to penetrate into the alcove of every home. We transmuted facts into myths, twisted them into grotesque sensations, made them emerge in distorted contours, surrounded them with the magic of a modern epic. We were the verbal mirrors of the city's explosive tumult, we responded to the morbid hunger of the mass unconscious. Of course we made a show of being objective, but we were also aware that we were prejudiced and sought only the titillation of the senses. We somehow felt that we were engaged in the creation of a living folklore, that we were myth-makers in the industrial chaos. We invented heroic-comic figures that corresponded to age-old modes of thinking and to the yearning of the masses for simplification of life's enigmas. When we discovered the "bootleg queen," for instance, we felt we had added a new myth to the many we had launched already. In reality, however, we were simply echoing the epoch's anarchic individualism, the cheap era of "Papa" Browning and Peaches, the rule of the mercantile philistine, the new attitude toward sexual freedom. We were chiming the collective belief in unending progress and perfectibility, the triumph of the machine.

The New York of my boyhood had changed, but I participated in its gaudy post-war mood with a kind of elation. I learned to know it more intimately than any city I had ever lived in. Chinatown was no stranger to me, after I had roamed through Mott Street looking for stories with a shifty-eyed, ragged old tramp, who was also a stool pigeon and a dope fiend. I was assigned to the East Side, where I covered everything from murders and hold-ups to the system of the *Schaedsche*. I was privy to the secrets of Hell's Kitchen, I covered immigrant yarns on Ellis Island and was sometimes sent to the piers as a ship-news reporter. I knew the outlying Brooklyn sections well, and was sent out on many a police story in the most dubious neighborhoods. Since taxis were not allowed, I had to use the subways and the "L," and I pounded the pavements for long stretches in the rotting slums behind Flatbush and Prospect Park. I slunk through malodorous hallways where I saw a sum of human bleakness, degradation and misery that filled me with pity. These scenes brought back my own days of extreme poverty in the forlorn tenement-houses of Manhattan's West Side, and an indescribable fear invaded my nerves.

Working with me on the *News* was a brilliant and comradely group of reporters and editors, many of whom had ambitions to become poets, playwrights, novelists, even scientists, and our conversations were frequently tinctured with literary and scientific speculation. Paul Gallico, who worked beside me, wrote about sports in a personal and coruscating style. Vincent ("Jimmy") Sheehan, our star reporter, had a keen love for France and an awareness of French pioneering in letters. Jack Chapman, who combined reporting and photography, evinced interest in the theater. Dick Clarke did a really excellent job as picture editor. Clifford Laube, the assistant city-editor, let me read his mystic poems. Lamar Middleton, one of the most imaginative newsmen I have ever known, always had a string of stories about New York, which he told with scintillating humor. The erudite British-American Montgomery Belgion, who worked on the copy desk, entertained us with tales of literary Europe. Bernardine Szold was the star "girl reporter." Mabel McElliot and Lorette King wrote conspicuously good movie criticisms.

The tabloid style was dynamic and brief. We strove for a new writing technique that would differ from the venerable tradition of our *confrères* on the more conservative papers. We wanted our vocabulary to be lush and game-flavored, earthy and daring. We rivaled with one another in the invention of new words and even encouraged our readers in the use of "slanguage." It is undoubtedly true, too, that in mirroring the New York logos, with its polyglot intonations, provincial distortions, aggressive neologisms and illogical sound-twangs, we constituted a sort of advance-guard of a future journalism that, for better or for worse, would appear to have come to stay.

I was eventually taken off "the street" and given the job of caption writer, which challenged both my imagination and my sense of precision. For it required a lurid use of words and the capacity to work at high speed, especially around edition time. When the Sunday edition was organized, I was given an assistant editorship, and covered as well unusual stories emanating from the municipal courts or from the numerous other sources of sordid news items scattered throughout the five boroughs. With George T. Frye, a superlatively gifted reporter, I helped prepare the "pre-date" edition for expedition outside New York, a task that involved the nerve-searing duties of make-up editor, working directly in the composing-room. We filled this edition with the most phantasmagoric material we could unearth. Among other usable features, I discovered a monthly review entitled *Science and Invention,* edited by Hugo Gernsback a few blocks from our office. Gernsback was an editor with a futurist vision who combined journalistic acumen with creative imagination. He let us use mats of sketches showing fantastic anticipations in urban construction, new ideas in aeronautics, astro-mental utopias, and a general transformation of the world around us. These were reproduced in the Sunday *News* and helped not only our own circulation but also that of the review.

The Prohibition era, with its social and psychic tremors, was in full swing, and the blasphemous emblem of hypocrisy lay like a blight over our lives. Clandestine drinking became our principal source of liberation from the tedium of the tragic conflicts mirrored in our stories, with the result that we consumed bathtub gin and other ersatz concoctions to excess, often stumbling home three sheets to the wind. The war had left its wreckage on the storm-bruised shingle of contemporary history and we were swept along by an almost sickly restlessness toward a sybaritism that became characteristic of the age. In fact we were propelled unconsciously by the moral disorder around us into a veritable saturnalia of the senses. This general atmosphere of nihilism undoubtedly weakened our nervous stamina.

The more feverishly reporting activities kept me whirling in the perversities and aberrations of urban life, the more I sought escape in poetry. I soon began to retreat into a mystical world of the logos, to detach myself from the almost paranoiac delirium in which I felt enchained. I spent many of my free hours in second-hand bookshops and Carnegie libraries, and became particularly enthusiastic about modern American poetry. I read everything I could find, from Whitman to Oppenheim, from Scollard to Sandburg, from Underwood to Kreymborg. It was haphazard reading; to be sure, without critical acumen, but it helped me stabilize my disturbed nerves.

BEFORE PRESS-TIME

The clink of typewriters challenged the cynic hours —
While we brooded over the morbid adventures of the day —
We juggled bagatelles in the limelight of the future,
Lingered over them with the sing-song of our fancy,
And smiled, remembering hidden sins.

Outside, the winter storms rattled at the barred windows —
Sometimes a late reporter stumbled in, covered with snow,

Bringing the sneaking gossip of one who had seen too much of misery,
Too much of darkness to long for the sun.

And over us came the queer fantasy of a longing
For the music of strings and the voices of children,
For moon-white villages with shimmering gables,
For tranquil words weighted with love.

Our dreams were the shriveled fingers of a reliquiae,
And we were caught in the ache which nothing can heal —
Until the black night comes with its endless silences.

By now I felt confident that I should eventually make a conquest of the
English language, including the colloquialisms of the day, and I prided myself on being a real "scribe" of the newspaper profession. I felt, too, that the
German words with which I had crossed the ocean had now been replaced
forever by an Anglo-American amalgam of sounds. But although I was
living in the post-war excitement of the great city as an American reporter,
I realized that my journalistic education was not yet complete. News from
my family in Lorraine stressed the great political and psychological readjustments after Versailles. Still I had no great desire to return. I was very
ambitious, and I wanted to complete my training in America. Meanwhile,
although the New York scene was stimulating and I liked the comradeship
with the men and women working on the paper, I began to sense that I
needed the systematic technique of a small-town newspaper. The migratory urge was needling me once more. In response to an ad in *The Fourth
Estate,* I applied for a position in a New England town. My letter brought a
quick answer, and I entered the Yankee world.

I reached Waterbury, Connecticut, on a coppery autumn day and went
at once to the office of the *Republican,* where the city-editor, Joe Keene,
introduced me to the technique of the "police beat." The industrial city had
an essentially New England character, and I was struck by the examples of
typical colonial architecture side by side with modern office buildings and
factories. In the center of the town was the traditional green, flanked by
white ivy-covered churches. The mills (and slums) were situated on a hill,
while on the other side the residential district, with its porticoed houses
and wide lawns, dozed in comfortable sufficiency. At night the street-lamps
flared up on Exchange Place, which was where the local politicos met their
friends for news and gossip. The autumnal streets were shadowed by russet-
flaming elm trees.

Police headquarters was in the city hall, which soon became my daily mecca. From two in the afternoon until the same hour in the morning I went back and forth between the city-room and headquarters, where a laconic Irish captain informed me of the latest arrests or accidents. For details concerning the background of this savage tom-tom of crime and wretchedness, I consulted the chief of detectives. I covered murders, suicides, arrests of all sorts, interviewed prisoners in their cells, followed up [on] fires, kept in touch with the hospitals. I watched raids on brothels and gambling dens. I accompanied federal agents banging their way into the rooms of Red agitators during the famous Palmer raids. I saw a young servant girl who had kidnapped her master's child, cowering in a cell under the watchful eye of the police matron. I watched the police line-up in the morning, and the gimlet eyes of the criminals, fear-roving to the ceiling. I soliloquized in rain and storm and blizzards and heat. I felt an irresistible curiosity, a morbid itch to be "in" on the moving world outside; an unhealthy appetite for the latest developments.

On my days off I sought escape from the industrial anomalies and disfigurements of the town in the woods and fields, frequently wandering as far as the attractive Woodbury region. I had been reading Thoreau's *Walden*, and experienced no difficulty in evoking the Concord setting in which this Yankee individualist had spent a memorable two years a century before. I speculated on the problem of time, trying to synthesize the currents of prehistory, history and the present that flowed around me in organic and inorganic life. I learned the English names for plants and flowers and was fascinated by such words as "sumach," "goldenrod," "johnswort," "Queen Anne's lace." I recall sitting in rapt revery in a meadow near a farm, watching the sun on bush and rock and marveling at the thought that the Indians must have been there long before the white man had trod this ground.

By the end of my working week, which was set against a background of eternally clattering telephones and typewriters, Mergenthalers and passing motor-cars, little remained of the illusory calm afforded by these outings, and I gradually developed an almost obsessional aversion to everything mechanical. Not only the automobile, but all the inventions of our modern technological existence began to assume for me the figures of diabolical instruments that had but one aim: to de-spiritualize the life of the individual. Against this mechanization of the human spirit I posited the catalystic powers of poetry and art.

As my facility in handling the new language increased, I became captivated by the study of the sound and values of individual words, and between assignments, whenever I had a few moments to spare, I would hurry to the Bronson Library, just opposite police headquarters. These visits were of an almost ritualistic nature; I walked into the silent premises as though I were entering a sacred temple, and leafed reverently through volumes of philosophy and poetry. It was here that I became acquainted with the works of Swinburne, Coleridge, Tennyson, Lowell, Byron, and other English and American poets, and I made every effort to attune my alien ear to their rhythms. Such contemporary American poets as John Gould Fletcher, E. A. Robinson, e. e. cummings, Conrad Aiken and a few others seemed to me to possess inventive power and grace. Imagism, however, struck me even then, as being rather an aesthetic fraud. I never tired of reading Webster's *New International Dictionary of the English Language,* and, in fact, I grew enamored, fairly hypnotized, by the beauty and enchantment of many words. Obsolete and rare words, especially, had an extraordinary appeal for me, and I determined to increase my knowledge of them by a systematic study of their meanings. Paradoxically, in my reading of that time, I lived more in the idiom of England than in that of America, for I was convinced that only in this way could the true sources of the language be learned. I also became aware of the fact that modern American was essentially a blend, and I decided to take English as the model for my own efforts.

Although my speech habits had now been formed, my American reporter friends still referred smilingly to my foreign accent. These inadequacies of mine irritated me, but I realize today that they could hardly have been avoided, for I had undoubtedly come to the language too late to free myself of all accent. Nor did the fact that I had absorbed its first sounds in the gutters of Manhattan facilitate matters. I was aware, however, that in my English poems I was using a language different from that I used in my news-stories. Intuitively I felt that the functions of language were of a dual nature — that of suggestion and that of communication, and I attributed to the poetic use of words a superiority over that of everyday communication. I even began to take an almost abnormal pleasure in bringing out this difference in my own experiments. When I tried to obtain confirmation of these conclusions from my fellow reporter, Ray Fanning, a sensitive lad of Irish extraction, he would have none of them, and quoted lines by Whitman, who, he said, had used everyday words poetically. He did not convince me, however, and as I walked through the mean streets of the mill-town, I continued to seek an emotional outlet by repeating to myself litanies composed of rare, obsolete and fantastic words gleaned during the hours spent in the Bronson Library, or invented for my own use.

Out of my experience as a newspaperman I wrote expressionistic poems which I later grouped under the title *Ink,* and in which I tried to achieve a lyrical humanitarianism that would express my journalistic universe. I thought in terms of machine words and tried to make the newspaper rhythm the basis of my inspiration. In the early twenties Oscar Williams's review, *Rhythmus,* devoted one issue to my *Ink* collection.

METAMORPHOSIS

My words went into a sonata by Scarlatti,
They chanted night-hymns to the girl;
They lingered over archaic symbols.

My words explored the ecstasis of dusk,
They floated against the troubled light,
Between waking and sleeping,
Between bats and dreaming;
They were filled with forgotten rites.

My words grew ethereal with the saga-hours.
They besang the white trance of the girl
Who had kissed me in the bloom-park,
When the city light-sparkled below
And the mills floomed phantasmata

My words looked at themselves in the dancing mirror
They were inebriate with the music of their wishes.

On my day off I liked to visit Manhattan's theaters and concert-halls. The New York theater of that period was under the aegis of the Expressionist movement and Toller, Werfel, Kaiser, Rice and Čapek were the dramaturgic names most in view. This movement, with its gospel of world-embracing fraternity, fascinated me, although I occasionally felt that this essentially Central European attitude tended to become pure vaporing. Once or twice I ventured to Greenwich Village to listen to lectures by Frank Harris. I had sent some of my poems to his magazine, *Pearson's,* and received an invitation to call on him at the Chelsea Hotel, where he was staying with his beautiful, tawny-haired wife. He spoke good German, and insisted on conversing in that language all evening, as we walked through the downtown streets.

"You came to English too late to become a real poet in our language," he said to me. "There is, in fact, no example in history of a poet who abandoned his native language in adolescence, and later succeeded in penetrating the mysteries of a new one. There are so many grammatical pitfalls that can never be overcome, unless the words have been felt in childhood. What you heard from your mother or your 'nanny' is important. That is what give the tone to your style. All the rest is artificial."

But I was not convinced: I even began to argue. I said that the violence of my life in American cities had made me experience the English language in a heightened manner, that I felt I was a lyric poet with the words I had snatched from casual conversations during the years of my Americanization, that I had deliberately submerged my root languages in order to feel the music of English. I read him some of my poems. He thought they did, indeed, show an awareness of the genius of the English language, but, he added, "only a reduced awareness." And then he began to question this phrase and that *tournure,* this rhythm and that rhythm. When I left him I felt deeply disturbed. I knew passionately that I wanted to be an American poet and not a German or a French poet. I wanted to bring the melting-pot into America's poetic idiom.

I had covered murders and burglaries, I had interviewed politicians and divorcées, I had witnessed strike-riots, and gradually these horrors had begun to create a kind of psychic malady in me. The reporter's constant contact with the sensational in crime and aberration had produced in my unconscious a vicarious sense of collective culpability for humanity's miseries. Even my dream life during that volcanic period became more and more nightmarish, and a feeling of guilt played a leading role in these nocturnal visions, in addition to which the jangle-noises of the town also penetrated my night thinking. These dreams led my imagination into the realm of satanism, a paroxysmal world in which the orgies of the spirit developed a veritable doctrine, and an almost hedonistic joy in crime and vice tainted all my ratiocinations. I seemed to be wandering through a tenebrous romanticism in which my oneiric life wallowed in proliferations of succubi and vampires, of sacrilegious rituals, of bacchantic outbursts. I was in rebellion against Providence, and on the side of the demons. My preoccupation with the demonic soul (cf. Dostoyevsky's "subterranean man") undoubtedly produced something approaching a mental disorder, which I was to have difficulty in shaking off.

Once more I became obsessed by *Wanderlust,* by an almost sick impulse to move on, to take to the road again. This antithesis of languor seems to me to correspond to something characteristically American. Is it a part of the immigrant neurosis? Or could it be a part of the Indian heritage that has come down to the modern city-dweller on the new continent? But I was also driven by the conviction that somewhere, where I was not, there existed a paradise. The pace of my life was growing too delirious for me. I decided to leave. I thought of the West; the name of San Francisco became a conjuration. But I knew nobody there, and there was no one in Waterbury or New York who could help me to go there. I was in love with America and wanted to see others of its cities and meet others of its people. But I also dreamed of ships and oceans.

A strange tedium settled over me as the months went on. James Joyce's *Portrait of the Artist as a Young Man* fell into my hands, and I found in it many disturbing analogies with my own life in the Lorraine seminary I had once attended. I read Schopenhauer, Carlyle, Nietzsche. I was also beginning to take an interest in political philosophy; I believed in progress as an immutable law of nature, in ever-ascending scales of human advance. Some of my newspaper friends were socialists, and they talked enthusiastically about "that experiment in Russia." But I was an individualist; I hated political and economic dictatorships. The reading of Stirner fostered my apolitical tendencies.

Letters from Europe were becoming more frequent and their contents seemed more real to me. They spoke of the latest metamorphosis of the frontier, the new conflicts, the liberation from German militarism. Passing by a steamship agency one day, I stopped to look at pictures of boats and harbors. I was lured by an unnamed desire. I had little money saved, but by practically starving myself for several months, I was finally able to purchase a steerage ticket, which I paid for in installments. The boat, the name of which was, symbolically, *La Lorraine,* was to leave New York some weeks later. When the day of my departure arrived, I wandered once more through the familiar city-room and listened to the noise of the Mergenthalers and typewriters. I said good-bye to my New England friends, the boys and girls in the office who had become my democratic comrades, whose friendship, I felt, had marked my inner Americanization.

But the mood of homesickness was dominant:

NOTE TO ANOTHER CIVILIZATION

My nostalgias seek your moods
In every meditative dusk,
When I am tired with the tedium of machines,
This age is distorted with madness . . .
Fever stalks through the cities of stone,
Through misery-echoing hospitals and police stations,
Through tenement houses in factory towns,
Through streets lonely with desire-furrowed faces.
And life goes through a metamorphosis of lies

Hidden in the noise of stammering accents
And laughter is dying

My soul hungers for your vanished sublimities
For the ecstasies of your primitive spirits
For the reaching magic of Gothic minsters.

4
RETURN TO THE OLD WORLD

The shock of seeing Europe again stirred me: I was going back to my roots, to the cradle of my psychic beginnings, to mythic archetypes, the images of which had lain dormant in my unconscious for more than a decade. The atmosphere of the ravaged continent after the cataclysm evoked scenes from the Thirty Years' War, glimpsed in old almanacs decades ago, and although autumn spilled its cornucopia over the landscape, not only the works of man but nature itself seemed paralyzed by an infinite sadness. Nevertheless, I felt a sense of release from technological pragmatism and machinism, and I envisioned the future in terms of utopian plans to report my European experiences to America in prose and poetry couched in apocalyptic accents.

Our soot-covered, somewhat archaic train left Le Havre early in the morning, dragging its damaged cars across France. As we approached the Eastern provinces, I saw numerous scars left by the recent war: rusting barbed wire scattered about the fields, shell-maimed houses, the anguished look in people's eyes. My home-town of Forbach appeared uncannily quiet as the train pulled into the familiar station late that night. Nobody expected me, since I had not written that I was coming. I trudged like a sleep-walker through the deserted streets, until I reached the house from where I had left ten years earlier to engage in the great American adventure. All the windows were dark except one, but I could see that someone was still up in the living room. The old-fashioned street-lamp opposite threw a dull reflection across the pavement. From the tavern next door came melancholy accordion-music. I knocked. Mother opened the window. Who's there? There was a cry and a rush to the door.

My brothers and my sister hurried downstairs to look at the American brother, and we stayed up very late that night, exchanging broken syllables about the years behind us. Mother and Father were affectionately happy to see the returned wanderer. But despite the warmth of their reception, I was somehow fearful lest a spring had broken in our relationship; I felt a stranger among my own.

As I gradually re-entered family life, I realized that it was good to be part of a large household that had a closely knit common past. At each meal a cascade of questions splashed around me in patois-spindrift. But looking about the long table, I was struck by the fact that every face was marked by the terrors it had witnessed. I thought of the grotesque political fate of my parents: they had passed through the war as Germans; once they had been Americans; now they were French citizens.

My four brothers, whom I had not seen since their early childhood, had grown into young men. They seemed to me excessively European, so much so that they showed little interest in my tales of America. In reality, too, they were mature beyond their years. Their childhood had been plowed under in the madness of the war, and they had grown up in a period of violent transition. Now they talked cynically about the immediate past: the wild, undisciplined life they had led in the early days of the fighting; the screaming of the sirens at night, when Allied planes had strafed the nearby Saar war-plants and they had had to hurry to the cellar; their roustabout existence since the end of hostilities. They remembered the German armies on their way to the front, sweeping like automata through the main street of Forbach. They remembered huge cannon rumbling towards France. But they also remembered them coming back, beaten and humbled. They re-membered the arrival, after the armistice, of the first American and French regiments, which were welcomed by the townspeople in an outburst of delirium. Above all, they remembered hunger. As I listened while they told about these years, I found them disturbed, nervous, anarchic.

For several days, I looked with incredulous eyes at the room I had once shared with my American brother, Jacques, before we had emigrated. It had hardly changed. The old-fashioned oil lamp was still standing on the deal table, where it had sputtered over our heads while we toiled at our lessons. On the dusty shelves of a bookcase I fingered again the books we had used before our westward journey: Tacitus, Cicero, *Anabasis,* French grammars, German readers, a history book now out of date. In a corner, a much-thumbed volume of *Robinson Crusoe,* a book about Columbus, copies of the *Limping Messenger of Strasbourg,* an anachronistic atlas; some old American magazines brought back the memory of my parents after their American stay.

From the window I could see the market-place. Housewives crowded

6. A family reunion of the Jolas family in the early 1920s. Front row: Grandmother (Oma), Maria, Grandfather, Eugene; back row: Emile, Armand, Jean, Jacques, and Charles. Used by permission.

in front of booths where peasant women from the villages, in picturesque garb, bargained and gossiped. There were swallows' nests under the eaves, and the acacia tree was still standing in front of Hayo's house, shedding its autumn-tinted leaves onto the asphalt. The old hospital chapel, where we had served as altar boys, stood stiffly gray in the afternoon light. The shops were the same, only the names were changed: the *Spezereiwarenhandlung* was now an *épicerie*, the *Weinhandlung*, a *débit de vin*. The streets, too, had been rebaptized, and I mused over the new name of the *Wagnergässchen*, now the Rue des Charretiers.

Rummaging among old papers, I found letters I had written home during that first chaotic, apprehensive immigrant year in New York. The sheets were beginning to yellow . . . "Today is Sunday and I am free this afternoon. . . . I shall probably go for a walk along the Hudson. . . . Nobody to talk to. . . . The work is hard. . . . Sometimes I feel homesick." I looked at the adolescent handwriting; it might have been another person's life I was reading about. The letters had been scribbled in the furnished room of a West Side tenement-house. Digging further, I found some faded notebooks: Latin and French lessons. The decade whirled around me.

My immigrant trunk—the same one I had taken with me to America—finally arrived and was opened before the entire family. The young people's faces betrayed their shattered expectations, as the inventory of my humble belongings revealed the truth of my transatlantic adventure: some worn clothes, a few books, disorderly manuscripts of poems, a broken violin. I had brought back none of the fabulous wealth that was said to lie in the streets of American cities, and there was evident disappointment.

Soon my insomnia-lacerated years in America began to take their revenge and I slept heavily, always late into the day. I felt an abnormal, savage need to lose consciousness, and it seemed that only in dreamless sleep could I find compensation for the restless nights in cities. My mother did everything to make the transition to Europe and to home life as easy as possible, and in reality so little had changed in the family routine that my long exile soon began to recede from my consciousness.

I found anchorage in my ancestral home. In our peaceful old house, my wanderings had temporarily come to a close. Reading French, German and English books and writing lyric poetry now became my principal occupations. For a while I hardly left the house, save for walks with my brothers, or an occasional aperitif in one of Forbach's numerous taverns. I found it difficult to talk to people I had known; there seemed to be no bridge between us, for their minds could not project themselves into the far-away American reality. I read most of Huysmans's works, and Baudelaire's *Le Spleen de Paris;* I re-discovered the German Romantics: Jean Paul, Tieck, Novalis, and made the acquaintance of some modern Expressionist poets, particularly Georg Trakl, whose lyrics I marveled at. I had brought with me from New York an American anthology of modern poets. I myself began to scribble in a kind of psychic automatism, influenced by the style of certain folk poetry with which I had recently become acquainted. I wrote poems now in English, now in German, now in French, and by way of experiment, translated them from one language into the other.

As I had in my childhood, I went on numerous bicycle trips with my father through the Metz, Nancy and Verdun regions. On one of these occasions we visited the war-battered fort of Douaumont where a number of our French cousins had fought, been wounded or killed. The spectacle of ruined villages was everywhere to be seen.

Several times I pedaled to Strasbourg. I had always had an affectionate regard for this city, and these visits permitted me to relive the moments of childhood wonder I had experienced before the beauties of its Gothic architecture. The war had left many unsolved problems which the transfer from one regime to another had not eliminated. Local *comités de triage* were still functioning, and each day recent immigrants from Germany were being forcibly driven across the nearby Rhine bridge, at Kehl. In the schools French had become the official linguistic medium and the study of German was a matter of individual choice. At first, this so-called *méthode directe* threatened to become a source of great pedagogical confusion, but, in the end, it proved to be the right solution, and a decade later, the young people of Alsace-Lorraine were using French with ease and flexibility; they even seemed to prefer speaking it.

There was undoubtedly, however, a certain malaise which, fanned as it was by German sympathizers, grew apace, and one was frequently re-minded of the well-known folk verse "Der Hans im Schnokeloch" (Hans in the Skeeter Hole) in which the Alsatian has caricatured his own ambivalence.

> Hans in the skeeter hole
> Has everything he needs
> But what he's got
> He doesn't want;
> And what he wants,
> He hasn't got.
> Hans in the Skeeter Hole
> Has everything he needs.

I myself continued to be haunted by the dream-image of a frontierless Europe and took no part in the political debates around me. Strasbourg, I felt, came nearer than any other city in Europe to making realizations of that ideal possible. Here was a typical border-city, one that possessed all the elements of a marginal *urbs,* and in which the spirits of France and Germany could blend in possible harmony. Long before it was chosen as the seat of European discussions, Alsace had a supranational aura, and it even gave me a certain satisfaction to listen to the two basic European languages quarreling with each other or falling fraternally into each other's arms against this background. This process, to be sure, did not produce a mellifluous tongue, but the bilingualism of the border had abundant vigor and imagery, nevertheless.

In one of the small *Weinstuben* near the cathedral, I met Henri Solveen, poet and painter, a robust man of old Alsatian stock, who wore old-fashioned sideburns and dressed in a decidedly rustic manner. He had never been to "inner" France, but spoke French and German equally well. In World War I, he had been among the Alsatians compelled to fight with the German army on the Russian front, where he was severely wounded. At the time I came to know him, he was freed of all military service in the French army. His wit was famous in Strasbourg, and his contagious good humor and Bohemian manner of living attracted around him the best poets and painters of the region.

Despite his mocking manner, his was a genuinely religious spirit. As we grew to know each other better, he read me his poems aloud. I was impressed by the solemnity of his lyric creations, which had a mystic dimension quite at odds with his more frivolous nature. So far he had published relatively little except in an Alsace-Lorraine almanac to which he also contributed portraits and landscape drawings. We found a common interest in the great movement that had flourished in Europe a hundred years before under the name of Romanticism.

Solveen lived in a small flat, with his somewhat dowdy wife and child, not far from the Ill, and evidently they were in somewhat straitened circumstances. He nevertheless possessed a fine collection of Romantic books and documents as well as numerous books dealing with the Alsatian world — Alsatica — especially rare texts and books by and about the Strasbourg Friends of God, that mysterious fraternity of mystics who flourished in the Middle Ages. Skeletons and crucifixes said to have been saved from the Swedish invasion during the Thirty Years' War entered into his somewhat macabre notion of interior decoration.

At the same time, Solveen had a strong feeling for the new in the arts and was constantly engaged in experiments of the imagination. Dada and Expressionism interested him intensely. He had followed closely the artistic and literary developments of both France and Germany, and was himself an active participant in the lyric revolution then in progress. He was an admirer of Kurt Schwitters, the Dadaist, and of Hans Arp. Through his young Strasbourg friend Marcel Noll, who knew the Paris Dadaists, he also met some of their leaders, among whom was Louis Aragon. He liked to quote Rilke, Morgenstern, Trakl, Baudelaire, Jammes and Jacob.

Although a number of "little magazines" appeared in Strasbourg during that period, none of them survived, because there was no centralizing agency capable of gathering together all the creative forces then existing in Alsace. The French reorientation, which had begun after the return of Alsace to France, had created a certain confusion among the writers, and the linguistic problem dominated all others. In reality, three languages were being used: French, the Alsatian dialect, and High German. The Alsatian poets who were still writing in High German, however, did so because they had been reared under the German regime, and simply had not had an opportunity to absorb the French grammar.

Solveen decided to launch a bilingual review, *Les Nouveaux Cahiers Alsaciens / Neue Elsässer Hefte,* that would gather together these various elements and present a platform for the tendencies in Alsatian writing. The first numbers contained poems by Raymond Buchert, George Schaffner, Henri Solveen, Sylvain Kahn and myself, as well as texts in both French and the Alsatian dialects. The review had an excellent reception and seemed destined for a brilliant career.

In his editorials, Solveen envisaged the role of his review as an organ of "the European spirit." He reminded his readers that men like Herder, Goethe, Hugo, Delacroix, Barrès had always loved and praised the Romanticism of Alsace, from which they had drawn considerable creative nourishment. They had all felt the humanistic beauty of the region, and had been interested by the complex psychology of its people situated between two European races and spirits. Solveen wanted to make Alsace a supranational bridge between two cultures and languages. As examples of this cosmopolitan spirit he cited the works of René Schickele, Maurice Betz and Albert Schweitzer.

At the same time, he pointed out the frontier fate. Alsace and Lorraine, he indicated, had been the battlefield of numerous races in the past, and the memory of the bloodshed for national and religious ideas on the soil of the borderland was still alive in the regional consciousness. It was still a continuous mutation, he insisted, and history in the land between Rhine and Moselle would continue to march steadily, with terrifying logic, towards ever-new changes. "The love of our land and its history," he declared, "is the basis of our action; the love of its mystic and Romantic creations, throughout the centuries."

The younger poets, Buchert, Reinacher, Sébas, Katz, Matthis; the younger playwrights, Reinholt, Fuchs, Maegelen; the younger novelists, Odilé, Dieterlen and Betz, all became contributors. They drew pictures of the local urban and rustic landscapes, and in all three languages managed to create a European nostalgia. Betz, a native of Colmar, where his family, even before 1914, had always been militantly Francophile, chose French as his instrument of expression. He may be considered to have been the leader of the French group. His novel, *Rouge et blanc,* deals with an adolescent evolution in the transition period of Alsace after 1918. His knowledge of

German and German letters as well as his mastery of French made him the ideal interpreter in France of contemporary German literature. He was the first translator of Rainer Maria Rilke, who was his great friend, and he continued this idealistic task until his death in 1946.

One of Solveen's contributors and his friend of long standing was René Schickele, the native Expressionist poet, playwright and novelist. We often met in a wine tavern at night and listened to his rude, vehement speech. He was a remarkable story-teller, and had the peasant-like stubbornness so characteristic of his countrymen.

Schickele had left Strasbourg at the beginning of the First World War for Zurich, where he came to know James Joyce, Hugo Ball, Tristan Tzara, Hans Arp, and the painter Paul Klee. He told us the story of his flight: in August 1914, he had received orders from the German military authorities to report to barracks at Strasbourg. He sent the document back with the reply: "Gentlemen, I regret very much my inability to participate in your undertaking. Signed, Schickele," and vanished by next train to Switzerland. "The liveried scoundrels did not like me either on this side or on the other side of the Rhine," was his added comment.

Schickele, although Alsatian and as such a French citizen by reason of the Versailles treaty, decided to show his "good Europeanism" by living in Germany, opposite Strasbourg. He chose a little town called Badenweiler, in the Black Forest, from which he could look across into Alsace, and see the Rhine winding its shimmering way towards the sea. His love of the Alsatian homeland was a deep emotion with him, concerned his own province and its people. Whenever he had to cross the Kehl Bridge to reach Strasbourg, he continued to complain about the "liveried scoundrels" on the border.

Before the war he had lived for many years in Paris, and his dream had always been to bring about a reconciliation between the French and German cultures. He envisaged this as being possible through Germany's absorption of France's democratic spirit, and all his writings of that period reflected this desire. Schickele assumed a leading role in the battle of Expressionism which broke out in Germany some years before the cataclysm, and during his years in Switzerland he founded a brilliant review, *Die Weißen Blätter,* in which he published the work of the German and French dissidents. He told us that the greatest day of his life was when he received the news that the revolution had broken out in Germany.

The years 1924–25 were rich ones throughout European literature, and the Alsatian writers who contributed to the new review were conscious of the enormous fermentation that was taking place. Schickele was an excellent fulcrum, and his ideas of an Alsatian humanism that was to transcend the temporary frontiers became a slogan in our group. He talked a great deal of Thomas Mann, who was his friend. He speculated about his vision of the Alsatian intelligence as a quintessential European direction with Celtic sources that would weld all the other European elements into one. We discussed this question frequently in our meetings. As a Lorraine-American who had also tried to absorb English and American literature and the English language, I was unable to share his views. He had the typical continental European's prejudice against the American intelligence, and all he really knew about America was the work of Whitman.

To me that was not enough. At that time I was reading Van Wyck Brooks's *The Pilgrimage of Henry James,* a book which I liked very much and which marked a phase in my development. I translated some of its passages to Schickele, but he waved it aside. I felt to my disappointment that there was a gulf between the American and the European viewpoints that might be hard to bridge, and I have since had many occasions to confirm this impression.

On one of these rather wine-happy evenings, Solveen launched an idea that gave rise to endless discussions among writers and artists in Alsace. He felt that a movement starting from the Alsatian matrix could become really European and be an active link across the Franco-German frontiers only if a central force were welded together in Strasbourg. It was his desire, therefore, to organize an activistic "system of affinities" under the name of l'Arc, and he asked his friends for their approval. There was unanimous agreement with the suggestion, and he got to work to draw up the necessary articles of faith.

A week later he read a printed manifesto, part of which stated: "The sky above our city once echoed the voices of the victorious Roman civilization; it echoed the incomparable glamour of Gottfried von Straßburg's language, as well as that of the Alsatian minnesingers, the spirit of Geiler von Kaysersberg and the rude witticisms of Fischart. It echoed the clear wisdom and the imaged beauty of preachers and scientists, the fruits of richly talented poets and artists, not forgetting the cry for liberty which announced France's Great Revolution of 1789. But it also echoed the cruel sound of the bells that tolled the tocsin of the years 1870 and 1914."

Solveen distributed this manifesto throughout the land. It was taken up by newspapers and reviews, and a battle began that was to last several years. His internationalism, or rather cosmopolitanism, contrasted sharply with the nationalist forces that were beginning to assert themselves in Alsace, forces that had their roots in political ideologies such as that of the Action Française. Academic *littérateurs,* however, also joined the fray against him, for it was primarily a battle of languages. The insistence of the Arc manifesto on the retention of a link with the historic past clashed decisively with the nationalist notion that the French language should henceforth be the instrument of all creative manifestation.

As an outsider, and one whose American background made it possible to remain above the mêlée, I could hardly take sides on this issue. Yet I could see that it was really a question of organic linguistics, for the Alsatians who had been reared in the German language could hardly be expected to change overnight. This constituted an inner problem for each individual that could only be solved after long evolution. I felt the "Bridge" should be content to start as a sort of symphonic aspiration, in which all the linguistic voices might be heard.

The Arc anthology got under way. It was to contain poems, plays, stories and essays in French, German, the Alsatian patois, the Lorraine patois, and English (my own contributions). The "Bridgemen," as Solveen used to refer to his little band of dreamers, met regularly, and as the creative *Internationale* came nearer realization, a growing excitement possessed them. All the contributors—Schickele, Buchert, Solveen, Reinholt, Betz, Kahn, Mannoni, Fourmann—were aware that a great renewal of language had been taking place in both French and German during the past decade. Hatred of the traditional sentence, abomination of the decorative phrase were shared characteristics. A new richness had entered expression, and the metaphysical essence of the word was becoming more and more apparent. Hölderlin, de Nerval, Achim von Arnim and other nineteenth-century Romantic precursors were often quoted.

Like the Romantics, these men found themselves in violent opposition to the bourgeois philistine. The very words they used constituted manifestos against the Strasbourg burgher, whom they considered their arch-enemy, the eternal chameleon, changing with every political wind—before 1914 the German patriot cringing before the military and commercial privileged classes, and now the ardent French nationalist, thanks to a quick change of fortune. Buchert, especially, distinguished himself by an uncompromising attitude to which his sensitive lyrics offered a curious contrast.

New elements began to join the group. There was Hans Arp, a native Strasbourger, and friend of Schickele. With the Dutch painter, Theo van Doesburg, he was engaged in doing some remarkable murals for the palatial Aubette café on the Place Kléber. I had known Arp's work for some time, and liked it. Poems from his *Der Pyramidenrock* had been read before our group. They were more like verbal fantasias, or magic tales, than poems. He spoke the Alsatian dialect with great ease, and his dream-language was often a savage caricature of philistinism. Only recently Arp had returned from Zurich, where he had participated with Tristan Tzara, Hugo Ball, Richard Huelsenbeck in the founding of the already famous Dada movement. He was still a Dadaist, a quaint, primitive type of man, whose Swiss wife, the sculptress Sophie Taeuber, was a fellow Dadaist. Both plastic artist and poet, writing only in German, Arp proved to be a strange mixture of irrationalism and mysticism. A prodigious reader, especially of the works of Jakob Böhme and medieval German baroque literature, he would surprise us at one moment by speculating on theological questions, and at the next by plunging into savage scatology—a habit that proved disconcerting to many of his friends. He had a heretic kind of humor, and although he was an admirer of Jacques Maritain, he was nevertheless capable of poking fun at him with merciless wit. Arp talked to me of his friend Hugo Ball, the real founder of Dada in Zurich, who after a year of Dada dementia, had become converted to Catholicism and was then living like a medieval monk in a Swiss mountain village.

From Paris came the manuscripts of Yvan and Claire Goll who also joined the Arc group at that time. Goll, a native of Lorraine, having been reared in Metz, had played a role in the Expressionist movement in Germany before the war, and since his flight to Zurich early in August 1914 to escape military service, he had begun to write in French. Another French poet who joined the Arc direction was a young Alsatian Romantic, Maxime Alexandre, who later joined the Surrealists, writing his poems and prose texts in an irrationalist manner.

One of our lustiest insurgents was Marcel Noll, a young Dada anarch, who wrote his poems of violence without ever allowing them to be published. He had a genius for subversion, and our forays with him into the world of the "envious, sexless brood of philistines" usually ended in fistfights with the Boeotians of the border. Noll's admiration for Rimbaud, from whose *Une saison en enfer* he would quote whole pages, amounted to a religion. His style, too, was decidedly influenced by Rimbaud.

A transitional mood dominated all these writers. They were determined to help build a new humanity in a democratic European brotherhood. They were out to smash, with verbal bombs, the exploiting classes, to terrorize the bourgeois and his system, with word-guns and pictorial disfigurements. Their idea was to change the world—"Changer le monde," as Rimbaud had said—at all costs.

The second anthology was ready to be published when a hitch occurred that threw significant light on the inherent provincialism of the region. Solveen's printing was done by the Catholic firm Alsatia. The material, which was brilliant and revolutionary, had already been set up when Solveen received a letter from the official censor of the Strasbourg bishopric to the effect that Catholic objection had been taken to a great many texts in the book. Arp, Goll, Schickele and myself were particularly resented as subversive agencies. Solveen took the matter to the court, but from the first the battle was hopeless. The case dragged on for months, and it was only a year later that permission to print elsewhere was granted.

Meanwhile, the newspaperman in me began to grow impatient, and I decided to look for feature stories in the Rhineland, which, I heard, was in the grip of a decidedly *Weltuntergangsstimmung* (an end-of-the-world mood). I made a leisurely journey to Bingen, Koblenz, Mainz and Frankfurt during a week of unforgettable Indian summer splendor. The collapse of the middle class, with accompanying poverty and despair, dominated the scene. A relative who had been a well-to-do wine grower near Mainz had suddenly found himself obliged to work as a menial; indeed most of the persons I talked with were ill clad and seemed both glum and wretched. The Weimar Republic was feeling its way, but the militaristic spirit was still extant, and I had the impression that the political ideal of democracy meant nothing to the average German now that his dream of world conquest had ended in disaster. The newspapers contained little news, their pages being given over to the *feuilleton*—that half-literary, half-informative journalistic genre which I was, later, to have such difficulty in uprooting from the vitiated Nazi press. But the theater was flourishing and I attended performances of old and new plays by Maeterlinck, Wedekind, Sorge, Strindberg, Kaiser, etc., that were staged with intelligence and great beauty. Echoes of Dadaism and Expressionism could be heard in every provincial town.

But despite this dramatic raw material, I did not succeed in marketing my stories quickly enough to permit me to stay on in Germany, and I was soon obliged to return to Forbach. Also, financial conditions at home had deteriorated, so that Father could not help me. I wrote letters to the editors of the Paris editions of the *Chicago Tribune* and the *New York Herald,* as well as to several American news agencies. Finally, I received a letter from David Darrah, managing editor of the *Tribune,* offering me a position with his paper. A few days later I arrived in Paris, in the sheen of spring.

5

REPORTER IN PARIS

I was now working as an American newspaperman in the Seine cosmopolis and during the following years was to realize my ambition to serve as interpreter of European civilization to my native America and of American culture to Europe. The next fourteen years of my life in Paris were to be frequently interrupted by western voyages—both real and visionary—to the Americas, which I saw increasingly as America Romantica, America Phantastica, America Mystica. It was during these years, too, that I set forth on a long pilgrimage through language, a journey of exploration through the titanic forest of words, many thousands of words, a columbiad through the empires of three languages, in search of a new language which I envisioned as the synthesis of a future tongue. My renewed contact with the linguistic life of the Lorraine frontier had sharpened my awareness of the bilingual spirit of my childhood. But meanwhile the American language, which had been the most passionate experience of my adult years, fought slowly for supremacy and although I was to write poems in French and German as well, it was the lyric feeling of the last-acquired language that I strove for most. I was drawn by the concept of a kind of Eur-American philology, an intercontinental idealism of the word that soon dominated my waking and sleeping hours. But I also suffered language.

After some months, David Darrah took me off the night desk and assigned me to a reportorial job. It was exciting to have the privilege of seeing the inner and outer phenomena of the French city at close range, to be privy to its multifarious riddles and paradoxes, to listen to its nervous heartbeat. Not only Paris but all Europe of that period spun around Versailles and the League of Nations. Locarno came, with an apparent promise of long peace between France and Germany. Politics was radical and democratic and the German danger seemed remote, smothered as it was in the fiction of Weimar.

For a while I covered foreign news at the Quai d'Orsay, along with other Anglo-American journalists. I was present at sessions of the Chamber of Deputies, when I heard Aristide Briand and Edouard Herriot electrify their listeners with the splendor of their verbal improvisations, against a background of boisterous Communist and Action Française caconyms roaring between the antipodal brethren. I attended the weekly luncheons of the American Club of Paris, where I heard Otto H. Kahn eulogize Mussolini for getting Italian trains to run on time, Senator Capper explain the agrarian problems of the United States, Senator La Follette expound his social theories, and numerous other eloquent or dull visitors to Paris, who did not hesitate to edify us with their frequently "hick" impressions. I interviewed so-called prominent men and women — many of them movie stars — who arrived at the Gare St.-Lazare in a blowzy cloud of publicity. It was easy enough to elicit their volatile, gewgaw phrases. I saw Gloria Swanson become Marquise de la Falaise de la Coudraye, and was struck by her beauty. I interviewed Mrs. Annie Besant, the occultist leader, and heard, to my surprise, that California was about to produce a new race of mystics. I covered the American Embassy and noted down at banquets and other gatherings the amiable speeches of Ambassador Herrick. I covered the American Legion's activities, lectures at the Sorbonne supposed to be of interest to Americans, cafés and clubs on the Left Bank where students, artists and adventurers from all over the world were expressing their revolt against bourgeois life. I reported police stories, hospital stories and divorce stories — for Paris was then the mecca of hundreds of ladies and gentlemen from every part of the world, eager to break their conjugal bonds in an atmosphere of inexpensive, guaranteed amusement.

When our city-editor returned to America, I was appointed his successor. I plunged into the new work with enthusiasm: I wanted to mirror the kaleidoscope of Paris in the columns of the paper, and I decided to apply methods of journalism that I had known in the United States. We had a serious rival in the Paris edition of the *New York Herald*, but the *Chicago Tribune* style differed deliberately from that of the rather conservative *Herald*. In fact, we made an effort to "jazz up" our reports, often growing lurid and sensational over the leads, applying the tabloid technique. We invented our own grotesque cable stories as fillers, and played gaily with nerve-demoralizing headlines. But also we tried especially to emphasize the new intellectual and aesthetic developments in Paris, and whenever possible, to scoop the *Herald* with unusual stories and interviews.

The office of the *Chicago Tribune* being located on the edge of Montmartre, not far from the Gare de l'Est—the big station for the Eastern provinces of France—I naturally sought my first habitat in that gaudy commune. It was a cheap little hotel called the Hôtel de Nancy et de Commercy, with plush-bottom chairs in the reception room and, for *patronne,* an antique, brawling termagant, always on the lookout for trouble and for money, who knew everything that went on in the house—love affairs and lovers' quarrels, for the most part. When a lodger failed to pay the *note,* she subjected him to sinister forms of compulsion. On these occasions she would become ruthless and vicious and scream "voleur," "espèce de voyou," "va sur le trottoir, toi," at the unfortunate man or woman who happened to be in dire straits.

Several of my colleagues lived in the same hotel, or in hotels nearby. We were, in fact, known in the neighborhood as "les Chicagos"—with the stress on the first syllable—and we benefited greatly from the prestige of that name. We had our meals in a little restaurant in the Rue Lamartine, where for a few francs we were given a tough steak—horsemeat—with a glass of dulcified Algerian wine. Other indigent and sometimes underfed persons from the *quartier* ate at the same restaurant. We grew to know them, listened to their stories of amatory and domestic felicities and misfortunes, and had a drink with them occasionally, whenever we happened to be flush. Now and then one or other of the "Chicagos" would bring in a *belle de nuit,* and there being no sense of moral or social hierarchy in our group, the peripatetic lady was accepted with grace and old-world courtesy by the other customers. At the hotel these girls made themselves at home, and before anyone knew what was happening, they were there to stay.

That epoch was characterized by a rush for pleasure that swept us all into its maelstrom. The four terrible war years were ended. The threat of death that had been over France was now dissipated. It was natural that people should seek to forget the macabre nightmare, just as, in the days of the Directoire, French youth had plunged into festivities to find relief after the horrors of the guillotine. The *incroyables* had their counterparts in the youth of the 1920s.

A typical incident that threw a harsh light on the *mores* of some of the U.S. exiles then living in Paris occurred one night in the editorial rooms where a number of us were preparing the next day's issue. We were banging away on our typewriters, when suddenly there appeared in the doorway Scott Fitzgerald and his wife, Zelda, both a bit under the weather alcoholically. Fitzgerald began to mumble something that resembled a speech and ended with the information that he had just visited a bordel situated very near the *Petit Journal* building. "Grand place," he said unsteadily, "you fellows ought to go there and see what life is really like." As the couple stumbled out of the office, there was a short silence of complete astonishment that was soon broken by sarcastic jeers hurled after the departing sybarites.

Once a year the staff of the *Tribune* received a visit from the newspaper's editor-dictator, Col. Bert McCormick of Chicago. This event was invariably accompanied by a week of chaotic living, part of the tradition of which was a copious *déjeuner* for the entire staff, which took place at the inn of La Mère Catherine, in Montmartre. Before we settled down to gigantic libations of excellent *crus* from the Côte d'Or, there was always a speech by the "boss," who on these occasions, tried his best to play the *bon enfant* in the midst of his hedonistically inclined employees.

Rumor had it that the sour-looking gentleman from Lake Michigan was hankering for the rosette of the French *Légion d'Honneur,* and we heard that he had entrusted the task of obtaining it for him to our colleague Eugène Rosetti (could it have been because of his name?). This gifted linguist — he wrote and spoke Rumanian, German, French and English — who also acted as our legal expert, was a friend of Senator Caillaux and, in consequence, was confident that he would be able to arrange the matter of coveted ribbon through this and other connections at the Palais du Luxembourg. When Caillaux became Minister of Finance, we thought the plan would certainly succeed. Some hitch occurred however, and as a result, poor Rosetti was dismissed for inefficiency.

But neither the "Col.," through his pep-talks, nor the managing editor, through his toughness, succeeded in creating an efficient organism modeled on the lines of the home-town paper. For we were all anarchs at heart, and the disorder that reigned in the editorial rooms was an exact reflection of our state of mind. The sorcery of Paris made seductive music all around us, and we were generally out for fun and trouble. Also we were all trying to write novels or poems of our own, and literary discussions interested us more than technical debates about headlines and news-stories.

In the spring of 1925, my brother Jacques and his wife arrived in Paris and settled in a little apartment on the Avenue de la Bourdonnais, near the Eiffel Tower. Somewhat shocked by the chaotic way in which I was living, they kindly invited me to stay with them, an invitation I eagerly accepted. Jacques was studying piano with the eminent Maître Isidore Philip, and I found myself once more in the musical sphere I had always liked. He was practicing two concerti, one by Mozart and one by Schumann, as well as compositions by Scarlatti and Scriabin, and his delicate, sparkling virtuoso art furnished a leitmotif to my own reflections. In fact, I found it a joy to wake up in the morning with piano exercises ringing in my ears.

The Champ de Mars neighborhood has great loveliness in spring, and we often strolled in the gardens beneath the Eiffel Tower after a joyous déjeuner at the nearby Ferrari Restaurant, where Jacques's gold watch was occasionally left in escrow to pay for some particularly Lucullan menu. Or else we would meet friends at the bar of Chez Francis, just across the Alma bridge, on the right bank of the Seine. I usually went to the newspaper office at dusk, and I remember the daily aesthetic shock I received as the AC bus rumbled across the bridge and my eye caught sight of the Moorish towers of the old Trocadéro Museum high up on the hills of Passy. This falsely oriental structure has since disappeared from the Paris horizon, but it remains in the mind's eye of many for whom, like myself, it was for years the familiar *réplique* to the Eiffel Tower.

Once a week Jacques organized a musical soiree, when American, French, British and Scandinavian friends would come to listen to his playing of Scarlatti, Bach, Mozart, Brahms, Poulenc and Scriabin. Our bohemian friend Rosalie Campbell, a genial Scottish spinster who was also mysteriously related to several aristocratic French families, helped us receive our guests, and introduced into the circle a number of sensitive music-lovers whose presence added to the enjoyment of these evenings. Among them was Paul Rosenstand, a tall Danish *boulevardier* who bore his poverty with imaginative grace, and who, as he said, preferred to "live in Paris like a gentleman" than to vegetate in the crotchety atmosphere of Copenhagen. There were also Jacques's and my American friends: Dwight Fiske, Jacques Leclercq, Chester McKee, Edmund Pendleton, and George Antheil, whose brilliant, almost barbaric compositions, in the vein of a modern machine romanticism, I liked.

Dwight Fiske was studying composition, and Jacques played his "Preludes" at several concerts. In addition, Dwight's *badinage* and pleasantries diverted us, for he was already beginning to entertain close friends with the pianistic buffooneries he was later to present with such success to a wide public in America and England.

Jacques Leclerq, who used the *nom de plume* of Paul Tanaquil, had already published several volumes of poems and was engaged in writing a group of short stories under the title *Show Cases*. These were savage portraits of American exiles in the upper social brackets, whose disordered love lives he pilloried without mercy. He lived on the Île Saint-Louis and was ostensibly studying at the Sorbonne. Although a true bohemian, he curiously enough also took a certain pride in the fact that his godfather was Premier Clemenceau, who had been a friend of his father.

Chester McKee, a native Pittsburgher and a former army "buddy" of mine, had studied music in Paris before 1914. Now he wanted to be a conductor, and he worked for some time as assistant to a number of French *chefs d'orchestre*. An incorrigible romantic, Chester felt he had realized in France his dream of a paradise on earth, and he soon learned to speak French like a Frenchman.

Edmund Pendleton looked rather like Beethoven and was at once pianist, organist and composer. He also had a remarkable gift for mimicry, coupled with a rollicking sense of humor, and he frequently diverted us with his one-man performances, which included imitations of French opera singers, German *Lieder* singers and Italian tenors, presented in slapstick style. At that time he had already lived in Paris for over a decade—during the last war he roamed the French countryside, disguised as a shepherd— and he is today one of the few Americans I have known who have become thoroughly French.

When my brother gave a recital at the *Salle du Conservatoire* or in the *Salle des Agriculteurs,* our little group used to attend in a body. Jacques was quite a virtuoso and played Mozart and Chopin with rare brio and lyricism. As the date of a concert approached, I grew even more nervous than he, but as soon as the first measures were played, I felt reassured and enjoyed listening. After the concerts there was always a little fête Chez Francis, when quantities of white wine were consumed to celebrate the event.

One winter we decided to organize a group concert, in which Jacques, Fiske, McKee and Pendleton would all participate. They named me their "publicity manager," and soon numerous exuberant items about my friends and their collective musical genius began to find their way into the columns of the *Chicago Tribune.* These stories were picked up by the agencies, and we even received inquiries from the United States. Encouraged, I peppered away. The boys had engaged the Conservatoire orchestra, and Jacques was rehearsing the Schumann concerto under the baton of McKee. Meanwhile, Dwight Fiske was setting some of my poems to music, to be sung by the well-known French singer, Geneviève Vix.

The great day arrived and there was a final rehearsal in the morning. It went badly, however, and the nerves of all the performers were decidedly on edge as a result. Dwight Fiske had not yet finished his orchestration of my songs, and was still working in one corner of the concert-hall with the help of Pendleton, while Mlle. Vix tried her rather inadequate English on my texts. Chester McKee had difficulty in getting the maximum effect out of the more recalcitrant members of the orchestra, and his rebellious locks waved madly over his forehead as he strained to keep the instrumentalists together. We were all quite depressed when the rehearsal was over, and anticipated disaster for that evening. But somehow the concert went off well. Dwight got an ovation for a remarkable job of invention and orchestration, and Jacques and McKee received many bravos for their performance of the Schumann concerto. I, meanwhile, kept the wires burning with publicity material about this "triumph of American musicianship."

A dream I had cherished throughout my years of migration and struggle in America had now become a reality. I was living in Paris as an American reporter. The French language, which I had heard in my childhood in Lorraine, but which the long years in the linguistic universe of Anglo-American had almost obliterated, was again emerging; I was beginning to think in it and even to dream in its colloquial weft. I began to bathe in the idiom of Paris: I listened to it on autobuses, I studied the popular speech in the *métro* and on the boulevards. I was in an ecstasy of words that traversed me like an electric current. And then there was the sky of Paris, which was unlike any I had ever seen before. As I walked through the old quarters near the Île de la Cité, the ever-changing sky was for me a fabulous spectacle. I understood now the springs at which the French painting genius had found its inspiration.

One day David Darrah asked me to edit the *Tribune*'s "literary page," which he had inaugurated some months before. Till then it had been in the hands of the English writer Ford Madox Ford, but Darrah said he wanted a newspaperman to do it. Ford was a famous writer, and I hesitated considerably at the idea of becoming his successor in such a prominent spot, but Darrah insisted that I should try it. Thus I began the weekly column I called "Rambles Through Literary Paris," and made my entry into literary journalism. For the next year this activity kept me busy, for I had to combine it with my function as city-editor. My aim was to apply American reporting methods to the creative and aesthetic issues of the day. I considered myself primarily a reportorial observer and recorder of the ideological currents in post-war Paris.

Not that I had abandoned the writing of poems. On the contrary, this was a particularly fertile period, and when I returned to my hotel room at night, I scribbled countless prose-poems in French which I called *Monologues sur les Boulevards,* for the most part studies in the grotesque and the macabre. I told myself that I belonged to the spiritual family of Jean Paul Richter and Gérard de Nerval, of Novalis and Brentano, and unconsciously

I looked around me in search of similar contemporary minds. I loved the French Symbolist poets with an absorbing passion, and especially those in the anthology published by the *Mercure de France,* in which Henri de Régnier and the American Symbolist Stuart Merrill appeared side by side with Saint Pol-Roux-le-Magnifique and Jules Laforgue.

Reporting now became a real adventure of the intellect, for many contemporary French writers began to come within my purview. As a rule I found them urbane and human, but a few appeared to me to be egocentric and pretentious. Some were American enthusiasts, others had a penchant for Moscow. Many impressed me as mere *hommes de lettres,* intellectuals from the Ecole Normale or the Sorbonne, who were far removed from the stream of life. But there were real poets among them, both major and minor, creators blessed with the vision of a noumenal reality.

I liked especially Jean Giraudoux. He invited me to his home in the Rue aux Clercs, and I found him the gracious *homme de lettres* of the old school. He had gone to the United States during the war with a French commission and had written a tribute to America entitled *Amica America,* a copy of which he gave me. He was a tall, slender, bespectacled intellectual, who had a ready wit and seemed to enjoy the ordeal of the interview. He had just completed a new novel, he told me, to which he had given the title: *L'Europe sentimentale,* but he had heard that morning that his friend Paul Morand had quite unwittingly chosen the identical title for a new book of short stories contemplated for early publication. Giraudoux relinquished his priority right to the title and decided to look for another.

Then there was François Mauriac, whom I interviewed in his Passy Tusculum. The Dadaists were vociferously active and he told me with a sense of hurt pride that he could not understand the violent enmity to his work shown by such young men as Aragon and Breton. "What have they against me?" he wondered. I told him of my own admiration for his first novel, *Genitrix,* which had remained in my memory as a graphic portrait of a pathological matriarch. We spoke of the Catholic spirit in France, which he felt was going towards a revival. He himself was a convinced and practicing Catholic, and his novels mirrored the disquiet of people who retained a sense of the conflict of good and evil. I always thought that, fortunately for creative literature, he was more on the side of the Devil than on that of the angels.

Philippe Soupault, young and dynamic, flashed on my horizon. He arrived at the Deux Magots, where we had a rendez-vous one evening, with a copy of his newly published *Le Bar de l'Amour* under his arm. He talked with brilliance and charm of Dada and the then nascent Surrealist movement, of his friends André Breton and Louis Aragon, and expressed admiration for two young American writers he had met in Paris, Malcolm Cowley and Matthew Josephson. We became friends, and he invited me to his home in Auteuil, where he and his wife, Marie-Louise, were living in a pleasant *garçonnière*.

Jacques Rivière was editor of the *Nouvelle Revue Française*. I had met him several times, and was glad to accept an invitation to tea at his home, where the contributors to the review frequently gathered. Rivière had published a book of essays, *Etudes,* which I greatly admired and in which he had analyzed the work of Gide, Claudel, Matisse, Rimbaud, Bach and others in a highly sensitive style. In fact, he anticipated many of the currents that were to emerge in the later twenties. He had been taken prisoner in the First World War, from which he brought back a book of incisive psychological insight devoted to a study of the German, *L'Allemand.* It was at his home, in which his charming wife, Isabelle, presided as hostess, that I was presented to André Gide for the first time.

I had been reading *Les nourritures terrestres* with growing enthusiasm, and my meeting with the writer was an event in my life. At this first meeting, however, he seemed quite shy and taciturn, and my reportorial ambition was not satisfied until later, when I succeeded in knowing him better. A collection of his critical works, published under the title *Prétextes,* had revealed a subtle intelligence and artistic integrity, and what I admired particularly in Gide was the mixture of classical consciousness and romantic exaltation that marked his strongly individualistic will. Seated beside him in the Rivière salon, I observed his sharply chiseled features and his deeply sunken eyes, with their smoldering fire. But he seemed melancholy, and I do not remember seeing a single smile pass across his face that day. Rivière, a gentle, almost timid man, hovered around him with filial respect, and the other writers of the younger generation seemed hardly to dare approach the *maître.* Gide spoke to me of Nietzsche, but denied that his *Nourritures terrestres* had been influenced by *Thus Spake Zarathustra.* Rivière felt that *La symphonie pastorale* was Gide's most representative work (Joyce also admired it); others preferred *Les caves du Vatican* or *Paludes.*

I was also presented to the Catholic metaphysician Charles Du Bos, a friend of Gide's, and a most engaging person. He spoke excellent English and was familiar with the work of both British and American writers. Then there was the younger generation: young men just out of the army or the Ecole Normale, even adolescents. Each one seemed either to have a book to his credit, to have contributed to the *NRF,* or to have a book in preparation. The *Nouvelle Revue Française* was closely connected with the publishing house of Gallimard, which had been founded a decade before by André Gide, André Schlumberger and Gallimard. The young men talked about Paul Valéry and his aesthetic theories, about Gide and his Lafcadio, about Dada and Surrealism. The more radical representatives of the two latter movements, however, were never to be seen in the sacred precincts of the Rivière salon. Jean Prévost, who had just published a first novel dealing with his youth during the war, told me with pride that he was also a boxer and had had a few bouts with Ernest Hemingway. There were others: Pierre Drieu La Rochelle, Jean-Richard Bloch, the mysterious Pierre-Jean Jouve and Pierre MacOrlan, all up-and-coming young poets and novelists. Shining metaphors glimmered, daring images played across the room. The name of Rimbaud was frequently mentioned. Many names, some still unfamiliar to me, aroused my curiosity. A young man recited a line from a poem by Saint Pol-Roux-le-Magnifique, the aged Breton poet, once the magus of the symbolist epoch. To the former grocery boy, these were exhilarating, formative moments.

Léon-Paul Fargue I met elsewhere. In the little Rue de l'Odéon there were two bookshops that were already famous in Paris, and soon to become known to the entire European world of letters. One was Shakespeare & Co. run by an American woman, Sylvia Beach, and the other La Librairie des Amis du Livre, run by her French friend Adrienne Monnier. In these intelligently hospitable shops one met the great, the near-great and the authentic bookworms. Blaise Cendrars might appear beside Jules Romains on one side of the street, while on the other, you could run into James Joyce, Ernest Hemingway or Robert McAlmon. If a writer had obtained the imprimatur of Adrienne or of Sylvia, he was made, at least on the Left Bank, and from there news traveled fast to the outside world. I interviewed both of them, and was told many interesting things about Fargue, Joyce and the other habitués.

Mlle. Monnier expressed great admiration for Fargue, a visionary who was also a poet of the fabulous reality of Paris, and whose poems she described as lyrical transfigurations. She had encouraged him a good deal, she said, for Fargue was a frankly lazy writer, and had published only one volume thus far; he preferred to "speak" his poems. However, that one little volume, *Poèmes, suivis de Pour la musique,* which had appeared before the war, was now making its influence felt on contemporary poetry. Fargue was living his poetry, experiencing personally the nocturnal wonder of his native city as he wandered from boîte to boîte till the early morning hours. Mlle. Monnier had induced a mutual friend, the poet and novelist Valéry Larbaud, to join her in a conspiracy to get Fargue to work. The result was that Larbaud invited Fargue to his home in Vichy (where the Larbaud family owned the mineral springs). But Fargue, who enjoyed the Vichy climate, merely lazed around, as was his habit. One day Larbaud locked him in his room and refused to let him out until he had finished setting down in black and white one of his lyrical prose-poems. Gradually Fargue himself became interested, and soon a number of metaphoric luminosities were ready for publication. Larbaud sent these post-haste to Mlle. Monnier, and they appeared soon after in the great review *Commerce*, which Paul Valéry and others were editing.

In those years Fargue's poetry seemed to me to represent the very essence of lyrical creation. In the early poems there had been traces of the influence of Rimbaud, Verlaine, Jarry, and even Laforgue, but there was also a distinctly personal note, so personal, in fact, that it could never be mistaken for anybody else's expression. It had a purity, a quality of incantation, and a metaphoric feeling for language that I admired. Now he was inventing a language of his own, and his prose-poems contained strange neologisms that anticipated another epoch. In my opinion, he found his real vein in *Vulturne* and later on in *D'après Paris*. Our night wanderings frequently brought us to the same places, and we subsequently became good friends. What an opulent imagination he had! An inveterate reader, he was able to incorporate his vast heterogeneous knowledge into a very personal vocabulary, and to disseminate it in exquisitely cisellated *mots bijoux*. I was particularly attracted by his poetic interest in the stars and planets. He knew a good deal about both astronomy and astrology, and throughout his works one can find countless examples of this astral awareness. He was a born *raconteur* and his table-talk was often filled with references to obscure esoteric lore acquired no one knew where. He was certainly at his best late at night, when he was usually to be found in the Boulevard St.-Germain quarter, and the last hours at Lipp's in his company have a shining place in my memory. He could be Rabelaisian at will, and since he was usually savagely critical of his contemporaries, his conversation never lacked spice. He had a great love for music, which is evident in his prose-poems, and his friendship with Debussy and Ravel was no accident.

The *Chicago Tribune*'s "Rambles Through Literary Paris" achieved a certain vogue, and I gradually became more adept in the technique of the literary interview. Among the persons I interrogated was Marcel Raval, the editor of an advance-guard magazine called *Feuilles Libres*. He had just published an issue containing poems by the Dadaist *anti-philosophe* Tristan Tzara, and was preparing a special number to consist entirely of tributes to Léon-Paul Fargue. Raval presented me to Tzara, who had come to Paris from Zurich a few months before and was creating something of a sensation. He wrote prose-poems of great verbal felicity, and showed an aggressive daring that the Surrealists were to use to good advantage later on. He also presided over public manifestations, the aim of which was to spread the gospel of Dada, as it had been proclaimed in Zurich: "mix everything together: futurism, *bruitisme, simultanéisme,* poetic license; sneer at bourgeois prejudice, create a maniacal tom-tom of illogic. The result if you wish will be a new kind of beauty." However, the newly founded school of Surrealism, whose leader, André Breton, had decreed the official demise of Dada, refused to admit Tzara into the fold. This exclusion followed a personal quarrel between Breton and Tzara that was not patched up until some years later. When I first met Tzara he seemed, in consequence, to be rather at a loose end.

The Alsatian sculptor-poet Hans Arp, also one of the original members of the Zurich Dada group, had settled in the suburb of Meudon. Here he and his wife, the painter Sophie Taeuber-Arp, lived in an ultra-modern house where he worked at his queerly deformed "concretions"—monolithic sculptures of titanic dimensions. Tzara introduced us and we soon became friends—for like myself, Arp was a man of the border. He had a sharp sense of humor, and his companionship was always agreeable. He came to Paris very frequently, and we used to meet at some convenient café on the boulevards or on the Left Bank, or else near the Gare de l'Est, for which district he shared my own enthusiasm. On these occasions we usually spoke German together. Arp was full of scintillating talk, either amusing gossip from the artistic camps or else reminiscences about Dada. For even after the Surrealists had systematized Dada irrationalism and lured him into their fold, he remained the picaresque, laughing troubadour of Strasbourg and Zurich.

I never succeeded in interviewing James Joyce. In 1924, when I was presented to him by Sylvia Beach at a testimonial dinner given for Valéry Larbaud, he was already aureoled by the fame of *Ulysses.* The banquet turned out to be a rather lugubrious affair, even though *tout Paris littéraire* was there to pay homage to the author of *Barnabooth.* Paul Morand acted as toastmaster, but his speech could be heard only in snatches, because of the noise made by some of the more ebullient younger American writers present, among whom was Robert McAlmon. In fact, the only speech of interest, in my opinion, was that made by Gérard Bauer, the well-known *feuilletoniste.* It had the cool, Cartesian structure of the best French prose, and silhouetted quite perfectly Larbaud's delicate, if minor, art.

James Joyce sat quietly at one of the smaller tables and seemed far removed from this urbane French gathering of *hommes de lettres*, although he liked the guest of honor personally, and in later years never forgot the help Larbaud had given him on his arrival in Paris; for it was Larbaud who introduced Joyce in France.

When *Ulysses* appeared in the *Little Review*, Larbaud translated a fragment of it for a French magazine, and it was he who first presented the Irish poet to a French audience, in a now-famous lecture that took place in Adrienne Monnier's shop. Later, he undertook the arduous task of supervising Auguste Morel's French translation of the entire book, a task to the ultimate accomplishment of which Stuart Gilbert also lent valuable assistance.

This, my first meeting with Joyce, was to be followed later by years of close friendship. But already that evening, I was immediately struck by his Old-World courtesy. Having recently written something about him, which I myself had thought quite inadequate, I was astonished to hear Joyce thank me for my interest in his work.

My reporter's mind immediately envisaged a possible interview. In fact, I asked him point-blank if I might call on him for that purpose. Hearing this, Sylvia Beach, who was sitting opposite me, gestured so negatively and looked at me so reprovingly that I soon realized I had committed *lèse-Dedalus*, and desisted at once.

For apparently Joyce made it a rule never to give interviews, and even the important literary journalist Frédéric Lefèvre, to whom few had said no, had been obliged to admit defeat.

After this first meeting I frequently ran into Joyce, but I did not get to know him well until several years later, when I launched *transition* with Elliot Paul.

I was reading *Ulysses* with growing interest, and his audacity in the treatment of language fascinated me, because I was myself engaged in a personal insurrection against conventional syntax and vocabulary. That night at the Larbaud dinner, Mlle. Adrienne Monnier, who published the French translation of *Ulysses*, told me that a fragment from Joyce's latest and as yet untitled work would soon appear in a new review which Valéry Larbaud was to edit under her imprimatur. The review was to be called *Le Navire d'Argent*.

After the banquet, I was invited by Valéry Larbaud to join his group at the Fantasio Café in Montmartre. A number of his friends were there, among them several lovely girls who approached him with adulation and called him *maître*. As we watched the dancing, he told us about a collection of tin soldiers he had made, and invited us all to come and watch him maneuver his miniature martial robots. I questioned the author of *Poésies de*

A. O. Barnabooth about his globe-trotting, for I admired his slightly Whitmanized yet very French epic of a traveling humanist. His eyes gleamed with interest as we spoke, but he told me that he was at present engaged only in literary voyages. Being a remarkable linguist, he contributed a Paris letter in Spanish to *La Nación,* the great Buenos Aires newspaper.

One day Miss Beach introduced me to Ernest Hemingway, whose *In Our Time* Robert McAlmon's Contact Editions had just published in Paris. For a while I saw a good deal of him for there was something breezy and slightly swaggering about him—the antithesis, in fact, of some of the pallid, over-cerebral French writers I had met—that I liked. He lived next to a planing mill on the Left Bank, and told me he enjoyed working in the proximity of this noise, because it reminded him of his Chicago days. In the morning I often met him walking in the Luxembourg Garden, or in the vicinity of the Odéon, holding his small son by the hand and looking alert and proud. He usually wore workman's clothes and was always most careful to avoid being taken for a literary man. His speech was simple and human. It was also tough, and he seemed to have a preference for intermingling his vocabulary with strong four-letter words. Frequently, however, these gave the impression of being carefully calculated.

One day, at his home, Hemingway introduced us to Gertrude Stein and Alice Toklas, who had come "visiting," like two maiden aunts. It was my first encounter with Miss Stein, and I thought her rotundity and garrulousness rather pleasant. At that time I knew practically nothing about her writings, the only work of hers I had seen being *Three Lives.* "What are you doing in Paris?" she asked me. I said I was a reporter who was trying to write poetry. This did not seem to impress her and there was an embarrassed silence. Alice Toklas sat watching and smiling, and I began to feel more and more uncomfortable. Brusquely, Miss Stein rose and left the room, followed by Miss Toklas. At the door she exchanged a few pleasantries with Mr. and Mrs. Hemingway, then walked majestically into the Paris afternoon, leaving me with my discomfiture.

One day Hemingway and I sat talking at a café on the Boulevard St.-Michel. After expressing his admiration for a pair of magnificent dray-horses pulling a van down the boulevard, he showed me an envelope from which he took a proof sheet. It was titled "The Undefeated" and had been sent him by the Anglo-American advance-guard review, *This Quarter,* published in Monte Carlo by Ernest Walsh, an American poet, and Ethel Moorhead, a Scottish novelist. I liked the story immensely and told him so.

"I write rather slowly," he said, "but sometimes when I get going there is no stopping me. Glad you like it."

"There's something Zolaesque in your writing," I commented. "I haven't read Zola yet," was his answer. Then he said, "You're still writing poems?" "I'm still scribbling," I said. "Why don't you send some of your stuff to Walsh? He seems to like poetry."

I took his advice and dispatched some new poems, written in a mystic vein, to *This Quarter.* Walsh wrote an enthusiastic letter accepting three of them, but he warned me that "writing about God is a bigger job than most poets realize." Walsh was a generous evangelist of letters, a fighting editor who wrote truculent criticisms of the American literary scene with a pen dipped in acid. Besides Hemingway, he brought out Kay Boyle, Robert McAlmon, some of James Joyce's new work, and several other new English and American writers. His pioneering role was an important one. I did not realize at that time that he was suffering from a lung ailment caused by an airplane crack-up during the war. His early death was a great loss.

When Hemingway published a violent poem in *Der Querschnitt,* in which he hurled scatological insults at Ezra Pound and other contemporaries, I wrote him an open letter in my "Rambles" column, advising him to stick to his story-telling. He answered this blast with an amusing note and our friendly relationship was not affected by the exchange.

American writers were landing in force, and Paris was beginning to have a rather large American literary colony. Sinclair Lewis, fresh from his triumph as the author of *Main Street,* arrived one summer with his wife and a friend named Woodward, author of a book called *Bunk.* An American newspaper friend insisted that I meet Lewis, and asked me to join him and the Lewises at the Harcourt restaurant, on the Boulevard St.-Michel. Lewis was in a rather belligerent mood when we arrived, I was introduced, and Mrs. Lewis began carefully to note down my name and background. There was a bottle of excellent sparkling burgundy on the table and we were served generously. My friend and Lewis talked literature, while I chatted with Mrs. Lewis and Mr. and Mrs. Woodward. Out of one ear I heard Lewis expressing his disdain for Europe in no uncertain terms.

"I wouldn't think of living as an expatriate writer over here," he said, "I can only work in America . . ."

My friend and Lewis argued back and forth, but there was no sign that the vehemence of Lewis's convictions was weakening. I noticed that things were going badly at the other end of the table, and I began to grow nervous.

"Can't we stop those two from quarreling?" I asked Mrs. Lewis. She smiled and continued asking me questions about Paris. Then I heard the newspaperman, who also dabbled in literature, asking Lewis about modern American letters. The name of Dreiser occurred several times. My friend then suggested that he would like to write an essay on Lewis, and even went into the subject at great length. But Lewis flew into a rage: "I don't need any of your damned eulogies. Critics over here don't interest me. What has Paris got to do with my being an American writer? I have nothing to do with all this . . ."

With that he paid the bill — each one paid his share — and we all rose in great embarrassment. My friend was flustered and seemed taken aback. When we reached the coat-room, Lewis turned to me and said: "Why don't you come along with us? You look like a nice enough guy. Let's go have a drink somewhere." But because I had been my friend's guest, I declined, and thus ended my first and last encounter with Sinclair Lewis.

I followed assiduously all the new books and reviews that were appearing in great number. "Little magazines" particularly had begun to abound and one felt a nervous excitement in the air. Daring experimenters from every part of the globe were hammering out their visions in the atmosphere of liberty which the French city represented and encouraged. This romantic emotion was very much in evidence among the American newspapermen with whom I was working. There were men who had come to Paris in quest of adventure from all parts of America; they had wandered all over the States, as I myself had done; some had worked in South America, some in the Far East. A number had been in the war and had brought from it the spiritual disquiet, that peculiar American restlessness which characterized so many of our compatriots at that time. Most of them felt they wanted to stay on in the splendor of the Seine capital in order to participate in the activities of the new French creators.

André Breton, *chef d'école* of the Surrealists, whom I met for the first time in 1924, represented a peculiarly electric force in the period of renovation. He belonged to the poetic line of such men as de Nerval and was one of the discoverers of new dimensions and new myths who are able to crash open hitherto closed gates of consciousness. Having served in the psychoneurotic branch of the French Army, Breton decided to apply his observations to the creative processes, and he inaugurated an inner revolution, which had as its objective nothing less than the complete emancipation and transformation of man, by introducing into modern French creative life the dream and the night-mind. At his Montmartre home, in the Rue Fontaine, where the walls were covered with paintings by Picasso, Ernst, Malkine, Masson, Tanguy, de Chirico, etc., Breton received me one summer evening for an interview that had been arranged by Paul Eluard. We were alone in the phantom-cluttered studio and I listened to him for a whole hour, spellbound by the brilliance of his style. It was almost a soliloquy, delivered by a master of the French language. He talked of his Romantic precursors and emphasized the fact that the poetic conflagration which passed through England, France and Germany between the French Revolution and about 1835 had not really left behind a unifying doctrine. It had had constantly to fight, in fact, for its own definitions. Now he, Breton, had laid down such a doctrine in his manifestos.

When the first issue of the *Révolution Surréaliste* appeared, it was for many a disappointment. It contained manifestos, essays, and poems by diverse persons, some of whom were more or less loosely connected with the new group, but somehow it did not seem to hold together. With the fourth issue, however, Breton himself took over the editorship, and from then on it was truly "the world's most scandalous review." For it became the laboratory of the subrational forces, publishing automatic dialogues, dreams, *textes surréalistes*, hypnological experiences, erotic investigations with emphasis on Freudian pan-sexualism, poems, reproductions of photos, painting, sculptures and heteroclite objects of all kinds. Each number seemed to whip the collective delirium more savagely than the preceding one. During this period, Breton also organized a dream-laboratory in the Rue de Grenelle. But this did not last long, because of the intrusion of a curiosity-seeking bourgeois element, not to mention certain aristocratic hangers-on.

A number of younger writers gathered around the Surrealist banner, some of them remaining in the group for years, while others, like Raymond Queneau, refusing the doctrinaire shackles, revolted early in the game. Together they contributed towards obtaining that liberation which was, I believe, the chief characteristic of the Surrealist dynamism. Among the Surrealists I liked best in those early days, both personally and creatively, was Paul Eluard. He was a sparkling conversationalist, and I enjoyed listening to his beautifully formed phrases as we walked about the city together. He had just returned from a voyage to Easter Island and other parts of the Antipodes but he seemed reluctant to discuss his experiences. Sometimes, in a bistro, he would ask for a piece of note-paper in order to write down a poem.

At that time Eluard was married to the brilliant if rather sharp-tongued Gala (since become Mme. Dali), and I used to visit them in their suburban home in Eaubonne, with their painter friend Max Ernst. Eluard had a remarkable collection of Picassos of the "blue" period, as well as canvasses by such Surrealist painters as Ernst, de Chirico and Masson. But he had little feeling for music. On one of these visits Jacques joined me and, as usual, we spoke animatedly about music. Eluard told us that he was anti-musical, an attitude that was very much in vogue among the Surrealists of that period.

Jacques and I were shocked at the irreverent manner in which he disposed of an art we both loved as much as we did poetry. When I met Eluard again in the early thirties, he told me smilingly that he had changed his mind about music, and had begun to enjoy it. His poems have since been set to music by Poulenc and other modernist French composers.

In that mad crucible of the Paris of 1924 and 1925 I recall Michel Leiris, neurotic and unpredictable, who decomposed the words of the dictionary in order to reconstitute it with poetic *calembours;* Raymond Queneau, less lyrical than the others, a humorist with a mathematical type of mind, who had great difficulty in making obeisance to the hierarchy; Joseph Delteil, who was already ill, yet worked feverishly in his Montmartre room (a vehement quarrel broke out between him and Breton, after he published his *Jeanne d'Arc,* which Breton considered to be an act of treason to the Surrealist program); Roger Vitrac, who wanted to reintroduce the drinking of absinthe, and who, with Antonin Artaud, founded a Surrealist theater based on Jarry and his grotesque humor. Vitrac did not stay long in the group, being quickly at loggerheads with the policies of Breton. He "slammed the door" as he left.

Robert Desnos was a pure lyric poet, who also had strong mediumistic gifts, and Breton organized séances, at which Desnos's occultistic talents were the center of interest. On these occasions he seemed really to be living in a universe of the unconscious, and his automatic writings were undoubtedly genuine. At that time, he wrote certain of his poems in what he called a *langage cuit* (cooked language) that often resulted in striking word fantasies. His inventive virtuosity, which derived from the Dada experiences, added new color to Surrealism. Max Morise wrote comparatively little. He was, as he called himself, *un grand dormeur*—a great sleeper, who entertained the group with recitals of his dreams the way others tell stories of actual events. He took the anti-literary tenets of the movement quite seriously, and simply refused to publish in magazines or books.

Last, but far from least, there was Marcel Duchamp, who had very consciously abandoned all artistic ambition and spent his time playing chess in Paris cafés. The creator of the *Nude Descending a Staircase,* which, to his distaste, catapulted him to fame in the United States in 1916, continued to wield great influence on the Surrealists, who frequently quoted his picaresque *Rrose Sélavy* for its punning aphorisms.

Meanwhile I had met another American "exile," Maria McDonald, of Louisville, Kentucky, who was studying singing in Paris. We soon became engaged and decided to get married almost immediately. Before I embarked for New York, where the wedding was to take place, my friend

Philippe Soupault, who was acting as literary adviser to the Paris publishing house of Kra, suggested that while in the United States, I should collect material for a French-language anthology of modern American poets. He also encouraged Maria and me to prepare, together, a little volume of Negro spirituals, to appear in French translation under the title of *Le nègre qui chante.* These anthologies were published in Paris two years later.

I found New York in the euphoric atmosphere of an incredible boom. The literary platitudes of Greenwich Village, however, quickly became tiresome, and I felt little inclination to share in this life which, at the same time, it would have been difficult for me to avoid. With the result that when I heard of a reporting vacancy on the New Orleans *Item Tribune,* I made an application, and we left soon after for the Southern city. We settled in St. Peter's Street, in the Vieux Carré, in a typically French colonial atmosphere of wrought-iron balustrades, Greek porticoes and "galleries." The Mississippi was only a short walk from our house, and I never tired of listening to the music of the calliopes, wafted from the river-boats. Indeed, the river and its "levee" soon became the mecca of many of my nocturnal pilgrimages.

In my capacity of feature reporter I was given a special "beat" that included the hotels and local clubs. At stated hours I made the rounds of the city, visiting its different caravansaries in monotonous routine, in the hope that some celebrated "lion" would present himself to be interviewed. For the most part I talked to club presidents, political leaders, businessmen and theatrical people. Now and then I came across a South American visitor who gave me a good story, as for instance when the new President of Cuba passed through the city and I managed to elicit from him a vigorous condemnation of the Volstead Act.

Once a new film was scheduled to be shown at one of the biggest moviehouses in town. The Hollywood press agents had decided to import for the occasion a number of pretty starlets, together with the comedian Buster Keaton. When I entered the rooms of the Hotel Roosevelt, where they were having their party, I found the comedian in the process of manipulating a cocktail shaker, and I was invited to share in the illicit liquid. Much to my disappointment, however, Buster proved to be almost mute; he appeared not to understand a single question I put to him, and I had to depend on bright remarks by the girls to make my story palatable.

One of the visitors to New Orleans that year was Edmund Wilson, who came there to do a series of features for the *New Republic.* His rather cynical, critical mind bewildered me at first. I learned later, however, that he was not only a critic but also a poet and short story writer, which made him very congenial to me. Wilson proposed to accompany me on certain of my newspaper rounds, and as soon as the opportunity presented itself, we started forth together. The Rotary Clubs of America had called a national meeting in the city, and a feature of their program was a big banquet. It proved to be a dreary affair, but I had to cover the fatuous, banal speeches with as much thoroughness as though the contrary had been true. Wilson was highly amused.

Occasionally on my rounds I heard Creole French spoken, by both whites and Negroes, and the mellifluous deformations of Hugo's tongue fascinated me. On my day off Maria and I would drive out into the Cajun country, where we had opportunities of exchanging conversation with the descendants of transplanted French Canadians from Nova Scotia. The bayou French of these people differed from the New Orleans patois and at first it was difficult to understand. They, in turn, said they found that we spoke "parisien," an almost alien language to them. Their children were named Ulysse, Télémaque, Olélia, Omen.

After a few weeks Maria unearthed some childhood friends from Kentucky, and we soon found ourselves the recipients of overwhelming hospitality. We met the editors of that excellent *revue* the *Double Dealer,* Lilian Marcus and Julius Friend, as well as Hamilton Basso, James Feibleman, Lyle Saxon, Bill Spratling, Natalie Scott and Fred Oechsner. Getting to know Sherwood Anderson and his wife, who were living not far from us on Bourbon Street, was a stimulating experience.

What a contrast Anderson's happy personality seemed to offer to his rather pessimistic writings! For he was really in love with life. He talked endlessly about America, in Whitmanesque dithyrambs, and his lyrical faith had something contagious in it. One day I found sufficient courage to show him my American poems. His comment, that they had an "American ring," pleased me more than anything that could have been said about them. He showed me new poems from his own *Testament,* and I began to translate a number of these into French.

Anderson was at his best when speaking of his native folklore; for although capable of flights of the imagination, he was inclined to reduce most ideas to a very personal, often rather elementary plane. He was extremely simple, humble even, about many things. But he could also be vain, the way an actor or a race-horse tout is vain. He was delighted to be taken for either, in fact, and it amused him no end to play-act these parts.

"In America," he once said, "we have an infinite pattern of life, such as cannot be duplicated anywhere else."

"Am I part of this pattern?" I asked him.

"You're an Alsatian-American," he replied. "You belong to the immigrant class, but you are an American in feeling and words." Alsatian and Lorrainer were the same, as far as Anderson was concerned.

"What difference does this or that European background really make?" he mused.

"A great deal of difference," I replied. "Although born in America, I, for instance, happen to be both French and German as well, and this combination makes of me a neo-American, a kind of European-American."

"True. But do we in American pay any attention to that? In my opinion, the days of the melting-pot are over."

"You yourself take pride in having had an Italian mother," I insisted. "Has this fact no significance in the make-up of your character, or in your writing?"

He admitted it had influenced him to a certain extent. He continued, however, to ignore the fact that over forty million foreigners who had immigrated to the United States during the past hundred years had perhaps altered the great cauldron's brew. "They forget Europe," he said, "and America soon becomes the only reality for them."

Although I did not share many of his convictions, knowing Anderson was for me a fine human experience. I loved listening to his yarns, told with a lazy Middle-Western drawl, about quite ordinary folk, his fantastic speculations concerning the human tragedies he sensed about him, his sometimes baroque fictions. For he was a great inventor and a born story-teller. He never lost his daydreaming propensities, his extra-literary feeling for humanity. Once, as we were strolling along Royal Street, he began to talk about a novel he had been working on for some time. I listened to his monologue: "I don't seem to get anywhere with it," he said. I hesitated to inquire into the details of his problems, for I know too well the almost occult shyness sensitive writers feel about revealing the inner mechanism of their creations while they are working.

"You see," he said as we passed an early colonial house with a wrought-iron balcony, "it's about one of these houses. . . . I call my story 'The Other Man's House.' What is happening in there, I wonder. Take our mutual friend X. . . . I have a hunch as to what goes on in his house. . . . Did I never tell you about it? No? Well . . ." He suddenly broke off, and I realized I would never know what he thought he knew.

The *Double Dealer* having become moribund, Maria and I several times discussed the possibility of taking it over. I felt, however, that I wanted to build a laboratory of my own in which I could tackle my personal language problems without having to consider an exclusively American audience. We soon reached the conclusion that such a review could only be issued from the vantage point of Paris. My ambition was to build a bridge between Europe and America, and particularly, to make known to America the new aesthetic currents in Europe. After six months we returned to Paris, with plans for an intercontinental magazine in our minds.

Shortly before our departure the Andersons moved to Virginia, where Sherwood had bought a small country newspaper. There was genuine sadness at the separation, and a number of us went to the station to see them off. As Katherine, their colored maid, began to weep huge tears, Sherwood threw his friendly arms around her and kissed her good-bye. Then the train pulled out, in the quiet way of American trains. Our little group stood for a while on the platform, conscious that what had been an unusually happy period had come to an end. The extraordinary warmth that radiated from Anderson's rare personality was gone from our midst.

My book of poems *Cinema* was about to be published in New York. Sherwood was kind enough to write the following introduction:

I met Eugene Jolas in New Orleans last winter. He was working there on a newspaper. My son, who also worked on the paper, came home one day all excited. "There is a real poet down there, working on our paper," he said. Later I found Eugene Jolas just the poet. He is unsure of himself, quick and sensitive to the life about him. Most young poets are impossible as companions. They are so dreadfully sure no poets have ever lived before their time. Jolas is not like that.

He is an Alsace-Lorrainer, with a mixture of German and French blood, married to an American woman. As a lad he came over here to live, and he has been coming back over here ever since. At this moment I have on my desk a letter from him. He is just sailing for Europe. The letter is full of regret that he must go. "I'll be back," is the burden of it.

Jolas is a poet feeling his way. The energy of America, the fast pace here, the growth and development of our industrial life, Pittsburgh, Chicago, the Kentucky Derby, the bootlegger, our skyscrapers, our great mills, the Ford. All of these things excite and fascinate the man.

He wants to be thought of as an American himself. Well, his heart is here.

He is one of the young poets intent on expressing the age in which he lives and he believes America best expresses the present age.

He is, I am very sure, one of the few important new singers here lifting up his voice to America.

6

VOYAGES OF DISCOVERY

It is difficult today to project oneself from the tenebrous era of the *univers concentrationnaire,* with its accompanying *esthétique* of epigones, to that period of felicity and effervescence in the nineteen-twenties and thirties, when writers of the Anglo-American literary colony in Paris competed with their French contemporaries in imagining new mental landscapes, in an atmosphere of complete intellectual liberty. We seem now to have been living in a golden age of the logos. Many of us had taken refuge from the bleakness of the Volstead regime in the more friendly climate of Montparnasse and Montmartre, and we were hell-bent on discovering new continents of the mind as well. Daring experimentation with words, colors and sounds was the chief preoccupation of an intercontinental avant-garde that extended across continents and did not pause until that day in 1929 when Wall Street "laid its historic egg." Most of the British and Americans went home then, but a few die-hards remained until the Nazis' attempt to conquer the Occident.

In the late fall of 1926, I began preparations to launch the review the following spring. I needed an editorial assistant, and had the names of several newspapermen then living in Paris under consideration. Elliot Paul seemed my best choice and I decided to invite him to join me. He gave enthusiastic acquiescence to the plan, which included a small salary that permitted him to quit the newspaper work entirely and devote himself exclusively to the task. He came to our apartment in the Rue Valenteen-Huy every day, and we began to discuss details with growing excitement. After a few weeks, having outgrown our dining-room table, Paul and I hired a room in a modest hotel on the Place des Invalides, where we hung out the *transition* shingle. Our "offices," as Paul used to call our cluttered-up ex-bedroom (complete with all French plumbing fixtures), were eventually to become the mecca of numerous manuscript-laden "exiled" writers from every state in the Union.

For some months the problem of a name troubled us, and numerous suggestions were weighed and rejected. For a time "Bridge" and "Continents" seemed to be the favorites. Then Edwin Muir's collection of essays appeared in London, and the title struck our fancy. We finally settled upon this same title, because it seemed best to symbolize the epoch. I insisted, however, that it be printed with a lowercase *t*. As an old newspaperman, I knew that the critics would give it a howling reception, and anyway it was the fashion among many continental "little magazines" of the day.

Sherwood Anderson came to Paris that winter, and we were happy to see him again. I met him at the Gare du Nord, and a news-story I wrote about him brought many requests for interviews from the French press. But Sherwood did not really like Paris.

He knew no French and felt ill at ease in consequence, for he was essentially the Middle-Western type, and it irked him that he should not be able to talk to the workers of Paris in their native argot. I can still see him standing at a little bar where he had invited some workers for a drink, smiling and trying with gestures to approach their minds. He was a frequent visitor in our house, and he also saw a good deal of his old friend Gertrude Stein, concerning whose peculiarities he entertained us. "Use your head, Sherwood," she would say to him, whenever he lazily played with some Middle-Western "notion" of his. One day he arranged to bring Gertrude Stein and Alice Toklas to our home. At his insistence, Maria sang some of the American songs he had liked to hear in New Orleans. Miss Stein seemed pleased, although I doubt if her interest in music was more than platonic. With Virgil Thomson, who was also present, the conversation turned to the Gregorian chant, Antheil, Milhaud and Honegger. It was not a wholly successful evening. It constituted, however, an accurate preview of our future relationship with Miss Stein, which was also to be never wholly successful.

Editing the review seemed to entail such an alarming amount of social activity that we decided to look for a place outside the capital, preferably well in the country. When we heard of an old house for rent in the Haute-Marne, near Chaumont, we decided to make a tour of inspection and invited the Andersons to join us. After a three-hour train ride we arrived in an ancient, almost abandoned village called Colombey-les-deux-Eglises, and put up at the only hotel in the place, the Cheval Blanc. The "estate," which consisted of a roomy house and garden, surrounded by meadows and forests, had great charm. While we visited it in detail, Sherwood gossiped, or tried to gossip, with the villagers, especially the village belles, and seemed to derive much pleasure from the experience, despite linguistic difficulties. He was curious about their love affairs, their social relations, the harvest, anything they could tell of their lives, and he kept me busy translating back and forth. He was amused by the revelations of village customs which were told him without false modesty, and he enjoyed to the last drop the excellent near-Champagne wine of the region offered by M. Poulnot, the hotel proprietor. We liked Colombey-les-deux-Eglises and decided to rent it — for Fr. 4,000 a year. The move was planned for early spring.

I urged Sherwood to give us a manuscript for the review, but he firmly refused; perhaps he was a bit jealous of the Paris writers. Or was he afraid? I never knew. Paul and I were now in communication with writers in England, France, Germany and the United States. We went through countless manuscripts in French, English and German, and began to translate pieces not only from these languages, but, with the aid of experts, from Spanish, Russian and Yugoslav as well. We went to the Shakespeare Bookshop in the Rue de l'Odéon and asked Sylvia Beach to speak in our favor to James Joyce. This she very kindly did and within a few days, overjoyed, we held in our hands a bulky manuscript bearing the title "Work in Progress."

One Sunday afternoon, at the end of 1926, Joyce invited Miss Beach, Mlle. Monnier, Paul, Maria and myself to his home in the Square Robiac, to listen to him read from the opening pages of his manuscript, which was subsequently to appear in the first issue of *transition*. He read in a well-modulated, musical voice, and often a smile went over his face when he reached a particularly witty passage. We were staggered by the revolutionary aspect of this fragment. After he had finished, he asked each one of us separately: "What do you think of it?" There was little to be said; it was obvious that we were faced with a unique literary work, one before which all critical canons would have to be abandoned. For Joyce had apparently found a solution of his language problem that was essentially his own, a solution that was also exclusively applicable to the English language, to which he gave a polysynthetic quality. We knew that while the technique of the "interior monologue," or "stream of consciousness," used in *Ulysses*, had found a number of supporters (and imitators), the new work, which was based rather on the canon of the "stream of unconsciousness," would in all probability find few sympathizers. We nevertheless had complete faith in the ultimate value of the work, and were proud to contribute in a modest way to its unfolding.

Paul was in constant contact with Gertrude Stein, who let him see a batch of her manuscripts that had been gathering dust in her Rue de Fleurus home. I never shared Paul's enthusiasm for the repetitiveness of Gertrude

Stein's writings, but I did not oppose publishing them, because she, too, was experimenting with language.

I myself was in touch with the Surrealists, and Paul Eluard gave me not only his own poems for translation, but poems by other Surrealist friends as well. One of these, Marcel Noll, an old Strasbourg friend, who had just been appointed director of the new Galerie Surréaliste, let me have reproductions of Tanguy, Miró, Arp, Picasso, Ernst and others. The writers and artists of the Surrealist group were at that time under orders from Breton not to collaborate with any French review other than their own, *La Révolution Surréaliste,* and it was something of a triumph, therefore, when in 1927 *transition* published the Surrealists — many years before they became the fashion in New York and London. In fact, a proposed anthology to be composed of translations of Surrealist prose and poetry, with illustrations of the painters and sculptors identified with the movement, was turned down by a number of New York publishers when they were approached by Maria in 1928. "Nobody would be interested," was the invariable reply.

Archibald MacLeish, Raymond Larsson, Kay Boyle, Ernest Hemingway, Malcolm Cowley, Hart Crane, Matthew Josephson, Ludwig Lewisohn were among the many American writers who gave us manuscripts without hesitation. Their work, however, differed from the French orientation, for it contained a kind of American Expressionism, a humanistic quality that was lacking in the cerebral torridity of the French writing of that epoch. There were indeed no Surrealist tendencies evident in American writing during those years. It was all the more interesting, as time went on and Breton's doctrines became known, to see the results of this excursion away from literary isolationism on the part of a whole generation of U.S. writers. Among the German Expressionist works which had by then more or less dropped into oblivion, I chose "Busekow," by Carl Sternheim, and a short story by Gottfried Benn. I dictated the translation of Sternheim's psychological study of a Berlin policeman to Paul, who took it down on the typewriter, while we both laughed hilariously.

It so happened that a few months before our review appeared, Ezra Pound started his new review, *Exile.* He wrote us from Rapallo, where he was then living, that if he had known that Paul and I were planning a review, he would never have burdened himself with the ungrateful task. His review I believe lasted only three numbers.

Finally, all the translations were made, the original texts were carefully checked, and the whole manuscript was in the printers' hands. In a state of nervous excitement we awaited the result of our effort, for we were planning to bring out the first number in February 1927. But just here something happened that seemed of almost saturnine origin and which, in any case, proved to be prophetic of the stormy career that lay ahead of our revolutionary magazine.

One gray, wind-blustery day, Paul and I went to the Gare des Invalides to entrain for the town of Mayenne, where we were to supervise the make-up of the first issue directly in the print-shop. We stopped by our "offices" — our room in the little Hôtel de la Gare des Invalides on the Rue Fabert — to pick up whatever mail might be there. We found a letter from an American poet angrily withdrawing his contribution because, in our advance announcement, we had inadvertently printed his name in what he felt to be an inferior and therefore unflattering position. Since his poem was to be printed in the first number, this manifestation of wounded *amour-propre* upset us considerably. Before taking the train, I hurried to a nearby telegraph office and wired the irate poet our regret and the pious hope that he would reconsider his decision. Arrived in Mayenne, we found a wire from him, liquidating the difficulty. Finally we were ready to go ahead.

Mayenne is a quiet old town in Normandy, about ten hours away from Paris. Immediately upon arrival we installed ourselves in the office of the print-shop, where we began to read final proof. The excellent cider of the region soon found two eager amateurs, and the three days we spent in the town remain among my happiest memories. Finally, everything seemed to be in order, and we gave the *bon à tirer* — the signal for the printer to go ahead. I returned to Paris and took the next train to Colombey-les-deux-Eglises, where we had moved a week earlier. While waiting for the first number to appear, I welcomed the pastoral quiet of our new home. It soon became evident, however, that this quiet would be only relative.

First there was Gertrude Stein. A few hours after we had received our advance copy of the review, a special-delivery letter arrived. Maria and I were already in a rather disappointed state, for we felt we might have done better; we even criticized the number rather harshly, and were discussing the elimination of certain defects we had noticed. But Miss Stein had another complaint: one of the pages of her contribution entitled, ironically enough, "An Elucidation," which was to have explained her technique in her own style, had been printed in the wrong place, thus creating a certain confusion — oh, quite a disarray! Her letter was virulent enough and demanded a rectification. I got hold of Paul by telephone and we agreed that we would try to print a correction; but this proved technically difficult and we finally decided to order a special reprint of her entire contribution, to be inserted in the number as a supplement. This involved considerable expense. However, Gertrude Stein was propitiated. The supplement had quite a success later on, and critics in England and America seized upon the whole incident as an excellent theme for spoofing both author and editors.

But our troubles were not yet over. The first few copies were beginning to arrive in Paris, and we were feeling that relief which any technical difficulty well conquered always gives, when the police stepped in. This incident proved to be even more serious than Miss Stein's misplaced page, and it kept us on tenterhooks for almost two weeks. Meanwhile, orders had been coming in from every part of the globe, and it was maddening that we should be stalled.

Just before we left Mayenne, the printer, who printed a number of reviews and should therefore have known better, had asked us for the name of our *gérant;* for every newspaper or periodical printed in France is required by law to have an agent legally responsible for its contents. In Germany, I believe, this gentleman is known, or was known, as the *Sitzredakteur,* because it was he who "sat" in the hoosegow if the review became suspicious to the authorities. We told the printer that we would *both* act as gérants. We were unaware, however, that only French citizens could assume that honor. When the *préfet* of the Mayenne département inspected our effort, the only words he understood were the words *gérants* and our names. The police machinery was immediately set in motion, and Paul and I received orders in Paris to report to the police *commissariat* of our quarter. When we arrived there, we were told very seriously of our heinous crime. We tried to look innocent, and I even camouflaged my knowledge of French in order to impress the uniformed gentleman behind the desk with the innocence of our behavior; but he wagged his head and seemed to think that the case was *extrêmement grave.* Paul assumed a blank expression. In any case, there could be no question of releasing the issue for some time, and the *flic* impressed on us that we should be obliged to hold ourselves at the disposal of the authorities.

This was a nice kettle of fish and, however ridiculous, we were quite gloomy over the prospects of our intellectual child. When we returned to the office, I had an idea: the son-in-law of our hotel proprietor was a policeman, an authentic one, and it just so happened that this station where we had been questioned was his own commissariat. I suggested to Paul that we use his influence somehow to get out of the mess. A hundred-franc *pourboire* did wonders, and we heard no more from the police authorities. We were cautious enough, however, to wait another week before actually putting the issue on sale in Paris.

The second number appeared, and the third. We were quite astonished to realize that the review was being discussed, criticized, vilified, admired.

From England, Ireland, the United States, South Africa, India, Australia came reactions of every shade of opinion. We were frequently amused by the violence of the echoes, for we had expected a very small group of readers, and were suddenly confronted with the necessity of ourselves taking our mad effort more seriously than we had at first anticipated. The bookshop demand was growing rapidly.

To me, *transition* was not only a workshop, but a kind of higher journalism, a simultaneous attempt to report to the English-speaking world the main intellectual movements of the continent, and to introduce to European readers the work of English-language writers. And since I felt that realism, imagism, the photographic, had become the chief enemies of the modern creator, I posited as my main objective the dictum of a "transformation of reality." In my manifesto, "Suggestions for a New Magic," published in Number 3, 1927, I stated: "We need new words, new abstractions, new hieroglyphics, new symbols, new myths . . ." This was my guide-post throughout the *transition* decade. I wanted to encourage the creation of a modern romanticism, a pan-romantic movement in literature and the arts.

For this reason I welcomed individual Surrealist contributions, from the beginning until the last issue in 1938; and, in fact, *transition* was the first review to present Surrealist poems, texts, dreams, etc., in English; the first non-French review to reproduce photos of Surrealist and abstract objects and paintings. Not that I was ever a member of the Surrealist clan, but I sympathized with André Breton's early efforts, with his discovery of the "surrealist text" in *Les champs magnétiques* (written collectively by him and Philippe Soupault), with his discovery of automatic writing as a possible basis of a new type of literary creation. To be sure, he deviated from his first idea often enough, and I made it plain by the end of 1927 that I was violently opposed to the political aberrations of Surrealism—that I was chiefly interested in its *neo-idealistic* tendencies. Surrealism as a post-Romantic manifestation has today become a world movement. But when I knew it first, it was confined to limited circles, even in Paris. It was *transition* that made it known to the Anglo-American world.

I myself had been under the neo-romanticist influence of Surrealism since 1924, and had trained myself in the notation of my dreams. I kept a notebook on my night-table and after a while was able to note down, even in the dark, the images that I had experienced, each time I awoke. I filled many of these books with sketches written in various languages. I saw that in nocturnal life there was a new life, that there were juxtapositions of which the waking life was apparently unaware. The most heterogeneous images were tumbled together and became friendly and coherent. Many of these dream-and-daydream sketches were included later in my book *I Have Seen Monsters and Angels.*

At that time the Breton-Soupault experiment was the sensation of Paris. Many young poets used it and finally developed into a *poncif*—a stereotyped system. Aragon, then a member of the Surrealist group, explained it in his "A Wave of Dreams," published in the magazine *Commerce,* in the following manner: "What strikes the writer is that he seems to possess a power he did not know he had, an incomparable ease, a liberation of the spirit, a production of images without precedent, and his writings assume a supernatural quality. He recognizes in everything that thus emerges from him—without feeling in any way responsible for it—all the incomparable qualities of the few books, the few words that still move him."

Some years later Aragon renounced all this and joined the Communist Party. A strange evolution for an idealist, even for a nominalist mystic!

Being at that time more or less swept up into the Surrealist avalanche, I witnessed a number of public manifestations organized by Breton. Among others I was present at the Vieux Colombier theater when the Surrealists forgathered to boo a *matinée poétique* featuring a recital of poems by de Musset and other poets of his type. It should be added that de Musset was their *bête noire,* as he had been that of Rimbaud. In the midst of a grandiloquent reading of the pseudo-Romantic poet's works by an effeminate-looking gentleman, Breton rose and shouted: "C'est une saloperie!" At this point there began a wild scramble to the stage. Benjamin Peret shouted imprecations, while Eluard climbed on a chair and began to harangue the fevered crowd of society ladies and gentlemen whose mild enjoyment of "poetry" was being so rudely interrupted. The management called for police protection, and in the midst of the greatest excitement, Breton, Eluard, Peret and others were conducted to a nearby police station. There they were booked on the egregious charge of *bagarre entre intellectuels.* A few telephone calls to certain of their friends in the Ministry of the Interior brought about their liberation several hours later.

As our task grew heavier, we began to look for an editorial assistant, and I decided to engage Robert Sage, a young American writer also working with the *Chicago Tribune,* for the position. Paul, Sage and I used to meet in one or the other of the Left Bank cafés we had chosen as annex, and it was during one of these discussions that we tried out Breton's technique of automatic writing as it had been explained by Soupault. We soon began to try our hand at composing collective poems in prose, stemming directly from the unconscious, and felt exhilarated by the boldness of the images, and the liberation of the imagination that resulted. There was no doubt that there was a method worthy of the age of psychoanalysis; a method which would still need the curbing hand of critical reason, but which opened up new and unsuspected veins of wealth to the poet.

The importunities of would-be contributors in Paris, added to the need to economize, soon drove us completely to Colombey-les-deux-Eglises, and by the early summer of 1927 practically all the editorial work was being done from there, leaving only the "office" in Paris.

The Colombey house was a large, rambling affair, covered with ivy, and isolated from the country road by a high wall. Lilac trees were in bloom along the wall when we arrived, and we could look from there into a far land of rye and clover waving in the wind. A beautiful, wild park surrounded the house, and below it was a hillock covered with furze and fern. Beyond the fields lay a tangled, mysterious forest called *la forêt de la lune,* in which big game was abundant. At night the inn-keeper's wife watched stout-heartedly for wild boars, of which she usually managed to shoot one specimen during the season. The peasants, who called this country la Champagne Pouilleuse (to distinguish it from the real Champagne country, contiguous to it), still lived in a machineless age. They cultivated their fields and vineyards with the same stubborn love of the loam which their ancestors had shown, and their meager existence was made more difficult through the fact that most of the younger men and girls had left the village to seek less monotonous work in the cities. They made a wine from local vineyards which I always thought was as good as any of the better known white wines. Their rather hard, eastern patois reminded me of that spoken in nearby Lorraine.

Tranquil weeks at the "Boisserie," our hermitage! Paul would come down from the nerve-mad city to mediate and prepare new issues of *transition* with me. He liked to stay with us in this pastoral quiet, but never for very long, for he was restless and led a somewhat complex personal life that often made it necessary for him to return to Paris on very short notice. Other friends came for weekends: Philippe and Marie-Louise Soupault, Stuart and Moune Gilbert, Robert and Maeve Sage, Whit Burnett and Martha Foley, Carl and Lyda Einstein, Harry and Caresse Crosby, and others, joined us in our rustic retreat, in order to forget for a while the dynamo-whirl of the capital. We were told that Clemenceau used to visit there as the guest of a friend, before 1914; and a curious quirk of fate was the fact that after our final departure, in late 1929, the place was sold to a French colonel named Charles de Gaulle.

This old house, which was conceived originally as a hunting-lodge by the wealthy nineteenth-century merchant who built it, had had a somewhat lurid existence: in 1917–18 it housed American troops who left their names and drawings on the attic wall; from 1927 till 1929 it housed ourselves, our growing family, and *transition;* in 1940 it was confiscated by the Vichy government as being the home of France's first *résistant,* and during the second war it was occupied by German troops. Today, it has become the little Versailles of the Gaullist movement, the goal of all new recruits to the RPF. (*Rassemblement du Peuple Français*), the center from which their leader launches most of his political statements.

For the most part we were not interested in social problems, in economics, or in any particular political complex. We thought of our fight as good, clean aesthetic fun, nothing else. We baited the Babbitt with monstrous paradoxes, we prodded him with topsy-turvy asseverations. We saw ourselves as modern barbarians who did not hesitate to shout their nervous prejudices into the faces of well-to-do, streamlined, shallow minds. We were rebels against everything that did not participate in flights of wild, burning imagination. We were the Romantics of the twentieth century, launched on voyages of discovery.

James Joyce was our bellwether. In his "Work in Progress" he was building a colossal elegy to the night-mind, a creation in which the ancestral night was wedded to the individual, modern night in grandiose transformations. We lived in this night-world of his in which he was transmuting not only the myth of Finn Macool, but all myths. At his side we felt no fear in our own pilgrimage through the *Nox,* in the walk from dusk to dawn.

Around us were French poets who were also in love with the night, for Breton was leading his little band toward what he called magical Surrealist art, and a revival of interest in the dream and everything connected with the nocturnal processes of the unconscious was the result. He even went so far as to dig up certain early "black" Romantic writers, such as Raabe, Borel and von Arnim, whom he proposed as models to his disciples. Although all the Surrealists were conscious of this nocturnal universe, this was particularly true of Antonin Artaud, Paul Eluard and Robert Desnos.

I myself tried independently to revive interest in the "white" Romantic poet Novalis, and translated for *transition* his *Hymns to the Night,* with a short preface of my own. I also published a pamphlet entitled *The Language of Night,* in which I sought to analyze Novalis's vision of night and his expression of that vision. My translation of poems by Hölderlin, written while the poet was living in a state of mental alienation, was a further attempt to place *transition* at the service of "white" as opposed to "black" romanticism.

Meanwhile I continued to study the writings, not only of Freud, but of all his group, and in the review *Imago,* as well as in the *Psychoanalytische Rund-*

schau, I found many possible applications to the creative processes. Stekel's studies in psychic criminology interested me particularly, and I asked myself if the curiosity concerning Sade evinced by some of the younger Frenchmen, as well as their predilection for crime novels and crimes *tout court,* did not indicate that the taste for cruelty went well beyond the limits of the criminal unconscious. The "diabolical principle" which had undoubtedly inspired Lautréamont's work, for instance, was certainly part of our own mental heritage. It could be found in many of Baudelaire's lines, and Edgar Allan Poe's necrophilia offered another example, as did certain works of Barbey d'Aurévilly, Villiers de l'Isle Adam, and others. *Les contes cruels* had their prolongation in most of the early Surrealist writings, as well as in those which this group recommended for study. The French words *supplice, viol, délire, ivresse, volupté,* assumed a significance for us that the English equivalents did not possess. We were living in a world of *sorcellerie.*

This preoccupation with the night-mind elicited a violent onslaught against *transition* from the British writer Wyndham Lewis, father of the vorticist movement. Lewis published two books — *Time and Western Man* and *The Diabolical Principle* — in which he grew nearly hysterical about *transition*'s efforts. He denounced the review as a Surrealist challenge to modern letters, forgetting that it published, as well, Expressionist, Dadaist and futurist writers. He attacked particularly James Joyce, who replied in his "Work in Progress" with an Aesopian allegory, "The Ondt and the Gracehoper." Meanwhile, Paul, Sage and I also engaged in a somewhat ironic and acrid debate with "the Enemy," as Lewis called himself. We pointed out that *transition* was not a Surrealist organ, but had published some of these writers because they were allies in the pan-romantic battle. I had written an essay in *transition,* "Enter the Imagination," in which I analyzed the *Maldoror* by Lautréamont from my own personal and somewhat theological standpoint. I pointed out that the "diabolical principle" inherent in Lautréamont's monologues had its genesis in religious perversion. The Promethean revolt, I wrote, was evident in this poem. I asserted that there was a spiritual element in his frenzy of agnostic and bestial imagery. I could have added that he had such distinguished precursors as Milton and Dante. Lewis pounced on the term "diabolical principle," which he used as the title of his new book, making it the point of departure for a virulent denunciation of the entire *transition* direction.

Mayenne, where the first three issues were printed, was in Normandy, and we were now living in the heart of the east, at the other end of France. It became necessary, therefore, to look for a new printer. In our antique Ford, we decided to scour the villages and towns of Haute-Marne in search of one. We first tried Langres, the attractive medieval town beyond Chaumont. We next tried Chaumont itself. But the print-shops in both towns were unsatisfactory. We finally discovered an excellent printer in the industrial town of St.-Dizier, at the other end of the département. The print-shop of M. André Bruillard became our headquarters until the review was temporarily suspended, in 1930.

Many European writers, especially those of the advance-guard, were published in *transition*. We had our own team of translators, for I regarded this as an essential feature of the mediatory action of my early conception. During the first year, *transition* published Franz Kafka, in a translation, made by myself, of his short story "The Sentence." Unless I am mistaken, this was his introduction to Anglo-American readers. As the years went on, his grotesque and anguished narratives continued to appear in the review, the last of them being *Metamorphosis,* which we published in 1938. *Transition* can probably justly claim, therefore, to have fathered the interest in Kafka's work which has since swept the Anglo-American world.

In addition to numerous writers of continental Europe, chosen from the Expressionist, Dada and Surrealist camps, *transition* gave many young and older writers of the English-speaking world an opportunity to present not only their finished work, but also their experimental efforts. Sylvia Beach was our Paris representative, and Frances Steloff's Gotham Book Mart acted as our American agency. During the first year I was extremely busy, for I had not yet finished my French anthology of American poets. I also undertook for Joyce the rather arduous task of reading proof on the German version of *Ulysses.*

For several days each month, St.-Dizier became our temporary headquarters. Paul and I installed ourselves in a little room put at our disposal by the printer, which we did not leave until the *bon à tirer* was given. The Bruillard print-shop had been in the same family for many generations, and a leisurely, paternalistic system prevailed there. All the printers were French, which of course complicated matters considerably, and our special foreman—a wizened little man named Monsieur Noël whom Paul dubbed Father Christmas—was always worrying about the numerous changes we often had to make at the last minute.

As a rule things went smoothly enough until the final proofs of James Joyce's "Work in Progress" came from Paris. A first proof, in overlarge type, had already been set up, on which additions were made in Paris by Joyce. He then sent this back to "St. Dizzier" (as he called it), in a condition that more resembled an esoteric scroll than typesetter's copy. At this stage of the work, Joyce's friends were usually enlisted for the task of deciphering the many notebooks in which, for years, he had been jotting down his bold inventions. Stuart Gilbert, Giorgio Joyce, the latter's wife Helen, Elliot Paul, Padraic Colum, Thomas McGreevy, Samuel Beckett, Paul Léon, Maria and myself all shared in this task. The proofs went back and forth, each time with new inventions, until the pages had often doubled in number. For Joyce would improvise whenever something particularly interesting occurred to him during the reading, and occasionally even allow a *coquille* — a typographical error — to stand, if it seemed to satisfy his encyclopedic mind, or appeal to his sense of grotesque hazard. Often, however, his last-minute additions really taxed the patience of the excitable Monsieur Noël. "Joyce, *alors!*" he would shout, while the editors kept discreetly silent. Joyce chuckled when I told him that his name was being used as an objurgation.

Once, I remember, I had just finished reading the last page of final proof and had given orders to go ahead with the printing. Although somewhat exhausted, I felt happy at the thought that another number was ready to appear. I dropped in at the nearby Café du Commerce to join Paul, who was already ensconced before a shimmering glass of what he had baptized an ironworker's cocktail. (This invention of Paul's consisted, if I remember rightly, of generous portions of cognac, rum, armagnac, champagne, and a dash of Alsatian kirsch, and was guaranteed to create at least a temporary Dionysian ecstasy.) As we settled back comfortably, the telephone rang. An excited voice announced that a heavy special-delivery letter from Paris had just arrived for us at the print-shop. Joyce wanted to make further additions, one of them probably the longest he had yet invented: an onomatopoeia of over fifty letters expressing collective coughing in a church during a sermon. It was included.

In Paris, Joyce, who was then living in the Square Robiac, also on the Left Bank, would sometimes climb the four flights of stairs to our office, to talk with "his editors" about "Work in Progress." He was very anxious to have people like the work, and seemed astonished that the first reactions were for the most part negative in tone. He would look carefully over the list of our subscribers in France, England, Ireland and the United States, and sometimes suggest names for circulation. One visit I particularly remember was the occasion of Marshal Foch's funeral. Joyce stood for a long time at the window, field-glasses in hand, profoundly engrossed by the spectacle of the procession of dignitaries leaving the Invalides. A mythological version of the funeral of another "great man," H. C. E., was incorporated into "Work in Progress" shortly afterwards.

At Joyce's suggestion, Paul wrote an interpretative article about "Work in Progress" for *transition,* and I followed with another. We then decided to ask other sympathizers with the new work to contribute further essays, and thus published a number of articles on the subject by writers of several nationalities, among whom were Samuel Beckett, Marcel Brion, Frank Budgen, Stuart Gilbert, Victor Llona, Robert McAlmon, Thomas McGreevy, Elliot Paul, John Rodker, Robert Sage, and William Carlos Williams. Some time later, Sylvia Beach brought out those essays in book form, under the title *Our Exagmination Round His Factification for Incamination of a Work in Progress*—a title which, needless to say, was suggested by Joyce himself. In addition to the *transition* essays, this volume contained an unsigned article which was included in order that, symbolically, the "disciples" or "apostles" might be twelve.

During the summer of 1927, Joyce had let me read his entire manuscript. It was not more than 120 pages long, and had been written, he said, over a period of five weeks during a stay on the Riviera in 1922. Yet it was already complete in itself, organically compressed, containing the outline of the entire saga. Even the title had been chosen, he indicated, but only he and Mrs. Joyce knew it. It was still a primitive version, to which he had begun to add numberless paragraphs, phrases and individual words. In a moment of confidence he told me something about the genesis of the idea. His friend and admirer, Miss Harriet Weaver who, some years before, like a Maecenas of other days, had made it possible for the struggling writer to be freed of financial worry, had asked him one day with what book he was planning to follow *Ulysses*. He replied now that *Ulysses* was out, he considered himself as a man without a job: "I am like a tailor who wants to try his hand at making a new-style suit," he continued. "Will you order one?" Some weeks later Miss Weaver handed him a pamphlet written by a village priest, that contained a description of a giant's grave discovered in a parish lot. "Why not try the story of this giant?" she asked. It was the giant's narrative that ultimately became the story of Finn Macool, or *Finnegans Wake.*

The first issues of *transition* containing installments from what was then known as "Work in Progress" (Joyce told me that his provisional title was the invention of Ford Madox Ford, who had previously published a fragment in his *transatlantic review*) created a fanfare of sensational outbursts on many continents. For the most part, the confused critics in France, England and the United States simply snorted their violent disapproval. Miss Weaver herself was quoted as having expressed the fear that Joyce was wasting his genius, an incident which disturbed Joyce profoundly, for, after all, it was for her that the "tailor" was working. His French friend, Valéry Larbaud, said he regarded the work as a *divertissement philologique,* and of no great importance in Joyce's creative evolution. H. G. Wells wrote that he still had a number of books to write and could not spare the time needed to decipher Joyce's experiment. Ezra Pound, after expressing the opinion that "Work in Progress" reminded him of a description of some venereal disease, advised him to put the manuscript into the family album together with his poems. This Joyce resented, and since Pound had only recently eulogized the poems of an American poet named Dunning, Joyce bought a copy of the book in question, to see what it was like. "If that's Pound's idea of poetry," he said to me, "I'm quite safe." As time went on, the reactions to "Work in Progress" became more and more vehement, and on the whole, journalistically stereotyped. Joyce continued working at this vision.

To those who knew him intimately during the late twenties, James Joyce was a man of great warmth and charm, although at first approach his personality could seem almost forbidding. As a point of fact, it always took him some time to accept easy comradeship in social intercourse. At first he appeared to be on his guard, an attitude that was particularly noticeable during the explosion of fame that followed the publication of *Ulysses*. Later, as his own personal tragedy deepened, a dour and almost inhuman passion seemed to impinge on all his outside relationships, and he was able to live in his cavern of despair with what appeared to be pitiless indifference to events that did not touch him directly or, through friends, indirectly. Once he had given his friendship, however, nothing could swerve him from his loyalty, and he was capable of extreme delicacy towards those he felt were his friends. He was never an ebullient man, and his moments of silence and introspection frequently weighed even on his immediate surroundings. Usually, however, there would finally come a festive pause, when he would begin to sing, or even dance, and on these occasions he frequently showed flashes of gaiety and wit that approached a kind of delirium.

I never knew Joyce to be an easy conversationalist. He had a tendency to rather monosyllabic utterances. Nor did he relish being questioned on any subject. Nevertheless, when he was in the mood, his conversation, couched in the mellifluous Dublin speech, was a ripple of illuminating ideas and words, and once he had left his anarchic, misanthropic isolation, he could enjoy the companionship of his friends with a conviviality that brought out his essential nature. Above all, he eschewed esotericism. He was interested in human relations, human behavior, human thought and customs. His range of interests was a wide one: poetry prodigiously remembered and faultlessly recited; music and musicians, especially singing, of which his technical knowledge was astonishing; the theater, where his preferences went to Ibsen, Hauptmann, Scribe; the various liturgies; education; anthropology; philology; certain sciences, particularly physics, geometry and mathematics. He was little interested in pure politics or economics, although he followed events faithfully and his occasional barbed comments revealed complete awareness of all that was happening.

My memories of the first year of *transition* are inextricably associated with the personality of Elliot Paul. Paul was a New Englander who loved his native heath, but who had also rebelled against it ever since he could remember. I believe, in fact, that this emotion was dominant with him, and that the ambivalence of his attitude towards his birthplace colored his thinking processes. Once he told me: "If I ever go back to Boston, it'll be on a steamer that will stop off-shore to let down a raft from which I can jeer at that damned town . . ." One felt, at the same time, that he was secretly in love with the harbor city of his youth, for somehow he never allowed an outsider to criticize it. His conversation had the Yankee quality of terseness, but also an indefinable spirit of whimsy that made his listeners chuckle. He was a philosophical anarch — in the word's primitive semantics — and routine, bureaucracy, red tape were the enemies from which he escaped by a series of well-thought-out machinations of his own. He was an excellent story-teller and often entertained us with autobiographical sagas of his wander-years, or accounts of amative exploits. His sense of tolerance and personal liberty was a profound, an essential part of his religion. As for work, even the most satisfying job could become irksome to him if he felt that his freedom was in any way threatened, and whenever this happened, he simply faded into insubstantiality. Literary persons and facts he took *cum grano salis,* and even the overtowering figure of Joyce did not escape his tart comment: because of the Dubliner's proud withdrawal into himself, he frequently referred to him in letters to me as Camphor James.

Paul had an intuitive appreciation of literature, and nobody could detect a fake or piece of plagiarism more speedily than he. When manuscripts came pouring in from every part of the globe, it did not take him long to look them over with his keen, clear-seeing eye, and a gesture sufficed to inform Maeve Sage that they were to be put in the envelope destined to take the road back to the author. In spite of limitations, his instinctive feeling for language allowed him to see through forgery or distorted fabrication with astonishing directness. He hated counterfeit and simulation, and I was often surprised to see him read certain difficult and relatively *précieux* French writers and reject them with an infallible judgment of values. When I showed him my translation of Franz Kafka's "The Sentence," he immediately recognized the Czech writer's greatness, although at that time there were perhaps only a dozen or so writers anywhere who were aware of Kafka's existence and importance. Paul shared my admiration for André

Breton's "Discourse on the Dearth of Reality," and did not hesitate to acknowledge the talent of certain other young Surrealist writers.

We undoubtedly had misunderstandings, but these were only minor human aberrations of one kind or another, and we usually agreed instinctively on almost everything we selected, translated and published. In spite of his occasional animadversions with regard to contemporary American literature — and he had some powerful, very personal convictions on that score — he was genuinely optimistic about American letters and his *critiques* were marked by an essentially American perspective. All in all, however, I should say that at that time — for our lives have not crossed since — Paul was a man without pose or artificiality, whose imagination tended towards the absurd and the droll rather than towards the tragic. As the first turbulent year of *transition* came to a close, we wrote a final joint editorial, after which we separated. Paul told me that he was going to return to the United States, and I decided to abandon monthly for quarterly appearances.

Returning from Paris for brief visits to Lorraine and Alsace during this period, I became aware of the increasingly frenzied tone of the autonomist agitation there. Posters appeared overnight denouncing the French regime in gross, patois words. Mass meetings were held at which the chief agitators ranted and shouted their grievances. In Forbach I attended some of these meetings and watched the disorder steadily gaining ground.

There appeared, however, to be no real unity about objectives. Some claimed that they did not envisage secession from France. Others I heard complained about individual mistreatment and went so far as to demand complete independence. Some explained that they only wanted Alsace-Lorraine to be freed from the complex machinery of the French departmental system so that the frontier-land could have its own laws and regulations. An appeal to this effect was addressed to the League of Nations.

The leaders of the group — an illogical mixture of clericals, communists, and frank Alsace-Lorraine nationalists — had won a political victory when they were elected in a body to the municipal council of Strasbourg. The mayor, a former communist named Maur, declared himself for "limited autonomy within the framework of the French democratic regime." But it was obvious from the start that other leaders had different plans. Dr. Roos, for instance, made no bones about his hopes for complete independence, with the ulterior aim of handing the land over to Germany, in case of success. He was charged with treason a few years later, and in the winter of 1940 was executed by a French firing squad, at Nancy.

The French government could not sit idly by and let the disquiet of the border continue, and orders were given to confiscate the autonomist newspaper *Die Zukunft,* which had over a million readers. It was high time, for the aggressive insolence of the editors had been rapidly increasing in violence. Editorials appearing in that newspaper openly declared for revolt against the French system of education and against the French administration.

But local leaders did not abandon the battle. Charles Hauss, an autonomist from Strasbourg and a notorious Germanophile, now entered the fray. He was the son of the late Dr. Hauss, also a well-known pro-German, who had tried to save Alsace for the German Reich in the disastrous days before the armistice of 1918. Young Hauss was a prosperous printer in Strasbourg, and he made immediate plans for launching a new daily newspaper with autonomist tendencies. It was called *Elsass-Lothringische Zeitung,* or *Elz,* and it quickly became the most scurrilous propaganda sheet of the German wing in Alsace. Its anti-French spirit had the tone of the gutter.

More and more, an atmosphere of civil war prevailed in the borderland. Bitter brawls between the pro-French citizens and the pro-Germans or autonomists became frequent. The political antagonists engaged in fistfights whenever they met, and the Alsatians, who are somewhat brutal by temperament, with a peasant stubbornness, plunged into this internecine struggle with grim earnestness. Invectives were hurled about, and the altercations in inn and tavern resounded with a metallic clack of hate.

Warrants charging the principal autonomist leaders in Alsace with subversive activities against the safety of the French state were issued in the winter of 1927. It took the police a long time to arrest the agitators, for they were hiding in remote peasant houses or in the larger cities. Finally, they were all behind bars, fourteen of them.

The news was received throughout France with much relief. The activities of the fifth columnists—for although this term had not yet been invented, there was no doubt that they were acting in that capacity for Germany—had been growing in impudence and disorder for months. French public opinion, which had been waiting for fifty years for the return of the stolen border provinces and had finally seen the victorious conclusion of the struggle with great enthusiasm, was now convinced that the German neighbor had not given up the plan of reconquest. The situation, which had been growing worse from day to day, had finally gotten out of hand.

The case was set for trial in Colmar. Paris newspapers and foreign agencies had sent a small army of correspondents to cover the trial and the town had the atmosphere of a country fair. The hearings lasted many weary weeks, and in spite of their denials, the accused were finally led to admit that their autonomist aspirations were motivated by an anti-French feeling which, translated into the opposite, meant that they hankered for a German regime.

Yet was that really the issue? The defendants denied this obvious fact, declaring they were interested only in the preservation of their ancient local customs, which they claimed the centralized French state encroached upon. Be that as it may, it was a nauseating spectacle to watch these philistines who were so obviously lying, so obviously hiding their real motives. There was no longer any question in my mind, as the trial continued, that treasonable things were going on in the Alsatian borderland. The documents presented by the prosecution seemed irrefutable.

To my genuine sorrow, Solveen was among those arrested. For some time past he had seemed to become more and more embittered and lonely. His friends had left him, and he drank a good deal in the company of the cheap politicians of the municipal government of Strasbourg, who were the most fanatic dissidents. Solveen's entrance into the political fight, and his abandonment of the purely creative action to which he had dedicated himself in The Bridge, were now bearing bitter fruit. Although I had personally known him to be guilty, I was convinced that he had acted out of a mistaken idealism, more through accident than through any real anti-French bias. He had become lured into the net of the plotters through his artistic honesty, an honesty that sought to preserve the regional form of expression—always his chief desideratum. That he was acquitted at the end of the trial proved his integrity of character, but I had no further illusions as to his subtlety of intelligence.

The jury acquitted a further four men and found the other ten guilty. But the objective observer could not help feeling that a worm had begun to gnaw in the tree of France. A sense of demoralization was apparent, and the German danger seemed a very real one.

A few months later, legislative elections were held throughout France. In Alsace the former autonomists, under new party names, presented a long list of candidates. The election campaign was a bitter one. In the streets and meeting halls of the towns, the partisans of the German-inspired section often came to blows with the French democratic loyalists. This situation finally resulted in a reign of terror.

The election returns shocked the people of France, for all the autonomist candidates in Alsace won. Among them were several of the very men who had been involved in the Colmar trial. Some of the cases had even been especially compromising, proof having been established by the prosecutors that Berlin money had financed their treacherous activities. Nevertheless, these men now wanted to take their seats at the Palais Bourbon, in Paris.

In the Chamber of Deputies, they were received with glacial indifference. Democratic fair play permitted the autonomists to make their presentation speeches, and the chamber voted their admission, with the exception of two, whose treason was too obvious.

In Lorraine the elections did not have the significance of the autonomist-nationalist antithesis. There it was the clerical against the left-winger, communist against clerical, socialist against clerical. The clericals, who were also the bourgeois or the pro-capitalists, won.

My friend Dr. Dupuy, who had run on a ticket of militant republicanism — he was a radical socialist — had fought bitterly during a campaign that was marked by personal venom and violence. He stood for social reform, and as a doctor whose contact with suffering humanity had been long and close, he demanded better housing for the miners, a crèche for the babies of the poor, and other modern legislation.

His wily enemy Liétard, the clerical editor, who had boasted of being a member of the Souvenir Français, made his vicious campaign entirely on grounds of French patriotism and preservation of the Code Napoléon in the reannexed provinces, and used all his political experience, aided by a few shrewd country priests, to blacken the character of the good doctor. Vile insinuations were flung about. Dr. Dupuy was in the pay of the Devil. Dr. Dupuy was in the pay of the League of Nations Commission in Saarbrücken. Dr. Dupuy had had illicit love affairs with patients in town. The result was that Dr. Dupuy was snowed under. A pious but shrewd clerical nobody became the new deputy from the Forbach district.

The malaise in the borderland in the twenties was a deep and cancerous growth. On the other side of the frontier could be heard the first rumblings of the Nazi revolution. Thus far its repercussions in the borderland were faint. But those who knew the situation well were aware that certain elements of subversion were at work. In spite of the prosperity in the rest of the world, this land, so rich in coal, iron, oil and other raw materials, became a place where the poor became poorer and the rich richer.

Alsace-Lorraine stood at the crossroads.

7

QUEST FOR NEW WORDS

Transition interested me more and more as an adventure in language. I became intensely aware of the interrelationship of three great tongues, each of which was part of my own patrimony, and all three, I felt, were passing through a crisis. Experiencing this pathology on a triple plane, I prodded other writers into answering questions concerning their own linguistic experiences, with the result that the review gradually became a laboratory into which I tried to gather the forces that sympathized with my desire for a renewed logos. I sought a new style, something between prose and poetry, with which to express the experiences of the inner "I," as well as the unconscious experiences of dreams, daydreams and hypnogogic hallucinations. In Anglo-Saxon writing, the language of poetry began here and there to show the influence of our experiments. Poets seemed to become more language-conscious, and some of them began to abandon "imagistic" fatuities in favor of a richer and more sensitized style. We stimulated interest in the new narrative or paramyth, which encompasses the night-mind, in the Kafka-like grotesque, the fantastic fairy tale. We encouraged word innovations even to the point of absurdity, as well as syntactical research. We elicited new metaphors and made possible word-associations that were not only more musical but created a quite different universe. We gave a free rein to what I called "mantic writing," in sonorous incantations; a trend that was to be imitated in Paris after World War II by the literary school known as lettrism.

To crystallize my own mood of insurrection against the "malady of language," I wrote a manifesto to which I gave the title "Revolution of the Word." I stated as my dicta that "the literary creator has the right to disintegrate the primal matter of words imposed on him by textbooks and dictionaries"; that "he has the right to use words of his own fashioning and to disregard existing grammatical and syntactical laws"; I concluded with the insolent asseveration: "The plain reader be damned." This manifesto, which bore fifteen signatures, apparently struck the imagination of my contemporaries, for it quickly became a winged word in Paris, London and New York, and columnists, critics and editors of Sunday supplements used it as a bugaboo to pillory the insensate doings of the so-called Paris exiles. Even today, however, it remains for me the basis of a possible renovation of creative language to which I can still adhere.

Certain critics in France, England and America—not forgetting the Central European countries—attacked this manifesto with great violence, accusing us of satanic schemes against the classical traditions of grammar. Other—they were few, however—defended it half-heartedly. As a matter of fact, the manifesto was simply an aphoristic expression of my own convictions, an echo of my own concrete experiences. I had been caught in the labyrinth of idiomatic interfusions and transformations since early childhood. I had lived in a climate of word-interpolations before emigrating to America. In my boyhood I had heard not only two major tongues at war, but also a blending of their patois. In city-rooms I had experienced intimately the American language, as well as the numerous languages of the melting-pot: alloyages of assimilated nouns and verbs in the crucible of New York, the speech of mill-towns, southern types of Anglo-Saxon English, Creole English, Afro-American. Nor should it be forgotten that I had participated in the linguistic reorientation of Alsace-Lorraine since the end of the First World War.

The great example of James Joyce was naturally an added fillip. His experience had been without parallel: in addition to his native English he had been in intimate contact with Italian, German, Swiss German and French. To these he had added the study of Danish, Norwegian, Slovenian, and many other living and dead tongues. He had published the results of his experiments in *Ulysses*. Now that "Work in Progress" was appearing in my review, the problem was certainly before me.

But it was probably newspaper work, more than anything else, that had made me so conscious of the "malady of language." I should like to ask any sensitive police reporter, any political or city hall reporter, any correspondent, any feature writer what he really thinks of the iterant, trite words he is compelled to use, day in, day out. Does he not finally come to feel repugnance at having to continue to use the same overworked, hollowed-out phraseology? As an admirer of American journalism and the marvels of modern information services, I felt, by virtue of my first-hand experience, that a reformation of the newspaperman's vocabulary was a categorical imperative. I was convinced that the journalist's task would be facilitated if his vocabulary could in some way be enlarged, if he were given the possibility of using a more precise, richer and more fluid speech. In the face of sneers on the part of old-time newspapermen, I defended the tabloid language revolution which I had witnessed on the New York *Daily News*. In order to back up my manifesto I published in *transition* a New York "slanguage" dictionary, in which the inventions of Walter Winchell were given prominent place. Winchell, I felt, was a neologist of genius, for he had an instinctive sense of the kinetic word, of the word needed for the expression of new experiences and sensations in daily life.

An expansion of language seemed necessary, also, in English and American poetry. Work on my translation of American poets had impressed me with the paucity of vocabulary and the poverty of the lyrical phrase, both of which seemed to me to be meager and often pedestrian. This, I felt, prevented the poet from expressing the deeper emotions which his unconscious might have evoked. I myself invented a poet I called Theo Rutra, in order to project certain of my own neologistic work, and soon this fellow Rutra became my alter ego. I enjoyed playing him up to my friends, to whom I described in detail the "Czech immigrant living in Brooklyn." He was also alleged to be a newspaperman working as a reporter in the jungles of Myrtle Avenue. Rutra wrote:

FAULA AND FLONA

The lilygushes ring and ting the bilbels in the ivilleyo. Liloos sart slingslongdang into the clish of sun. The pool dries must. The morrowley loors in the neaves. The sardine-swungs flir flar and meere. A flishflashfling hoohoos and haas. Long shill the mellohoolooloos. The rangomane clanks jungling light. The elegoat mickmacks and crools. A rabotick ringrangs the stam. A plutocrass with throat of steel. And matemaids clock for dartalays . . .

And there were also sonorous incantations:

TO THE TREMENDUM

You are silverglast in starspace
Slowly lood the millarales of our hungers
Filla oo bilda alastara tinka
Es ist warm im eiswirbel deiner nacht

Lilla me malilla istoon tl lassa
Minna thone neenuna glustamiloo
Meilavo grola atlanty ganasta
Il fait chaud dans la neigeade de ta nuit

Lilla mo malilla istoon tl lassa
Hallali leetara runlee dra reesto
Brensa ioneersi paeondra alpantanta
Shhhh oina milla ma milalla loo

The "Revolution of the Word" provoked an intercontinental controversy that raged for several years. In France, such critics as the late Benjamin Crémieux (who died during the war at the hands of the Gestapo), Marcel Brion, and a few others argued in our favor. Crémieux wanted to relate our revolt to the futurist "words in liberty." Others, such as Roger Vitrac, evoked Rabelais and Fargue. In London the commentators had a field day.

Among Americans, the debate was particularly violent and, in consequence, fruitful. V. F. Calverton, editor of the *Modern Quarterly,* sent a letter challenging the editors of *transition* to a public debate on the problem. I cabled my acquiescence immediately, and it was agreed that members of the *transition* group should defend their principles of linguistic reformation in the next issue of the *Modern Quarterly.* Robert Sage, Stuart Gilbert and myself met at Colombey-les-deux-Eglises and worked out our *apologia pro verbo nostro.* Harold Salemson also joined our group, and in a few days we had our *pensum* ready to send off to New York. The Manhattanites were represented by Calverton, Herbert Gorman, S. D. Schmalhausen and Pierre Loving. The battle was fought almost entirely on the basis of social language versus language as expression. It was, in other words, the conflict between the Marxist and the romantic view of language. I answered Calverton's assertions point by point in the following anti-materialist vein:

> The creator is always an individualist. This does not prevent him from seeing his work in relation to the general mythology of his group. But he always sees himself as an autonomist of the spirit, a nonconformist, a rebel, a subversive element in any group as far as his inner life is concerned. If that were not the case, and he were merely running along the line of the social movement, he would doubtless be obliged to lower his intellectual values in order to reach the masses. He would have to give the replica of mass-hierarchy in his creative expression. He would have to play the role of the polite journalist who is the echo of the powers that

be. The creator, no matter what specific social structure surrounds him, is contemporaneous only by chance.

My conclusion was born out of personal experience and my faith in the American future:

> The mystique surrounding the "purity" of the English language has, I believe, lost its force. In the crucible of the immense racial fusion of indigenous and immigrant America we see today an astounding creation that ultimately will make the American language, because of its greater richness and pliancy and nearness to life, the successor of British English. This is already happening in speech, and as soon as the age-old delusion that there must be a difference between the written and the spoken word has had its day, we shall probably see the American language colonize England and all English-speaking countries . . . It is in the immigrant development of the new America that the potentialities for a fundamental revolution of the word are inherent. Here the foreign background, the word mythos lying dormant and being blended with the reality of the new continent, will eventually sweep the word-lore of the mother country away — although retaining the latter's primal elements — and thus will bring to fruition the language of the centuries to come . . .

Some time later, the poet and translator Samuel Putnam, who launched the *New Review*, returned to the attack. He was a Parisian American with intellectual energy and a great capacity for work, who showed fine awareness of modern literature. His personal dynamism soon made his review a much-talked-of organ of letters, which during a short life published, among others, Henry Miller, Wambly Bald, Peter Neagoe, James Farrell. Putnam launched an assault on *transition*'s word-revolutionary program, but before I was able to prepare a counter-offensive, the *New Review* folded up and the editor returned to the United States. I felt that the *New Review* was too much under the influence of the egregious Ezra Pound, whose poetry and fascist neuroses usually left me indifferent.

Matthew Josephson and certain of his friends in New York also took exception to the "Revolution of the Word." Most of his group had been in Paris for brief visits and they were apt to consider themselves arbiters of things emanating from France, though at the same time they professed a certain disdain for those of us who continued to live there. When Hart Crane, who had signed the document with me, arrived in New York, he was received amid a shower of ironic comment that raised doubts in his mind.

The fact remains, however, that Crane approved the proclamation when he signed it, and objected to none of its points. I felt that he did not "do quite right" by *transition* when he repudiated his endorsement under pressure of the boys "in old New York." However, in view of the fact that Josephson had also rejected *Ulysses* on its appearance, I was less discouraged than I might have been.

Invention, above all, invention, became the raging desire of my creative unconscious. During those Paris years of speculation and impending gloom, I worked on an "Atlantic dictionary" of my own, with the ambition to exhaust the greatest possible number of word-mintings. It was here too that I wrote a book of French neologistic poems under the title *Mots-Déluge*, which was later published by the Editions des Cahiers Libres. A *Comoedia* critic pronounced it "halfway between madness and genius." To mark the occasion, Joyce sent me a limerick that ran like this:

VERSAILLES 1933

There's a genial young poetriarch Euge
Who hollers with heartiness huge:
Let sick souls sob for solace
So the jeunes joy with Jolas
Book your berths: Après mot le déluge!

With the publication of *Mots-Déluge* I had now reached a phase of my poetic evolution that I had always hoped to attain one day: that of poet in each of my three languages. Not that the poets born to these languages really accepted me as one of their own; quite frankly, they did not, and I was not surprised to find myself eventually in a volume entitled *Poètes à l'Ecart/Dichtung der Abseitigen* (Poets off the beaten track). However, this activity constituted something of a *tour de force*, and I was interested at that time to discover analogies in literary history. I knew of a few bilingual poets, but was unable to discover any trilingual ones. In Paris there were my Lorraine friends, Yvan and Claire Goll, both of whom wrote poems in German and in French. There was also Tristan Tzara, whose native tongue was Rumanian, but who never wrote and published in anything but French. My friend Hans Arp, the Alsatian Dadaist, wrote in both German and French — better in German than in French. Two Americans, I recalled, had become French poets and even played a role in the symbolist movement, Francis Vielé-Griffin, a native Virginian, and Stuart Merrill, a New Yorker. Most of these poets, however, had chosen a new language without returning to their original idiom. My case remained troublesome, because I could not bring myself to abandon any one of the three languages, and my tendency was to write now in one, now in the other. I soon began to amalgamate my words, as in the following fragment from "Polyvocables":

now I stand in the wounded prairie the rhythms of a glocke
in my hands and the aeons lie hymnic over the gables
lallwords darklehaunt the heart and the corybantic light-music
s'enfuit dans les ombres and the caverns hide the weary birds and
je monte au-dessus des forêts a snowstorm dans les cheveux

As these experiments progressed, I became increasingly absorbed by the nocturnal mind. I studied my dreams and tried to perfect an instrument for expressing them. In those days of psychic tension in Europe, when the great economic temblor was at its height and totalitarianism had begun to cast its sinister shadow across the political horizon, I found that my unconscious life somehow mirrored these phenomena of the sick world-soul. My dreams and daydreams in Paris and in my frequent roaming around Europe were marked by this preoccupation with primordial things.

Above all, I was haunted by the following question: Is it I who am dreaming, or am I being dreamed? Were the Romantics right in assuming that in the dream we witness a game of polarity between the powers of the subhuman and those of the transcendental world? Is the dream the theater of an incessant struggle between the demonic and celestial agencies? Between monsters and angels? Between cherubic and Luciferian perspectives? I became convinced that in the dream man is in the grip of an enigmatic power, an other-world agency, and that he is really *being* dreamed. In the night life, I felt, especially during such a transitional, apocalyptic period as our own, when the lower and properly irrational forces seem to have been given power over us, we are possessed.

Thus I believed I had discovered the principle of polarity functioning in my dreams. The clash between the subrational forces of the past and the cosmological forces of the future was discernible in the new sense of time revealed by the night life. I found that my unconscious life aspired towards ascension. According to C. G. Jung, archaic man is still with us. In my own dreams of those years I saw analogies with ancient myths that were living realities to me. The mythological world was revealed to me in definite reconstructions of the following images: Death and resurrection; *Magna mater;* cosmic fear; the biblical motif of conflict between Satan and Michael; possession and descent into Hell; nostalgia for a lost paradise; inter-racial fraternity; the tower of Babel; the birth of planets; the legend of flying or the conquest of gravitation; the fall of the angels; the creation of the world.

I quote from a dream transcription, "The Grala," written during that period:

My friends had invited me for dinner in their Auteuil home. It was brumewinter. The city rumbled as if struck by vague apprehensions. Their apartment was warmquiet.

Bread and wine were on the table. Both were happy to see me after a long absence beyond frontiers. There was lighttrialogue, and then my friend's wife grew nervous and had tears in her eyes. He smiled obstinately and talked in long melodious phrases about Baudelaire.

I looked up from the table and saw, opposite me, on the studiowall a large, white animal, slow-moving, glittering in the lamplight's shaft. It's a spider, I mused. As I looked more carefully, I noticed that it was not of flesh, but of marble or skullbone.

A stubborn silence came over us. I could not understand what had happened. My friend looked at me and tried to smile. I observed that the animal did not attract the attention of my friends. A hurdy-gurdy began to play from somewhere in the street outside. Then silence again, like a menace.

Now the animal seemed to grow bigger. It continued to slowroam on the wall. At one time it tried to fly. But its wings apparently were glued to its body, for in spite of a violent effort, it could not move.

I had the feeling that the animal belonged to the household, for the indifference to its presence on the part of my friends seemed to indicate that they were accustomed to it. I tried to ask a question about it. But my words lipstuck. I could not, try as I might, recall the French word for "spider." I grew iresome. Finally I stammered, more to interrupt this intolerable silence than to get any information: ". . . Die Weiße Spinne."

My friend looked up and laughed. Only now did he become aware of the chimerapresence on the wall. He got up and walked over to a bookshelf where he hastily thumbed a *Larousse*. But he evidently did not find what he was looking for.

The telephone shrilljingled. My friend came back into the room after he had answered it and informed me that a writer named Galsworthy wanted to talk to me. He pronounced the name with French phonetics and it took me some time to understand it. Then I thought of the word: *Justice.*

I phonehallooed, but there was no answer. I whinecried. I bellow-squeaked. I wrathshook schimpfnouns into the receiver. The silence wirehummed spectrally.

My friend was sitting alone in the room, his face in his hands. He starewondered at a white page in front of him. Then he wrote, swift-fingering, for a long time. I did not interrupt him. I stood near the window watching children playrunning in the street.

The silence in the room grew terrordark. I was no longer able to bear it. I took the *Larousse* and, turmoilblustering, looked at the animal pictures. There was nothing there resembling the species on the wall.

I tore the inkburdened paper out of my friend's hand and read in endless repetition:

GRALA GRALA GRALA GRALA GRALA GRALA GRALA . . .

I flashsaw: I was face to face with the apocalyptic beast. I awestared into the past and into the future. The room turned vertigomad around me.

Nearly all my writings of this time reflected these tendencies, and, as they began to appear in *transition* and such other magazines as *Les Cahiers du Sud, Bifur, Aman, Documents,* etc., as well as in trilingual books and pamphlets, critics either strongly approved or indignantly rejected the innovations. *Mots-Déluge, Epivocables of 3, Hypnolog des Scheitelauges, I Have Seen Monsters and Angels* were the titles, and their reception was never one of indifference. To the Jesuit Father Leonard Feeney in New York's *America,* I was a "curious word welder." The critic of the *Irish Times* found that *Monsters and Angels* represented "honest work on the part of a man who is undoubtedly an artist interested in pure poetry." I learned of this surprising appreciation through James Joyce who called me up to tell me about it, adding that he too felt "it was a very important book." *The London Star,* on the other hand, thought my multilingual efforts were "spine-shuddering." "Subliminal subtleties," said the *Cincinnati Inquirer,* while others in America called it "poppycock," "schizophrenic," "gibberish." Stephen Spender, writing in the *New Statesman,* thought that my psychic drama represented "an unfortunate development." The most comprehending reactions came from France, where the *Mercure de France,* among others, gave my verbal experiences a commendatory reception.

James Laughlin, editor of *New Directions,* contributed an essay "New Words for Old" to the magazine *Story,* in which he said: "And what has all this to do with experimental writing? Just this: that the writer, the serious writer, is rendered by his occupation most sensitive to language deficiency. It is not by accident that Stein and Joyce, that Cummings and Jolas, that basic English and surrealism are coeval to a major crisis of civilization. Working intimately with words, the writer becomes aware of their bad habits as well as their persuasive power."

Between the wars, Gertrude Stein was the *doyenne* among American writers in Paris. At that time, she was living in the Rue de Fleurus with her life-long friend Alice Toklas, and from where she radiated her esoteric stammering. Her mental attitude was remote from anything I felt and thought. For not only did she seem to be quite devoid of metaphysical awareness but I also found her aesthetic approach both gratuitous and lacking in substance. Unfortunately, too, she seemed to have an almost pathological need for adulation — of which she later received a great deal — and her nervous reflexes were violent and contradictory.

Frankly, we never got along very well. I used to accept her occasional invitations to tea in her salon, where paintings by Picasso, Gris and Matisse heightened the modernity of the background. One could at times meet "interesting" people there, painters and writers, but the atmosphere was also apt to be laden with electricity. Whenever there was a lull in the conversation, Miss Stein would nervously signal to Miss Toklas to relinquish the guest she had engaged in dialogue and pursue the talk with another. She was fond of gossip, but could talk engrossingly as well on a great variety of subjects, even on American advertising methods, which she had studied for years.

At the time I began to know her well, she was just emerging from a long literary eclipse. Her resurrection was made possible thanks to Elliot Paul, for his articles about her in the *Chicago Tribune* re-awakened public interest in her work, and *transition* completed the job. Paul visited her frequently, and usually left with a batch of manuscripts which she chose among many in a huge filing case. We published a number of her compositions in *transition,* although I am obliged to say that I saw, and see today, little inventiveness in her writing. The "little household words" so dear to Sherwood Anderson never impressed me, for my tendency was always in the other direction. I wanted an enrichment of language, new words, millions of words, even, and for my part, I was in search of these millions of words. I was, however, occasionally diverted by certain of her rhythmic enchainments, and even today can find a pleasing quality in her incantatory repetition of ordinary words. Curiously enough, when I included a short piece of hers in my *Anthologie de la nouvelle poésie américaine,* I was the first to make a translation of her work into French.

In 1928 I had republished Miss Stein's *Tender Buttons,* which had long been out of print, and a year later printed the first version of *Four Saints in Three Acts,* six years before American audiences heard Virgil Thomson's ingenious score of the work in New York. After that, we saw little of each other, except for occasional chance meetings. We were not enemies, nor were we friends. A strange temperamental antinomy existed between us, and I felt we irritated each other. One bright morning in 1931, I visited her with the intention of asking her for another manuscript. The conversation went along smoothly enough, until suddenly she began to upbraid me for publishing James Joyce more frequently than herself. "Joyce is a third-rate Irish politician," she declared, and she added: "The greatest living writer of the age is Gertrude Stein." I begged to disagree with her, and left, mentally slamming the door.

A year later I received a telephone call from her.

"Jolas," she said, "I have just put in a telephone and I am phoning my friends to test it. You're the first one." I could not help laughing. We began to see her again, and I published her latest work once more.

After the Second World War, someone sent me Gertrude Stein's *Portraits and Prayers,* which somehow I had missed when it was first published in 1934. In it I found a portrait of myself entitled "A Play Without Roses" which afforded me a good laugh. We were hardly friends.

And yet I recall that when our baby girl Georgia died, she and Miss Toklas were among the few Americans to call and bring flowers. I have never forgotten this very human gesture on her part.

The motive of exile or expatriation was a dominating one among Americans in Paris. Many of the writers, painters and musicians who had fled from prohibition and Babbittism felt they were engaged in a conscious revolt against their native land, and marked this rebellion by an exaggerated admiration for all things European. However, the heaping up of cultured clichés about Continental superiority over America sometimes threw me into angry outbursts, for I never shared this particular prejudice. I was rooted in Europe, of course, but my American nostalgia was an unhealed wound. When my book of poems *Cinema* appeared in New York in 1926, its Americanophilism elicited irreverent quips from my Parisian colleagues. Some said it was a romantic absurdity on my part, that the tradition of Henry James was the only intelligent line open to young American writers and artists. Even in my French poems the American nostalgia remained a primal emotion:

Je m'arrête aux routes de l'Europe et j'entends ta voix
J'entends l'orchestre gonflé de ton coeur
Dans les nuits ensanglantées quand le sol tremble dans la peur

Dans les midis lourds d'hommes osseux et de femmes-vampires
J'entends les syllabes de ta langue d'airain
J'entends le tourbillon ronfler contre tes gratte-ciels
Je vois ton rêve printanier caresser les tiges du désespoir
Je m'arrête dans la rue et je vois ta verticalité blanche
Je vois ta marche de titane trébuchante à travers le temps libéré
Je regarde tes mouvements électriques et tes seins de baigneuse
Tes horizons sans fin où la flamme descend sur la mer
Tes nuits qui s'agenouillent devant les assassinats des espaces
Je vois le coquillage rouge de tes amours
Et l'élan de tes violences grammaticales

. . .

But the problem remained a burning one, and I decided to publish a symposium of opinion from the exiled in answer to the question, "Why do Americans live in Europe?" Gertrude Stein gave the typically paradoxical reply: "The United States is just now the oldest country in the world. There always is an oldest country and she is it, it is she who is the mother of the twentieth century civilization. . . . It is a country the right age to have been born in and the wrong age to live in." Hilaire Hiler thought: "In America there are no facilities for the enjoyment of leisure or apparatuses for reflection." Robert McAlmon felt he preferred Europe, that is France, to America because "there is less interference with private life here." The composer George Antheil asserted that "musically it is absolutely impossible to live in America." Kay Boyle exclaimed, "I am too proud and too young to need the grandeur of physical America which one can accept only at the price of one's dignity. . . . I am making a voyage into poverty because I am too proud to find nourishment in a situation that is more successful than myself." A. Lincoln Gillespie, Jr., vaticinated: "a) because in Europe I find meaningscurry in their organise-self-Divert-hours loll here simmer-rife — Except-lush-stat, Get in less necessary. b) because of the absence of Tight-blank faces here and c) liquor-gamme abroad somewhat breathelier." There were also lively answers by Walter Lowenfels, Pierre Loving, Emily Holmes Coleman, Berenice Abbott, Lansing Warren, Harold J. Salemson, and Kathleen Cannell.

As I expected, the critics on both sides of the ocean pounced on the inquiry and soon there was a terrific exchange of verbal blows. Paul Morand contributed a long essay to a Paris magazine in which he asserted that he preferred Americans living in the United States to the Parisian Americans of Montparnasse. New York, Chicago and other critics kicked the exile protests around like a football, and the cartoonists began to add their skill to the general brouhaha. The satiric review *Life,* predecessor to the present-day magazine, had a full-page caricature showing a couple of inebriate American gentlemen seated behind a pile of saucers in a Montparnasse café, while at their feet lay abandoned copies of Hemingway's *The Sun Also Rises* and — *transition.* The caption read: "First American: 'What's that the band is playing?' The garçon de café: 'Why, that's the "Star-Spangled Banner," Sir.'"

Editing *transition* remained throughout a high adventure. For one thing, I reached intensely to the mood of invention and experiment in which a few writers and artists of the Western world seemed to be working during those years. I believed, too, that such a review could become a sort of center around which would gravitate all those who shared what I felt was a universal impulse to push back the frontiers of the mind and its means of expression. This, to a border-man like myself, was the quintessence of action. I decided to give *transition* the subtitle "An International Quarterly for Creative Experiment." It was later to become an "Intercontinental Workshop for Vertigralist Transmutation." But this is another story.

Those ten years brought many friends and sympathizers. They also brought enemies, and intrigues were frequent. Yet somehow we seemed to weather them. The little magazine drew into its orbit practically all the neo-romanticist currents that were to be found on both sides of the Atlantic. Most of these writers and artists seemed sincere, even illuminated by a vision they had evidently cherished in solitude for a long while, and I was convinced that we stood before a general explosion of the imagination throughout the Occident.

I had been reading with increasing pleasure the poems of St.-John Perse, pen-name of Alexis Léger. For a long time he had been a mysterious figure to me, for I was unaware that he occupied a high diplomatic position at the Quai d'Orsay in Paris. Then I learned from friends that he had given up writing poetry many years earlier, after publishing a few small *plaquettes,* and was devoting all his efforts to his career as permanent General Secretary of the Ministry of Foreign Affairs, where he was second to Aristide Briand and other Prime Ministers in the formulation of French foreign policy. A native of the West Indies, his work showed traces of the tropical luxuriance of his childhood background. *Eloges, Anabase, L'amitié du prince* and *Pour une enfance* enthralled the young French poets.

I had translated some excerpts from the collection, *Eloges* and *Pour une enfance,* which I hoped to publish in *transition.* So one day I took my courage in hand and went to the Quai d'Orsay to ask permission to do so. I sent in a copy of *transition,* with a note requesting an interview. A short while later the poet appeared, a handsome man with intelligent eyes in a typically Creole face. He said he had very little time, so we plunged immediately into the subject of my visit. He spoke with scintillating charm about the mystery of language, said he had given up writing entirely but was following modern movements with interest. Of the poets in the Surrealist group he said that they might produce important works if they could rid themselves of their preoccupation with purely political dynamism. To my surprise he knew about *transition,* and gave me permission to publish his poems. The interview lasted almost an hour, and as I left I noticed a number of important-looking gentlemen waiting impatiently for their turn to speak with Léger the diplomat. In 1940 Léger came to Washington, where he is still active in the French Section of the Library of Congress.

St.-John Perse is one of the really great poets of our time. T. S. Eliot and I were the first to translate him into English, simultaneously in fact, and I take pride in this. The influence of this French poet-diplomat on contemporary British and American poets is very evident.

In Paris I came to know personally many of the contributors of *transition.* Most of those who visited the city from abroad took time off to call at the "office," or we would meet in cafés and at the homes of other writers. They were of many nationalities, and all seemed to agree on one point: they were little interested in action as such; they wanted to express their own visions, dreams, fantasies, even their hallucinations and nightmares.

I first met Harry and Caresse Crosby in 1928, when they sent me some manuscripts in which I found lively imagery and a marked surrealist tendency. I published some of their work, and we met them later. Harry's interest in *transition* was warmly genuine, and I recall with gratitude that he helped me financially on two occasions when the bills were more than we could meet alone.

When Hart Crane came to Paris, he looked me up. I introduced him to Crosby, who greatly admired Crane's Elizabethan wealth of language. Crane's greatest desire was to create an American myth, and he read us passages from his long poem *The Bridge,* on which he was then working. His notebooks were filled with unusual esoteric words which he said he would eventually incorporate in the stanzas of his poem. Crosby asked Crane to allow him to publish *The Bridge* with his Black Sun Press, and Crane accepted. At about the same time, Kay Boyle, whom I had also introduced to Crosby, gave him a collection of her short stories. Joyce contributed a fragment from his "Work in Progress," "Tales of Shem and Shaun," and I gave him my own *Secession in Astropolis,* an astronomic fantasy in the style I later called verticalist. These were the first incursions into general publishing to be made by Crosby's Black Sun Press.

The Crosbys left for America after the appearance of the eighteenth number of *transition,* in which I announced that Harry Crosby would henceforth be associate editor. I saw a good deal of him shortly before his departure. He had taken up flying with ecstatic enjoyment and often described to me his aeronautic emotions, his reckless daredevil flights. When I bade him good-bye I noticed his restlessness, an almost mad need for mobility. He expressed admiration for a story by the Surrealist poet René Crevel, which I had asked Kay Boyle to translate for *transition* and which had appeared in the new number. He said he wanted this tale to be published by the Black Sun Press as a separate book, as soon as he returned from America. By now he had gone completely Surrealist, and he gave me a little volume he had just published with his press, *Dormir Ensemble,* containing dreams and fantasies. A few weeks later a cable brought news of Harry Crosby's suicide in New York. Only a few days before, I had received a hastily scribbled letter thanking me for having helped him in his work and proposing an expansion of the *transition* movement after his return to France.

Kay Boyle, whose sensitive poems and short stories I had been publishing since the first issue of *transition,* came to Paris from England in 1928. She was a lank, striking girl whom we all liked instantly and whose caustic wit and brilliancy was admired. She wrote her early stories in a feverish mood of lyricism and expressed her violent appreciations and acid dismissals of certain of her contemporaries in no uncertain terms. She had been part of the *This Quarter* group and, like Ernest Walsh and Ethel Moorhead, had a combative spirit with which I occasionally disagreed, but which could be loyal in defense and frequently was so towards me. She introduced me to Robert McAlmon, whose narrative talent she greatly admired. Two years later she married Laurence Vail, a fragment of whose Surrealist novel *Murder, Murder* I had just published in *transition.* At a party in our Paris flat, we presented Kay to Gertrude Stein. There were a number of writers present who had been published in *transition:* Archibald MacLeish, Philippe Soupault, Georges Ribemont-Dessaignes. But whereas the other guests seemed to get along well, Kay and Miss Stein were soon at odds, I forget about what. Kay was one of the few young American writers who persistently refused to pay homage to the genius of the Rue de Fleurus.

Matthew and Hannah Josephson introduced the New York rhythm, for Matty was imbued with a strong economic-materialistic romanticism and talked excitedly about the machine millennium he thought he saw on the

Detroit horizon. I asked him to prepare a group manifestation on the subject for *transition* as soon as he returned to New York. A few months later we received a bulky manuscript written by him and some of his Manhattan friends, which I published under the title of "New York 1928." I was rather disappointed in the result. It was in many respects witty and pertinent, but it was also too optimistic concerning the future of the machine civilization for my taste.

When Robert Graves and Laura Riding came to Paris from London, I organized a lunch-party to which I also invited Kay Boyle. But the two women proved to be poles apart in their literary tastes; so much so, in fact, that a slightly acrid discussion of Hart Crane's poetry soon degenerated into what threatened to become an open antagonism. I intervened with the suggestion that each one present her opinion in the pages of *transition*. When the debate appeared, certain of Crane's friends, among whom I recall Yvor Winters was the most vocal, withdrew their own collaboration with the review by way of protest. Kay and Laura's incompatibility was to be further evidenced when I presented the latter to Miss Stein. Unless I am mistaken, a genuine friendship that lasted over several years developed immediately between these two transplanted American writers.

Another English writer to look us up was Richard Aldington. I had published some of his poems in *transition* and he had written sympathetically of the review in the *Times Literary Supplement*. I invited Philippe and Marie Louise Soupault to meet him. Although the bilingual dialogue was electric and plans for collective actions were enthusiastic, I fear that these were never realized. Aldington was beginning to write poems in French, some of which he showed us. Soupault liked them, but felt they were occasionally too greatly influenced by Surrealism. I recall that Aldington spoke very critically of T. S. Eliot's recent conversion to Catholicism.

As a result of my renewed acquaintance with Alsace and Lorraine, the German language began again to play a certain role in my creative life. Through *transition* I was in friendly correspondence with several German writers and my translations of Kafka, Sternheim, Benn, Trakl and others stimulated further contacts with the literary scene beyond the Rhine. In addition, the signature of the Locarno pact by France, Great Britain, and Germany seemed to announce a new era in Europe's blood-stained history. Maria and I often discussed plans for a visit to the Weimar Republic.

The Expressionist movement which had been triumphant in Germany since 1910 was nearing its end, and I was anxious to witness its last phenomena on the home ground. Although this movement had seemed to be little else than the modern prolongation of early romanticism, it soon became evident that it was also an expression of world crisis which the first war had brought to fruition. For it was a universal manifestation, embracing not only the creative arts but also philosophical and political-social zones of thinking, and it even contained certain religious-metaphysical elements. During a period when hatred and chauvinism seemed to reign supreme, the representatives of this *Weltanschauung* preached peace and fraternization. A tempestuous pathos characterized this break with tradition, and the analogy with the Sturm und Drang period in Goethe's time was often striking. It was primarily an emotional sirocco of youth, an experience of what was termed the new mythos dominated all the poems, dramas, and narratives of that group, and a polemical attitude towards the horrors of war, accompanied by a longing for dream and wonder, was common to them all. Expressionism gave the German language new syntactical associations, and the sound-poems of August Stramm foreshadowed the Dada insurrection. Over it all there hovered the spirit of pre-existentialism, the philosophical climate of Scheler, Husserl, Heidegger and Jaspers.

In Paris, my friend the German-Jewish Expressionist writer Carl Einstein often suggested that I visit Berlin in order to collect what he called "the last echoes of the Expressionistic era," before they became buried in a "nationalistic realism." He felt that a new and dangerous jingoism was coming up in Germany and that the "Prussian spirit was not dead." "Expressionism was the last form of the human equation in German," he said. "What is now developing there, looks like the sterile echo of the creative mind. I see nothing of interest in the works of the younger men — they're drifting towards the spirit of Teutonic megalomania; they're the true epigones who might become dangerous to European peace."

He did not believe, however, that the racist infantilism of the nascent Nazi movement would ever triumph. "The German is organically ambivalent," he would say. "Sentimentalism and power lust are in him in equal portions; but there are still a few humanists left who will prevent the Teuton berserk spirit from getting the upper hand. Even Thomas Mann, whom I do not like, as you know, will have enough influence over the young writers to stop the evolution towards military nationalism."

Einstein, Hans Arp and myself spent hours in Einstein's book-cluttered studio near the Boulevard de Grenelle, talking about poetry in the German language. Einstein was determined to launch a cry of revolt against what he called the Fichte spirit among the German poets then writing on the other side of the Rhine. "Let's hurl something in their faces," he said. "The two or three poets left there will thank us!"

He had grandiose plans for a collection of poetry plaquettes to be issued in German from Paris. We discussed the project at great length, wrote manifestos, gathered a number of possible manuscripts, but in the end nothing came of it — Arp was bound by his Surrealist allegiance, and I was working to complete some poems in French for a volume that was to appear shortly.

Einstein had one bête noire among the German writers — Goethe — and he often amused us with his violent broadsides. "The greatest bore on the European continent, that ruined antiquarian of letters," that "little burgher who worked to preserve his fame after his death" were but a few of the expressions he used to describe the "Sage of Weimar." I asked him to prepare an essay for the hundredth anniversary of Goethe's death, and he went at it hammer and tongs. I made the translation and it was published in *transition.* He insisted again and again that I should look at Weimar Germany before it might be too late. "Weimar still exists," Einstein said. "But we can't say how long it will resist the jingoism of the new littérateurs. "I don't trust these fellows," he used to say; "they like too well to march in goose-step and wear *Pickelhauben;* and then they usually go mad. . . . You should go to see Döblin, or my friend Grosz."

We read poems by Gottfried Benn, Georg Heym, Georg Trakl, Alfred Mombert, Ernst Stadler and others, who were the first to launch the Expressionistic revolt in poetry and prose. In all this poetry one felt a desperate attempt to save the human being from technological enslavement. Deeply impressed by this, I decided to visit Germany in 1929, before the creative force of this hymnic group should be destroyed.

In the winter of 1929–30, Berlin was cold and inclement. Its intellectual life under the liberal Weimar regime was, however, still vigorous. We settled in a comfortable boarding house recommended by American friends, where our fellow boarders were for the most part American, English, German and Swiss psychoanalytical students, who spoke of Freud with filial devotion but rejected all Jungian and Adlerian "heresies" with amusing violence. We met most of the poets and writers with whom I had been in correspondence, as well as new writers whose work I was planning to translate for future numbers of the review.

Among these was Alfred Döblin, whose *Berlin Alexanderplatz* was undoubtedly the most discussed novel in Berlin that season. I visited Dr. Döblin in the Frankfurter Allee, in the workers' district. On this occasion I told him of my project to present fragments from his book to English-speaking readers. We talked, of course, about James Joyce, whose *Ulysses* had appeared sometime before in an excellent translation by Georg Goyert. Although he admired *Ulysses* immensely, Döblin denied that his new book had been in any way influenced by it. During our conversation Döblin mentioned that his publishers, S. Fischer, had just completed negotiations with Viking Press in New York for the English translation of his novel and was looking for a translator. He suggested I try it and arrange a meeting with Dr. Gottfried Bermann at the Fischer office. After Mr. Huebsch had seen a sample of the translation intended for *transition*, he sent a contract, and the work was completed within a year. In 1933, when Hitler's barbarism overwhelmed the democratic regime, Döblin emigrated with his family.

A few days after my meeting with Döblin I was introduced to the playwright Carl Sternheim, whose work I had presented in *transition*. His goal, he said, was the destruction of German philistinism, which he held responsible for Prussian militarism and the Kaiser's will to conquest. We attended a dinner at which his wife, Thea, announced smilingly that she and Sternheim would divorce within a few weeks, and that he would marry Pamela Wedekind, daughter of Frank Wedekind, the playwright. Pamela Wedekind was many years younger than Sternheim, but he was deeply in love with the gifted, beautiful girl. "I think it an admirable thing," Sternheim commented, "that with our marriage, two of the greatest play-writing families in Europe should be united."

A few years later we were to see Carl and Pamela Sternheim again, in Brussels, where they occupied a delightful, modern apartment. But they seemed lonely and isolated from the rest of the world. "We decided to quit Germany forever," Sternheim said sadly. "Es ist und bleibt ein kulturloses Volk." Pamela sang for us her own settings of German poems, to the accompaniment of a lute, and Sternheim related with great vehemence that Chancellor Brüning had stolen all his ideas for a new foreign policy from him — from Sternheim, the greatest playwright of Weimar Germany. It was a painful visit.

At a restaurant frequented by writers and newsmen, I was introduced to one of the Ullstein brothers. He seemed to think that the nationalist revolution would not succeed, and showed a blind belief in the stability of the Weimar Republic that astonished me even then, for signs of the approaching storm were only too evident. The news kiosks were already displaying racist and anti-Semitic newspapers, as well as a plethora of little sheets with occultistic predictions that were always on the side of the swastika. There were also frequent parades and skirmishes that foretold violence. But in the great *Ullstein-Haus* it was apparently easy to lull oneself into the illusory notion that the republican regime had a journalistic fortress that would withstand all assaults.

Alfred Flechtheim, the former "wheat king," who at that time owned the leading modern picture gallery in Berlin, showed us his great collection of paintings by Picasso, Braque, Klee, Grosz, Hofer and many others. One Sunday we were invited to lunch at Flechtheim's magnificent home near the Spree. There were present representatives of intellectual and artistic Berlin, as well as visiting writers and artists from other countries. The apartment was a veritable gallery, and it was a joy to wander through the rooms, whose walls were literally covered with well-chosen manifestations of contemporary paintings.

That was a pleasant luncheon, a gathering I like to recall. Around a perfectly appointed table, the twenty-odd guests spoke in almost every European language, and it was about art, not politics, that they chatted. I sat next to a little hunch-backed man, Max Herrmann-Neisse, a poet who spoke his lyrics with intoxicated introspection. At the other end of the table, George Grosz talked eagerly with his neighbor, a bearded gentleman whose German sounded laborious, and who turned out to be a well-known Hungarian writer. French still seemed to be a common medium of communication. For that brief hour one had the impression of a European community capable of finding a meeting-ground, at least in the arts.

A few years later, most of these artists and writers were in exile: in France, in Switzerland, in England or in the United States. Flechtheim, the lusty patron of the arts, died during the blitz in London. Herrmann-Neisse, after several months there, passed away out of grief for his homeland's degradation. Thomas and Heinrich Mann, Walter Mehring, Alfred Neumann, Theodor Plivier, Erich Maria Remarque, Ernst Toller, Berthold Viertel, Franz Werfel, Paul Zech, Stefan Zweig escaped to North or South America. When Hitler came to power and instituted his low-browed action against what he called degenerate art, I often thought of that luncheon in Berlin. Exile and death have been the lot of most of those who sat around that table.

Döblin told me to see his friend Gottfried Benn, whose work I had translated and printed in *transition*. A dermatologist by profession, he was also a leading Expressionist poet. He lived in the workers' quarter of Berlin, and was apparently well liked by his proletarian patients. According to Döblin, Benn had seen war and malady at close range, so he had a sense of Europe's decay, and his writings were direct expressions of his pessimism. I had several conversations with Benn, in which I remember his repetitive insistence on "the bankruptcy of the antithetical structure." He agreed with me as to the poet's right to a new vocabulary and syntax. Haunted by the self-imposed problem of what he called the "southerly word," Benn has undoubtedly written a few of the great poems in modern German.

He told me, however, that he had given up writing poetry because the growing naturalism which he felt to be part of a vast process of disintegration could no longer be expressed in the language used by his day. He was tending toward a new sense of the personality, and at that time was trying to give expression to his philosophy of life: a kind of synthesis of his medical-biological experience and his evolution as a word-coiner. The budding science of characterology interested him above all else, and he was a friend and admirer of its leading propounder, Kretschmer. What he wanted to do was to explore the "geology of the I." I felt that as a doctor and a poet he was eminently fitted to make the deductions from the "body-soul unity" idea which Klages and Prinzhorn were then developing. He told me he wanted to establish contact with the primitive "I." He spoke of the Dionysian intoxication with lyrical ecstasy.

One day he said quite out of the blue, and with absolute coldness: "I knew Nurse Cavell. She was a traitor. It was I who wrote her death certificate." This sudden revelation of Prussian callousness, especially in so sensitive a poet, sent a shudder right through me. As time went on, however, I detected in his conversations a strong Nordic bias. He told me that he found the germ of a nationalist movement in Germany, which, he felt, would crystallize in a few years. To be sure, I had been aware of this current ever since I had arrived in Germany, for the Weimar Republic was being assaulted from every side. And yet, at that time, in early 1930, democratic Germany impressed the visitor as leading the country towards a possible renaissance in liberalism and the arts. There was a definite feeling of liberty in the air, and the writers, artists and film producers all seemed to be working in an atmosphere of fertile pioneering. New experimental ideas flashed across the horizon and anything seemed possible.

The nationalist movement was undoubtedly making headway. Wherever I went with Benn, I ran across partisans of this creed, and the books of Rosenberg, Moeller van den Bruck, and other ideologists of racial barbarism were being eagerly discussed in salons and on public platforms. Against this fermentation, democrats and socialists as well as Thälmann's Communists battled constantly. Often I saw the Nazi parades, closed in by armed police, marching through the streets. Elsewhere the Red banner could be seen waving above ragged masses in the proletarian quarters.

One evening in a well-known restaurant, a drunken student, hearing my wife and me speaking English, approached our table and began a violent tirade against England and the United States. "We'll get you yet," he shouted, and he became more and more offensive until he was dragged away to another table by his Nazi friends. At that moment, I understood that the idea of revenge for defeat was rankling in the breasts of the racists, and that democracy was greatly endangered in Germany.

When I told Benn of this incident, he smiled and said it was natural that the renaissance in Germany should come, but that he deplored such violence and boorishness. Benn came out openly for Hitler in 1933, but apparently recognized his mistake some time later. His post-war writings, still tainted with certain Nazi ideas, are influencing the new generation of Germans.

George Grosz, the satirist and painter, still living in Berlin, was a close friend of Dr. Benn, who arranged a meeting between us at his bachelor quarters in the Belle-Alliance-Straße. A delicious meal was served for the three of us, and an excellent Rhine wine soon whetted the conversation. Grosz, whose savage depiction of the German philistine constituted at that time a gesture of defiance to every nationalist in Germany, was a gay and eager talker, and the discussion waxed high when the question arose as to the role of the artist in the social convulsions threatening Europe. Benn defended the conception of the ivory tower, "the high colloquies of the best spirits," against the artist's participation in any social action. Grosz, on the contrary, defended a sociological approach, although at that time he had virtually abandoned his ironic vein for work of a purely aesthetic character. We continued the discussion in Benn's favorite beer tavern, frequented by workers of the neighborhood, many of whom, as Benn smilingly indicated to us, were his venereal patients.

At a reasonable hour, Benn left us, and Grosz began to talk amusingly of his war experiences. He had been drafted in 1914, but since he did not have the slightest intention of serving in the war machine, he developed a malingering technique based on his study of psychiatry, which landed him in numerous hospitals and jails, but which in the end kept him out of the army. He had many diverting tales to tell about the post-war period in Berlin, when he and my Paris friend Carl Einstein had edited a Dada review called *Der blutige Ernst,* of which only three issues appeared, all three immediately seized by the authorities. He spoke of the Dada *Rummel* with rollicking laughter. He asked me many questions about America and told me that he wanted to emigrate. Europe, he felt, was a dying world which he would leave to its fate. He also foresaw the arrival of a dictatorship in Germany. Seven years later I met Grosz, on Long Island. He spoke enthusiastically of the folklore to be found in the Sears Roebuck catalog. I realized that he had found his ultima Thule.

After a few weeks, Berlin proved disquieting and fatiguing, so we left for Zurich, where I hoped to complete my search for literary and psychological material to be used in *transition.*

That winter Maria's Louisville friend, Dr. Cary Baynes, was working in Zurich in close collaboration with the psychoanalyst Dr. C. G. Jung. At our request, she arranged a meeting with him at her home, on order that I might discuss with him a possible article for *transition.* I found Jung a jovial, solidly built man who, in addition to all the rest, had a capacity for congenial conversation, and we got along well. He chatted much about Surrealism that night, and asked me particularly about Yves Tanguy, whose work delighted him. He had bought a new Tanguy painting, concerning which he outlined to me a fascinating analysis based on his doctrine of the collective unconscious.

I called on Dr. Jung several days later in order to discuss in greater detail his contribution to the review. He showed me a series of strange automatic sketches made by one of his American patients and compared them with reproductions of ancient Chinese mandalas. The resemblance between these two creations, originating from such widely distant regions, helped him to formulate new psychological theories. With the vague idea in mind that I myself might undertake a psychoanalysis, I related to him certain of my dreams which he interpreted with profound sagacity and intuition. He advised me, however, to "put my disquiet into creative work." He talked interestingly and at length about his researches on the subject of the source of aesthetic creation. When I left him, it was with a copy of his essay entitled "Poetry and Psychology" in my pocket, and his permission to translate it for *transition.*

The Jung "seminary," frequented mostly by patients and visiting scientists, was a workshop in which Jung read his new essays, or else spoke freely about the many problems being studied. There were always fruitful discussions, especially since he often spoke without restraint, very personally. The talks were taken down by a stenographer, and later re-arranged, or left untouched for posthumous publication. There he talked of his relations with Freud, giving a thorough history of the famous break with his former teacher. He indicated that he, Jung, had discovered the unconscious theory independently of Freud, and that he could have asserted his priority, if loyalty had not prevented him from pressing the claim. He retained the greatest respect for Freud, and in many of his writings he pays homage to the pioneer of Vienna. He told me that after publishing *Wandlungen der Libido,* he had sent a copy to Freud, who wrote him a very brief note saying:

"This is not what we set out to do together." And that was the last he had heard from Freud, whose disciples, using the methods of psychoanalysis, characterize the break as a "revolt against the father."

Personally I was strongly attracted by Jung's theories, and I liked especially their religious and mythic implications. His theory that the language of the unconscious was the symbol which emerges again and again from the depths of the collective unconscious as a creative function appealed especially to the poet, for he explained that the symbol is the eternal wisdom of the ages, of art as well as of religion. Everything, feeling, imagination and will, as well as instinct, participated in this. Thus the myth becomes living.

Zurich, where the Dada movement was born in 1916, was now somewhat lethargic as regards artistic creation. The memory of Dada was almost extinct, except with an occasional newspaperman who had some vivid recollections of the carnival. My friend Hans Arp, who was one of the earliest Dadaists, had asked me in Paris to visit his friends the architect Dr. Siegfried Giedion and his wife, Carola, who, he said, would be able to tell me a good deal about the Dada period. Arp had often talked to me about those mad days with amusing frankness, revealing many inside stories of the genesis of Dada.

I visited the Giedions and liked them immediately, especially since Carola Giedion-Welcker, who was herself a writer on aesthetic subjects, was also a personal friend and great admirer of Joyce. She described to me a séance at Dr. Jung's seminary during which Jung had lectured on *Ulysses*. It was a destructive analysis, and had become especially irritating to her when Jung declared that he had been bored by *Ulysses* and unable to finish it. Carola Giedion-Welcker made a violent protest from the floor, but I heard no further echoes of the incident. Some time later it was reported to Joyce, who, fittingly, included it in "Work in Progress."

I was eager to visit the place where the Dada movement was born, the Café Voltaire, but it no longer existed. I did, however, see the house where Joyce had lived during the war. I was particularly interested in the real founder of Dada, Hugo Ball, who had died two years before. As I found another copy of his diary record of the period, *Flight Out of Time,* in a second-hand bookshop, the whole Dada tumult assumed new perspectives for me. Here was an intimate, day by day record of this artistic nihilism and its development. It also showed the integrity of its founder, who, having launched the movement, relinquished it almost a year later, to join the Catholic faith of his youth.

Ball, who hailed from the Rhineland, went to Zurich at the outbreak of the First World War, because he found himself unable to sympathize with the German aims. He had previously been active in Munich as an Expressionist playwright and poet. He and his wife, Emmy Hennings-Ball, poet and actress, lived in great poverty for a year in Zurich, and finally he managed to eke out a scant existence by founding an itinerant cabaret. From this developed the famous Café Voltaire, where the Dada movement really began.

"The café was overcrowded," Ball related in his diary, after the first evening. "Many were unable to find room. Towards six o'clock, while we were still busy hammering and hanging up futurist and cubist paintings and posters, there appeared an oriental-looking deputation of four little men, with briefcases and pictures under their arms, discreetly bowing and scraping. They introduced themselves as Marcel Janco, the painter, Tristan Tzara, the poet, Georges Janco and a fourth gentlemen whose name escapes me now. Arp, too, happened to be there, and we understood each other without exchanging many words. Soon Janco's generous archangels were hanging on the wall, together with the other beautiful things, and that same evening Tzara read verses in an earlier vein which he took out of his coat pocket in a not unsympathetic manner."

It always seemed curious to me that Dada should have been born in Zurich, which is so definitely a town of old-fashioned bourgeois comfort. I discussed this question once while walking through Zurich with Dr. Max Rychner, the young Swiss editor of *La Nouvelle Revue Suisse*. Rychner was a keen observer of the literary scene, and had many documents on the Dada venture. He replied that he felt the Zurich genesis of Dada was due to the action of the law of polarity.

Rychner represented a type of Swiss nationalism that appealed to me. For quadrolingual Switzerland had always been to Europe in nuce, and the city of Zurich, situated as it is at the linguistic crossroads of continental Europe, a laboratory of the modern spirit. Rychner had conceived his review as an expression of this concept, and he published articles in French, German, English and other languages.

Shortly after New Year in 1933, I visited Zurich again at Joyce's invitation to join him there. We worked together each morning at his hotel on a fragment of "Work in Progress" which he was preparing for publication in the coming issue of *transition*. In the company of the Irish poet I felt far removed from all political considerations; we were living in a world of linguistic alchemy that offered me the absorbing spectacle of watching Joyce's creative genius in action.

I met again his Zurich friends, Siegfried Giedion and his wife Carola Giedion-Welcker, who sympathized with "Work in Progress." The Giedions

7. James Joyce and Eugene Jolas, Stein am Rhein, 1936 (photo: Sigfried Giedion). Copyright Zurich James Joyce Foundation. Used by permission.

8. James Joyce, Eugene Jolas, Nora Joyce, and Carola Giedion-Welcker, Stein am Rhein, 1936 (photo: Sigfried Giedion). Copyright Zurich James Joyce Foundation. Used by permission.

and other *Zurichois,* who knew a good deal of what was happening in the German prison camps, spoke with bitterness and loathing of the sadistic intolerance of the Nazis and of their efforts to extirpate the creative spirit. Stories of violence against intellectuals and Jews had begun to trickle through. We even heard, among other things, that a copy of *transition,* with a cover by Arp, had been burned in Munich. The poet Erich Mühsam had been murdered by SS men who cut his nose and ears off before massacring him. German writers and artists were fleeing to the hospitable soil of Switzerland to escape the Gestapo, and Zurich began to harbor many exiles. We used to meet them in the little restaurants that Joyce and I frequented near the lake. I recall seeing there Max Herrmann-Neisse, Else Lasker-Schüler and many others.

One Sunday the Giedions took us in their car on an excursion to the Rhinefall of Schaffhausen, on the Swiss-German border. We lunched at a little inn in the frontier-town of Stein, and from a window we watched the course of the wildly swirling Rhine which, only a few kilometers away, had passed through the Lake of Constance. The Rhine trout was excellent and the Valais wine was cool and herby. After lunch we continued our pilgrimage to the Rhinefall itself. As we watched the grandiose spectacle of the falls from the broad terrace, Joyce appeared almost indifferent. In reality, however, he stood in great awe of natural phenomena, and it is more than probable that what seemed to be indifference was his way of hiding his emotions. Rivers and mountains are among the recurrent themes of *Finnegans Wake.*

While we were sitting on the terrace facing the iridescent waters, we suddenly noticed at nearby tables several grotesquely garbed Nazi youths who had crossed the border for a Sunday excursion. They wore their Hitlerite insignia with ostentation and seemed evidently proud of this affiliation. Soon we heard their raucous voices in a dull Germanic tavern song, and I could not help recalling the days in my childhood, when we used to hear the drunken voices of the Kaiser's soldiers in the little inn next to our house. Nothing had changed. Almost immediately this invasion robbed the place of its charm, and we soon left. On the way home, Joyce, who seldom seemed to abandon his apolitical stoicism, whispered to me: "Did you get that whiff from Boeotia?"

8

GOG AND MAGOG

The middle thirties were nomadic years for me, during which I traveled back and forth between Paris and Strasbourg, Paris and Forbach, Paris and New York. Neurotically, I sought escape from the threatening collapse of a world in the throes of primeval possession. The dogma of "blood and soil" had been proclaimed by the illiterates who dominated Central Europe, and I could feel the first tremors of the imminent earthquake whenever I visited Alsace-Lorraine, where the futile Maginot Line was being hastily constructed as a bulwark against militaristic aggressiveness and intolerance. On the frontier men recalled the Apocalypse: "And when the thousand years are expired, Satan shall be locked out of his prison. . . . and shall go out to deceive the nations which are in the four quarters of the earth, Gog and Magog, to gather them together to battle, the number of whom is as the sand of the sea." Daniel's beast was roaming the earth.

By 1935 I had grown weary of Europe generally, and even Paris had become depressing. Magazine journalism and *avant-gardisme* were beginning to pall and I longed to return to straight reporting. For this it seemed to me that Manhattan offered more interesting opportunities than Paris to a newspaperman with European training, even though Paris remained the crossroads of international news and some of the best newspapermen in the world were stationed there. I knew and liked many of them, among whom were such Americans as William Bird, Will Barbour, Morris Gilbert, Lansing Warren, Edgar Mowrer and Leland Stowe. But the return to the States of thousands of Paris Americans had forced the Paris edition of the *Chicago Tribune* to fuse with that of the *New York Herald,* and jobs were scant. For a while I considered working on a French-language paper in Paris, but that would have meant staying in Europe indefinitely. I finally decided to try my luck again in New York.

Before sailing I spent some weeks with relatives in Strasbourg and For-bach. Everywhere I heard stories of the persecution of Jews in the con-tiguous Saar and Baden regions, and echoes of militarist rage crashed daily across the border. My brother Emile, who owned a truck garden near the Saar frontier, described the barbarism of which he was a constant witness. Hardly a night passed without panic-stricken Jewish refugees who had tramped all night through woods and fields knocking at his door to beg for shelter.

One day as he stood talking with some Lorraine friends near the oaken beam that marked the border, a Nazi official approached from the other side and began to listen in on the conversation.

"You're attacking our Führer!" he suddenly shouted.

"To hell with your Führer!" was Emile's reply. "The sooner you get rid of him, the better it will be for us all."

At that moment, an SS man who had been hiding nearby moved towards the French side of the line and, with a lunge across it, seized my brother, whom he dragged to the German side, with the aid of other Nazis. Once in-side the German customs-house Emile was beaten. Later he was transferred to prison in Saarbrücken.

In Paris we haunted government offices in order to obtain his release. Certain American newspapers took up the fight, for although he was not an American citizen, he was the French brother of American citizens. At the Quai d'Orsay, officials seemed embarrassed.

"*Tout de même,* you don't expect us to go to war on account of a minor frontier incident," said one of them, adding that these incidents were be-coming more and more frequent.

After two months, we finally won out. Quite as suddenly and with-out warning as he had been arrested, Emile was released. He was deeply shaken by the brutal treatment he had undergone at the hands of the Nazis, who had subjected him each day to long interrogations, during which they forced him to stand rigid against a wall with his hands on his trouser seams. They also beat him with blackjacks and threatened him with prison and execution. Emile survived all this, but his hatred of his eastern neighbors was by now a dogma. The harsh reality of racist arrogance was at our doors. The book-burning thugs were beginning to shake the pillars of European civilization.

This frontier-terror haunted me:

One more spring along the Maginot Line
The village slowly dug itself out of winter

The lark climbed chanting above the growing fields
Where the farmer ploughed and plodded beside a turret
Where the horses steamed beside the gun-caisson

The broom-golden spring would soon be here again
But could we think of seed-time and cuckoo-shout
When the greenwood and the berry-ravine were gleaming
With the tangle of many sharp-toothed barricades
And the soil was heavy with the menace of dynamite?

Whitsun would soon come into the greening world
The forests would be flaming with blossoms
There would be a festival in the clover-fields
But the soldiers waited in the rose-shrouded trenches
For the phonehello of an anguish-aching voice

Earlier that year, a plebiscite had been held in the Saarland. Drawn by the impact of a European political drama that was obviously developing, I crossed the border sometimes and noticed a tension in the streets and shops of the city. Huge swastikas were hanging from a few business houses along the Bahnhofstraße. The posters were graphic and exhortatory: *Zurück zu Mutter!* Others had shrill, minatory overtones. But the posters of the democratic groups had a more powerful appeal. They spoke the language of the West, the words of the great liberal tradition. The former were backed by the Nazis, and the latter by the socialists, the liberals, the progressives. At night the streets were black with an almost neurotic crowd that milled up and down, discussing in Teutonic fashion the events of the day. One noticed numerous swastikas on the lapels of the men. French poilus were still roaming through the streets. The taverns were crowded with a drunken Prussian mass of burghers who made no bones about the hopes they had for a Nazi triumph.

The day after the plebiscite, my old newspaper instinct awoke in me and would not be downed. I heard through Paris newspapers that Saarbrücken was filled with French, British and American newspapermen, and I hoped to run into one my old friends. But when I arrived, the crowds were thick in all the streets, and it was difficult to find anyone. Armand, Emile and I walked through this tumult listening to the repetitive slogan song of the Saar: "Deutsch ist die Saar, deutsch immerdar . . ." None of my American friends were to be found in this mob of madmen. Only some years later my friend Bill Shirer, who was the CBS correspondent for continental Europe, told me in Paris that he was there that day and that he and some friends crossed in the evening into Forbach. He told me of his joy at being in a French town again after the Prussian grotesquerie, and they had dined hilariously in a Forbach tavern. When I told him that it was my town which he had visited, he said, "Well, it was a great liberation to be in France after the Nazi farce we had just witnessed."

That day Hitler arrived. The word had spread like a sirocco in the town, and the Nazi flag was soon to be seen everywhere. It was beginning to rain and then to pour, but the masses remained glued in the streets waiting for the man who was to plunge the world into war a few years later. The mob of Saarlanders was a Nazi mob. Anybody could see it in their faces, where expectancy and that peculiar German dullness that comes over them in moments of collective sentimentality was now visible.

Hitler stood erect in an open automobile, his hair disheveled by the rain, his arm outstretched in the Fascist salute before these newly converted automata. Then we heard a roar from thousands of animal throats. The car containing the ex-painter and his party drove through the principal streets finally arriving at city hall, where the reception became official. Standing here, packed in among the ever-increasing crowd of men and women, I could not help thinking that this manifestation of communal dementia had something in it that was pathological and repellent. These miners of the Sarre, who had not wanted this to happen, who had fought violently in their newspapers against the Nazis, now suddenly seemed to be transformed. They knew that his Gestapo was in town, that it was already at work dressing lists of the democratic suspects, yet they stood there in a mystic trance, saluting the demagogue and shouting their obeisance to him.

I was able to watch the man whose destiny was beginning to disquiet the world. The pale and embittered fanatic received the applause of the Sarre with a faint smile. When he spoke—those mendacious words he repeated since so frequently, that promise that this was his last territorial claim in Europe—it sounded like a rasping tirade. The words were catapulted over the heads of the naive and already Nazified mob, and they had to me an ungrammatical ring, as if spoken by an illiterate.

Then the roar began once more, and this time it seemed like an irrational grunt emitted by one huge throat. It flew against the houses of this archaic quarter from where the Prussians of another day had started on their forward march of robbery and massacre in two wars. It seemed to echo a collective Pan-Germanic will.

That evening, as my brothers and I tramped home, we saw the roads leading to France crowded with numberless refugees to get out before the terror began. Already SS troops were stationed at strategic points to register the stragglers, and, if possible, challenge and terrorize them. As yet they could only indulge in objurgations, for Hitler's triumph was not yet officially ratified. The border between France and Germany was still under the jurisdiction of France and the League of Nations; but although a customs union existed between the Sarre and Lorraine under the Treaty of Versailles, French customs officers were still stationed at strategic points along our frontier.

So the defeated wended their way through the gathering night, and the commotion caused by the slowly moving autos and cars lent an eerie mood to the region. We passed hundreds of Jewish families on foot, often with older members of the family hobbling wearily along. At the Brème d'Or, where the actual frontier was, each case was examined by French officials as rapidly and effectively as possible. The French government had thrown the border open for the men and women threatened by the Gestapo, but it was also prudently winnowing the cases to ward off possible infiltrations of enemy agents. We saw weeping women and children on the point of leaving their homes for an unknown fate. Rich and poor were crowded together before they were released and allowed to enter France's promised land. I noticed a number of Catholic priests in the crowd of new exiles.

As I myself crossed the border, I realized that I never wanted to see Germany any more. And indeed, since 1933, I have never again set foot on totalitarian German soil.

The people of Forbach were shocked by the turn of events in the Sarre. Most of them had entertained hopes that the Sarre would at least vote retention of the League of Nations regime, and the realization that it had deliberately voted itself into the Nazi camp came as a stunning blow. The Lorrainers' old suspicion of the *Prussien* now began to assert itself again. During the Weimar days the tendency was to regard Germany as on the way to a stable democratic regime. Now the fact that the new neighbor would be the anti-Catholic, anti-Semitic, anti-liberal Nazi trouble-maker caused a deep disquiet among the population of the Lorraine land.

I found New York greatly changed. The "depression" was still evident and the unemployed numerous. I settled in a skyscraper hotel from where at night I liked to watch the motley movement below. Grand Central Terminal and the Empire State Building gleamed in an eruption of lights, and from my stone summit I could follow the stream of night-beings zigzagging into darkness. Occasionally I listened to the panic-weary conversation of old friends; their faith in the benefits of a machine civilization of the masses seemed to have been severely shaken. Soon I too joined the army of job hunters. I wandered the city of my youth, which was now metamorphosed by a number of immense new structures; I rode up and down precipitous elevators; my goal once more: a newspaper job. Through the intercession of a friend, I finally found employment as staff correspondent with the New York office of the French Havas News Agency. My chief was Percy Winner, and others working there were Fernand Auberjonois and André Peron. Our task was to send cable stories in the French language — general American and Central American news — to Paris. It was both an editorial and a mechanical job; often we had to manipulate the teletype machines ourselves.

Working on the fourteenth floor of a New York skyscraper, I sometimes found myself alone in the newsroom in the early morning hours. The American editors — Adrian Berwick, Leon Edel, Samuel Dashiell — who transmitted European news from French into English, stopped work at midnight. From then till morning the solitude was complete except for the three teletype machines behind my desk beating out their savage binary rhythms. It was a metallic monotone that caressed the nerves in the watches of the nights, as I typed my own French items. At two o'clock the windows of the neighboring skyscrapers grew dark, and only the Radio City Tower seemed still to be burning with energy. Sometimes my hours were shifted, and I was on hand from dawn till four o'clock in the afternoon, or from four o'clock until midnight. This broken work rhythm was particularly tiring. Despite the continual change of hours, however, I enjoyed being a newspaperman again. I relived the earlier days of my passionate search for news — now in another language, in the language of Rimbaud and Gide, but otherwise identical with the mechanics of the American technique. I discovered that I had not entirely lost my old dexterity.

Yet I saw more clearly than before that news gathering is really a very subtle problem. The vital facts of a nation's life are never truly reported. For there occurs in the transmission of these facts an inevitable subjective deformation that makes it impossible to arrive at more than an approximation of the truth. I observed the infinitely variegated versions of specific events reflecting the point of view of the individual newsmen. Rarely, if ever, did three of four eye — or ear — witnesses relate exactly the same story. Something happened between the moment of the occurrence and its impingement on eye and ear. Did this mean that our senses were becoming dulled? Or was it that the machinery for gathering news is, in itself, defective?

These lobster-shifts during sultry New York summer nights were an experience in introspection and depression. The teletype machines continued to clang and jangle. But some nights there was no news worth transmitting. Through the windows I could see the lights of nocturnal Midtown; at the Hotel Roosevelt opposite, little intimate tête-à-têtes could be glimpsed through dimly lighted windows; below, in the streets near Grand Central Station, life in the hot night, although reduced in intensity, was still going on. In those moments I experimented with what I termed cable poems, in which I intermingled words from several languages.

On the early shift, I felt less alone in my office. The men working in the American section, on the other side of the room from me, were full of pranks, and there was often an atmosphere of hilarious sociability among them. Sometimes, during a lull in work, we would gather in little knots to chat. On these occasions we talked of our migrant newspaper days or debated the stupidities and eccentricities of politicians, cynicism being one of the journalist's prime characteristics. We also detailed the psychodramas of criminals we had encountered—described our sensations while witnessing electrocutions, hangings, or shootings—talked of our emotional lives or our wrenching habits. Stories of malice, conflict, and violence abounded, and I often wondered at the almost cruel insensitivity we showed. Nearly all these men had read the works of Freud, but they seemed to have retained little of his humanity. I became friendly with one of them, Leon Edel, a Canadian writer who was interested in James Joyce and Henry James, and who often entertained me with tales of his newspaper days in Montreal.

At that time the New Deal was a reality, and this work, which kept me in touch not only with its functioning but also with individuals who were literally fighting for their daily existence, revived in me a sense of social communion which the aesthetic life of Paris had undoubtedly attenuated. I felt a heightened sense of human togetherness, and I enjoyed increasingly the camaraderie of my fellow workers. In the office I was obliged to follow closely the intricate Washington dispatches, and this made me understand more completely than I had before the significance of the plan for social betterment being elaborated in the nation's capital. I also began to take a real interest in the complexities of national politics, it being my duty to selec: the most salient features for transmission to France. Drew Pearson was our Washington correspondent, and the French desk had to gallicize his prose for relay to Paris and South America.

During these New York months, I fell in love with Manhattan all over again. I made pilgrimages to all the places associated with my early years there: the Upper West Side (the tenement-house in which I had spent my first New York year still existed); Hell's Kitchen (where I had attended evening high school to learn English); the Park Row district (where I had once dreamed of a journalistic career); Battery Park, Central Park, Riverside Drive Park, and many other neighborhoods closely identified with the hopes and discouragements of my immigrant years.

I saw some of my old colleagues of the *Daily News,* with whom I discussed the careers of mutual friends. Jack Chapman had succeeded Burns Mantle as drama critic, and Gene McHugh was now news chief. Dick Clarke, my old boss, was managing editor of the vast establishment. It was indeed a far cry from the provincial little brick building in lower New York where the *News* had begun to the glamorous miracle-skyscraper in the forties, where the paper was being published. But somehow, I had no desire to work with that sensation-hungry organization again.

New York had already begun to receive refugees from Hitler's tyranny. Our chief at Havas, M. Lemercier, had been one of the first to be expelled from Germany by Goebbels's henchmen because, as chief of the Berlin Havas bureau, he had dared tell the truth about the regime. Lemercier was a charming, easily inflammable Frenchman, and, as a member of the International Press Club, he seized every opportunity to tell his Nazi colleagues what he thought of them. His sudden death a few years later left many American and foreign friends with a genuine sense of loss.

I met Dr. Richard Huelsenbeck through my old Berlin acquaintance, the painter George Grosz. Huelsenbeck, a medical man and a poet, was one of the founders of the Zurich Dada movement. His name was less known, however, than that of Tristan Tzara, who, he insisted, had been able to claim more credit than was his due, simply because the real founders either were dead, as in the case of Hugo Ball, or had emigrated. Huelsenbeck's wife was Jewish, but he declared that this was not his only reason for emigrating: a former Dadaist, he said, could not live in Hitleria. He told me that a wealthy relative of his wife, who lived somewhere in New Jersey, had commissioned him to write the story of his emigration to America. Somehow his title, *Geschichte eines Auswanderers* (Emigrant's story), stirred me.

Dr. Huelsenbeck and I spoke German together, since at that time his knowledge of English was still very imperfect. He was particularly proud of his connection with the early days of the Dada movement, and when I told him that his name was rarely spoken of in this connection in Paris, he grew furious. I mentioned that I had read Hugo Ball's *Flucht aus der Zeit,* in which Ball told how he had recounted to Huelsenbeck a mystic revelation he had had in connection with the word "D.A.D.A." (Ball recalls in this diary that he was engaged in writing his *Byzanthinisches Christentum,* when one day — evidently while he was reading Dionysius Areopagita — he heard the recondite word "D.A.D.A." and knew immediately that the nihilistic movement he had unleashed at the Café Voltaire in Zurich should be baptized Dada.) Huelsenbeck claimed, however, that the genesis of the name "Dada" was quite different, and he told me the following story. He and Ball were discussing what to name the new movement. Huelsenbeck opened a dictionary, and his eye fell by chance on the word *dada*, which in French nursery language, means a hobby-horse, or simply "hobby." I asked him to write down this version, which he did, and I translated it for the twenty-fifth issue of *transition,* which was brought out in New York. Thus there exist four different versions of the birth of Dada: Hugo Ball's, Huelsenbeck's, Tristan Tzara's, and finally Hans Arp's. For Arp has always told me that he came upon the word one day while drinking a glass of beer and at the same time holding his nose, in order to cure an attack of hiccoughs. The chance that an authentic version may eventually emerge from these conflicting claims is indeed slim.

While working with Havas, I edited three American issues of *transition* with the help of James Johnson Sweeney, whom I had met in Paris several years before at the home of our mutual friend Carl Einstein. On their annual visit to Paris, the Sweeneys—James, Laura, and their fast-growing family—always stayed at the Crillon, from where James carried on his somewhat ambivalent activities of businessman and art critic. He was undoubtedly more attracted by the latter role, and this interest in *transition* was genuine and, to me, extremely welcome. In New York, he offered to act as assistant editor, and his skyscraper home on the East River became the scene of many spirited debates on subjects that interested us both.

I was eager to obtain American contributions, particularly in the realm of the fantastic story, or *paramyth,* a term I had recently introduced in *transition.* A few of the younger American poets were beginning to write in the style *transition* had initiated and nurtured. Kafka was beginning to be known; Surrealism was fast becoming the fashion. An eager young poet and publisher, James Laughlin IV, had begun his *New Directions* editions by dedicating the first volume "to *transition* and the Revolution of the Word." There was undoubtedly a creative element to be discovered in what I had named America Fantastica. I saw it in the comics, the tabloids, the cinema, as well as in the new language that was developing with almost Elizabethan opulence, especially in New York. But although this phantasmatic reality existed all about us, the literature of the day bore little or no trace of it, and most New York writers seemed hell-bent on discovering social *misère* and nothing else. To find the true representative of the type of writing I was after, one had to dig. We did finally, however, discover a few. A very gifted new writer of chimeras was Wayne Andrews, a young Harvard student, whose creations had the qualities of a modern Hawthorne's. Among the poets whose work I liked were James Agee, Horace Gregory, Muriel Rukeyser, Oliver Wells — all of whom lived in New York — and a rather mysterious fellow named Charles Tracy, who wrote from somewhere in the Far West. Most of these contributors were guests at the Sweeney apartment during that period, as was also "Sandy" Calder, the sculptor, who was generous with his own contributions and gave many helpful suggestions concerning our reproductions. Sandy's studio in Connecticut was reminiscent of an alchemist's laboratory, particularly when all the "mobiles" — which covered walls, floor, and ceiling — were set in motion by the wind.

To me who had lived abroad during the early years of the review, publication in the U.S. was a unique experience, for I had never before had the satisfaction of watching at close range the reactions of American critical opinion to the appearance of a number. A *Herald Tribune* editorial writer devoted a long and facetious meditation to certain of my linguistic innovations (perhaps I should have sent him a controversial reply, but somehow I never got around to it), and the *New York Times* devoted almost an entire page of a Sunday issue to what it called the transition movement. This elicited a plethora of replies from many parts of the United States, and for a brief moment *transition* seemed to be the target of considerable American comment. For the most part, however, it was unfriendly, full of jeers and gibes and titterings. Of course I could have answered my critics with the fact that I was holding down a disciplined newspaperman's job at the same time that I was engaged in word-revolutionary activities. But it hardly seemed worthwhile; *transition* had been knocked before.

One sultry morning, after working all night on the lobster-shift — o nocturnal solitude on the skyscraper, o dark and ailing fatigue of the morning hours — I had just fallen asleep in my hotel room when the telephone began to ring. It turned out to be a team of *Time* reporters and photographers who were downstairs asking for an interview. Recalling my own impudent reportorial incursions back in the *Daily News* days, I projected myself into the minds of the numerous victims of my early journalistic zeal, and scrambling out of bed, called to say that I would meet them on the roof of the hotel in a quarter of an hour. A young woman, accompanied by two men and another girl, introduced herself, and we were soon engaged in an amusing polylogue, while flashbulbs were popping. When the interview was over I crept back to bed, exhausted. But my old friends the newsmen would not let me sleep that day. Two hours later I was once more dragged from bed by the insistent buzzing of my arch-enemy, the telephone. This time it was a member of the *News-Week* staff who was eager to have me explain the "esotericism" of *transition*. Of the two articles, *News-Week*'s was the more ironic, but it also showed a better grasp of *transition*'s aims.

The French painter Fernand Léger was living temporarily in New York, and his studio was the meeting place of many who were interested in modern painting. During his stay in America he designed a special cover for *transition,* which stirred up considerable controversy. Léger was genuinely interested in the Manhattan cosmopolis and appreciated particularly its architectural novelty. He often told me, in fact, that he was in love with New York, and he undoubtedly knew as much about the romantic aspects of the city as any native-born New Yorker. He liked to roam around at night in all kinds of out-of-the-way places: in Hell's Kitchen, on nocturnal Broadway, or in the Afro-American milieu of Harlem. He even introduced us — the old New Yorkers — to the crazy thaumaturgy of Father Divine.

In a manner of speaking, I was now living in a new diaspora, a Gallic one, this time, and I experienced in a kind of hypnosis the ideas and feelings of a Frenchman recently emigrated from one of France's eastern provinces. I thought bilingually, with the accent on French, wrote journalistically in the grammatical style of a *lycéen,* followed the rhythm of the great French classics. Many of my new friends were French or French-Swiss, and I seemed to be living in the French colony of New York.

But the interlinguistic vastness of Manhattan is so pronounced that no one can remain in one area for long without coming into contact with other national elements from all over the world. Even today, New York is still the melting-pot, and the cosmopolitan aspect of the city is evident in a multitude of phonemes from both East and West. This gives the New York speech used in the streets and offices, on the beaches and in the subways, a variegated tonality that often leads ordinary talk into uncharted regions. It is not the American tongue one finds in the newspapers or magazines, but an American language with both ancestral and futuristic shadings.

As I walked about the city, I discovered a recent German-Jewish refugee group on the West Side, a Czech quarter on the East Side, representatives of Greek, Italian and other Mediterranean countries scattered throughout the megalopolis. There were also Canadians and metropolitan French living in small colonies here and there. And everywhere was the picture of the frontierless world! At Father Divine's frenetic evenings in Harlem I listened to pious, grotesquely neologistic sermons. At the opera in Chinatown, weirdly unfamiliar gesturings and exclamations and harsh, metallic costumes symbolized bewilderingly the eternal and universal motifs of human drama. In the delicatessen shops and hotels of the Upper West Side, where Jewish intellectuals, artists and writers continued the traditions of pre-Hitler liberalism and humanism, I was catapulted into Austria and Weimar Germany. At press gatherings, or at the homes of individuals, I was drawn into social relations with American, French, Italian, Spanish and Mexican journalists. Here domestic and world affairs were discussed, and the pro- or anti-fascist attitude was quickly gauged in casual conversation. In this vast variety of sounds I was beginning to hear the new language I had dreamed of so long.

For I too belonged to this migratory mass of word experimenters. In this whirling cauldron of the new vocabulary, I often retraced the cease-less journeys of my own language across America and Europe. I thought of Pittsburgh and the days of my first newspaper job that had required a knowledge of my mother's tongue. I thought of the American city-rooms in New York and elsewhere on the continent where I had begun to write in the language of the land, in the language of Walt Whitman and Henry James and Emily Dickinson. In three decades I had passed through the German, English and French languages on a continuous voyage in the company of editors, reporters, printers and pressmen.

I reflected upon the romance of news-gathering and news-writing, and its dynamics obsessed me. "Hard" news and news features excited me more than editorial writing as such. Nor was I much interested in liter-ary criticism, theater reviews, movie chronicles, or any of the numerous other forms of so-called intellectual journalism. My interest was focused on reporting, headline writing, make-up. I was indeed a romantic of the Gutenberg mythos. I liked the tension of edition time, the fevered activity of jingling telephones, clanking typewriters, telescriptors, the shouts and staccato conversations that accompanied the writing of each lead and story. I liked to haunt the composing rooms, to listen to the mechanical rhythm of the Mergenthalers, to help the printers with the make-up of difficult pages. I admired the esthetics of *information,* news, *Nachrichten.* I fell in love with the countless words that went into the execution of my trilingual tasks. As the process of metamorphosis advanced I heard them change meaning, then emerge from the lexicological crucible as new words.

As I recalled my life in New York, I became aware that personally I be-longed to an indefinable poetic category. The fact that I was an immigrant American sufficed to make me different from the other American poets I knew. For I was an immigrant who had never lost contact with his native speech, with the evolution of his European sources, and who had felt the enormous problem of language in daily living. Was I wrong in thinking that my case was unique? In New York I felt that one could be a European poet as well as an American poet, that one could be an intercontinental poet as well as a French and German poet. I belonged to the European tradition and language as well as to the American tradition. I was a neo-American poet.

I decided to make an experiment in inter-racial philology. I haunted all the quarters of Manhattan and Brooklyn as far off as Long Island, which I had known in the past. I listened to the conversation of so-called foreigners, and to that of the second generation. As a result I made some interesting discoveries. Although the English language was the magnet which attracted all the other elements, in most cases these remained independent and there was an infinite variety of speech to be heard in the city, a fantasia of many-tongued words. I was especially interested in the speech metamorphoses of the new European exiles from Nazism. It was in fact astonishing to note how much of Europe one could detect in the speech habits of the inhabitants of the five boroughs. For a time I took down almost stenographic accounts of conversations overheard in street-cars, on the streets, in bars, in shops. It was a very fruitful experience.

A synthetic language was undoubtedly being spoken, although it had no name as yet. Nor was it used by writers of prose or verse. Yet it struck me as having very real existence. It was not even H. L. Mencken's American Language, but an intensification and expansion of it, a super-Occidental form of expression with polyglot overtones. Millions spoke it throughout America, and to me it was the embryonic language of the future. I called it the Atlantic, or Crucible, language, for it was the result of the inter-racial synthesis that was going on in the United States, Latin America and Canada. It was American English, with an Anglo-Saxon basis, plus many grammatical and lexical additions from more than a hundred tongues. All these, together with the Indian "subsoil" languages, are now being spoken in America. They form an intercontinental idiom used by millions of neo-Americans, an idiom that is the result of the ceaseless migrations of peoples of all races and tongues going forever westward during the past two hundred years. It is the attempt by the autonomous tongues to retain certain sound-values from the past, which they incorporate naturally with archetypal myths and images, into the scheme of the existing American language.

An idea came to me one night that had a deeply lyrical appeal: here I was in the New York crucible, I the inter-racial man who had emerged from this crucible, and I was seeing America again with the eyes of the immigrant. I still perceived it with the consciousness of the immigrant, and yet it was not entirely the same. The urban cosmopolis lay sleeping, its millions of inhabitants probably locked in dreams. Dreams of what? Did they recall in their deep sleep words from the vanished European past? It was with this thought that I wrote "America Mystica," the end of which mirrored the skyscraper aspiration, the American idea of continuous ascension toward new spiritual realities:

> The horizontal world is dying we want to rise higher than the Andes higher than the Empire State Building higher than Yggdrasyl voici venir l'ère de l'Atlantide
>
> Je vous salue inconnus pleins de grace o vous qui rêvez un avenir de cristal que les anges vous gardent du tumulte des bêtes démoniaques qui se tapissent dans les caves pourries
>
> The voyage goes upward veergulls drift farewells in foam rhythms we stand before the conjuration of the lonely beings who wait for the ripplechants of their redemption
>
> The continent is incandescent with the cries of the mutilated hearts the vision of the new age of glass glisters the ships are freighted with ecstatic men and women.
>
> We hear news from ungeheuren zeiten da die scheitelaeugler sternsuechtig in das weltall sannen the moundbuilders are here and the sky-storming Aztecs
>
> Go obsidian-swinging into the migratory march we join a skyworld without horizon we dream one tongue from Alaska to Tierra del Fuego
>
> We dream a new race visionary with the logos of God.

Havas supplied the Canadian Associated Press with French-language feature stories which we in New York were asked to write. We were in close touch with the French-language newspapers of Montreal and Quebec and read them eagerly, always anxious to continue our comparative studies of journalistic techniques. These French-Canadian papers, as well as such French-language papers as *Le Travailleur,* published in certain upper New England mill-towns, had an American appearance, even though they retained a certain Old-World atmosphere.

The story of New France in the Americas gradually became a subject of major interest to me. I read all the works of Francis Parkman, author of a prolific romance-steeped historical epos about the New World, a story of discoverers and evangelists, of struggle and triumph and defeat. His *Pio-*

neers of France in the New World, La Salle and the Discovery of the Great West, The Old Regime in Canada, and other volumes on kindred subjects, deepened my interest in early America. The important contribution of French missionaries seemed to me to have been neglected in the modern teaching of history, and I had a strong desire to see for myself what was left, to breathe the air of these historic transplantations, to absorb their living poetry, if possible. I decided to go to Canada as soon as vacation time should come around.

In the Franco-American journalistic world I experienced intensely the anti-Nazi, anti-totalitarian orientation that was to dominate my life for years to come. In Europe, like many of my friends, I had been more or less indifferent to the political aspects of events. Joyce, who in his youth had undoubtedly suffered greatly from the wrangles of his compatriots, seemed to have an almost physical loathing for anything connected with politics, and I had not entirely escaped this irradiation. In New York, on the other hand, I began to face the problem logically and humanly, and I gradually came to feel that a poet had not the right to remain entirely aloof. As a newspaperman, or even as a simple human being, I felt I could not stand aside, although as a poet my course would have to follow the line of conscious as well as unconscious expression. In New York literary circles there was more and more talk of a new proletarian literature, and attempts were made to persuade me to join the ranks of the "proletarian" writers. But there was something in their attitude that didn't ring quite true to me, and I found that I had almost as little in common with the obviously well-fed, well-paid "people's" writers as with the smugly affluent creators of "best-sellers." Not that I was in any less sympathy with the disinherited, the homeless, the prisoners of life; I had been one of them too long. But mediocre journalism disguised as literature seemed to me to be without interest, and I felt that only the poet had the necessary vision and imagination to combat the evils from which these conditions stemmed.

In summer Maria came to New York with our two daughters, Betsy and Tina, and we talked at length of the alternative: Europe versus America. I felt tempted gradually to liquidate our life in Europe with a view to settling permanently in the United States. But there were still many problems to be taken into consideration.

I did not want our children to repeat my experience; I did not want them to belong to a "lost" generation that has one foot on one continent and the other thousands of miles away. Above all, I did not want them to become linguistic hybrids, like their father.

I myself should have liked to live in America, to shake off once and for all the European burden. But would that be possible? I was an American, but like millions of other immigrants, from the times of the earliest settlers to the most recent wave, I carried my European unconscious with me. I felt that perhaps the geographical remoteness of Europe might ultimately do the trick; that eventually I should be absorbed into the American cauldron, like the others. I almost envied my American friends. To be sure, I felt, they must have their own psychological problems, but they did not suffer from my particular trauma. Should I ever achieve my dream? Should I ever be entirely rid of the European malady, would I ever be able to take my place as an American among Americans?

One day, with the children and their young cousin, I took the "L" to South Ferry. It was a sun-golden day, and as we walked through Battery Park, the three little girls exclaimed over the boats in the harbor and the surf of the Hudson roaring into the Atlantic. They recognized the distant Statue of Liberty from having seen the original model on a bridge over the Seine. Leaving the Battery, we walked up lower Broadway and I explained to them how, hardly three hundred years earlier, all this part of the island had been Indian land. When we reached the Woolworth Building, I invited them to go up to the roof and look down on Manhattan. How they thrilled to the spectacle below! On Park Place, we could distinguish a number of old-fashioned factories and office buildings that had once been Newspaper Row. The names Greeley, Bennet, Pulitzer, Dana, Hearst, and Patterson still shone in my journalistic memory, even now that the great period of Newspaper Row was over. We lunched in an old Dutch tavern on John Street, then wandered up on Nassau Street. The afternoon was carefree, and the little out-of-the-way shops reminded me of the *Rue Nationale* of any French provincial town. As we walked on toward Brooklyn Bridge, a mnemonic mood seized me: spring days in my early immigrant years came back with a rush. I said: I will stay in Europe a few months, liquidate everything and return. At the end of summer the children went back to France with their mother, and I followed soon after.

Was the fabulous America only in my mind? I have yet to find the answer to that question.

Back in Paris I found a Popular Front government in power and a general atmosphere of liberal thinking. But already a dark pall was being lowered over the Continental landscape, and each day brought further evidence that no amount of social legislation would stay its inevitable envelopment. I made up my mind to remain in Europe only long enough to prepare a new and what I wanted to be a final issue of *transition*. Also, I decided to do some free-lance journalistic work before returning, I hoped for good, to America; there seemed to be little to hold me any longer on the unhappy Continent, where one sensed a cracking in the beams of its ancient civilization, which appeared likely to offer little to the creative spirit for years to come. It was a time of all-engulfing floods, of the bursting of titanic dikes; a time when the very towers of Babylon stood ready to tumble. A rapid regression to a primitive, barbaric mentality seemed inevitable.

As a result of my recent stay in America, my thoughts were turned towards the Western hemisphere, and in the disquietude of Europe this nostalgia could not be dismissed. It came back again and again with an insistent romanticism that evoked landscapes quite different from those of Europe—winters more glacial, springs more sudden and violent. My boyhood had been spent on the European continent, but my adolescent eyes had seen America, and could not forget what they had seen. I recalled a fond project of those earlier years, when I had seen myself roaming, in peripatetic imagination, across America. Then I had wanted to be a newspaper nomad. I had wanted to travel the length and breadth of the vast continent. I remembered an article I had read many years before, in which Vachel Lindsay described his rambles through the Middle West, and how he had lived by reciting his poems in farm kitchens. The idea had attracted me, and, in my mind's eye, I had seen long tramps along wind-moaning roads with, for reward, homey talks with friendly people of the soil.

Paris, in that winter of 1938, was gay and slightly hysterical. French friends often said, "If only this false peace would end! We would rather be on the firing-line than continue this exasperating waiting for the crash." Meanwhile, the cafés were crowded. The Exposition Trente-sept, which had had such difficulty in getting under way, stood light-wreathed along the Seine and on the Place de l'Alma. From the terrace of Chez Francis we gazed at the flash of lights on the Eiffel Tower or at the grotesquely heroic couple that topped the Soviet Russian building just opposite the dour, swastika-wreathed eagle of the Nazis. The Champs-Elysées was crowded day and night, and its numerous cafés echoed with the multilingual conversations of cosmopolitan masses. But the temper of these crowds was short, and there were frequent heated political discussions during social hours on the terraces.

Amid great financial and technical difficulties, preparations for launching the tenth anniversary issue of *transition* finally got under way. However, the printer to whom I entrusted the job was so lackadaisical and irresponsible that what should have taken three or four months took almost a year to complete. Acting on a too hastily accepted recommendation, I had left

9. Maria and Eugene Jolas with daughters Betsy and Tina and their Russian governess, Bormes les Mimosa, 1933–34. Used by permission.

our old-fashioned, efficient printer in the provinces and had fallen into the hands of an adventurer, for whom the virtues of honest work and technical integrity, which I had always associated with the French craftsman, were nonexistent. A manuscript was lost in a taxi by the printer's devil. At one time the printer himself disappeared for two months. In addition to all this, the print-shop was far from immaculate. To this day, I ask myself how that issue, which contained many illustrations and texts in several languages, could finally have emerged from such disorder.

This issue represented a last attempt on my part to gather together such intellectual and artistic forces of Europe and America as were not already enslaved by the shallow realism that had been introduced by the totalitarians. I wanted again to emphasize experiments in nocturnal images and their expression, as well as other new currants in art and letters. I wanted the final number of *transition* to bring together the various romanticist tendencies of the epoch: Expressionism, Dadaism, Surrealism, even simultaneism.

In those last years before the war, two historical phenomena dominated the French literary scene: a marked interest in England's Elizabethan literature and a return to nineteenth-century Romanticism. The Franco-Swiss philologist, Albert Béguin, was beginning to publish a remarkable study of the latter period, and I asked permission to translate his chapter on the night-mind for *transition*. Jean Ballard, the editor of *Cahiers du Sud,* was preparing an entirely Romantic issue to which a number of writers were in-

10. Jolas and daughters on a trip back to Colombey-les-Deux-Eglises in 1937. Used by permission.

11. The Jolas brothers in Forbach, 1938. Standing: Armand, Charles, Jacques, Eugene, Emile; sitting: grandmother (Oma) and sister Maria. Used by permission.

vited to contribute. In *transition* I initiated an *enquête* on "the dream and language." For the most part, however, the replies, save that of Herbert Read, were disappointing.

After a long silence, Joyce was beginning to work again. His London publisher, in the person of T. S. Eliot, of the firm Faber & Faber, was planning to bring out "Work in Progress" in book form, under the title *Finnegans Wake,* and he had begun to receive proof. Joyce wanted to have one more fragment of his work published in *transition* before the book should appear. He gave me a long manuscript, dealing principally with the Russian "general," which I sent to our lethargic printers. "This book of mine must appear before the war comes," he said wearily. "Otherwise, no one will read it." That a catastrophe was threatening Europe was no longer a matter for discussion; it had obviously become inevitable. *Transition* finally appeared.

The Paris of that period had become a hot-bed of intrigue, both political and artistic. We were living in the suburb of Neuilly, where Maria conducted her very successful Franco-American school, and I rarely went to the Left Bank. Most of the writers I had known were drifting into the communist or fascist camps, and only a few still believed in the organic efficacy of democracy. Joyce was my only real companion at that time. Even with him, however, I sensed an occasionally irritating aloofness, despite the fact that the electricity of his creative genius and his aesthetic integrity called forth my constant admiration. But how I loathed the quacks, the shoddy intellectuals, the sycophants, the mandarins, the littérateurs, the hypocrites, the fellow-travelers, the Nazi and Soviet apologists of all sorts who were slowly but surely making of Paris a nightmare! There were also the sincere eccentrics, the mad tragic poets, the men of the apocalyptic vision. Indeed, many referred to the Apocalypse, and in spite of the growing threat of Nazi aggression, numerous manifestos and ephemeral *petites revues* continued to appear. Jean Wahl, Julien Benda, and other leaders of modern philosophical thought were engaged in passionate discussion of Kierkegaard, Heidegger and Hegel. I began to see something of Henry Miller, who combined a genius for scatological fury with lyric sensitiveness, and whose sketches were appearing in *Mesures, Volontés, The Booster* and *transition*. We were poles apart in our objectives, but we agreed on the necessity of a cosmic means of expression, of a "language of night."

I was reading mystic, metaphysical and even occultist literature. For a long time I had studied Kierkegaard's *Fear and Trembling,* and I recognized that my own sense of apprehension, born of my border past, was a universal emotion. I could also see it plainly in Kafka's stories. This was an archaic sensation, an existential *angoisse* which reflected the mood of our age. I read Leon Bloy and Thomas Aquinas and Dostoyevsky and Soloviev, and even the *Tertium Organum* of Ouspensky. Ouspensky, who had seen *transition* in London, came to see me in Paris, and I was much interested to talk with him. The work of the English mystic Richard Jefferies also came to my attention. I felt an elective affinity with his spirit.

Poetic experience became, for me, mystic experience with an objective validity, and poetry itself became an ontological process, a kind of continuous cognition. Although I was a dissident Catholic, I was nevertheless *still* a Catholic, whose goal was the *via mystica* outlined by the poet Saint John of the Cross. The Spanish mystics attracted me especially, because of the precision with which they had succeeded in describing their inner transformations and illuminations. But the language of Blake and Böhme captivated me too, and I became interested in inventing new forms for expressing similar research: liturgical forms, for the most part, to embody the hunger for the Supreme Reality. Henry Vaughan, Francis Thompson and Paul Claudel guided me poetically.

My great directive was the Ascent of Mount Carmel. I wanted to leave the caverns for heights and light. I read eagerly the poems of O. V. de L. Milosz, the Lithuanian-French poet who had been reintroduced by the

Belgian Pierre-Louis Flouquet, in his *Journal des Poètes.* The mysticism of Milosz excited me. When I was invited to a banquet given in his honor by the Belgian journal, I saw a tall, sad, inward-looking man who listened in humility and silence to the eulogies heaped on him. His esoteric qualities approximated to a religious conviction, and the memory of his childhood in his native Lithuania was always mingled in his verses with biblical imagism. Milosz sought a fourth dimension of thinking. Some years later I was to translate one of his longer poems for a volume entitled *Vertical.*

I personally was seeking a *constructive,* a *white,* a *sidereal* romanticism. "Revive our sense of wonder," said Stuart Gilbert. He admired Algernon Blackwood and often quoted O'Malley, the protagonist of *The Centaur,* on this great search: "Far beyond the words it lies, as difficult of full recovery as the dreams of deep sleep, as the ecstasy of the religious, elusive as the mystery of Kubla Khan or the Patmos visions of St. John. Full recapture, I am convinced, is not possible at all in words." I called the new tendency verticalist or vertigralist and in a "vertigralist" pamphlet I discussed "existential anguish" (later to become a "winged word," the point of departure of Sartre's existentialist teaching) and liberation from the three-dimensional law of gravitation as a possible creative objective. I wrote:

> We are afraid. A nameless apprehension lies over us like a stupor. We bend under the weight of cosmic fear, an existential anguish, a Weltangst, which are the mark of our collective emotion. . . . Through Kierkegaard, Heidegger and Kafka we understand what a primordial role this sensation of primordial fear plays in the life of man. . . .
>
> The poet exorcises this possession through the mantic word. For the will to ascension still slumbers in us. . . . Our racial memory is still preoccupied with the dream of flying. . . .
>
> I am convinced that the creative instinct should be identical with the instinct of ascension. The arts are analogous to existential mysticism and, as such, should once more become conjuration, a mantic means of liberation or exorcism.

The verticalist principle of ascent and descent in the psychic sphere became a new source of spiritual activity. I began to write poems based on this principle. In the third issue of *transition,* in 1927, I had already mentioned this "vertical urge" and in my poem *Secession in Astropolis* the astronomic imagination had proved fertile. In 1932 I published in *transition* a manifesto entitled *Poetry Is Vertical,* and in my essay *The Language of Night* I revived ideologically the archaic concept of the third eye, *le troisième oeil* of Descartes, *das Scheitelauge,* the *cosmological eye,* positing the imperative of a new form of expression for such phenomena as "the dream," the day-dream and "hypnogogic hallucinations." I sought an identity between the mystic-romantic conception of life and this tendency. But I also tried to go beyond my predecessors by demanding an "expansion of the frontiers of language" to keep pace with the expansion of consciousness. I was in favor of the metaphysical word, the word as sacrament, exorcism, conjuration.

Vertical aimed to be an astro-mental vision of a pluralistic universe. I believed in the existence of other worlds, of beings living on planets, of a cosmological conception.

In some of my experiments with the "vertical duologue" in which the ascending and descending principle becomes a voluntary principle, I sensed definite therapeutic and creative properties. Certain poems I called verticalist-poems, or *Planets and Angels,* or Alchemical Poems were written in this spirit. Following are a few fragments.

> Nous volons dans un blizzard de satellites
> A côté de la voie lactée
> Nous volons éblouis
> Nous regardons un soleil tomber
> Sur les montagnes antarctiques
> Nous regardons les milliers de bolides
> Emerger du fond des nuages roses
> Nous sommes devenus des yeux
> Nous sommes devenus des oreilles
> Au-dessus de nos métamorphoses
> Au-dessus de nos cheveux en flammes
> Nous regardons le festival des nébuleuses
> Dans lequel les oiseaux volent
> Portant dans leurs becs géants des étoiles
> Pleines d'étincelles rouges
> Nous volons dans un paroxysme de feu
> Dans une grande explosion sidérale
>
> ferner stimmen aetherschwall ruft
> berueckend im reigen des nachtchors
> der die namenlosen umschwebt
> in der glanzfeier der lebenden gestirne

im feuertraum der auferstandenen toten
und klanguebersprueht ragen wir
verbunden in die heiterkeit der wunderpilger

We grow huge and visionary
We play with spiral nebulae
With the angelic spheres
And ride upward
In a vertigo of fire streams
We swarm in stellar dew
We are racing through burst-flames
Into a time without frontiers

Then came the signal of Hitler's aggression against the free world:

We saw the men being mobilized
We saw the crying women in the streets
And the mountain looked down on us
Looked sneeringly down on us

We knew this was the age of the dominators
It was the time of the tenebrous beings
Who unleashed the satanic insurrection
Against the army of luminous wingmen
In the space of the delirious metalcrash

We heard the blasphemous monologues
Blasting through the sultry afternoon
In the blistering motion of time
Which had lost the sigil of eternal things
We heard the dourwords shouted from the caverns
With an aura of the crawling larvae
And the mutilated houses bent in the hot squall

The brave men walked
In the dustwhirl of the roarblaze
In the pilgrimage to the marred hour

*   *   *

Speak not you said
This is the hour of the fluent crisis
The great wrath lifts its vertigo
The alpine eagles are still and stunned
O Autumn will come with dying.

We will not see the flamehair any longer
The tatters of the sunken memory weep
The victims will lose their summer
The hunters will not stalk the dawn
A senile thunder will flail the crags

Words lie in rust you said
The ancient crucible has collapsed
The alchemy has closed its eyes
All the sacred words are in ruins
It is an age of trickling silences

It is the time of the primitives
And the savage era comes on tip-toe

9

ANANKE STRIKES THE POET

Back in Paris, I found Joyce still working on his magnum opus, but under great psychic difficulties. His daughter, a lovely, gifted girl in her early twenties, had begun to show alarming signs of mental derangement. There had always existed a great affection between the father and daughter, and her increasingly serious malady soon became a nightmare from which he could never free himself. Lucia, whose principal interest was the ballet, but who also had a sensitive talent for the medieval art of illuminated lettering, had become engaged to a young friend of the family, and Joyce had arranged an informal celebration of the event. A few days later, however, after announcing that she would have to break the engagement, she began to talk irrationally and showed signs of aberration. At Joyce's request, Padraic and Mary Colum invited her to visit them, but they soon noticed that her case was much more serious than had at first been believed.

The sudden death of his father, which had occurred only a few months previously, had also been a profound shock to Joyce. He had never made any secret of his deep affection for his father, and the autobiographical elements of his work reveal this in symbolical and mythological allusions. *Ulysses* was man in search of his father, and *Finnegans Wake* takes up this theme again in a different manner. In those days he dreamed much about him, and one evening he said to me: "I wonder where he is." Sometimes he would tell tales of his father's waggish wit. I remember one that concerned the old gentleman's reaction to the sketch made of him by Brancusi, and which consisted merely of a geometrical spiral study of the ear. "Well, Jim hasn't changed much," commented his father drily, when the portrait was shown him in Dublin.

I was preparing a new number of *transition* and had decided to pay homage to Joyce on his turning the half-century mark. Among other features, I had ordered a sketch to be made of him by the Spanish artist César Abin. The result was an impressive study of a distinguished homme de lettres, with pen in hand and his own volumes reverentially piled beside him. But Joyce would have none of it, and insisted in giving the cartoonist precise instructions for the design and execution of the job. He wanted it, first of all, to look like a question mark, because friends had once told him that he resembled a question mark, when seen standing meditatively on a street corner. For more than two weeks he kept making new suggestions, until he was at last satisfied. He asked to be drawn with a battered old derby hung with spider's webs and bearing a ticket on which should be inscribed the fatal number 13. He asked that a star be put on the tip of his nose, in memory of an English criticaster's description of him as "a blue-nosed comedian"; that his feet be suspended perilously over a globe labeled Ireland, on which only Dublin was visible; that he have patches on the knees of his trousers; that out of his pockets there should emerge the manuscript of a song entitled "Let Me Like a Soldier Fall." For his "luck," his "fate," had already started down the somber path it never left again. It was as though already at that time he had a premonition of the immense trials that lay before him.

Joyce's family life had always been a happy one, and his humor was a natural manifestation of this. Yet even then it was rather what André Breton has called somewhere "un humour noir." It had an Elizabethan tang and robustness. During the economic crisis, when even mirth-loving Paris began to assume a dreary face, Joyce celebrated, on the same day, his fiftieth birthday and the tenth anniversary of the publication of *Ulysses.* The two events were hardly noticed by the literary world, which was discovering social realism and considered Joyce outmoded. To mark this occasion we gave a small dinner at our home in Paris, attended by Thomas McGreevy, Samuel Beckett, Lucie and Paul Léon, Padraic and Mary Colum, Helen and Giorgio Joyce, and a few others. The birthday cake was decorated with an ingenious candy replica of a copy of *Ulysses,* in its blue jacket. Called out to cut the cake, Joyce looked at it a moment and said: "Accipite et manducate ex hoc omnes: Hoc est enim corpus meum." At table the talk turned to the subject of popular sayings. Someone expressed a suspicion of all of them and gave voice to his dislike for the adage "In vino veritas," which experience had shown him to be untrue and bromidic. Joyce agreed warmly, adding: "It should really be 'In riso veritas,' for nothing [so] reveals us as our laughter." He was always astonished that so few people commented on the comic element in his writings.

It was shortly after this event that he suggested we organize a *bal de la purée* (which is French for "general insolvency"), since the depression was beginning to be felt more and more. The party was held at our house, and we invited a number of friends, among whom was the operatic tenor John Sullivan. For several years, Joyce had been urging all his friends to go to the opera and listen to what he considered the world's greatest tenor voice. Sullivan sang that night, and his powerful voice rang through the house, to the delight of all present. The gaiest of the guests was Joyce himself, who finally inveigled all the ladies present into giving him first prize for his costume: that of an old Irish stage character, famous once as "Handy Andy."

The doctor advised Joyce to send Lucia to the mountains, and at his request we took her with us on a trip we had planned to Feldkirch, a little medieval town in Austria, near the Swiss border. Her parents remained in nearby Zurich, because it was the doctor's theory that Joyce's own tension might be partly responsible for her condition. And in fact, the mountain air and the isolation and quiet seemed for a while to do her good. She began to smile and took long walks, always accompanied by a nurse, however.

I was busy working, and looked forward to a fertile summer. One day there came a telephone call from Joyce, asking me to come to Zurich. I took the next train, and found him in great distress. He said that he had received a disturbing letter from his daughter and he wanted to know my impression. I told him I felt she was living a quiet life, but that her condition had not fundamentally changed. It was decided that Mrs. Joyce would accompany me to the Austrian town, and that he would follow later, which was done.

Now began a tragic period. Lucia's condition was worsening day by day, and both her parents were deeply grieved at the turn her health was taking. They were staying at a hotel in the center of town, while we had taken a little house nearby. Joyce seemed utterly bewildered by the blow which fate had struck him.

He had not been writing for some time, due partly to intense worry over his daughter's condition, but also to the general mood of inertia caused by the depression. So we took walks together along the swirling mountain river Ill, nearby, or we climbed the wooded hills. He had a love for mountains and rivers, because, he said, "they are the phenomena that will remain when all the peoples and their governments will have vanished." Yet he was not at all a nature romantic, but rather a man of the megalopolis.

Towards dusk, after a siesta, he would go walking again. Eight o'clock was the hour he had set himself many decades before as the time for his first glass of wine of the day. That summer he evolved a sort of ritual which, to me, had an almost grotesque fascination. At half past seven, he would suddenly race for the railroad station, where the famous Orient Express was due to stop for ten minutes each day. He would walk quietly up and down the platform. "Over there, on those tracks," he said one evening, "the fate of *Ulysses* was decided in 1915." He referred to the fact that in this very Austrian border-town he had almost been prevented by some jinx from crossing into Switzerland during the First World War. When the train finally came in, he would hurry to the nearest car in order to examine the French, German and Yugoslav inscriptions, and he felt for the embossed metal letters with the sensitive fingers of defective vision. Then he would ask me questions about the persons getting on or off the train, or he would listen to their conversations. In those moments his fine ear for dialectal nuances in German often astonished me. As the train continued on its way into the usually foggy night, he stood on the platform waving his hat, as if he had just bid Godspeed to a dear friend. With eight o'clock approaching, he almost skipped back to the hotel, for his first draught of *Tischwein* — or, as Mrs. Joyce, who thought the drink of rather inferior quality, used to say, "dishwine."

We thus spent a month of idling and worry. Joyce talked about his Austrian days before the First World War, and Mrs. Joyce especially liked to reminisce about Trieste. She laughingly said she had loved Emperor Francis Joseph like a father, and Joyce expressed his conviction that the Austro-Hungarian federation had been one of the most efficacious political regimes of modern times. Lucia and her parents always spoke Italian among themselves, which gave our little party a multilingual ambiance.

One day I told Joyce that I was preparing a new issue of *transition*, after having let almost a year go by without publishing anything. This acted as a fillip to him, and he began to write again, for he said he wanted to appear in the new issue. He attacked his work with almost savage energy. "How difficult it is to put pen to paper again," he said one evening. "Those first sentences have cost me much pain." But gradually he got the task in hand. This fragment was to be known later as "The Mime of Mick, Nick and the Maggies." During the remaining months he wrote steadily on this fragment, in spite of his anxiety about the health of his daughter, and his own increasing nervousness. We worked in the afternoon at his hotel, and one day as I arrived there he handed me a closely written foolscap sheet beginning with the words: "Every evening at lighting up o'clock sharp and until further notice . . . ," which I typed for him. After a few pages had been thus transcribed, we began to look through the notebooks; and the additions, set down years ago for a still unwritten text, became more and more numerous. The manuscript grew to some thirty pages and was not yet finished.

Joyce never changed a word. There was in fact always a certain inevitability, an almost volcanic affirmativeness about his primal choice of words. He only added ceaselessly, like a worker in mosaic, enriching the original pattern with ever new inventions. His black notebooks had esoteric titles and signs, which he used to indicate the various characters of his story. He had a special love for Earwicker, the hero of the book, and to my astonishment I noticed one day that the ancient arms of the town of Feldkirch had precisely the same sign as Earwicker. He smiled, when I called his attention to it; but he never seemed to be over-astonished at fantastic coincidences in his life.

"There really is no coincidence in this book," he said during one of our walks. "I might easily have written this story in the traditional manner. . . . Every novelist knows the recipe. . . . It is not very difficult to follow a simple, chronological scheme. . . . But I am, after all, trying to tell the story of the Chapelizod family in a new way. . . . Time and the river and the mountain are the real heroes of this book. . . . Yet the elements are exactly what every novelist might use: man and woman, birth, childhood, night, sleep, marriage, prayer, death. . . . There is nothing paradoxical about this. . . . Only I am trying to tell my story on many planes. . . . Did you ever read Laurence Sterne?"

We read together Goethe's account of his experiments with color, but he finally said he could use nothing from it. He was interested in a comic version of Leibniz's essay on theodicy, and he asked me to obtain from the local Jesuits in charge of the famous Catholic preparatory school Stella Matutina a certain Augustinian text. We discussed Vico's theory of the origin of language, and the Viconian conception of the cyclical evolution of civilizations born from each other, like the phoenix from the ashes, haunted him. He began to speculate on the new physics, and the theory of an expanding universe. Sometimes while walking with him I was obsessed with the notion that he was not really in an Austrian town but in his native Dublin.

The children's game called Devils and Angels which is one of the themes of "Mime" riveted his attention for a long while. He read a number of gnostic books, and was interested in the Manichean idea of light and darkness. The news of the discovery in Egypt of an ancient Manichean text interested him. Besides the purely theological construction of the Irish game—which he remembered vividly having played in the streets of Dublin—he was bent on incorporating into the text children's games from many languages. In a kind of abstracted way, he sometimes watched our two little girls as they played in the garden of our house, and he did not fail to use one of their games and their Joycified names in his fragment.

The "Mime" was completed in Zurich, after our return there. In the late afternoon, Joyce and I often took a motorboat for a ride on the lake. Or else we would go walking up the hill to the zoo, where one evening he quoted to me the magnificent nocturne of Phoenix Park with the verbal magic of animal sounds dying off in the gathering night. He had just finished it, and he seemed to be pleased with the result. Joyce had a love for Zurich, its rivers and mountains, its lake, its well-ordered life. In the forenoon he liked to walk along the busy Bahnhofstraße, which runs from the railroad station to the lake. In those moments he was always very quiet and introspective, and I remember that sometimes we would walk for an hour without either one of us saying a word.

He usually lunched at a vegetarian restaurant where vegetables were served camouflaged as meat dishes, which always amused him. He knew all the Swiss-German dishes and some of them he recommended heartily. But in the evening nothing could keep him from the Kronenhalle, which he preferred to the more colorful Zum Pfauen that had been his *Stammlokal* during the First World War, and where he used to meet his friends. The Kronenhalle was near the lake, and its cuisine and cellar were excellent. He was very fond of the Swiss fondant wine from the Valais, and rarely drank any other. He did not like to drink red wine, which he found "unpalatable." He used to say that white wine had an electric quality which all wine should have. In that we were thoroughly in agreement; all my life I have preferred white to red wine. His preferences were: Swiss Fondant, Alsatian Riesling or Traminer, Niersteiner or some acrid Moselle wine, French chablis or *champagne nature.*

Among Joyce's Swiss friends were, beside the Giedions, Prof. Bernhard Fehr from Zurich University, Dr. Borach, one of his World War I English pupils, and Edmund Brauchbar, who had apparently served as model for the figure of Bloom in *Ulysses.* With these friends Joyce never entirely lost a certain reserve which was so characteristic of him. I remember that during another of my visits with him in Zurich, the *Neue Zürcher Zeitung* was publishing excerpts from Dr. Borach's diary; notations Borach had made of his conversations with his teacher during the World War, with verbatim quotations. Joyce was somewhat upset about this, since he did not like to be quoted for publication. He never gave an interview, and it used to be a source for amusement in Paris literary circles that even Frédéric Lefèvre, the demon interviewer of the *Nouvelles Littéraires,* was never able to batter down Joyce's resistance on this point. Joyce forgave Borach, however, for he had great loyalty to old friendships.

One day a British critic wrote that Joyce was trying to revive Swift's little language to Stella. "Not at all," was Joyce's comment; "I am using a Big Language." And he added: "I have discovered that I can do anything I want with language." His linguistic memory was extraordinary and he seemed to be constantly on the look-out, listening rather than talking. "Really, it is not I who am writing this crazy book," he said in a whimsical way. "It is you and you and you and that girl over there and that man in the corner." One day I found him in a Zurich tea-shop laughing quietly to himself. "Have you won the *gros lot?*" I asked. He explained that he had asked the waitress for a glass of lemon squash. The somewhat obtuse Swiss girl looked puzzled. Then she had an inspiration: "Oh, you mean *Lebensquatsch?*" she stammered. (Her German neologism might be translated by "life's piffle.") Joyce remembered all the scraps of conversations, the lopped-off syllables, pronounced in moments of inertia or fatigue, *jeux de mots,* alcoholically deformed words, slips of the tongue — all the verbal grotesqueries and fantasies which he heard said around him in unconscious moments.

Often he would give his friends strange, out-of-the-way books on science, philology, philosophy, theology, psychology to read and ask them to extract such words — or ideas — from them as he could use in his work. Or else he would ask one of us to read the books aloud to him. I remember reading Mauthner's German volume on language to him, and he was much interested in certain of the conclusions which seemed to harmonize with his own. On these occasions he lay on a sofa, his thin legs tangled almost inextricably in the air, listening intently, making constant notes, jesting. He would thus extract numerous words which found their place somewhere in the vast pattern of his story.

Joyce had great dislike for ready-made phrases and particularly for much of the modern medical vocabulary. Whenever anyone in his presence used words from the psychological dictionary, he would become almost impatient, and with a certain insistence he usually succeeded in obtaining the same thing in other words. This was in line with his intellectual indifference to the psychoanalytical school of thinking. While in Zurich I read to him an article on *Ulysses* by Dr. Jung, but he felt it was unimportant. "The Rev. Dr. Jung," as he called the distinguished psychologist, seemed to him less a figure to be reckoned with than Dr. Freud, whom he did not readily accept either, but whose pioneering genius he nevertheless admired.

Man's history, with its dreams, legends, myths, was the aim of the Joycean vision. Thus his language left the rules of logic to one side, although he always followed the conscious recorder. The usual meaning of words was destroyed by this revolutionary procedure. He was interested in a vast verbal metamorphosis, for his own construction of the history of mankind, with its repetitive cyclical return to eternal events, was being created in the panorama of the unconscious life. All linguistic borders had to be crossed in this progress towards a new universe. His new language must express night and sleep. Compared with this colossal attempt, the experiment of the Surrealists, who were also interested in digging into the nocturnal life, remains, to my mind, abortive. In this connection, Joyce was never interested in automatic writing. He was the rediscoverer of the great myths, and it was in a state of intense consciousness that he welded them "in the smithy of his soul."

During walks in Paris, we often talked about dreams. Sometimes I related to him my own dreams which, during the pre-war years, began to take on a strangely macabre and apocalyptic silhouette. He was always eager to discuss them, because they interested him as images of the nocturnal universe, though he was reluctant to attribute any transcendental or mystic function to them. He himself, he said, dreamed relatively little, but when he did his dreams were usually related to ideas, personal or mythical, with which he was occupied in his waking hours. He was very much attracted by Dunne's theory of serialism, and I read to him the author's brilliant *An Experiment with Time* which Joyce regarded highly. He told me one of his own dreams, in connection with which subsequent events seemed to confirm Dunne's serialistic conceptions. Joyce said he was walking through a big city and met three men who called themselves Minos, Eaque and Rhadamanthe. They suddenly stopped their conversation with him and became threatening. He had to run to escape from their screams of obloquy. Three weeks later I noticed a feature story in *Paris-Soir* to the effect that the police were looking for a crank who was sending explosives through the mail. This fanatic signed himself: Minos, Eaque, Rhadamanthe, the judges of Hell. One of Joyce's less complicated dreams, however, caused considerable chuckling each time he thought of it. This was a dream the climax of which was a vision of the titanic figure of Molly Bloom, seated on the side of a high hill. "As for you, James Joyce, I've had enough of you," she shouted. His reply he never remembered.

His excellent knowledge of French, German, Greek and Italian stood him in good stead, and he was constantly adding to his stock of linguistic information by studying Hebrew, Russian, Japanese, Chinese, Finnish and other tongues. At the basis of his vocabulary was also an immense command of Anglo-Irish words that only seem like neologisms to us today, because they have for the most part become obsolete. His revival of these words will one day interest philologists.

Language to him was a social as well as a subjective process. He was interested in the experiments of the French Jesuit Jousse and the English philologist Sir Paget, and *Finnegans Wake* is full of applications of their gesture theory. He spoke however with a certain derision of such auxiliary languages as Esperanto and Ido, which seemed to him to be without possibilities of any kind.

During those Zurich days I lived in the Pfauenstraße, and Joyce often walked up the hill to bring new additions to the "Mime," as he called it now. Despite his intense anxieties, he remained absorbed in his book.

His daughter was now under observation in a hospital near Zurich, and he went frequently to visit her. He hoped against hope that it would be possible to heal his child. He even went so far as to consult Dr. Jung, although he had little confidence in the result.

During this period he became increasingly absorbed by the problem of imaginative creation. He read Coleridge again, and discussed with me the Romantic poet's distinction between imagination and fancy. His approach was quite humble, and he even asked himself if he really possessed imagination. He read *Wuthering Heights*. "That woman had imagination," he said. "Kipling had it too, and certainly Yeats." In fact, his admiration for the Irish poet was boundless. A recent commentator, asserting that Joyce lacked reverence for the logos in poetry, inferred that he had little regard for Yeats. I can testify that this was not true. Joyce often recited Yeats's poems to us from memory. "No Surrealist poet can ever equal this for imagination," he said. Once when Yeats spoke over the radio, he telephoned us hastily to come and listen with him. I read "The Vision" out loud to him, and he was deeply absorbed by the colossal conception, only regretting that "Yeats did not pull all this into purely creative work." He was thrilled to discover that the hero of *Finnegans Wake* was described, both physically and psychically, as one of the human types Yeats presents in "The Vision." When Yeats died, Joyce sent a wreath to his grave at Antibes, and his emotion, on learning of his death, was very genuine. He always denied, almost vehemently, that he had said to Yeats in Dublin that he was too old to be influenced by him.

A favorite diversion during this time was a late-afternoon movie. He preferred English and French films to American, and was a keen judge of their aesthetic merit. He seemed to have very little sympathy with the problems of either North or South America, and judged the two continents entirely on the basis of their alleged dearth of aesthetic vision. He disliked all manifestations of American humor in the film, his particular bêtes noires being Charlie Chaplin and a comedian named Schnozzle.

We always depended on his remarkable judgment whenever we wanted to see a play in Paris, nor were we ever disappointed. The many plays we saw together and which he usually chose from a plethora of other, better "ballyhooed" ones, were nearly always striking and entertaining. I remember my great aesthetic pleasure when he and I went to see the Habima players in a play done in the Hebrew language, *Rachel*. He had a fine flair for little, out-of-the-way theaters, or for dusty old plays, especially at the Odéon Theater, where we saw plays by Scribe, whom he liked. Naturally, too, he never missed an Ibsen revival.

There was always an atmosphere of *fête* when Joyce went to the theater. Afterwards — since he was in the habit of dining late — we usually forgathered at Fouquet's, in the Champs-Elysées, or Chez Francis, and he quaffed his first glass of champagne nature with a gesture that was most diverting to watch. He usually ate little, but the carafe was never allowed to remain empty on the table until Mrs. Joyce interposed the final veto. He and I developed a trick we used in order to outwit the watchful eye of the spouses which I still use when that last drink seems desirable, and for this reason I shall not reveal it now.

Joyce's love of opera, especially Italian opera, and occasionally Wagner, has been noted by all who have ever written about him. Among opera singers he preferred the voice of his great friend John Sullivan, whom he considered to be the greatest tenor since Caruso. He also admired Lawrence Tibbett, the American baritone, and one or two Russian bassos whose voices he described as "coal mines." He had a hearty dislike for the music of Stravinsky and of most of his contemporaries, in fact. He liked to listen to piano music, especially Chopin.

I remember reading to him a German translation from a speech by Radek in which the Russian attacked *Ulysses* at the Congress of Kharkov as being the work of a bourgeois writer who lacked social consciousness. "They may say what they want," said Joyce, "but the fact is that all the characters in my books belong to the lower middle classes, and even the working class; and they are all quite poor." I know he was a convinced anti-fascist. He never returned to Italy under Mussolini, and only passed through Nazi Germany on his way to Hamburg, when he wanted to realize his life-long dream of seeing Copenhagen.

There are many human, all too human anecdotes about Joyce during those last years before the war that will bear recalling.

One sultry evening in July, Sylvia Beach organized a reading by Ernest Hemingway and Stephen Spender at the Shakespeare Bookshop, in the Rue de l'Odéon. Joyce, who liked Hemingway, decided to attend and asked me to accompany him. A good many American, English and French writers were already present when we arrived, rather late, in the midst of Hemingway's reading. Hemingway was seated at a small table with beside him a large mug of beer, from which he took an occasional sip. He was reading a fragment from the manuscript of his latest book, on Spain. He interrupted his reading for a moment while we were being seated, then took up again where he had left off.

As the reading progressed, Joyce began to yawn. In fact, he did it so frankly that everyone noticed it. However, Hemingway soon came to a pause and Stephen Spender read one of his poems of the Spanish revolution. Once more Hemingway took the floor. After a few sentences, Joyce pulled my sleeve: "Let's go . . ." I tried to persuade him to stay a little longer, but he would have none of it. To my great embarrassment he rose, and after stumbling over our neighbors' feet we left.

Joyce was undoubtedly allergic to any suggestion of politics.

Joyce had a keen sense of liturgy and was interested in the doctrine and rituals of all religions and confessions, both Roman and Orthodox Catholicism, Protestantism, Hinduism, Buddhism, Confucianism — all were grist to his writer's mill.

His relation to the Roman Catholic Church of his Dublin youth, although combative, was also one of analytical curiosity. He went to Notre Dame to hear the Lenten sermons of the famous Jesuit priest, the Rev. Père de la Boullaye de Pinard, and came back with numerous witty commentaries on the orator's name. He also followed the liturgy of the high feast days with almost ecclesiastical precision.

He resented intensely the personal attacks by certain Catholic circles in the United States who assailed him on the ground that his work represented an apparently heretic attitude. He often pointed out to me the enormous role of the concept of evil in Catholic theology. The paschal acolyte does not hesitate to eulogize "the sin of Adam" in a famous liturgical passage, and St. Augustine himself declared: "Felix culpa! O fortunatissimum Adae peccatum." The obscene distortions of gargoyles on Gothic cathedrals show the luxuriant imagination of the conformist architects. The satanic chimeras of the painting of such believers as Matthias Grünewald and Hieronymus Bosch lead us into the abyss of the grotesque. Joyce, who knew his Fathers of the Church, assumed the right which the Catholic Church has always given to the artist: to present the carnal side of man's consciousness with all the mystery of his verbal art.

"And what of the Book of Kells?" he asked. Once he gave me a volume of reproductions from that rare book of illuminated manuscripts. One picture in it showed a particularly hideous depiction of the Christ-child. "Doesn't he look as if he had just robbed the hen-house?" Joyce asked.

In the winter of 1938 someone sent him an issue of the *Osservatore Romano,* world organ of the Vatican, dated October 22, 1937. It contained a reference to Joyce which delighted him, and he quoted it frequently as we sat at Fouquet's one evening. In an essay on modern Irish literature, the pious Vatican essayist had written about Joyce: "And finally James Joyce, of European fame, iconoclast and rebel, who after having sought to renovate the old naturalism, attempted in *Ulysses* to translate plastically the inner reality, and, in 'Work in Progress,' in an oneiric and linguistic experiment, is seeking to open up new paths for the expression of human sentiments."

"We roaming Catholics," he used to say to me, whenever he wanted to introduce a reference to Jesuit theology.

Once an internationally known literary climber telephoned Joyce to ask for some biographical data to be used on the occasion of an evening which a group of Paris poets, les Amis de 1914, were planning in his honor. Joyce agreed to receive the lady in question, since she was to make the introductory speech at the meeting and he felt it was only courteous to have a brief talk with her beforehand. She arrived, elegantly dressed, and accompanied by a large dog, which did not make matters easier, since Joyce had a real aversion to dogs. Remembering vaguely that there was a certain city in which Joyce was particularly interested, the lady started out boldly: "When were you last in Edinburgh, Mr. Joyce?"

"I never saw Edinburgh in my life," was Joyce's reply, after which he fell back into his usual silence. A little confused, but undaunted, the lady then asked permission to photograph him for an article she was writing for the morning newspaper *Le Jour.* The photographer was waiting downstairs, she said, and he could do the job in a trice. In order to give a point to her story, she indicated that she would like to have her picture taken in conversation with Joyce. She had not reckoned, however, with the inventiveness of our friend Joyce. Excusing himself for a moment, he telephoned Paul Léon and myself and urged us to come immediately so that he should not be photographed alone with her.

Fortunately, we were both at home and very shortly afterwards, we arrived at his apartment, almost simultaneously. Joyce introduced us to the lady, but she was not very cordial and evidently resented the miscarriage of her carefully laid plans. The photograph was made, however, with Léon on Joyce's side and me on hers. The picture appeared the following morning in the *Jour,* spread over four columns, but lo and behold—both Léon and I had our heads chopped off by some artist in the newspaper studio. The lady, whose first name was Daisy, had won. Léon and I were highly amused, but Joyce was not pleased.

The following evening he recited a parody he had composed to the tune of "Daisy, Daisy, give me your answer, do . . ." I forget the middle lines but I remember it ended: "And won't we look sweet / Upon the seat / Of a photograph faked for two."

The night of the event, the lady read from the French translation of *Ulysses.* Joyce, who was seated on the platform, managed somehow to turn his back on her during the reading. I have often wondered if the experience gave much real satisfaction to her lion-hunter's heart.

As the political clouds gathered on the European horizon, Joyce grew saddened and lived in increasing isolation. We continued to meet regularly either at his or our house, or else for dinner at Fouquet's. The years brought great change in him, however: his hair became quite gray, and his old self-assurance seemed shaken. I felt he was more deeply human than formerly, more gentle, too. He even showed a certain curiosity about America, although he still adhered to his dogma that the great creative myths of humanity stemmed from Europe. I told him that I intended to bring out one more number of *transition* before relinquishing it, and he approved. "I'll have something for you," he said.

The terrible malady that had befallen his daughter was an ever-present heartbreak, and even his iron will was unable to discover the remedy that might cure her. Paul Léon, his old and trusted friend, was still helping him, but most of the friends of former, happier days had left France, and there was a deepening silence about him. Malevolent critics wrote sneeringly of the "clique around Joyce," which he ironically transformed into the "joyous click." There was little that was joyous about it, however, and we were hardly a "click." I myself was passionately interested in "Work in Progress," and I was proud of the fact that Joyce had confidence in me for the publication of his last great work. Yet I almost dreaded the moment when he said in his casual yet awfully deliberate manner: "I'll have something for you. When will you publish again?" For I knew it meant working with him night and day, it meant being at his beck and call for several months, until the number finally appeared.

Joyce did not explain. He wanted you to guess, to show aptitude at approximations, to have sudden intuitions. The "click" around him carried on arduously, and in fact we were like so many schoolboys working under the ever so slightly despotic whip of our Jesuitical *magister.* For that he was, indeed. It was not *ad majorem Dei gloriam,* but *ad majorem Jacobi gloriam,* and his cerebral intensity was over us like a rattan cane. His occasional impatience with the obtuseness of certain of the "students" was such that I almost anticipated chastisement for the offender. Yet we all felt affection for him, a kind of brotherly sense of protection which increased with his isolation.

I should like to say here a few words for those friendly followers of Joyce's work who did not fall by the wayside, as the years went on and the proletarian littérateurs with left-wing megalomania plodded through their inchoate program. I have in mind the men who wrote for the new Joyce at a time when few were interested in his neologistic innovations, when the majority of American and British writers felt they would have nothing to do with such novelties. They, after all, were only interested in the norm. They were interested in traditional values, in dramatic chronology, in fiction and poetry as handed down by their predecessors. They could not understand that a man who had written *Ulysses* and the *Portrait* might have continued in that vein, yet had decided heroically to forgo sure success in order to engage in a long calvary of creation. Nor did the professional critics distinguish themselves by great foresight in the years between 1927 and 1938. With a few exceptions, they waited for a signal from above. They waited for the moment when the literary stage was set and ready, before taking the bold step.

The men who set this stage were Joyce's friends, and some of them were my friends. We all felt that we were badly equipped for the task of interpreting a work which was not yet complete, and which we had seen only in disparate sections. We certainly had no conception of the whole as yet, only anticipatory presentiments of what it was to be. Elliot Paul was the first to take the step of explaining what we then considered to be the "plot" of "Work in Progress," and his essay on that subject in *transition* was a milestone. There was also Stuart Gilbert, who was ceaselessly at work deciphering the hermetic book. There were others, too, brilliant analysts all: Harry Levin, William Troy, Edmund Wilson, Alfred Kazin, Padraic Colum, Samuel Beckett.

Then there was Frank Budgen, the British writer and painter, who had been Joyce's friend in Zurich during World War I, and had written an engaging book on that period, *The Making of Ulysses.* An essay by him, which was published in *transition,* dealt with Joyce's use of Nordic mythology in "Work in Progress." When Budgen visited Paris we used to meet at Joyce's flat and then go on café-squatting Chez Francis. He talked wittily about the Zurich days — and, incidentally, was one of the few Anglo-Saxons I ever met who could speak faultless Zurich dialect.

Once in Zurich, when Joyce and I were walking in comparative silence through the Bahnhofstraße, I heard Joyce mumble Budgen's name. I remember that he and Budgen had been accustomed to meet at the Pfauen restaurant for nightly dinners and copious quaffs of "Waliser" wine during World War I when Budgen was employed at the British Consulate in Zurich. However, I said nothing more and we continued on our way. Suddenly Joyce turned down a side street called the Uraniastraße. It was dusk and there was a gossamer haze over the town. He stopped in front of a building, turned to me and said: "There he is." "Who?" "Budgen." I looked up and saw a number of nude sculptured figures gazing down at us. Joyce explained that Budgen had posed for the Swiss sculptor Suter, who had been commissioned by the city for the work. "Where is he?" I asked. "Labor," said Joyce laconically. Indeed, there stood the nude figure of Budgen on top of the world in all his paradisiacal glory. "Labor," mused Joyce, "the laziest man I ever knew . . ."

Another friend of Joyce was Samuel Beckett, the Irish poet who came to Paris to teach as exchange professor at the Ecole Normale. Joyce took a great liking to Beckett and through him we became friends. He was Anglo-Irish and in gesture and spirit resembled Joyce sometimes to such an extent that we were astonished. He was a young man of genuine talent, very original and creatively alive. Both as a poet and as a prose writer his personality imposed itself in all of us, and I enjoyed his brilliant albeit dour mind. He had an extraordinary verbal facility and inventiveness, and in that respect was, like his great countryman, *un beau ténébreux,* a Celtic visionary who was in love with France. Unlike Joyce, however, he wanted to simplify the English language rather than enrich it. For this reason he began to write in French exclusively shortly before World War II in order to retain simplicity by writing deliberately in a language he did not know as well as his native tongue. His French writings strike one as *dépouillés* and yet richly suggestive of his island background.

Six months before "Work in Progress" was scheduled to appear in book form, there was an amusing incident in connection with the title, which till then was known only to the author and Mrs. Joyce. Joyce had often challenged his friends to guess it, and he had even made a permanent offer to pay a thousand francs in cash to the person who succeeded. We all tried, Stuart Gilbert, Herbert Gorman, Samuel Beckett, Paul Léon, myself, but we failed miserably. One summer night while dining on the *terrasse* of Fouquet's, Joyce repeated his offer. The Riesling was especially good that night, and we were in fine spirits. Mrs. Joyce began to sing softly an Irish song about Mr. Flannagan and Mrs. Shannigan. Joyce looked up startled, urged her to stop. This she did, but when he saw no harm had been done, he very distinctly, as a singer does it, made the lip motions which seemed to indicate F and W. Maria's guess was "Fairy's Wake." Joyce looked astonished and said: "Brava! But something is missing."

At home we mulled over it for a few days. One morning I knew it was "Finnegans Wake," although it was only an intuition. That evening I suddenly threw the words in the air. Joyce blanched. Slowly he set down his wine-glass: "Ah, Jolas," he said, "you've taken something from me." When we parted that night he gave me the accolade, danced a few of his intricate steps, and asked: "How would you like to have the money?" I replied: "In sous." The following morning, during my absence from home, Joyce arrived with a bag filled with ten-franc pieces. He gave them to my daughters with instructions to serve them to me at lunch with the *hors d'oeuvres*. So it was "Finnegans Wake." We were sternly enjoined by Joyce not to reveal the title until he himself made the official announcement at a birthday dinner given by his son and daughter-in-law on the following February 2.

In the last few years of his life, Joyce circumscribed more and more his social activities. He was invited out very little — people had probably grown discouraged — and he rarely accepted the invitations he received. Thus he came to depend more and more on a few friends. Among others, I used to take frequent walks with him in the Bois de Boulogne, or go to a movie with him. On these occasions he was often silent, and seemed absorbed in his own world of meditations.

He was just the opposite, in fact, of the gregarious Gertrude Stein, whom he had never met in all the many years that they lived simultaneously in Paris. Shortly before the war, however, the American sculptor Jo Davidson, who was a good friend of both writers, decided to break the ice and invite them together to his studio. They were introduced, and shook hands. But that was all. Nor did Joyce ever meet Picasso, although I once saw them in the same restaurant. We were having a drink Chez Francis after a concert. Picasso was seated at a nearby table, in conversation with André Breton, Jacques Prévert and other Surrealist writers and artists. Informed of their presence, Joyce did not look up, although I noticed that the Picasso group seemed curious about him.

Joyce's devotion to his sick daughter knew no bounds. She was by now interned in a *maison de santé* near Paris, and he used to spend hours trying to amuse her, talking to her about the past, singing for her, or listening to her verbal fantasies with absolute patience. But sometimes his own nerves seemed to crack under the strain, and once I saw him weep bitterly.

"Why should this thing have happened to us?" he said. "We were so happy." Then, wanly: "And I am supposed to be writing a funny book . . ."

Although often despairing, he continued to read proof on *Finnegans Wake*. In addition to Mrs. Joyce, who literally never left him, Giorgio and Helen Joyce, Lucie and Paul Léon, Sam Beckett, Moune and Stuart Gilbert, Maria and I were his most constant companions. Usually one or the other of us went out with him each evening, and when he started brooding we tried to cheer him up.

One evening I received a telephone call from an unknown man who, it developed, was the proprietor of a little *bistro* in the Rue de Grenelle.

"Monsieur Jouasse," he said, "wants you to come down as soon as you can. The address is . . ."

I found Joyce standing in front of a bar, with a glass of pernod before him.

"Bon soir," I said, and ordered a pernod.

"Oh, there you are," he said, and fell into silence.

After a while he asked in a low whisper:

"Do you know the poet Mangan?"

And he began to recite "Dark Rosaleen" in his musical Dublin speech. One verse in particular struck me:

> I could scale the blue air,
> > I could plough the high hills,
> O, I could kneel all night in prayer,
> > To heal your many ills!
> And one beamy smile from you
> > Would float like light between
> My toils and me, my own, my true,
> > My Dark Rosaleen!
> > My fond Rosaleen!
> Would give me life and soul anew,
> A second life, a soul anew,
> > My Dark Rosaleen!

The months passed in great anxiety and Joyce became desirous of seeing his complex book appear before, as he said, "the storm broke." All his notes were carefully gone over by Léon, and together they adhered to a rigid working schedule. Even through its fragmentary publication in *tran-*

sition, we knew that the work constituted a challenge to contemporary speculation, as no other work had done for decades. To be sure, its partial appearance might have militated against immediate acceptance. On the other hand, public appetite had been whetted through the exegetical efforts of *transition* writers, and through the comments of connoisseurs, particularly in the United States.

We knew that it had been Joyce's ambition to write a book dealing with the night-mind of man. We had already followed most of the purgatorial, multiple characters blundering through their larval and anthropological transmigrations. We had glimpsed the titanic city-mountain synthesis of the wanderer Humphrey Chimpden Earwicker, and watched his countless human and pre-human metamorphoses. We had followed the pan-symbolic pattern in the creation of Anna Livia Plurabelle, the river-woman, the *magna mater*. Shem and Shaun, the antithetical brothers, sometimes called Jerry and Kevin; the daughter Isabelle, the washer-woman, the household slut, the topers and gossips of Chapelizod: all these contemporary and primitively barbaric evocations were familiar to *transition* readers. There were other characters too, most of them minor, but yet intricately interwoven in the narrative, with whom we were now acquainted. We knew the contour of the incessant conflict that takes place on the nocturnal stage; we saw the continuous mutation of locality, objects, events, languages, characters. Examining with new eyes Joyce's revolutionary idea of the paragraph, we tried to keep in mind that the dramatic dynamism of the book was based on Bruno's theory of knowledge through antinomies, as also on the Viconian philosophy of cyclic recurrence. History, for Joyce, was a nightmare, and he undoubtedly considered the present epoch to be the last phase of the Viconian cycle: man's fall, followed by chaos and resurrection. Like Goethe's, his was an Olympian eye. He looked on at the political scene with amusement and detachment.

As the war approached, Joyce manifested apparently little political awareness. I talked with him before and after Munich, but he remained non-committal. This was, in fact, a bewildering feature of my relation to him. For I was being gradually drawn into the anti-fascist, anti-totalitarian struggle, while Joyce, on the contrary, seemed almost to resent any reference to it. One day he said to me: "What can an individual do in times like these? I think he can only help personally those who are threatened." He was assiduous in his efforts to help Jewish friends escape from the Nazi clutches, and it is a fact that the Austrian novelist Hermann Broch and a number of other Central European friends were able to escape as a result of his intercessions on their behalf.

Paris was a rapidly changing city. There was constantly increasing social disturbance, and the resultant political fever all but paralyzed the functions of the state. The clash between the Croix de Feu, Action Française and other right-wing fascist groups on the one hand, and the left-wingers, led by the Communists, on the other, foreshadowed a cataclysm. One had the sensation that the time had come for the bursting of the dikes, for all-engulfing floods, for apocalyptic dementia. Hitler's persecution of racial minorities brought thousands of refugees to Paris and all the languages of Central Europe could now be heard on the boulevards. French friends often said: "*Pourvu que ça finisse!* If only this false peace would end! We would rather fight than wait helplessly."

Joyce gave me the last fragment of "Work in Progress" for inclusion in the new number of *transition* I was then preparing. This was the fragment relating the radio yarn of Butt and Taff, or how Buckley killed the Russian general. As usual, there were to be many changes before the final bon à tirer could be given. Joyce seemed to be living in the mythical inn of Chapelizod where the twelve uproariously drunken customers were engaged in recreating the world and fighting its battles — the brother-battles of Shem and Shaun, become Butt and Taff, and the protean transformations of sin-haunted HCE.

The first bound copy of *Finnegans Wake* reached Paris just in time for Joyce's birthday, on February 2, 1939. It naturally constituted an added attraction to the anniversary dinner which took place at his son's home, and to which French, Irish, British and American friends were invited. Joyce let each guest examine the precious volume, which T. S. Eliot, on behalf of the London publishing house, had just forwarded.

The Viconian cycle was coming to its inevitable climax. Two years later James Joyce died in Zurich.

10

IN THE MAELSTROM

Maria and our two little girls returned from France late in September of 1940, bringing with them a French boy, aged eight — Claude Duthuit, the son of Georges and Marguerite Duthuit — a grandson of the painter Henri Matisse. We celebrated our reunion on American soil, on a pier of my native state of New Jersey, where the *Exochorda* from Lisbon landed, after a long odyssey. It was a windy autumn day, and I remembered my own landing in New York many years before, when I was a youngster, hungry for the American utopia.

The travelers brought back the graphic story of the invasion of France. They brought their recitals of the war months, their own experiences and those of my relatives and friends. I heard the story of the débâcle, I heard intimate accounts of Nazi barbarism turned loose on the landscapes of France. A hundred human details gave me a picture of the catastrophe, a picture of complete despair and disaster, of tears and terror. Europe emerged from these conversations as a continent that was prey to a great darkness, like the one that once reigned during the Thirty Years' War.

The children, speaking their native French, looked at the great sky-scrapers of lower New York, as we crossed in the ferry, and expressed their admiration. They were happy to land. Now they were in the country where their mother's people had lived for two hundred years, where their father had been an immigrant. The hungry Spanish children who had stolen cakes from their plates on a Madrid terrace, the overcrowded, filthy trains, all the tragic images of the exodus were now things of the past. They were in America! They were American citizens, despite their French birth, and they embraced the land of great liberations with quick affection. It took weeks, however, before the entire story unfolded.

Maria said that the children — French, English and American — had adjusted themselves swiftly to the new regime of a rural school. In fact, they loved it, and, after the first weeks of confusion, everything ran along normal lines. They helped with the agricultural work. They learned to tend the horses, to round up the turkeys, to work in the fields and meadows with the old peasants. They had passed through the seasons with an increasing love of the earth, as they watched its ceaseless mutations. During the *Sitzkrieg* along the Maginot Line, they wrote to the soldiers and received grateful letters in return. They sent them gifts, mufflers and socks for the hard eastern winter, cigarettes and other delicacies.

Maria said that on Easter all the children went on vacation as usual, after which the last school term got under way. It was one of those gorgeous springs in France, the fields were filled with primroses and violets, the first mild April nights brought the nightingales whose singing they listened to so breathlessly. But the radio across the Rhine was becoming more and more threatening, more and more sinister in its dire prediction of what France's determined alliance with England would mean for her. Deep down in their hearts, people knew things could not go on as they had been.

"The moon," said an old friend to her on one of those nights, "is an awful enemy." Maria pushed her ominous thought from her mind.

Then came Friday, May 10. The three-day Whitsun holiday was to begin on that day. They expected several parents to visit their children, and other pupils were to join their parents elsewhere. A few teachers had already left. The telephone began to ring early: Paris calling. "Tell Jeannot I cannot come on account of the events." "What events?" asked Maria. This was the first time she had heard, but she was to hear more. Fifteen disappointed youngsters were told to stay where they were and be good on that day. Fifteen more children than she had counted on to be amused and cared for over the holiday. Fortunately the weather was perfect, so that they could be out of doors the entire time. But both teachers and children knew that the day had come, that from now on nothing would be as it had been before. A gymkhana, a picnic on the banks of the Allier river, grass-cutting, much choral singing and a bicycle hike — the three days passed somehow and school started again.

From that moment on, Maria has a memory of constant change. A few anxious parents came to fetch their children: "If anything happens, we shan't be separated . . ." Others came with new children. This or that region where military objectives were located was being bombarded. A little girl who arrived from Orléans had spent hours in the trench shelters of her school. Another from Fécamp was so frightened she could not work and had become almost mute. On May 19, a little girl of twelve made her first communion in the village church of St.-Gérand-le-Puy. Her father and mother arrived for the occasion. The father worked in an ammunition factory. "We have no stock at all for an emergency," he said; "the trucks wait before the door of the factory, while we finish enough shells to fill them." On June 3, another father and mother came to see Maria. "Here are some addresses in America," said the father; "I want the children to stay with you. We have some jewels that could be sold in America." "But what do you mean?" Maria questioned anxiously. "That we're going towards disaster," the father answered. "I am an aviator and my wife is driving an ambulance. One never knows what may happen." Maria pressed him. "Our aviation is quite inadequate," he continued. "I foresee that a large part of France will be occupied, even here" — he hesitated — "even Paris." Maria says her heart sank as this courageous young couple drove off, both of them in uniform.

This was the first time in her country retreat that she had admitted even to herself the possibility of defeat. It was not until two months later, after the armistice, that she received any news from this couple. They were both saved; for they were of the stuff that old France was made of and from which the new France will take her strength and courage. Here was no break with reality. They knew the truth and faced it without flinching. When her own decision was made to return to America three months after the armistice, Maria suggested that their two children accompany her until better times. "We've been very tempted," was the reply, "but have decided our children will know nothing of France's problems if they escape her suffering now. We've decided to keep them with us." Maria received the same answer from all of her teachers when she put them the tentative question. "Should I be able to reorganize my school in America, would you join me there?" Without exception, the reply came from each one: "Our place is here. France needs, now as never before, a population that is present and morally determined to work for her regeneration."

Paris fell June 14.

James, Nora and Giorgio Joyce arrived in St.-Gérand-le-Puy on the morning of the 16th from Vichy, where they had been staying in a hotel; for the latter was requisitioned by the authorities and they decided to install themselves near Maria. The Joyces and our friends Lucie Léon, their boy Alexis, Léon's sister, Mrs. Hirschmann, and their father arrived with friends and relatives from the Loire village whence they had fled. Maria depicted their pitiful fatigue, their fear before the invader. Paul Léon, Joyce's great friend, had been left somewhere south of the Loire, pushing a baby carriage filled with their valises and trunks. Maria told about her fatigue after a night passed at the St.-Gérand station trying to help the countless refugees, among whom were many terrified Jews.

She pictured the chaos: the little sales girl with her mother and beautiful baby: "Elle qui n'a été que dorlotée toute sa vie;" the exhausted people sleeping in tiers in the military dormitory; the crippled woman from Dijon who, at the first bombardment, had fled, not knowing where she was headed for; the two young women with babies, large bundles; two grandmothers, old and crippled with rheumatism; the old woman who fell unconscious on the floor of the train, on her knees, as they hurriedly lifted her in; the charming, high-bred Dominican nuns and the courtesy that everyone showed them; cattle cars with soldiers and civilians together; one car of young soldiers playing harmonicas in all the tumult; *les privés d'amour,* someone had chalked on the car; the politeness of the railway employees; the people sleeping on the floor of the dirty platform; the cute little girl of the Paris faubourg with two gay Poulbot lads, *plein d'esprit,* so happy to be washed at last; they had walked out of Paris, beyond Fontainebleau in order to board the train.

The little Alsatian-Lorraine colony of refugees consisting of my mother, my sister and her two children and my brother Charles's wife, Ginette, and their son who had installed themselves near Maria in the early days of the war were disturbed. There was no news from our soldier-brothers and relatives who were fighting somewhere on the Maginot Line in northern France. Maria said that my mother's courage was astonishing.

On June 15, Simone Chantalup, one of Maria's teachers, and Maria bicycled back to the school in the early dawn. The stars paled and the mists hung heavy over the fields. A peasant was already at work. At five thirty they crept into bed.

Monday, June 17, there were classes as usual. A father traveling by automobile offered his services. Maria quickly sent Miriam, Miron, Marie-Claire, Colette and others to their families in Vichy. Fewer mouths to feed, for food was growing very hard to find. "Armistice!" said someone. Was it true? But the Germans were still advancing!

In the night, the Reynaud government had fallen. Simone waked Maria to tell her this at 1:00 A.M. Pétain had taken over. At 2:00 A.M. there was an anguished visit from the owner of La Chapelle, Madame de Laire. Should they leave? Should she take the grandchildren away during their mother's absence? Excited, nervous departure of two cars. The voices in the courtyard. 5:00 A.M. French officers asking for gasoline. "None to be had."

The next day: St.-Gérand-le-Puy was filled with refugees and officers. The post office closed. They moved all of the teachers, pupils, etc., who had been staying in the village of St.-Gérand, to La Chapelle. The hotel occupied by crowds of poor people *en route—pour où?* Anywhere, where the Nazis were not. The mothers came from Paris, one by bicycle. Careworn hours about the radio.

The Germans were in the Yonne . . . The Germans were at Nevers . . . The Germans were at Moulins . . . Where were they not? Would they come here? If they did, what would Maria do? Would they carry off the big boys? Rumors flew thick and fast. They said, That's what they have done everywhere. What of the men? Had anybody a bicycle? Groups were forming in all the villages. Where would they go? Nobody knew. Away, anywhere out of the reach of the invaders. The cars poured by, all going south. Many had been bombarded. Mattresses attached to the roofs. Branches of trees. Household effects. Children, frightened and exhausted. Paris autobuses marked "Auteuil," "Passy," "Opéra."

Another car left with children from the school and a few parents. They were headed for Lourdes, Toulouse and the Pyrenees.

Afternoon. Paul Léon arrived in a donkey cart, worn out with fatigue. At the same time a French officer and about twenty French soldiers. Could they sleep in one of the barns? Of course they could.

Maria went to St.-Gérand-le-Puy to see how everybody was faring. Incredible spectacle of confused crowds of refugees, soldiers, townspeople. Everybody anxious. Many rumors. A drum in the streets. The announcer said: "The population is invited to refrain from all manifestations and to keep calm, no matter what happens."

What did this mean? That the Nazis were very near. Maria had to hurry back to La Chapelle to warn their French soldiers in the barn. On the road she met one of the farm women. "Oh, Madame, I have just been to see you. We are so anxious. Do you think they will take everything we have? My daughter-in-law is afraid they'll take her baby's clothes. And her wedding ring. Do you think they might take these things? *Oh, qu'on a bien du malheur!*" Maria tried to reason with her. She was not sure if she succeeded. She passed a French military contingent on the road. The cars of an état-major followed by armed side-car troops. The men grave, their cars battered. She said she saluted them affectionately. When she reached home, the French soldiers had already left. Later on she heard that their little truck of supplies was in a ditch and that they had emptied their valises on the road.

That evening, around eight o'clock, she returned to St.-Gérand to see if she could be of help. The village had suddenly become uncannily silent. Nobody was about. The streets were deserted. The village was awaiting the dreaded arrival of the Nazis.

My mother was calm, and her luminous faith dominated the household. My sister, Marie-Madeleine, could not hide her anguish. Ginette, my sister-in-law, was grave and resolute. James Joyce and his family, whom Maria had installed in a little flat in the village, seemed relatively calm. Joyce was seated on a sofa, listening to the radio. Churchill was speaking: "Marshal Pétain's melancholy decision . . ." "Dans l'honneur," Joyce commented ironically. He was never, for an instant, fooled. Mrs. Joyce made tea.

A grocer's family, around twenty-four persons, arrived from Nevers (children, men, women, dogs, chickens, canaries) and asked for lodging at the Hôtel du Commerce, which Maria had rented for the duration. It was naturally given them, and thanks to this, she did not have to lodge German soldiers.

On Wednesday, June 19, the first German soldiers arrived in St.-Gérand-le-Puy at 5:30 in the morning. The seventy-two-year-old handyman, who lived in the village, gave the group at the school the news at breakfast. Marthe de Terrier scolded him. How did he know they were Germans? Had he talked to them? Why exaggerate? She finally convinced him that he was mistaken.

But the Nazis were there, all right. For when Maria bicycled with two of her teachers towards the village a little later, she saw them. Once near the Vichy highway, the roar of motors stopped them. A continuous stream of trucks and motors filled with field-gray uniforms. Their hearts sank as they watched them. And at what pace they were going! The road being dangerous, the three women went across the fields, hiding behind the fences till the first large contingent had gone by. All three rode back slowly across the little side lanes. Abel had not deserved the scolding he had received.

The Germans were going fast somewhere. By radio the teachers heard that they were on their way to Lyons. The city fell into their hands shortly afterwards. All day Wednesday the school expected their visit at La Chapelle, which was a mile from the village. None came. They were evidently in a hurry, and the presence of the school did not interest them.

Later in the afternoon, Maria returned to St.-Gérand. The courtyard of the Hôtel du Commerce was a joy to behold. Entirely occupied by the grocer's family. Everybody was washing, eating, cooking. A bright red cover hung on a wire. The trucks were full of groceries. No *metteur en scène* could have done better. They were a clean, self-respecting lot, and they left four bottles of champagne in recompense for the hospitality.

On the main square, a real cantonment. Countless field-gray, heavy, well-equipped, well-armed trucks of all kinds (bridge construction, principally). German soldiers at the *mairie,* in the shops, in the cafés. They quickly bought up all the things no longer to be found in Germany—a little jeweler's shop emptied of everything, paid for in paper marks; yards of woolen material to be sent back to the Nazi families, silk stockings, perfumes, etc.

It saddened Maria to see that the attitude of the village population was not always perfect. Children on the square played with the soldiers. Among the younger women there was admiration of their uniforms, of their orderly, pedantic way of doing things. In one café a young woman lifted her champagne glass to theirs. Was this the result of the Stuttgart traitor's propaganda? Perhaps to a certain extent. Or nervousness, relief that they had not been burned and slaughtered, as they had feared? Both explanations were probably valid. The older generation, on the other hand, understood the tragedy of the moment and remained in quiet dignity at home.

Night and day the armies rolled on the two roads east and west of La Chapelle. Not one soldier came to the house, and school continued as usual in an atmosphere of calm work, which was a real tribute to the self-control of our teaching staff, many of whom were suffering from the uncertainty of the fate of their men. When school hours were over, they sat around the radio, but nothing came through, and no supposition of what might be the conditions of the armistice was forthcoming. All the adults in the house— sixteen, as opposed to twenty-six children—were tragically conscious of the fact that the fate of France was in the balance.

Gradually, most of the Nazi soldiers left. Still no telephone, no letters, no trains, no cars, no autobuses. Maria said it was like a long, long ocean voyage, and as always it was interesting to watch the reactions of the passengers to each other. They had in this house French, British, Turkish, Swiss, American pupils and teachers—mostly French, however. These last were sad and anguished at the fate of their men. Pierre de Terrier? My brothers, Armand, Charles, Emile? My brother-in-law Célestin? Did anybody know where they were? In the village my mother and the younger women were calm and took refuge in prayer.

The days passed; heavy, nameless. Maria said they were unforgettable weeks of anguish, fear, humiliation, relief, calm—the calm of complete resignation in a state that could not more nearly resemble death and not be death. Fortunately the line of demarcation was placed at Moulins, just above St.-Gérand. The school, of course, had to be abandoned, and Maria rented a little house in the village where she and our two children lived.

Their neighbors were the Joyces and the Léons. Joyce began to take notes for a new book and he wrapped himself up as usual in his impenetrable silence. From hints dropped to Léon, it appears he was contemplating a book that seemed to have been inspired by the village and Maria's school during and after the war. Maria said he would be found lying on the sofa, his legs twirled in an apparently inextricable manner, listening to the radio or working.

During this time, he asked Léon to go over the one copy of *Finnegans Wake* that he had. Every afternoon at three o'clock sharp, the two would work together, going over each sentence of the work, and marking the typographical errors — and there were a number of them — that had crept into the first edition of the book. Maria, when she returned to the United States, brought with her a copy of these corrections and gave them to his publisher, B. H. Huebsch.

Maria finally decided to return to America with our children. From what the children said, I gathered that the entire village saw them off, when they took the bus one gray morning for the long trip to Madrid and Lisbon.

Joyce realized that he could not stay in the Vichy country. He was deeply shocked by the surrender, and he decided to go to Switzerland, as he had done in the First World War. There were a great many difficulties. He went back and forth to Vichy to get the necessary papers, and there were obstacles. A large sum had to be deposited in Bern before he could enter the country, and it was his friends Dr. and Mrs. Giedion who finally deposited the sum.

Joyce did not want to leave without his mentally ill daughter, who was in an institution on the Atlantic coast. At that time a young Irish poet friend of his, Samuel Beckett, came to stay with Joyce, who had always had a particular affection for this very gifted poet. Beckett was charged by Joyce to go into the occupied zone and try to get his daughter to accompany them to Switzerland. The scheme was made impossible by the Nazis at the last minute. I know what sorrow this must have cost the Irish writer, for his love for his sick daughter was immense.

My mother and sister and other relatives left for Strasbourg a few weeks after Maria left. Somehow Maria seemed to have been the tower of strength around which they all clung, and when she returned to America, the little Allied colony broke up.

James, Nora and Giorgio Joyce left the little village of St.-Gérand-le-Puy a few weeks after Maria's departure. In Lisbon Maria found an affectionate telegram from our friend, ending with the impatient words: "J'ai soupé de St.-Gérand-le-Machin." Three months later we learned the heart-sorrowing news of his death in Zurich.

Along with the other millions, we were swept up in the great migrations un-leashed by the Nazis' war. The defeat of France put an abrupt end to all our activities there, and the autumn of 1940 found us once more in New York. The first months of distress and difficult readjustments were made more sorrowful by the shocking news, first of James Joyce's death in Zurich, then of the plight of my own family who, after having been driven from their border homes, were scattered all over France. It was not, in fact, until the following summer, which we spent in a wild and lively part of Connecticut, on the shores of Lake Wauramaug, that gradually our new life seemed to become oriented away from a sense of irreparable loss to one of hope in the future.

The presence of a few exiled French families who had settled in the same region lent an exotic note to the homely New England atmosphere. With other European children, some of whom had been in Maria's Neuilly school before the war, my two daughters Betsy and Tina began to re-create the happy childhood they had known in France. Among these "exile" friends were the former Surrealist painter André Masson, his wife Rose and two small sons. Preferring exile to the sacrifice of his liberty under the Pétain regime, Masson had come to America after the fall of France, along with the Surrealist leader, André Breton. They had stopped long enough in Mar-tinique to feel the spell of the tropics and make the acquaintance of the remarkable Negro poet, Aimé Césaire. Trepidating New York soon proved to be too disturbing, however, for Masson's highly sensitive nerves, and he decided to settle "for the duration" in Connecticut's bucolic landscape. He worked assiduously, for he liked the color of the American sky, al-though he found it quite different from that of Paris or the Île de France, which, he said, alone possessed the aerial freedom necessary to the modern painter.

I have always responded to the tormented quality of Masson's paintings of that period. When I first met him in Paris, in the twenties, I was struck by his preoccupation with the *coincidentia oppositorum* in the zoological world of monsters and grotesques. In America, I watched him establish contact with the New England fauna and flora which he later deformed with a con-vulsive touch. If Masson had not followed his painter's genius, he might well have had a writer's career, and our conversations, lasting often into the early dawn-hours, in the rustic little cottage beside the lake, were usually of a literary or philosophical nature. His mind was *bien meublé,* as they say in France, and he had a passion for analogies, a penchant for daring cerebrations. He suffered the sorrows of his time as few did, and his introspections invariably turned into sublime blasphemies. A mythological awareness, a love of the Dionysian myth and the self-lacerating idea of the god's death and resurrection, held his imagination captive. At that time he saw life as suffering, combat and massacre, and his plastic creations reflected this violence.

Many weekend guests came up from New York, among them the great and dour André Breton, who with his wife and little daughter Aube used to live in Masson's bungalow for the weekends. It was interesting to watch the difficult adjustments to America this Parisian *bohémien* had to make. In those sultry summer nights, we sat around in our shirt-sleeves, drinking vast quantities of California white wine and re-creating the stricken universe. He also indulged his hobby of chasing fabulously designed moths and night butterflies that abounded there and which he had never seen in Europe. Georges Duthuit, who was working with NBC, also appeared, and the three of us discussed the founding of a magazine, to be half in English, half in French, in which each of us would project his own ideas. The formula was a tempting one, and we began to discuss practical plans for its realization. I made it plain to Breton that I did not share all of his Surrealist convictions, despite my admiration for his own creative gifts, but that I was especially interested in continuing along the lines of my former interest in reviving the pan-romantic spirit. To this he agreed. He said there was no question of starting a purely Surrealist review, but one in which a number of kindred spirits could meet and commune.

Fortunately, some kind fate intervened; for had we gone through with the plan, I am sure it would have failed. As it happened, a dramatic event occurred that smashed our project: an article I had written a year before for a small, purely literary magazine, *Fantasy,* appeared in Pittsburgh, in which article I had bade definitive adieu to Surrealism, under the title of "Surrealism: Ave atque Vale." Here I had only expressed what I had felt for many years and what I had told Breton personally a few weeks before: that mere demonological resistance to the totalitarian menace was not enough. But when Breton read the article, he grew indignant, and after I met him again, he made no attempt to hide his displeasure. André Masson tried to pacify the storm, but Breton worked himself into bitter resentment. There was no longer any question of editing a review together, and Maria and I felt that even without the *Fantasy* article, the collaboration would probably have been impossible. However, this and other disagreements with Breton have never diminished my conviction that he is not only a writer of great distinction, but the most gifted and remarkable *animateur* of his generation of Frenchmen.

In those curious days immediately preceding the treacherous attack at Pearl Harbor, minatory headlines and apocalyptic stories filled the American newspapers. I pendulated between New York City and the suburban home in nearby Mount Vernon, to which we had moved in the fall of 1941, looking for a job and seeking at the same time to forget Hitler's monstrous world in the magical colloquies of esoteric literature, art and music. To be sure, America was physically far from the terrible massacre. Yet mentally we who had lived in Europe were in the midst of it. At long intervals, a Red Cross postal card containing a few prudent lines would arrive from my sister, or from old Paris friends. Otherwise, the past and present were engulfed in a fearful, nerve-shattering silence. Then one day news came that my mother had died in occupied France. We had no details other than those contained in the brief Red Cross communication received many months after the event.

New York had become more stimulating than ever before, not only because of its great museums, libraries, theaters and concert-halls, but also because of the presence of many representatives of Europe's intellectual advance-guard, particularly French writers, painters, journalists and politicians, who soon swept the Hudson city with a cyclone of ideas that brought a number of temperamental silhouettes into relief. The great physicist Jean Perrin, the mathematician Jacques Hadamard, the philosopher Jean Wahl, the architect Pierre Chareau; such writers as André Breton, Antoine de Saint-Exupéry, Denis de Rougemont, Georges Duthuit, Yvan Goll, Maurice Maeterlinck; the painters Fernand Léger, Yves Tanguy, André Masson, Moïse Kisling, Kurt Seligmann, Max Ernst; the composer Darius Milhaud, the playwright Henri Bernstein — there were probably others whose names escape me today — were all working under American skies. Not since the earliest days of immigration to the New World had a French colony of this quality existed in the United States.

It was perhaps inevitable that acrid political divisions should manifest themselves almost immediately. Pétain's ambassador, M. Henri Haye, was still in Washington with a large staff, and clashes between the Vichy adherents and those who had chosen the Cross of Lorraine for their symbol were frequent. Among the declared Gaullists were to be found such well-known politicians and journalists as Pertinax, Geneviève Tabouis, Henri de Kerillis, Pierre Lazareff, Raoul de Roussy de Sales, Emile Buré and Henri Torres. Later, after Gen. Giraud entered the fray, there was a further split, and the two French-language weeklies that had sprung up in New York — *Pour la Victoire* and *France-Amérique* — entered upon a period of journalistic feuding that lasted until the end of the war.

It was understandable enough that these French men and women should be far from happy, and there existed among them the same bitter rivalries and antipathies that have characterized political immigrants of all epochs and countries. But occasionally, too, there were gatherings at which a fraternal spirit prevailed. The Gaullist canteen La Marseillaise, which, with a Franco-American committee, Maria helped to organize and direct, was the scene of many such occasions, when visiting French servicemen and merchant seamen, fresh from France, allowed the exiled civilians to glimpse behind the curtain of their country's struggle.

Many of us had lived in the illusion that it was possible to remain aloof, to pursue the dynamism of the spirit by setting aside meditations on death and violence and crime, or through evocations of high poetry and art. It soon became evident, however, that this was a total war, that human freedom itself was at stake. Despite the coruscating attraction of gratuitous aesthetic life, I was eager to return to American journalism, to pull my small oar in the struggle. I had several offers almost immediately, but the work seemed to have little to do with helping the Allied cause directly. One day I met my old Paris friend Morris Gilbert, who had just returned from a mission to London. He told me of a war-time information service about to be organized in Washington. I immediately sent in my application.

Meanwhile, I was seeing something of New York literary circles. I attended banquets of the International Pen Club and the American Poetry Society. I even read my own poems at an evening organized by the Young Men's Hebrew Association, on a program that included two other poets, Oscar Williams and Robert Fitzgerald. On this occasion, I must admit, however, that I had a bad attack of stage fright. In addition, I made the mistake of reading some of my trilingual poems, in which French, German and English are mingled quite naturally. There was a good deal of criticism of this, since few in the audience understood either French or German, and I realized that my first public appearance in Manhattan (it was also my last) had been a fiasco. At that time these YMHA Poetry Evenings were under the direction of Norman MacLeod, who was himself a poet, and he managed to create a cultural center of genuine interest. W. H. Auden read his poems there for over two hours one night, and I recall other occasions when Alfred Kreymborg and William Carlos Williams read their works.

At the suggestion of my old friend Clifford Laube, I sent some of my translations of poems by Charles Péguy and a number of other French mystic poets to a Catholic poetry review called *Spirit*. At that time, Péguy was completely unknown in New York poetic circles. My surprise and indignation were great, however, when the editor sent them back with the remark: "Péguy is certainly not a real religious poet . . . No Catholic would speak this way about God." A few years later the Pantheon Press published translations of these same poems, by Julien Green, and the New York critics fell over themselves in their praises of the great "new" poet.

I later used certain of these transliterations in a "verticalist" anthology published by the Gotham Book Mart. In this collection I tried to summarize the spiritual disquiet of the pre-war years, as well as to give a cross-cut of mystical and ascensionist writing both past and present, on two continents. This volume, entitled *Vertical,* was probably one of the first literary manifestations of the so-called religious revival in American poetry. It also synthesized my own desperate attempts to find psychic freedom in a utopian conquest of the law of gravitation, and, to this extent, may be said to have been an early manifestation of the genre later known as science fiction. *Vertical* contained poems and prose by Léon-Paul Fargue, Pierre-Jean Jouve, Georges Duthuit, Raymond E. F. Larsson, O. V. de L. Milosz, Richard Eberhart, Paul Claudel, Kay Boyle, Charles Péguy and many others.

About this time, during a stay with Jacques in the Iowa college town Mount Vernon, where he was teaching, I made the acquaintance of Clyde Tull, a professor of English, who agreed with me that a spiritual renewal was inevitable in America. He liked my most recent poems, *Planets and Angels,* in which I had posited the existence of an angelic universe, and he had them hand-set by his pupils in a very nice edition. A few critics, among them the poet Richard Eberhart, writing in *Poetry,* spoke favorably of this little offering.

Another poem written during that period was:

TO MY MOTHER ENGULFED IN THE WAR

Suffering in the dogma of the era
This is the night of the fearful lacerations
The terrible fractures echo in my ears
It is the dance of death in the Manichean mind

Hitler is Daniel's beast with the iron teeth
He is the raucous voice smattering lies
But do not be afraid in the panting nocturne
The evangel of the angels wakes and is ready to strike

There's something keeps weeping in my heart while I think
Of you in the solitude of the darkling winter
The bombs shriek down on our land and the blackout shudders
And I think of you engulfed in the nightmare of Europe
And I send my stammering words to the abysmal skies

In James Laughlin's anthology *New Directions* I published a long poem, "Babel: 1940," which ends with the lines:

Clasta allagrona sil boala alamata
Cloa drim lister agrastoo
Cling aratoor
Es knistert es klappert es klirrt
On tonne on mugit on meugle
Toutes les ballades sont mortes
And we wonder in our deepest dream
Will the vocabularies never cease clashing
Werden die Woerterbuecher immer streiten
Will the bickerwords never grow silent
In the elegy of a great love
Will the liturgical word never come again
With the chorale of the frontierless voices
In a resurrection of the sacred tongue

Shortly after the attack on Pearl Harbor, I received notice that I had been accepted for an editorial position in the Office of the United States Co-ordinator of Information, as it was then called, on Madison Avenue. This section became the nucleus of the vast organization later to be known as the OWI—Office of War Information—which almost immediately occupied an entire building on West Fifty-seventh Street. I can honestly say that this was to be the greatest of my experiences as an American newspaperman. For while I was in the employ of Uncle Sam, first in New York, then in England, France and Germany, I was able to utilize the sum of my acquisitions in a professional trilingual capacity. I was to send millions of words in all three of my languages, words that soon became explosive as rockets against the Axis war-machine.

At the OWI I worked first with the German Section, writing news and feature items in German for the Stimme Amerikas (Voice of America) under Dick Hottelet, a former UP correspondent in Berlin, who knew the language. Some months later I was transferred to the French department, where I prepared news items for radio transmission in French to occupied

France. However, I did not like the inflammable and rather tempestuous atmosphere of that division, and was greatly relieved when the chief, Ed Barrett, suggested that I join him in a new section, in process of organization, to be called Cables Wireless. I now began to prepare a news-file in French "cable-ese," which was beamed to Léopoldville and Brazzaville, in the French and Belgian Congos, as well as to the Antilles. We worked a split-shift, twice a day (that is, from ten in the morning until twelve in the afternoon, and from six in the evening until midnight), and our task was to make the latest war news and other American news available—and palatable—to French listeners. The hours were tiring at first, but as time went on I grew used to them. The Cables Wireless service was in its infancy then and, besides Barrett and his assistants—Adrian Berwick, Ted Kaghan and John Dunning—the staff was limited to my old Paris friend Louis Atlas, and three others: Jim Sachs, Jack Iams and Jim MacDonald. It is amusing to recall this early stage of the operation, when one thinks that it eventually comprised some six hundred workers, many of whom, as the years passed, were sent on overseas service to the four corners of the globe. Under the direction of Adrian Berwick, the huge organization of American newsmen sent vital information about the far-flung battle lines to England, Scandinavia, Russia, French Africa, the Belgian Congo, the Far East and many other parts of the world. My desk was the only one, however, that "processed" the news into a foreign language. The press-wireless machines crackled day and night, sending out these millions of words of news and encouragement to our allies, sunk in the nightmare of Nazi and fascist occupation.

An additional task that I performed with love was the preparation of a daily file, in English, beamed to American soldiers stationed in Hawaii. This was pure fun, for its purpose was to entertain the GIs in the faraway zone with items about American life. It was composed of the kind of home-town news which brought me into intimate contact with America's smaller communities, and its preparation gave me the illusion of working once more in the atmosphere of a provincial news-office. I was the only French editor in the Cables-Wireless section until the end of 1942 when, after the landings in Africa, the staff was enlarged to supply news to Algeria and Casablanca, and later to other newly conquered regions. The personnel of OWI was representative of a true Allied "Internationale," composed of newspapermen, novelists, poets, cinema experts, photographers, publicity men, radio technicians and administrative agents from all the nations that, at that time, were at war with Hitler and his Axis. Two Americans, Joseph Barnes and Ed Johnson, controlled the entire outfit.

The French Section proper was headed by the American writer Lewis

Galantière and Pierre Lazareff, former editor of *Paris Soir*, who shared supervision of both radio and editorial activities. There was a considerable amount of cerebral force concentrated in this French group, and a collective energy, galvanized by the will to victory and the liberation of France, characterized their efforts. In fact, they were known throughout the service for a kind of wild and brilliant expenditure of intelligence that made their work a model for the other national groups.

I have known many remarkable newsmen in my life, but I think one of the cleverest anywhere is Pierre Lazareff. Unfortunately, he had a violent temper, and his ebullient outbursts were legendary, although he could also be exceeding ingratiating and charming. Because I was in charge of the French desk in the cables department, he tried for nearly a year to bring my service under his jurisdiction. Without success, however. When President Roosevelt recorded his address to the French, on the occasion of the invasion of North Africa, Lazareff was called to the White House as technical supervisor. There were some difficulties, he told us later on, for FDR's accent was not in the best French tradition, and when he said: "J'aime vos fermes, vos villes et vos châteaux," it sounded, at first, as though he had said: "J'aime vos femmes," etc. At Lazareff's suggestion, the president made a second record.

During those years, a number of well-known French literary figures were heard over la Voix de l'Amérique. André Breton presented regular special features, in a remarkably radiogenic voice that was more evocative of the *tribune* or popular orator than of the poet's traditionally pallid speech, and which lent itself admirably to the task in hand. He had one phobia, however, which never failed to arouse hilarious reactions among his colleagues: true to his anti-clericalist convictions, he absolutely refused to read the role of a French curé. Then there was the Franco-Swiss writer, Denis de Rougemont, who also worked in the French Section, as did Georges Duthuit, the French art critic, whose excellent voice and diction made him a valuable member of the group. In fact, Breton, Duthuit, and the ethnologist Lévi-Strauss became the ace speakers of the French radio section of OWI, which included, as well, Philippe Barrès, son of the great Maurice, and Patrick Waldberg, an American citizen who had been reared in France, and who had fought at Dunkirk with the French in 1940.

These men, along with numerous political refugees from Germany, Austria, Italy and other Axis-overrun countries, constituted a new immigration to America. To the other "immigrants" who, like myself, had arrived before the First World War, and who had passed through the desperate storms of inter-racial, linguistic, economic and psychological struggle, they seemed very different and their situation much easier than had been that of their predecessors. To begin with, they were not obliged to fight their way through the jungle of the cosmopolis. Nor were they compelled to live from hand to mouth, to inhabit tenements, to seek a balance in the wilderness of races and languages. Due to the circumstances of America's being at war, they were not even obliged to abandon their native tongue. Indeed everything was done to help them maintain the purity of their language, and the United States government gave them an opportunity not only to make a living, but also to fight the war through assertion of their native words in humanly comfortable circumstances. Certain of them even managed to continue their literary and artistic efforts, for their working hours were brief and pleasant.

For many, however, and I was among them, the purely aesthetic approach to life was now temporarily at an end. I noticed that dynamic news presentation as well as the writing of special features began to influence my style and I began to revert to the old newspaper technique I had used in the American city-rooms of another epoch. My mind, which had lived in the labyrinths of dream-words and "paramyths" for so long, was again in the realistic climate of facts, and linguistic coquetries were relegated to the past. The military vocabulary was filled with neologisms and audacious inventions that excited me, but it was often difficult to find French equivalents in moments of pressure.

Early in 1944 I was told to hold myself in readiness to leave for overseas, and a few weeks later I quit for good the clatter of the teletype machines, the staccato noise of the typewriters and the multilingual talk of my fellow workers in the OWI. That day, after leaving the office, as I walked up Broadway towards Columbus Circle, where the delicate shaft of the Genoese explorer's statue seemed to be storming heaven itself, I knew that I was eager to enter the fray. A raw wind was blowing in from the sea, and I walked through the familiar streets, my head still ringing with the thousands of words, the robust words that we had used in the office. In the war's inferno these words crashed, blasted, strafed, pounded, shelled, roared, wept and shrieked in my inner ear, now in French, now in English, now in German.

In the morning, I had talked over long distance to Jacques in Iowa, and conveyed to him in guarded terms the news of my imminent departure. His emotional reaction to this news had brought a rush of images to my mind. I recalled that most of these same buildings had been standing here when we first landed from Europe. New York had seemed then more like a city of small towns; it had had a quieter, almost Victorian rhythm, and the tall skyscrapers had not yet altered the skyline. Mechanically I walked towards the

DeWitt Clinton High School on Tenth Avenue, where I had once studied English in an alien diaspora. The building was still standing, and seeing it again brought back the nights when I used to arrive there breathless from the grocery store, to plunge into the mysteries of the new language. The grocery, the high school, the OWI — this narrow segment of West Side New York had been the stage on which much of my life had been played. Almost objectively, I wondered: Would I ever see it again? A few days later I left New York for Canada, to sail from "somewhere on the Atlantic coast" for the war zone. When Maria and the children saw me off at Grand Central Station, we little realized that we were not to see each other again for nearly three years. I felt sad, yet elated as the solemn voyage got under way.

I saw Montreal again, and reacted to it with a wing-storm of the imagination. The weather was wintry, the Saint Lawrence was frozen over, a keening wind was blowing through the streets. A few hours after my arrival it began to snow, first in tiny flakes, then in a welter of flurries, and the city became a glinting white vista. The French-Canadian radio announced a blizzard.

Then, one afternoon, the *Indo-Chinois,* with the Cross of Lorraine painted on its masthead, sailed forth from a Canadian port into the Atlantic mist. She was in reality a small freighter, remodeled to accommodate about forty passengers, and her cargo included a number of tanks, canvas-covered and lashed to the deck, for delivery to the war theater. The crew was composed of Norman sailors who had succeeded in reaching the British coast after Dunkirk. They were a rough and ready lot, whose captain too was something of an old sea-dog. Aboard there were a few English women and children, who had gone to Canada during the blitz of 1940, as well as several young English boys who had been sent to Canada during the early days of the war and were now about to enter the army.

The crossing was rough, and the danger from submarines was ever-present, for we were not convoyed. The captain ordered frequent maneuvers, and each time the ship's gun began to blaze, the war seemed to come very near. My "bunkies" were Charlie Eagle, a professional photographer, Sam Berman, a Morse specialist, and a radio expert whose name I forget. Charlie was very entertaining, for he was a good story-teller, and he and I talked and drank our way across the tempestuous wintry ocean. We landed in Liverpool, where we took a train for London. An alert was in progress as our train pulled into the station.

This time we wandered east we came from Canada
nous étions des voyageurs vers la bourrasque de feu
we roamed through space and time through day and night

into the continent of the great dying
nous marchions à travers les déluges et les convulsions
à travers le temps de babel vers une pentecôte de flammes

we were in the city of London on a dreamblue journey
we had crossed the wintersea and were now in ecstatic grief
we walked from early sunglow jusqu'au soir
in sacred tension through the great thundering
we raced through the huge guilt of the oor-father
nous étions en route pour la conquête de la terre des aieux

we roamed up and down in the fearful blackout
we followed the migratory masses of tanks and guns
we were chiliasts racing towards golden utopias
we sought our celestial origin dans la durée
we fearglided out of wombdark vers la mort
in a collective hunger for initiations

London in war-time had an intimate, proud quality, despite the constant aerial danger hovering over the ponderous, cyclopean dwellings, and one felt deep friendliness for its people, swarming fearlessly through the vast city in which countless raids had dug holes and left numerous fissures. At first we were billeted near Hyde Park. Here it seemed almost miraculous that in war-time the usual eccentric orators and dispensers of utopian *nostra* should still be able to say their word in an atmosphere of democratic liberty, as though the peace had never been disturbed. On the other hand, in the gloomy circumfusion of the blackouted masonry, we seemed to have returned to the time of Magdalenian man, and the sight of thousands of families living in the cavern-like shelters of the underground inspired a sense of genuine anguish.

I was assigned to the Psychological Warfare Division of SHAEF, a position that required me to work at night in a former cinema building on Wardour Street. At first the frequent alerts, with their wailing crescendos and decrescendos, rattled my nervous system considerably, and the weird sounds followed me into my sleep. Gradually, however, my friends and I grew used to the new acoustic climate, and soon we were able to jest about our life of chaos and the unwonted noises made by man's blatant engines. After a while, one seemed to be living in some sirius-far immensity, among astronomic nebulae, or on a vast, forgotten planet. Even our language began to take on an other-worldly quality of mystery and runic lore.

In our offices, British, American and French newsmen and women worked side by side, and a comradely spirit reigned among them. At first, I was part of a team that prepared a "basic news" file in English to be used for translation into other languages and beamed to occupied Europe and Africa. This service was organized with great efficiency by Jim Hart and his British counterpart, Merwyn Herbert, both top-flight journalists. A short time later, the service was moved to a large building near Bush House, on the Strand, where the British Broadcasting Station was located. When the buzz-bombs started coming over, the front seemed closer, and there were moments of deep anxiety when the house shook. Once we watched a bus being smashed by a bomb, and saw the dead and dying passengers lying on the pavement below. In the beginning the alert sounded each time, but this precaution was soon abandoned, and all one heard was the thunder of the diabolical machines in the air, as they raced over London. Somehow, one always expected to hear the explosive thud over one's own head. Towards the end of April, I moved from the English news-desk to the newly established French desk, where members of de Gaulle's Free French Ministry of Information were working.

During this period I got to know many Central European refugees who had escaped to London since 1938, men and women whose entire lives were centered on the hope of seeing their mutilated homes liberated and rebuilt after an Allied victory. They passed through this heart-harrowing period like other Londoners, uncomplainingly, and it was a tribute to English tolerance that they could speak their native tongues in buses, offices and other public places without remonstrance on the part of their hosts. However, they often expressed homesickness for their far-off lands and they liked to evoke the days when they had been free, democratic citizens of their various republics, living sheltered lives in what seemed now to have been tranquil ease. They talked of families they had left behind, and wondered anxiously when, if ever, they would meet again. They were Czechs, Poles, Austrians, Hungarians, Germans, and of course many Jews, from every country on the Continent. London was becoming a kind of New York melting-pot of races and languages, and I liked to listen to the multilingual utterances of my new neighbors.

In our Maida Vale boarding house, where many of these exiled nationals were living, the boarders all got up at night when V-1 bombs flew over London. They congregated in the basement, where our landlady and her pretty daughter served tea. On these occasions, the dog Brownie, sensing the outside disturbance, trembled violently. After a cemetery-like silence that seemed to last sometimes for an unconscionable period, suddenly all hell would break loose, and a terrific explosion would rock the house, while everyone sat pale and rigid. When the report came: "Quite a distance away!" we trekked sleepily back to bed.

Intellectual life in London during the height of the war was intense and daring. Cyril Connolly's *Horizon* put the accent on European-American contributions, and provided a platform for the best critical minds of the period. The poetry of such younger writers as Alex Comfort, Nicholas Moore, Ruthven Todd, Dylan Thomas, Francis Scarfe, Anne Ridler, Henry Treece, and many others, had a metaphysical quality. There was a violent controversy between Stephen Spender, who favored the poetic expression of positive faith in the democratic aims of the war, and Alex Comfort and his friends, who were for a poetry expressed in terms of suffering. A review, *La France Libre,* edited by André Labarthe, kept alive the traditions of French thought and managed to present a florilegium of distinguished writing.

Although we worked long hours in the news-room, I managed in odd moments to scribble a few poems that reflected the tormented visions of war-time London days and nights. Sometimes, when I returned home from the office, I saw entire families bedding down in the underground for a night of horror in the subterranean shelters. Among them were young and old women with sorrow-furrowed faces, as well as countless children living with their macabre nocturnes, while aboveground violent aerial combats filled the sky.

ANATHEMA

Lumor said
Curses on you, Hitler, defamer of the Sacred!
Black distorter of the Inventive Genius!
You have trodden underfoot the creative law of Man!

All your dreams are dreams of destruction
Your fantasies look into far spaces
Where rubbleruins gape into glareskies
Where mutilated children sing no longer
Their fairy-tale ditties of sleep and laughter
Your fantasies project the giant machines
That have lost the beneficent symbol
Of helping to soothe the ache-pain of mankind
The prehistoric anguish of the lonely
For your machines are Devil's work they sow

Terror over the planetary order
They are the monstrous reality of your evil brain
That carries the dark weight of your chimeras
They are in love with violent death they bruise
And slash and blight they hurt life's deepest nostalgia
For sheen-white hours for archangelic stillness
They try to kill man's hunger for the stars

Curses on you, Hitler, defamer of the Sacred!
And curses on your mother's evil womb!

On the night of June 6, 1944, I was working at Bush House with the French contingent, supervising the processing and radio transmission of news to the Continent. We were tense and tired, for we knew, from many signs, that the invasion of the Continent was quite near. British, American and French editors were busy transcribing the latest Moscow communiqués detailing advances in the East, and there was an electric mood among them, as the hours tick-tocked by. Shortly after midnight, we decided to go over to the mess-hall of the British Information Services for a brief midnight snack. London lay quietly under the bright rays of a full moon, and Fleet Street was deserted. Someone remarked, "A good time for the Nazis to come over . . ." We did not tarry long in the vast mess-hall where dozens of international journalists were seated at little tables, and were soon on our way back to the Bush House.

When we reached the clattering teletype machines the keyboard was hammering out the Reuters message: "INVASION ON, SAYS DNB." There was a tremendous shout of relief, but we had to wait a long time before the news was actually released officially. It had apparently been a great scoop for Reuters, and we learned later than one of their listening stations had obtained this first news of the landing through the German radio's broadcast of a dispatch from the Nazi agency, DNB (Deutsches Nachrichten-Bureau).

We did not go to bed at all that morning and, in fact, only left the office towards noon, after SHAEF had released the news. By that time everything was set to tell the French that we were on our way.

Our PWD-SHAEF convoy, consisting of a detachment of seventy men under the command of a regular U.S. officer, left London in jeeps and weapons-carriers in early July, for a point on the coast from where we were to embark for France. V-1 attacks had been growing in intensity, and news of additional Allied landings had heightened our desire to participate in the struggle on the soil of continental Europe. I had been appointed chief of an Anglo-American "Field Press Team," whose esprit de corps proved immediately to be exemplary. We rode all day through the lush English countryside, and by the time we reached the tent camp near the port of embarkation, a young moon was glimmering over the spectral landscape. That night we got little sleep, for we were alerted very early next morning in order to receive final instructions from our military chiefs. We were transported to the port in a driving rain. On the way, we joined combat soldiers in a Red Cross tent, where American and British girls were serving hot coffee and doughnuts. The ebullient banter and persiflage of this brief pause lifted our rain-soaked spirits.

We finally embarked on one of those miracles of modern nautical construction, the LST. Although we were packed in like the proverbial sardines, there was an almost collegiate joviality among the men, which took the form of card-playing in the cabins and ribald singing of songs from the North African campaign. The crossing was slowly and cautiously made and there were several alerts, but nothing serious happened. Towards dusk on the following day, we saw the outline of the French coast.

When we landed on "Utah Beach," on the tip of the Cotentin Peninsula, my bunk-mate Morris Gilbert and I performed a pre-arranged rite: we picked up a handful of French loam and put it in a little tin can to be deposited as a sacred souvenir in our musette bags. Facing us was the Atlantic Wall, now guarded by GIs, and we thought with gratitude of the boys who had breached it only a short time before. The day was windy, dark clouds were chasing across the sky, and we had to wait a long time in an open field while endless lines of U.S. infantrymen disembarked from the transports in the harbor; Sainte-Mère-l'Eglise, where terrific fighting had taken place, already looked deserted. Soon, however, a few Norman farmers arrived and began to talk to us.

That night we slept on board ship with a detachment of wounded American parachutists who had just captured Cherbourg and were returning to England. We listened, awed, to their stories of the battle. The next day our caravan passed through numerous ruined towns and villages, as we drove across the wild, summergreen Norman land, en route for Cherbourg. We bivouacked in a grainfield, our tents pitched in the open country as in Brady's pictures of the American Civil War. Towards midnight, enemy shelling began. Half seriously, half in jest, Sam Berman, the Morse specialist, left his tent and shouted: "You Nazi bastards! Don't you know I want to sleep?" It was just what was needed to relax our rather taut nerves. The next forenoon we arrived in the outskirts of Cherbourg, which showed signs of recent heavy fighting, although the center of the town was intact.

We settled provisionally in a house on the Rue Nationale, but were obliged to organize our mess in a building across the street, where the Nazis had kept a brothel for the Wehrmacht. This was evidenced by the fact that some of the girls were still about. All our rooms were littered with Nazi magazines and newspapers indicating that the enemy had counted on holding the Atlantic Wall.

Now our work began in earnest. I was assigned to act as censor for Radio Cherbourg, which Bravig Imbs and Ira Watkins were operating from an old fort on a hill outside the port. To this were added the duties of psychological censor of the local newspaper which my old Havas friend, Capt. Fernand Auberjonois, had just re-launched. In addition, I began to give French lessons to some of our men. We set up a monitoring system in the office, hired several local engineers and monitors, and were soon supplying the paper with news of the war's progress.

The owner of the paper had continued, during the German occupation, according to Goebbels's orders, and a perusal of the files showed a plethora of anti-British, anti-Gaullist, anti-American sentiments that might well have been written in Berlin. Soon a team from the Gaullist Ministry of Information, most of whose members I had known in London, arrived to interview the editor. With other Allied control officers, I listened as he pleaded his cause with his countrymen. At first the Gaullists maintained a contemptuous silence. Then they asked a few pointed questions, to which he replied with obvious embarrassment. When the proceedings were over, as we walked out of the office, Capt. Claude Dauphin, the well-known actor, took me aside: "*Le salaud*," he said, "he certainly did collaborate."

After the capture of Rennes, our team moved into the Breton capital, cheered by delirious crowds all along the way. This was especially true near Avrances, where the enemy was still resisting. In Rennes, where we were greeted with bottles of eau de vie, I took over from another press team headed by Jan Hasbrouck. A few days later we had repeated the Cherbourg experience and were ready to move on.

With two French comrades, Lt. Colin and Captain Lasalle, who belonged to the London Gaullist contingent, I was sent on a mission into the Breton maquis. On a bright, sunny morning, we jeeped into Dinan, then headed for Chatelaudren and St.-Brieuc. At every step our jeep was surrounded by jubilant crowds, and there were the same embracings and liquid liberalities on each occasion. Sometimes we were led to the main square of the town and treated to a sample of the Breton people's vengeance on traitors and collaborators. We watched several pretty girls in St.-Brieux being shorn of their locks under the gaze of the irreverent public, after which they were led around the town to be jeered at by the populace. In one street a caterwauling crowd surrounded quite an old woman who had been delivered to the barber because, we were told, "she had been kind to the Germans and unkind to the French during the occupation." It was not an edifying spectacle.

In each town we made an inventory of available printing establishments and the needs of the local press. Not a single newspaper was being published in the whole of Brittany, and people were relying for news on the village garagist or local electrician, who set up his radio with a loud-speaker at certain specified hours. To remedy this condition, we decided to have wall-sheets printed, and thus disseminate the war news through the larger towns.

A deep blue summer sky gleamed over the lovely Breton landscape as we jeeped from town to town. We came upon U.S. tank detachments getting ready to go into battle. We passed wretched refugees from Brest and St.-Malo tramping wearily along the white roads. We saw trucks filled with German prisoners of war, and observed the French crowds mocking and shouting at them.

The first night in Morlaix, where we stayed several days, was eventful. Although the greater part of the German forces had been driven into nearby Brest, large bands of stragglers were still roving the countryside, and the FFI were busy clearing them out. We had hardly gone upstairs to snatch a few hours' sleep when we heard the rattle of machine-guns, apparently directly in front of the house. We hurried down into the lobby and found that the FFI had brought in a number of German prisoners, several of them wounded, who had been caught in the town after the blackout. During a candlelight council of war, the American major in charge of the combat team that had taken the town two days before discussed plans for an attack, in which the FFI were to participate, on a German redoubt just outside the town. The plan was carried out successfully early next morning.

All day long trucks arrived packed with Wehrmacht prisoners captured during the sporadic battles of the Breton countryside. The men were taken to a school building in the center of the town, where they were lined up in the courtyard for the benefit of the crowds that stood outside watching the proceedings with amused delight. Our friends of the Resistance lent a welcome hand in organizing the prisoner convoys, comparing notes with American captors and occasionally weeding out a particularly notorious war criminal of the region.

One day, as a truck filled with Nazis drove up to the school, two French officers and I passed by in our jeep, on our way to a meeting with French newspapermen whom we suspected of having followed the Pétainist directives too closely. There was a roar of scoffing shouts from the townspeople, who immediately began to gather around the prisoners. One of the Germans, seeing American uniforms, looked our way and moaned: "Wasser, Wasser . . ." "Va demander à Hitler," a young member of the Maquis answered derisively.

We usually gathered at Resistance headquarters late in the evening. There we listened to heroic tales told by the members of the Maquis, several of whom had been wounded and crippled in encounters with the Germans. One evening, Lt. Col. Rolland, chief of the Maquis forces, related the circumstances of torture inflicted upon a comrade who, after having parachuted in, had been betrayed. "We caught the traitor a few days ago," he said, "and we shot him down like a dog." The same evening a member of his squad, armed with a *mitraillette,* burst into the room and tearfully insisted on seeing the chief privately. We waited a long time until Lt. Col. Rolland reappeared, somewhat excited, and told us that the *maquisard* had intervened on behalf of his *maîtresse,* a young girl the Resistance had just arrested for collaboration. This girl had apparently had a child by a German soldier during the occupation, and was in process of being questioned.

"What did you tell him?" we asked.

"I told him that his *putain* deserved *quelques balles dans la peau,*" came the prompt reply. Cruelty and oppression have rarely bred pity, and the French Maquis was no exception.

The following days were spent in making the usual inventory of the printing plants in the region. The principal shop housed that of the local paper—the *Journal de Brest et Morlaix*—which had issued its last pro-Nazi edition a few days earlier. We found, scattered about the now silent offices, numerous copies bristling with Goebbels and Vichy propaganda. It was an eerie experience, this trip through a newspaper plant in which the linotype machines were mute, the rotary presses motionless, and not a single worker to be seen anywhere. Several members of the staff, on hearing that we were making an investigation, hastened to explain why they had "collaborated" with the Nazis. But Lt. Colin, who had been a printer himself in Poitou, and had fled to England in 1941 in order to join the Gaullist forces, replied firmly: "The fact is, however, that you did *collaborate.* What you should have done was to close your shop and try to get other work."

After a few days we decided to push on to Quimperlé and, if possible, continue as far as Lorient. We started out by jeep in a south-westerly direction, but on hearing the roar of mortars and siege-guns, realized that we were in the neighborhood of Brest, which was under attack by American forces. We changed to a more southerly direction, and were soon in the heart of the Maquis, far removed from any Allied contingents. Lt. Colin was cheery, and fondled his mitraillette with loving hands. From the farmers we heard rumors of the sudden appearance of scattered German detachments in towns and villages, the murder of civilians, the seizure of hostages. In a number of Breton villages through which we passed, the people seemed frightened, for they felt the proximity of the ever-moving front.

As we reached the outskirts of one little village, we heard the noises of shooting. A girl came running towards us to say that the *Boches* were there, fighting it out with the FFIs. We stopped our jeep and decided to drive in slowly, while the two French officers held their mitraillettes in readiness. Just beyond the first house we could see a German truck backing into the road. The two Gaullists opened fire, but it was too late: the Germans escaped. Soon two civilians stepped out of a shed, and when they recognized Allied uniforms, started towards us. They told us that an attack had been made on the village by two truckloads of Germans who had killed several members of the FFI and wounded a woman. The Nazis had also liberated six of their own comrades who had been captured several days before and were being held for transfer to Quimper the following day. From each house, men, women and children began to emerge. Young boys, members of the FFI, appeared with their machine-guns. Meanwhile the two German trucks had been seen on the road to Quimper, and it was supposed that their former occupants were probably living in the nearby forest. There was great excitement on all faces, as details of the attack were told. "The next time, we won't take any prisoners," said one youth, fingering his machine-gun.

We continued our tour of inspection, which took us over the same road that the Nazis had undoubtedly taken before us. It was a hazardous thing to do, but we had to take the risk. We did not meet a single Allied vehicle, and we knew that if we were attacked we would have to depend on our own resources. As it turned out, the journey was quite uneventful, and we arrived at Quimper towards noon. Once more a great crowd gathered around our jeep, for it was the first Allied vehicle to reach the town since the FFIs had driven the Germans out two days before. The inhabitants told us with fear in their eyes that the Germans might come back any moment. "Tell the Americans to hurry," they urged.

We stopped at a print-shop, made the necessary inventory, and at ten had a quick bite in a hotel, where we met three Allied officers who had parachuted into the maquis a few weeks before the landing. One was British, one French, and the other American. The American told us that the situation was unsafe, and asked us to take a message to Allied headquarters in

Rennes. They needed reinforcements, he said, since the Nazis were just outside town. We delivered the message late that night in Rennes.

With the liberation of Paris, a cry of rhapsodic joy at deliverance from the Nazi incubus rose throughout France, and the summer itself became an elegiac poem. Not long after this event, our cars were speeding along through the Beauce countryside, past Chartres and Mantes, through the villages of the Île de France. When we finally sighted the Eiffel Tower we shouted in a kind of delirium. By now we were in a tangle of American jeeps and trucks to which were added a number of Paris autobuses returning from their four-year exile in the provinces. At dusk, as we crossed the Seine at Neuilly, I caught a glimpse of the house I had lived in before the war. We rolled down the Champs-Elysées through a mad whorl of frenetic Parisians yelling their heads off.

On the boulevards we were greeted by never-to-be-forgotten sights and sounds. The tanks of Gen. Leclerc's First Division were much in evidence, and the streets swarmed with Allied soldiers, accompanied by happy girls in wooden shoes, clop-clopping on the macadam. Others, on bicycles, rode gaily through the streets, their summer skirts swelling like sails. Although the blackout still obtained, and there was even an occasional enemy air attack, the population felt safe in the as yet almost incredible presence of friendly armies. American GIs conversed with the Parisians in a language all their own.

Our PWD was quartered in a building on the Rue Pierre Charron under the command of Gen. Robert A. McClure, with Luther Conant acting as press chief. I was given the immediate task of organizing a radio-monitoring bureau, and meanwhile, preparations for entering Germany were being mapped out. It was understood that I was later to become a member of the German-language staff.

In my off-moments, I wandered through the old, familiar streets. The city had lost none of its tenderness and beauty, none of its essential *sagesse*. Walking along the Seine, or leaning over the bridge-railings to watch its flow, an occasional yellowed leaf, gentle sign of coming autumn, evoked the languid Symbolist verses I had loved so much. I also took in a number of art exhibitions, among them one at the Palais de Chaillot, where Picasso was showing his war-time productions. Paris was still sick, but its fever was accompanied by clear vision, and one had a sense of stirring things to come. I met old friends who had spent the war in resistance to the enemy. I also heard of others who had been Pétainists or had even betrayed France and the Allies.

One forenoon Morris Gilbert and I went for a walk in the quarter I liked best, the famous *carrefour* of St.-Germain-des-Prés. As we took our seats on the *terrasse* of the Café de Flore, we felt content just to watch the crowds walk past in the sunlight. We recognized a number of painters and writers, among them my pre-war friend, Raymond Queneau. He had become slightly gray, but his eyes had lost none of their witty sparkle. We spoke of the difficult years of the occupation and the Resistance, and exchanged news of mutual friends scattered across two continents by the hazard of war. That day we lunched together at a black-market restaurant in the Rue de Bourgogne. Gilbert and I were a little astonished at the abundance of food served, but enjoyed the Lucullan meal none the less, and drank the delicious wine *con gusto*. Conversation was animated, and questions hailed from every corner of the restaurant; particularly concerning André Breton and those of his Surrealist friends who had been living and working in New York during the war years.

Queneau gave me a little book of his poems, *Les Ziaux*, which he had published during the war, and the title of which was a Joycean compound of *yeux* and *eaux*. He talked interestingly of his use of the spoken language, adding that he was experimenting with Paris slang and was planning a book in which it would be used. He also told us about the new school of Existentialist philosophy which had developed during the war, expressing admiration for certain creative manifestations of that doctrine.

As we sat there drinking a weak cognac, I watched the faces of several young men and women in gaudy shirts who were seated nearby. I also listened to their intellectual baragouin, a language of extraordinary argotisms and revolt. Superficially it was the vocabulary of the boogie-woogie, the be-bop and the jitterbug, but through it emerged a sense of tragedy and instability that was overpowering. Very evidently the Existentialist mythos dominated everything, and its prophet was Jean-Paul Sartre. Yet Sartre had already announced that these moths around the flame had nothing to do with him, or he with them. He had, however, seized upon the Zeitgeist with rare acuity, and certainly it was he who, whether intentionally or not, set in motion an "attitude" that lent itself only too easily to the kind of anarchic disorder these young people typified.

During the weeks that followed, I worked at headquarters and roamed the streets absorbing the mood of renascence which was beginning to be manifest throughout the sad and beautiful city. I sought out certain of my favorite cafés near the Gare du Nord, where one could sit under wind-rustling trees, or in the Gare St.-Lazare district, where a human swarm spread over the streets in a continuous metamorphosis of faces. On the terrasses, I entered into casual conversation with many young men and women, usually shoddily clad, and I found them, for the most part, intensely alive and intelligent. I was relieved to see that in this respect France had not changed; there was still ceaseless discussion, new and old names in literature and the arts sounded magically in the air. The name of Sartre cropped up again and again, and I recalled that back in the late thirties, when he was teaching at the Lycée Pasteur in Neuilly, he had patronized the same corner café as I did. Hearing these youngsters talk of him reminded me of the flaming conversations he used to have with his pupils in the little back room of the *tabac*. I remembered, too, with what excited interest I had read his early novel, *La Nausée,* just before the outbreak of the war.

But although there was much talk of Existentialism, Surrealism was not entirely forgotten, and the review *Fontaine,* which Max Pol Fouchet had founded in Algiers during the war, had just published Breton's prolegomena to a "new Surrealist manifesto." In fact, certain of the young men we talked with were awaiting Breton's return with great impatience. There was also much enthusiasm for American writing, and several people asked for news of Henry Miller and William Faulkner. Unfortunately, I was unable to satisfy their curiosity, not having seen either during my stay in the United States.

But how many specters walked with me through the streets of liberated Paris! At every street corner I was reminded that Joyce was gone; coming back to Paris had re-opened the wound. His great friend and adviser, Paul Léon, who was also my friend, had perished in a Nazi concentration camp. My German friend Carl Einstein, aware that the same fate awaited him, had committed suicide during the *exode,* after having set out, with his wife, for Spain. But there was not only the sense of personal loss. The whole population had witnessed numerous heroic deaths, and groups gathered daily around each spot where members of the Paris Maquis had fallen during the recent fighting for the liberation of the city. With the awe and respect for death so characteristic of the French, men, women and children stared silently at the little notices scrawled by bereaved hands, at the wreaths and bouquets that marked each hallowed bit of pavement.

There were other, less distressing street scenes, however, that one had always associated with Paris, and which seemed quite timeless in character. On the Place de la Bastille, a *foire* was in progress, the same sort of foire that had traveled from one neighborhood to another ever since I had known the city. The music of the merry-go-round was perhaps a little creakier than before, and at first the gaiety seemed a little forced. But as evening wore on and the square became enveloped in a crepuscular mist, crowds of young people began to gather and the age-old spectacle gradually became what it had always been. A familiar figure was the fire-eater, the only change in his act being that he now attributed his lowly state to the Boches. But he blew the same trumpet, drew the same crowds of curious onlookers, collected the same hatful of coins before swallowing the same mysterious flame. And even the feigned horror on people's faces, as they watched him wipe his soot-covered mouth with his filthy handkerchief, was the same. In spite of all its sufferings, the city had not really changed very much.

Our team being scheduled to Nancy, which, we understood, was now in American hands, I was sent in late September on a roving expedition to the eastern battle-line. With me were Lt. Jean Tessier, an officer of Gen. de Gaulle's Free French Forces, and an American Morse operator named Abraham Grober. We got no further than the ancient town of Toul, in Lorraine, where we learned from staff officers that the news of the capture of Nancy had been premature. At the Moselle River we joined a group of American officers and GIs waiting to cross. A barrage of fire was in progress on the other bank and the inhabitants were watching the phenomenon in a stupor of fear. "We'll probably reach Nancy tomorrow," an American captain told us, "but you boys'll have to be patient . . ." At that moment a shell crashed over our heads, then buried itself in an abandoned factory. Despite the fact that MPs advised us to turn back, we decided to remain in the region and succeeded in finding billets near headquarters for the night.

At noon on the following day, we were told that the road to Nancy was open, and our weapons-carrier got under way immediately. The damage in Toul was not very heavy, but as we neared Nancy we found destruction in many villages. We entered the Lorraine capital in the afternoon. Here one felt the excitement of the front; the town was filled with American troops, and heavy ordnance clattered almost incessantly through the charmingly designed districts of the liberated city. We halted on the Place Stanislas—one of the architectural wonders of the world—then signed in at headquarters where we were given billets with an infantry regiment near the station. I knew the town well, so decided to take a quick look around. There were few ruins, for the Germans had been obliged to pull out quickly, because of the speed of our advance. They were still in force on the other side of the Meurthe River, however, and the shooting was uncomfortably near.

That night I slept badly. It had begun to rain hard, and Grober and I sat disconsolately in the lobby of a billet to which was attached a GI mess. Outside, the big guns boomed and shook the house. A few frightened Nancyans came in to report the wild rumors circulating among the French population: that the Boches were about to re-enter the city; that the SS had recaptured a factory on the outskirts and were holding both men and women as hostages. We assured them that there was no truth in these stories. Around midnight I ran into Capt. Claude Dauphin, whom I had last seen in Cherbourg. He was accompanied by a beautiful girl, whom he introduced as a member of the Lorraine Resistance. She had just passed the line and been shot at by the enemy, as a result of which she had an ugly arm wound.

"She's come to get help for the Maquis," said Capt. Dauphin. She wanted to return that night, but we decided she should see a doctor first. I was much moved by this scene. Although deathly pale, this heroic girl had the flame of determination in her eyes. Later I learned that she had been treated by an American medical officer and had returned during the night, supplied with the material she had come for.

The next morning, Grober and I began working in the plant of the local paper, *L'Est Républicain,* where the building was fortunately intact. As Grober installed his Morse machine, I began to choose war news copy for the paper, which was about to reappear under the new name of *L'Est Républicain Libéré.* During the war the Nazis had called the paper *L'Echo de Nancy* (the people of Nancy had called it *L'Echo de Berlin*), and had made of it a typical Goebbels sheet, filled with Nazi propaganda and lies. Numerous copies of these occupation issues were still lying about, and it was interesting to see the degree of infamy to which totalitarian journalism had stooped. I felt strongly that one of the prerequisites of a democratic revival in Europe would be the spread of objective reporting, and determined that I would do everything in my power to introduce a more honest conception of journalism into Germany, once the war had reached the land of the enemy.

In Nancy I worked in close cooperation with members of the Maquis, and in a few days got to know their history. The head of the Lorraine Resistance movement was Jacques Zenner, a man of grave, provincial urbanity, who had been put in charge of the new paper. We had many illuminating talks, in the course of which he expatiated wittily on the clandestine struggle against the infiltration of turgid Germanic platitudes that had taken place during the four years just past. He was a native of Metz, I learned — a typical *homme de la frontière* — and had gone to school there before World War I. He spoke and wrote both French and German with equal facility. His French style, embodied in powerful editorials, struck me as possessing a quasi-classical texture. When I commented on this, he said casually that he had studied Latin and Greek in a Catholic lycée in Metz.

"Not Montigny?" I asked, intrigued.

"Precisely," he said. In other words, we had been schoolmates in the same school at about the same time, before my first return to the United

States. We talked at length of former teachers and companions, and evoked many half-forgotten personalities and incidents.

Electric current being available only for a restricted period, after 8:00 P.M., Grober and I usually worked at the plant throughout the night. I wrote news-stories and features, and helped with the make-up, whenever possible. It was an eerie experience, for the Meurthe battle was approaching its climax, and when, occasionally, the noisy grunt of artillery came very near, even the compositors standing before their Mergenthaler machines grew nervous. During that week there was an early curfew forbidding the civilian population to be in the streets after sundown, so I had to obtain special permits from headquarters for the editorial and technical staff. I fought many a skirmish with administrative pedants who, in war-time, could usually be defeated by a certain innocent ruthlessness. I was also in close touch with the special *commissaire* appointed by Gen. de Gaulle, and in his vast bureau, overlooking the Place Stanislas, sat in on deliberations concerning the fate to be meted out to certain pro-Nazi collaborators. Members of the Resistance were pursuing an *épuration* of their own, and they made short shrift of obvious traitors. There were others, however, whose avowed Pétainism required subtler measures.

Gen. de Gaulle visited the city during pouring rain, and addressed the population massed on the Place Stanislas. I had heard him make a speech under similar circumstances in Rennes, immediately after the capture of that city, when the enthusiasm had been great. Now I noticed that people seemed to manifest a certain critical reticence. I was also obliged to register the fact that American and other Allied participation in the victory was somewhat glossed over in his speech. But there was little time to waste on de Gaulle's personal and national pride. Now that the battle of Nancy was ended, American forces were driving towards the Saar, and Metz was already under siege by Gen. Patton's army. Grober and I continued to keep in touch with the editorial work, but since news communication had now become easier, we decided to return to Paris for new assignments.

As the Battle of the Bulge got under way, I was transferred to Radio Luxembourg to act as German-language supervisor, and, in this capacity, was ordered to join a large group of Psychological Warfare Division men near the front, where the Nazis were trying desperately to break through our lines. I left Paris in a weapons-carrier early one cold morning, but as we passed through the abandoned "Little Maginot Line," we ran into a blizzard which held us up for quite a while. We saw numerous American tanks rumbling to the front through the little French and Luxembourg villages, and the surrounding landscape was dotted with snow-covered, burned-out cars and tanks that looked like huge eviscerated insects. Shivering with cold, we arrived in the Luxembourg capital late in the afternoon. As we drove through one of the principal streets, a few enemy planes roared over the city, sending the ack-ack guns into action. The population, which had been anxiously watching the American tanks as they clattered over the wide, snow-crunched avenues, scattered rapidly in every direction. We new-comers soon had the impression of a city entirely deserted by its civilian inhabitants.

I called on Lt. Col. Rosenbaum, chief of the radio station, and he put me to work in the news-room that same night. Our announcers went on the air at regular intervals, speaking to Nazi Germany with news coverage on the progress of the war and special features designed to undermine the German will to fight. It was a savage war of words we were engaged in, and the young American soldiers who had been detached for this linguistic offensive were heart and soul in the battle. This strategic and technical job was conceived in terms of journalistic technique, for we were now speaking directly to the enemy population and even addressed the Wehrmacht during the fighting through means of "black," or clandestine, counter-propaganda.

Echoes of the battle came to us constantly, for the Germans were trying their best to recapture the city, especially the valuable and modernistically designed radio station, or *Funkhaus,* where, on entering a large vestibule, one was struck by a comic sight: a monumental statue of Hitler had been overthrown and was lying on the floor, face downward. Often during the day the guns sounded with a terrifying din that shook the building, and at night, when we walked through the blackout to the mess-hall for quick re-freshments, we could hear the crash of shells being hurled at the railroad station by enemy artillery. One soon grew used to the noise, however, and once we were back in our billets, we were so weary that we were even able to sleep through it.

While the battle was crashing against the city of Luxembourg, life among the natives went on with its customary quietude. A number of local young men and women, typists and technical experts, were working with us in the Funkhaus. I was struck by the joie de vivre of these people, their gen-erosity and courage—a characteristic to be found in this central zone of Western Europe all the way from Alsace to Holland. Despite the oppression from which Gen. Patton and his Third Army had freed them only a week before, despite their anxiety about the fate of some twelve thousand men whom the Nazis had forced into the Wehrmacht, the natural grit and equa-ble temperament of young and old were exemplary. Many war-mutilated men could be seen in the streets, and we heard stories of the deportation to Dachau and Auschwitz of over five thousand anti-Nazis and Jews.

I was struck by the architectural loveliness of this historic city, which had been politically free for centuries before Hitler destroyed its liberty. Above the Alzette and Petrusse Rivers could be seen many parts of the old town, and I recalled, from my history books, that this was a country through which war and devastation had always passed, that the city had been a fortress from time immemorial. Although a tiny monarchy, it had never been autocratic, and parliamentary democracy had been the outstanding feature of its evolution. In the shops on the main street could be seen large pictures of the beloved Grand Duchess Charlotte, then in exile in the United States, whose return was expected soon. But the GIs who passed through on their way to the front had no time to look around, for they were but part of the huge fighting machine. Many of them lie buried in a vast military cemetery at Hamm, in the wooded outskirts of Luxembourg City, where Gen. Patton, too, sleeps his eternal sleep.

Working hours at the radio station were long and tiring. News of the war was channeled through the Office of War Information in New York, and our staff had to process it into acceptable German. The German-speaking radio announcers then transmitted it to the enemy countries. Our words were martial and charged with printed psychological intentions.

A former Austro-Hungarian, Capt. Hans Habe, author of *A Thousand Shall Fall,* and himself a remarkable German-language journalist, was already editing a newspaper for the Germans called *Mitteilungen,* which was supervised by the Twelfth Army Group and dropped over the German lines. Every day at 2:00 P.M. there was a conference in the office of the PWD chief, Bill Hale, in the course of which the news and feature editors discussed the events of the day. These discussions were led by Hale and his deputy, a talented civilian named Newsome, formerly of the London BBC, whose duty it was to analyze the latest Nazi propaganda line as monitored by our service during the day. They then made specific recommendations as to the manner in which various developments at the front or in the political sphere were to be handled. Habe was supposed to edit his *Mitteilungen* from the standpoint of these directives, and we of the German radio section did the same. But when the *Mitteilungen* appeared, it was patterned on the style of pre-war Vienna newspapers — which were never real newspapers, in fact, only half-literary, half-editorial concoctions. I contended that the immediate use of American newspaper make-up and reportorial techniques would break the enemy reader's long habit, instilled in him by Goebbels, of reading "commentaries" on the day's news — or that other form of journalistic poison, the feuilleton—instead of information. Later, when I started the first German-language newspapers in Aachen and Heidelberg, I insisted upon their being strictly American in both style and make-up. I was gratified to see that this pattern, which had been instituted more for its shock value than with any illusion of possible survival, continued to be followed by certain German papers in the American zone even after they had been licensed for independent publication.

11

JOURNEY THROUGH RUBBLELAND

It was during that same bitter winter of 1944–45 that our special press-control team, under the command of Col. James Chesnutt, set out from Brussels for Germany. Our objective was Aachen, the newly captured Rhineland city in which we were to found the first local newspaper to be printed in the German language under the auspices of the American army. The Battle of the Bulge was still raging as our little convoy made its way through a blinding blizzard across Belgium and Holland to the German frontier. A few kilometers further on, Aachen emerged spectrally from out the white whorl. A harsh wind organed through the half-battered Hindenburgstraße, while we settled ourselves in the oil-stove–heated office of the former manager of the *Aachener Politisches Tageblatt.* The city being still in the immediate proximity of the front, the crash of big guns could be heard day and night. At first we were unnerved by the din, then gradually grew used to it.

In the old-fashioned three-story building that until only a short while before had housed the printing plant of the *Tageblatt,* we were soon deep in preparations for launching the new paper, and one week after our arrival the first issue of the *Aachener Nachrichten* appeared. For the position of German manager we settled upon an elderly printer, Heinrich Hollands, whose anti-Nazi record had impressed us. I myself was obliged temporarily to assume the function of general editor, local reporter, war news editor, headline writer, proof-reader and make-up man. It was not long, however, before we had succeeded in finding additional anti-Nazi printers and editorial assistants, including a number of young Germans, both men and women, in whom we succeeded in rapidly inculcating the spirit of American reporting. I introduced them to the summary court recently instituted

12. Press officer Jolas in Aachen, March 1945. Copyright Zurich James Joyce Foundation. Used by permission.

by the U.S. Army, and explained didactically how to handle the stories. I also went with them to Military Government headquarters. Although I personally reported the army's civilian reforms, we allowed the German reporters to cover developments in the German municipal administration which the army had set up soon after the capture of the town.

Among the goals we set ourselves, Maj. Chesnutt and I determined, if possible, to denazify the Aachen city administration. This Augean stable was in sad need of cleaning, not to say deodorizing, for the continued presence of genuine Nazis in the higher brackets of the city administration stank. There were some in every section, in fact, all of them protected by the *Oberbürgermeister*, whom we gradually came to identify as Enemy Number 1. We discussed with Maj. Jones, the American military governor, the problem of getting rid of these Nazis. He told us that there were several dozen still in the municipal services, and agreed that a clean-up was necessary. He therefore arranged with his assistant, Maj. Bradford, for their gradual dismissal. A few days later I was given a preliminary list of those who had been dropped, on the basis of which I wrote a careful story with an aggressive lead, which we published with a two-column head in the following issue.

Certain of those whose names were on the list wrote indignant letters to the editor. They even came to the office to explain that, although they had been *Parteigenossen* (party members), they had of course been only *Zwangsmitglieder*—compulsory members. This word was eventually to become a household joke in the office. Among the letters received, I should like to quote the following gem:

Frau Henny Wirtz
Aachen
Goethestraße 10   Aachen, 3.1.45

To the
Editorial direction of the *Aachener Nachrichten*, Aachen.

With reference to my letter of 2.10.45 I must inform you that we have canceled our subscription to your paper, the *Aachener Nachrichten*.

It would have been a simple matter for you to tell your readers that although Herr *Stadtamtmann* (city councillor), Dr. Joseph Wirtz, was a member of the party, he was never, in that capacity, an active member. Such a correction might have prevented a disastrous mistake. The following incident proves that your news item led to serious consequences which might easily have been brought about an even more dangerous situation.

When I inquired about a position in the office of the dental technician Dr. Hahne, 35 Wallstraße, I was attacked and insulted by that gentleman in a most grievous manner. When he heard our name, he began to shout to all the passers-by that he would no longer work for "Nazi swine," and that my husband was a "state criminal" who was responsible for the entire misery of war. He added that my husband must have admitted this before the CIC — *otherwise his name would not have been published in the newspaper.* As for me, who never was a party member, he declared loudly that I was a "Nazi whore."

A woman who happened to be passing by reproached the man for his insulting behavior and said that he could not have known the Wirtz family, or he would not have insulted persons who had suffered so greatly under the Nazi regime. This lady has assured us that she will be glad to testify in our favor when the time comes to do so.

Herr Hahne was not known to us before this incident, nor did any member of our family know him, so your newspaper alone is responsible for this insulting public defamation.

[Signed] Frau Henny Wirtz

Similar letters were received each time we published a new list of "Nazi swine." Usually, however, we threw these missives into the waste-paper basket.

Gradually the *Redaktionsstube* came to resemble a real American city-room, and it was a pleasure to watch the growing enthusiasm of the young German *Berichterstatter,* or reporters. They vied with each other in presenting their stories with frequently remarkable leads, and even in digging up straight facts. News was abundant in the ruined town, which was being used as a testing ground of the Allied informational reconstruction program for Germany. In fact, everything that was done in Aachen was closely watched by the Allied leaders during that glacial winter when Gen. Eisenhower was preparing the great spring offensive towards the Rhine.

Our global war news was furnished us by the New York Office of War Information, relayed with Morse and already processed into German by a London team called the Allied Press Service, working under the direction of Peter de Mendelssohn. In February 1945, local Military Government, in line with Gen. Eisenhower's directive, organized the first meeting of the new German labor unions. As it happened, their bellwether was our friend Hollands, who made the principal address before some two hundred delegates. It was the first opportunity given the good anti-Nazi Germans to express themselves publicly, and they made the most of it.

"Why, they use our language," whispered Maj. Bradford, the assistant civilian affairs chief, to me, during a speech by a woman delegate.

"Es ist eine Kulturschande," said this fiery woman delegate, "daß das Volk der Dichter und Denker unter Hitler zum Volk der Richter und Henker geworden ist." (It is a shame before civilization that, under Hitler, this people of poets and thinkers should have become a people of judges and executioners.) Even Mayor Oppenhoff—his title was Oberbürgermeister—made a speech that gave the American observers the impression that we might be witnessing the prologue to democratic reconstruction in Germany.

Soon after this event, rumors grew rife that Nazi parachuters had landed behind the Allied lines, and military control, especially at night, became very strict. Passwords were given out every afternoon, and we were again ordered to wear steel helmets in the streets. One morning, on reaching my office, I learned that the Oberbürgermeister had been shot dead by Nazi parachuters during the night for "collaborating" with the Americans. According to the story told me, Oppenhoff had been called away from a gathering of friends shortly after midnight to be confronted by the conspirators, who said they were members of Himmler's Werwolf organization, then shot him down. I printed the story with all the caution necessitated by military security. It was not until four years later that the Werwolf assassins were caught and sentenced.

As spring approached, the Allied advance towards the Rhine got under way. Firing in the nearby Huertgen Forest increased in intensity, and at night we saw great squalls of fume and flame tonguing into the air. Standing on the roof of the print-shop we watched violent aerial battles over the ruined houses of Aachen. When Cologne was captured, we were once more rushed to the newly taken city. On the other side of the Rhine the Germans were still resisting, and German shells would occasionally crash into the town.

When the front moved eastward, we began to liquidate our work in Aachen and another team arrived to take over after our departure. At night, after the paper had gone to press, we gathered in the living room of the former Nazi owner for a game of poker, to listen to the AFN radio, or else to read and write. The Belgian frontier was not very far, and our GI friends would occasionally jeep to some border town "to make whoopee." They usually returned with lurid stories of erotic encounters, told in a naively merry, even blasphemous style.

As the war progressed to its ineluctable climax, I was shifted about by PWD headquarters to Wiesbaden and finally to Heidelberg, where I edited another German-language newspaper for the area under the control of Gen. Devers's Sixth Army Corps. It was here that I experienced Nazi surrender and the war's end.

In Heidelberg we decided to bring out a four-page bi-weekly edition, for which I was given editorial carte blanche. I at once got in touch with Military Government officials, one of my principal directives being to help solve their administrative difficulties through close cooperation in the news pages. The chief, Capt. Haskell, gave me a long list of Nazi officials whom he had just eliminated from the city administration. We printed it under a three-column headline, giving not only names, but the position occupied by each one of them. Other stories followed quite naturally, and soon we had an entire page filled with legitimate local news.

As the weeks advanced, many of the ragged, sick men who had spent years behind the barbed wire of Hitler's infamous concentration camps found their way to the editorial room of the *Mitteilungen.* They wanted to talk about their experiences to Americans, who, they felt, would be interested in detailed accounts of the Nazi infernos recently liberated by American and British troops. Each of them had a gruesome story to tell. Listening to these martyrs, I could not but feel that every single German was somehow guilty of complicity in these crimes. It seemed incredible that they should have allowed this horror to exist without crying out against its sadism.

Among the DP visitors were numerous Jews, Russians, Poles, Czechs, even Germans. All had the mark of the beast on their bodies: one had a mutilated arm, another showed me his back lacerated by steel thongs, others told stories of intolerable hunger and thirst. They came for the most part from Dachau, and now that they were free again, they had but one idea, to tell the world about the atrocities they had experienced or witnessed. Some handed me written accounts, which I published in the newspaper. Reports about conditions in Celle, Belsen, Erla, Nordhausen and elsewhere were contained as well in correspondents' stories being relayed from London. To these I added further details gleaned from the stories of recent Allied visitors. One of the latter was Bill Hale who came directly to Heidelberg from Dachau. We also published a series of photographic documents showing how the guards of the *Konzentrationslager* had killed and tortured the prisoners during the Nazi regime. Whatever their pretended ignorance of these facts during the war, about which I am still skeptical, it soon became impossible for any German to say he "knew nothing."

One morning a young Jewish girl came into my office looking for translating work. She was well educated, and her story of suffering under Nazi barbarism was a moving one. Before 1933 her father and mother had been Social Democrats and enthusiastic trade-union members in Mainz. After Hitler's conquest of power, they were harassed by SA and SS visits, and even the Gestapo came frequently to their home in the early morning hours, armed with every kind of trumped-up charge. During the anti-Jewish persecutions inaugurated by Göring and Goebbels in November 1938, they were attacked in their homes, dragged into the street and unmercifully beaten by the police who were accompanied by the SS aides. When Hitler unleashed his war, they were both taken to Buchenwald, where they perished. The little girl, who was only eleven years old at the time, was left with friends of her mother's, but was obliged to wear the stigma of the Star of David whenever she appeared in the streets. As I listened to her tragic recital, I felt ashamed of the German blood in my veins, I cursed it even in revolt against this drama of inhumanity with which somehow I felt psychologically associated. In some strange way I, too, felt guilty. The girl was engaged as a member of the ever-growing staff of German employees.

During moments of leisure I visited one of the many university bookshops still open and picked up a number of German books, particularly German *Klassiker,* in the old Reclam edition. I wanted to refresh my memory, to see what evidence was to be found in German literature that the Germans are a nation of sadists. Is there something in the German past, I asked myself, that could explain this outburst of collective malevolence? I recalled that such French writers as de Nerval, Balzac, Madame de Staël and others had admired the Germany of the Romantics, which they had represented as a gentle nation of dreamers, a peaceful and noble nation. What had happened since that time? In re-reading Fichte, von Kleist, von Arnim and other Romantic poets and thinkers, I found, to my surprise, indications that these older writers had also a certain share of responsibility for the genesis of Nazi ideas. To be sure, they had never stooped to the low degree of satanic materialism manifested by their twentieth-century successors. Nevertheless, I found a definite predilection among the Romantics for the totalitarian state, for anti-Semitism and for the same sort of Pan-Germanic dementia which had recently encouraged practically the entire nation to undertake the conquest of Europe. I learned with horror that the poet von Arnim, whose collection of German folk songs, composed with the collaboration of another poet, Clemens Brentano, had elicited Goethe's admiration, had envisaged a "Christian Germanic Society" from which, he insisted, "Jews, Frenchmen and philistines must be excluded." I saw that Fichte had jubilated over the "superiority of German greatness," particularly of the German language over other tongues; that he had advised the Germans to build up a state with a planned "autarchic" economy, that he had preached in favor of a "new order" in Europe, with Germany as the leading nation; that he had been the first to demand *Lebensraum* for the Germans. There were of course many contradictions in this attitude. In their writings one could also detect a high idealism which had nothing whatever to do with the militaristic cruelty of the succeeding generations caught up in the cult of *Blut und Boden*. But the seed of German belief in German superiority had undoubtedly been sown a century before.

We press officers were doing a strictly pedagogical job, and the new press we were trying to introduce into Germany was designed primarily to help "re-educate" the Nazi-poisoned German mind. In countless conversations we tried to awaken a consciousness of Germany's national guilt among the editors and publishers. These gentlemen, however, usually succeeded in wriggling out of the necessity of accepting this fact; almost without exception they blamed the Nazis exclusively, and with ponderous German logic argued that they, as individuals, could not be held responsible. Through the good offices of OWI, in New York, we obtained articles by Thomas Mann, Franz Werfel and other democratic German writers living in exile, which we published prominently in the Heidelberg papers. Because the theme of German guilt was vigorously upheld by these émigré writers, some of our readers wrote furious denunciations of the viewpoints expressed. With typical cynicism, some even went so far as to use the term "inner emigration" in order to cover up their own abandonment of liberty during the Nazi era. But others were stung by the stern, ethical language of the exiles and tried to protect themselves from the obvious implications of the accusations made. A few honest Germans wrote letters of contrition; they acknowledged that they felt a sense of culpability before the heinousness of the crimes committed. But they were only a few.

To "implement" the theme of collective German guilt, I had two large wall-posters printed, with text and photographs. Military Government in Heidelberg liked both, and forty thousand copies were distributed in numerous towns throughout the country, from the Czechoslovakian border to Saarbrücken. The first was entitled *Wessen Schuld?* (Who is guilty?), and the second, *Diese Schandtaten — Eure Schuld!* (You are guilty of these infamies!). When one of our German printers saw the macabre photographs of emaciated skeletons piled up like cord-wood, he wept. "Did our people really do this?" asked another. "History will never forgive us." In the streets of Heidelberg I mingled with the large crowds that stood silently before these posters. They were obviously stricken with emotion. Was it shame or mere horror? I could not tell. Occasionally I noticed sneers or a faint smile of incredulity on certain faces. But I felt that at least the idea that Nazism was sadism had been driven home through this irrefutable documentation.

The question of German guilt became a subject of increasingly passionate discussion between Americans and Germans and among the Germans themselves. The existentialist philosopher Dr. Karl Jaspers, whom I came to know at that time in Heidelberg, agreed that there could be no question as to German culpability. He added, however, that the problem would have to be considered from various angles in the case of the individual German. A short time after this he published a pamphlet, *Die Schuldfrage* (The guilt question), which analyzed the complex problem very thoroughly and provoked violent debate. In general, however, I felt that the Germans were inclined to reject his justification in toto.

"We knew nothing about the existence of the KZs (concentration camps) and we cannot therefore be held responsible for the criminal death of millions," was the usual argument.

With true philosophical thoroughness, Jaspers defined four concepts of guilt: (1) criminal, i.e., responsibility for actions committed in defiance of man-made laws, which may be proved objectively and demand punishment; (2) political, resulting from the actions of statesmen with whom the individual is identified by virtue of common citizenship ("Each man shares responsibility for the manner in which he is governed"); (3) moral: Each man shares moral responsibility for actions concerning the merit or blame of which his conscience must be judge. This demands penitence and regeneration. Of (4) metaphysical guilt Jaspers wrote: "There is a solidarity existing between men as men which makes each of us responsible for all the wrongs and injustices throughout the world. . . . If I do not do what I can to prevent these, then, I, too, am guilty. . . . What is needed is transformation of our human liability before God." I personally met only a handful of devout Christians — both Catholics and Protestants — who were not only conscious of their fearful moral responsibility towards the victims of crimes committed in their name but also deeply penitent. *Attila* and *Usurpator* were among the epithets they used to describe the former *Führer*.

In spite of the grimness of the surrounding events, we worked in the former German newspaper plant in an atmosphere of almost lighthearted activity, for it had become evident that the war was moving toward its victorious conclusion. Nor did we mind the long hours, the hurried comings and goings between our editorial office and the composing-room, the numerous tedious consultations with the erstwhile German editor and owner, Dr. Karl Rüster. The Herr Doktor was a former Parteigenosse, but although we knew this, our operating chief from PWD decided to retain him temporarily, on the grounds that he was needed for the technical realization of our complicated job. We also knew that he had opposed physical resistance to an SS group who had tried to blow up the linotype machines shortly before the arrival of American troops in Heidelberg. I must admit, too, that despite his insolent smile, which was most irritating, Rüster was very helpful with the mechanics of printing. After a few weeks, however, he was dismissed, and we hired another German specialist, a Social Democrat and convinced anti-Nazi. Not one of the compositors or pressmen was a party member, although they had all belonged to the subsidiary Nazi labor organization known as the German Labor Front (DAF). Well before the invasion of Germany, SHAEF had decided that such technicians as these were indispensable, and that we should have to take what we could find to get the German press going again. But I found it necessary to read and re-read proof on every item that went into the paper, after which my friend Lt. Wolfe, our official censor, made a re-check before we finally went to press.

I myself wrote stories and headlines and supervised the make-up, always a nerve-lacerating job, but in this case a psychological operation as well. Heidelberg was overcrowded with DPs and other German war refugees, and the housing situation was very critical. The town had also become a haven for war criminals trying to disappear in the crowds. We worked hand in hand with various French and American missions in an effort to weed out this heteroclite population. There being no electrical power, the population was deprived of broadcast information, so that dependence on our paper became almost a categorical imperative. Occasionally we sent one of the German editorial assistants to listen to the conversations of the dour-looking mobs queuing up before the plant. We learned that they reacted negatively to the American technique of objective news, with which we had replaced their beloved feuilletons. But we persisted in giving them news, nothing but news. This was later to prove strikingly effective when we began to detail the utter defeat of their armies.

U.S. intelligence and publications sections were housed in the same building as the newspaper plant, and we worked in close touch with both groups, particularly the former, since many Germans stormed our office for jobs. I remember particularly in that section a number of young American officers and civilians of European origin whose contribution to the news press operations was very valuable. They were for the most part anti-Nazi Jewish refugees from Germany and Austria who had put their knowledge of the German language at the disposal of the Allied military forces. They had fled from Hitler's tyranny—some before 1933, others during the years just preceding the war—either to America or to England, where they had taken root and absorbed the language. A few had even begun to write in English. I talked with many of these men during those bitter days. All complained that in the new country they had felt psychically and linguistically uprooted, and they welcomed the opportunity to speak their native tongue again. They were indispensable in our task of fighting the Nazis with their own weapons and, later, in our attempt to denazify and democratize the German press.

Although I myself had renounced the German language forever—or so I had thought—during the First World War, I, too, was now working in that medium. I wrote headlines and stories in German and spoke to the German employees in their native tongue. I must confess, too, that I felt a certain psychic relief at being able to use this European language again, despite the fact that it had been so besmirched by the Nazis. During the past thirty years I had used English and French almost exclusively, more English than French, in fact. But my original language was still very much part of me. It emerged now as a living force from deep wells of the unconscious.

Curiously enough, however, this German experience was also an enriching one for my English linguistic store. In much the same way as during the First World War, I now found myself in daily contact with the popular vocabulary from nearly every state in the union, thanks to countless cross-country jeep rides with GI drivers with whom I had long conversations. From these men I heard new and old words, regional nuances of pronunciations and grammatical distortion, military slang and an erotic lexicon that, in addition to its original picturesqueness, was now being overlaid by numerous English-German amalgams. Rarely have I had such an opportunity to observe at their source the rapid mutations of American speech.

With the inexorable approach of "VE Day," we worked day and night preparing a special edition. When it finally appeared on Heidelberg's *Hauptstraße,* the crowds of news-hungry Germans trying to buy the paper were so huge that a riot was feared, and the military police had to be called out. The banner-line was suggested by Dick Crossman, British deputy chief of PWD, who later became a Labor member of Parliament. It was very simple: in huge, Gothic type was the one word

KAPITULATION.

The weather that day was hot and sunshiny, the occupation forces relaxed. Once the paper was out, we joined a group of Allied officers and civilians at a hotel where a heterogeneous orchestra made up of GI and DP musicians played lustily until the early morning hours. When we returned to the Redaktion, still shaken by the nocturnal tumult, we were happy to see that the DPs' mess-hall, next to the newspaper office, also showed evident signs of wassail and disorder.

The war receded quickly and Heidelberg soon began to assume the aspect of a garrison town. Blackout ceased automatically, we wore less formal uniforms, and the laws of the ETO were gradually relaxed. It was a good town to live in during the Dionysian summer days that followed, for in spite of the gloomy German faces, one sensed echoes of the student gaiety that had once lightened its atmosphere and would undoubtedly lighten it again.

12

NEWS FROM BABEL

The satanic epoch of annihilation that had gripped continental Europe was over. All around us were ruins and mutilations, reminders of the countless dead. But the survivors were determined to live, and having awakened from the long nightmare, they began once more to construct their lives with a certain euphoria and hope in the future. The German people entered upon a phase of active *Aufbau* (construction) that was both physical and intellectual.

We American journalists, however, refused to use their favorite word, *Wiederaufbau* (reconstruction), since what we were trying to build was something that the country had not known before: a free, democratic press. I must admit, too, that, at first, the task seemed almost an insuperable one.

A U.S. Military Government organization, Information Control Division (ICD) had replaced the war-time Psychological Warfare Division (PWD) and was now engaged in systematic elimination of all Nazi propaganda media, which were to be replaced as soon as possible by press, radio and stage activities freed from the authoritarian dicta of the Goebbels propaganda offices. In addition to instituting a wide search for personnel and machinery, we of the press found ourselves faced with the difficult pedagogical task of training new personnel in democratic methods of reporting, editorial make-up and the general handling of news. We were determined particularly to rid the "cubs" of the poisonous ingredients which the Nazis had injected into their minds during the totalitarian years. In the form of editorial and technological assistance to the nascent press, the U.S. Army played a generous role in the reorientation of German journalism towards a more objective concept of newspaper activity. It must be admitted, however, that subsequently little appreciation was shown by the recipients of this country.

In the late summer of 1945, army engineers began to provide mechanical equipment for a new operation which Gen. McClure, head of ICD, planned to launch in the famous watering place of Bad Nauheim. This was to be a news agency—the first to be set up in any zone—in the German language. AP, UP, and INS were to supply us with foreign news, and the new venture was to be modeled on their methods of organization. It was baptized DANA—Deutsche Allgemeine Nachrichten-Agentur—and put under the overall direction of Luther Conant, Lt. Leon Edel was named general editor and I was appointed editor-in-chief. I had worked with Edel in New York before the war, when we were both with the Havas Agency, and I was confident that we should succeed in doing a good job together. A large hotel in Bad Nauheim was requisitioned to house the growing activity, and by September, transmission to the few newspapers we had licensed was under way. For personnel, we began with a few GIs who knew German, and several former German newspapermen who had worked before the war with UP in Berlin and Amsterdam. Formal request for their services had to be made to prisoner-of-war camps in England and France. My immediate assistant was an American staff sergeant, Fred Jacobson, a former Vienna newspaperman, who did an outstanding job.

As in Aachen, our project was to make of the DANA staff the nucleus of a school of journalism, which we hoped would further the subsequent democratic evolution of German newspapers. At the very beginning, I issued a memorandum stating that American news techniques would form the basis of our work.

It took us some time to put this into effect, but we gradually succeeded in convincing the younger men of the excellence of our reporting. I fought with every means at my disposal the archaic German tendency to distort facts and to neutralize what to them seemed unpleasant events, or events they disapproved of, by warped and subjective commentaries. I also fought their proclivity for presenting news in feuilleton form. Indeed, I tried to hammer into their heads that "hard" facts alone can furnish the premises for discussion and analysis, and I emphasized the importance of objective, impartial, accurate reporting, as well as the American imperative according to which a news-story demands a *lead* containing the main facts and answering the questions: who, when, where, why, how? I tried to teach them that attribution of source in the lead or in the second paragraph was a prime directive; that the German translation must be accurate; that demilitarization and denazification of the corrupted German language should be unremittingly pursued. They were taught to separate fact from opinion, to avoid strictly all editorializing, and to eschew individual comment.

My first memorandum read as follows:

September 20, 1945

To: Staff German Desk
From: Eugene Jolas
Subject: News Style

1. DANA will henceforth adopt the American style of news-writing.
2. Essential facts should be given in the lead, that is, in the introductory paragraphs, to be followed by paragraphs dealing accumulatively with the chronological enumeration of details.
3. All editorial comment must be rigorously excluded from our stories and only objective facts should be presented.
4. Great care should be exercised in making accurate translations. The German style must be grammatically flawless. Too literal translations, however, should be avoided.
5. Elimination of all Nazi terms must be steadily kept in mind, and denazification of the vocabulary should be one of the prime tasks of every news-writer.
6. Members of the staff are advised to consult the files of American newspapers and to study the American style of news presentation.
7. Factual accuracy and ethical integrity in news-writing will be the hall-marks of the new democratic press we are seeking to create in Germany.

The staff grew rapidly. Within three months we had twenty-five editors at work, not one of whom had ever heard of objective reporting before, and all of whom had to be trained individually in the tricks of the new journalism. Many mistakes were made at first, for there were a number of half-tutored amateurs who were trying to learn the trade. But strange to say, nothing irreparable occurred, nothing was ever written which imperiled democratic reconstitution of the country, or contravened military security directives issued by the army. AP, UP, INS, Reuters and, finally, France Presse continued to supply foreign news which was forwarded from Luxembourg, where the Allied Press Services directed from London were still functioning. From Munich, Eddie Glynn sent Military Government news about Bavaria. We started a feature section and an economic section, both of which flourished at once and gave substantial assistance to the licensed German papers. An energetic American "news-hen," Sylvia Weiss, covered the Frankfurt military installations with the assistance of a little band of German cubs.

Some months later, Lt. Edel, who was the real genius behind this complex overall achievement, left the army to return to the United States. His successor for a few weeks was Don Gilbert, formerly of the Associated Press. Gilbert was followed by Jack Stuart, an American newspaperman, who took over with energy and roguish humor. It was he who, a year or so later, prepared the licensing of the agency to the Germans. He had learned rudimentary German in a New York Berlitz School, and his insistence on speaking the Teuton's own tongue to our editors often created amusing verbal imbroglios which could only be disentangled by vigorous efforts on the part of the interpreters staff.

Life among these anti-Nazi Germans was intense and often tumultuous. Frequent differences between individuals had to be smoothed out, and occasional violent jealousies made it necessary for the editor-in-chief to step in and restore normal relations. Neurotics with Napoleonic ambitions had to be curbed. There were also love affairs between men and women workers—for half of the editors were young girls—which at times interfered to such an extent with the efficiency of the employees affected that drastic measures had to be resorted to. Scrutiny control had also to be exercised with great care, for Nazi terms kept creeping into the stories and reprimands had to be issued.

From London had arrived a little group of German-speaking editors, originally from Germany, Austria and Czechoslovakia, but who, by international courtesy, were referred to as "stateless." They were all men who had been active as German-language newsmen before the Hitler regime and had emigrated from lucrative positions when Nazi persecutions got under way. Several of them had been in concentration camps in the early days of the oppression. We set them to work in the news-room, where we hoped that they would teach the younger Germans the ABCs of modern news handling. All these men were dexterous writers possessing intellectual perspicacity and political acumen, and they proved absolutely essential to the success of our operation. I listened to their stories, and in our dialogues found "bark and steel for the mind"; in fact, they were men with whom one could engage in high philosophical and political colloquies. They wrote a classical German that I liked to hold up as an example to our younger German editors, and their carefully thought-out interpretations of political events were based on minute studies of both pre-Nazi and Nazi viewpoints.

These "stateless" editors participated wholeheartedly in the Allied effort, and we worked together in wonderful consonance. All of them were interested in the very essential job we were engaged in, and all were determined anti-Nazis. Mercurial Egon Jameson, scholarly Franz Borkenau, melancholy Hans Gronauer, breezy Abe Strauss, and many others, contributed to the machinery of the news agency the force of their personality and the experience they had acquired in London and New York. All of them remained scrupulously loyal, save one — a former Ullstein journalist from Budapest, who hid his communist sympathies until he was in a position to join the Soviet propaganda machine in the eastern sector of Berlin.

Gronauer was my favorite "character," as we used to say in army parlance. He was a gentle little man with eyes that were veritable pools of human kindness. He seemed to be without nerves, and listening to him relate his tragic odyssey, I was always astounded to hear with what determination he had managed to elude the traps set for him by a hostile world. He was a native of Prague and before 1933 had worked as a feuilleton writer on the *Prager Tageblatt.* At that time he had been a friend of another editor, named Max Brod, the friend and discoverer of Franz Kafka, about whom he never tired of telling spirited anecdotes. He loved Prague with a lyrical homesickness that I always observed among my exiled Jewish friends of that epoch. He also spoke frequently of his wife and little daughter, whom he had not seen since Hitler's rape of Czechoslovakia. When, thanks to arrangements made by Edel, he finally was given a chance to visit Prague, he had tears in his eyes. He brought his daughter, by then grown to be a beautiful young woman, to Bad Nauheim. He was not able, however, to arrange an exit permit for his wife. This fact left a deep wound in his mind.

As the year 1946 went into autumn, he grew more and more taciturn. After his daughter had returned to her mother, he lived rather isolatedly in our requisitioned hotel, and participated only occasionally in the somewhat noisy wassail which one or the other of us organized. He had with him a German girl who was his typist and in whose company alone he seemed to feel at ease. But his mind was elsewhere. Often I used to watch him at his desk, lost in thought, looking out through the large French windows at the linden trees beyond. One rainy morning, his typist came into my office weeping bitterly: Gronauer had been found dead in his room. An empty veronal bottle was lying on his night-table.

DANA had a large office in the American sector of Berlin, which supplied us with news from the new quadripartite former capital. Press conferences held by Gen. Lucius D. Clay, the military governor, administrative measures taken by OMGUS (the overall office of American Military Government for Germany), and other information vital to the Germans reached us through this source. I made frequent visits to Berlin, traveling by rail or by motor through the Soviet zone, where stiff, apparently humorless Russian soldiers mounted guard. At that time East-West tensions were not yet apparent and the sequelae of the friendly war-time alliance against the Nazis were still perceptible in social and official relations. By the end of 1946, however, we began to notice an aggressive demeanor on the part of the Reds with whom we had official dealings, and it was obvious that a radical change of directive had taken place.

In the late fall 1945, in the company of a few American and British friends, I made a short trip to the former capital, in order to consult with our bureau on the possibility of improving technical details of our news transmissions. When we arrived, a melancholy rain was falling on the ruins of the vast city which I had known some fifteen years earlier, during the Weimar epoch, as a prosperous and optimistic megalopolis. Between official engagements, I visited the places I had enjoyed during that stay, which had coincided with the moment when the last phase of intellectual liberty had been filled with a sort of pagan gaiety and a passion for experimentation in every branch of the arts and technics. A few years later had begun the time of slavery and darkness, and preparations for Hitler's war of conquest. As I contemplated the fearful spectacle evocative of the most hallucinatory canvases of Goya or Bosch, it seemed as though centuries, rather than years, had elapsed.

I recalled the newspapermen and other writers I had known back in those pre-Nazi days, and I attempted to reconstruct their fates during the diabolical years. The playwright Carl Sternheim had died in his Brussels exile a few years before the war; Alfred Flechtheim had succumbed in London during the blitz; George Grosz was living in America; Franz Pfemfert was in Mexico City. Many others were scattered across the world, in Zurich, Geneva, London, the Americas. The only one who had stayed behind and come to terms with the Nazis was Gottfried Benn, the doctor-poet, who, I learned through licensed German newspapermen, had survived and was now trying to justify himself before the American authorities. In 1933 he had embraced Hitlerism with lyrical exaltation. A few years later he had apparently seen his error, and I was told that his professional activity during the war had been confined to that of medical officer. He now claimed that he had been prohibited from publishing anything, even poems, during the greater part of the Hitler regime. But, somehow, what he had described somewhere as his "double life" remained unconvincing, and his clandestinely pronounced "no" unheard by all except himself.

The names of older Expressionist writers, well known during the Weimar regime, were being mentioned again. I learned that some, such as Johannes Becher, who had spent the war years in Moscow, had become communists. I was introduced to a new writer, Elisabeth Langgässer, a heroic woman whose husband and children had been sent to a concentration camp, while she herself survived in hiding. She died early in 1950. Her novel *The Inextinguishable Seal*, published in 1946, started a new Catholic literary movement in post-war Germany. Ernst Jünger's much discussed "peace" pamphlet, addressed "to the youth of the world" was an irritating example of Teutonic obtuseness with regard to the Germans' aggressive role in the three European wars of their making.

In Berlin we stayed in a requisitioned villa in the Zehlendorf quarter which had been taken over as an American military compound. From time to time we would make explorations into the rubble-confusion of the other sectors, all of which presented a tragic appearance. On one of these occasions we went down into Hitler's bunker, near the smashed-up Reichskanzlei, where the two Russian guards stationed aboveground seemed happy to show us the way. In return, they indicated that they expected American cigarettes. We let them have a few packages, which they quickly and with evident satisfaction put into their wide pockets.

As we entered the underground wreck, I had the impression of a descent into hell. In the room where Hitler and Eva Braun had killed themselves, an American in the group, a former theology student now in the service of the U.S. Army's press division, quoted from the Book of the Apocalypse: "And the inhabitants on the earth shall wonder, seeing the beast that was, and is not." Everything was still intact, exactly as the Nazi bonzes had left it; furniture and mechanical equipment lay about as though the diabolical destroyer of civilization had left just a few minutes earlier. It was certainly an efficiently organized refuge, deep under the earth, safe from the shells and bombs that rained on Berlin in the days before the capture of the city. On our way out, the same Russian soldiers showed us smilingly the spot in the courtyard where the bodies of the Nazis — Hitler, Eva, Goebbels and his family — had been burned. This visit left an eerie sensation of horror.

On every side we heard stories of despair and exacerbated guilt, of hunger and starvation, of sudden suicides that had taken place in Berlin during those months of darkness. I went into German homes both in the western and eastern sectors with members of the DANA staff. Everywhere we saw misery and yawning indigence and hunger. I also heard countless jeremiads, and complaints of Russian brutality. One woman wept bitterly as she told her tale. I was tempted to answer: I can still hear your barbaric shouts and plaudits as you listened to the hate-inspired criminals who brought you to this fate. Along with his rapaciousness and cruelty the German's capacity for self-pity would appear to be inexhaustible.

Applicants for work came to Bad Nauheim from every part of the beaten country: young and old, men and women, each with an identical and yet different story to tell. I put them all through an examination, scrutinized their *Fragebogen* (questionnaires) and, whenever I was in doubt about their political background, completed our routine research with the aid of the intelligence sections. Many came and few were chosen. There were nuts, megalomaniacs, morons, crooks and secret Nazis among them, but also some politically reliable anti-Nazis. Some were dirty and malodorous, having spent long periods in filthy railroad cars or still filthier bunkers. Some of the stories were grotesquely and obviously invented; others were heart-rending in their accumulation of descriptive details of the sufferings endured during the Hitler years and since the capitulation. Some of these men were just plain liars, but we quickly found them out, and had no hesitancy about throwing them into jail whenever we found that they had deliberately falsified their Fragebogen. After a while, when the complete list of Nazi party membership was found in a barn, and a Central Document Section was installed in Berlin, all we had to do was to call Berlin by phone and ask for a scrutiny of the files.

One day I engaged two Jewish brothers with whose work I was very pleased. At last, here were the right types of high-minded reporters who had professional skill, and who had no reason to be lenient with Nazism or neo-Nazism. We became good friends, and the Americans on the staff helped them out with PX supplies that made their lives in those difficult days fairly bearable. The two boys had lost their father in the Dachau gas chambers, and their mother, who had come to live with them in Bad Nauheim, impressed us as a tragic and pitiful figure. We felt a special moral obligation for the well-being of this touching duo. One day the two lads came to see me, somewhat flustered and nervous. They had decided that they did not want to live in Germany any longer. "We've talked it over with Mother," they said, "and she agrees with us that the best thing we can do is to emigrate . . ." "Wir möchten nach Israel auswandern . . ." Their eyes were shining with hope. Although members of the American staff were sad to see them go, arrangements were made to facilitate their emigration along with a group of DPs. When we said good-bye to the two of them, we realized that they had started on the first lap of a journey that, until only a few weeks before, had surely seemed more than impossible of realization.

Those early post-war years in western Germany, before U.S. Military Government decided to apply a currency reform, were indeed dismal ones. The German employees were wan and their eyes were filled with an animal-like despair. Occasionally one of them would faint while at work, and our jeeps would be pressed into service to transport him home. Many complained that they were hungry, especially after eating the insufficient rations provided by their German mess. We did what we could to obtain food and medical supplies for them, and in this Eddie Glynn was a good Samaritan. He wrote to friends in the American Newspaper Guild and suggested that CARE packages be sent to these workers. Some months later a large shipment arrived. Its distribution spread much cheer. We finally persuaded Military Government to classify these editors as *Schwerarbeiter,* in order that they might receive heavy worker's rations, which relieved the situation somewhat. Undoubtedly the extra meal corresponded to a real need.

Reporting the first Nuremberg trials of big-wig Nazi war criminals was the first important task the new agency had to undertake. We were the voice of Military Government, and it was up to the American press-control officers to organize the machinery, obtain the necessary technical equipment and, in general, see that the German reportorial staff was ready for action; for it was evident that this would be a test case of our didactic operation. It was our duty to give an objective account of the trial and, at the same time, defend the Allied viewpoint.

The difficulties, which were mountainous, were discussed in hour-long conferences with military and civilian personnel. Finally Edel and I arranged to send Sam Grossman and Bill Stricker, both German-American experts, to Nuremberg, where they were to organize a team with offices in the Justizpalast. The army had installed special teletype lines to DANA in Bad Nauheim, and it was decided that a few German reporters would remain in Nuremberg during the entire trial. We next set up a special desk in DANA which was to "process" all material sent by the other agencies as well as by our own correspondents. Selection of these special Nuremberg correspondents was accompanied by certain difficulties; we needed men and women possessing not only a high degree of trained craftsmanship but also strong anti-Nazi convictions. Our first choice fell upon Suzanne Czapski and Ernst Michel, and they did not disappoint us.

Suzanne Czapski was a pretty, half-Jewish girl with raven-black hair and a pronounced sense of humor, who used to say in her rather disarming way: "Oh, I'm just a *Krautgirl,*" then laughed at her own joke. Under our tutelage she had learned the technique of reporting, and since she also had a very lively imagination she quickly become one of Nuremberg's star reporters, with her by-lines constantly appearing in the licensed papers.

Ernst Michel, a youngster of twenty, was more of a feature-writer, but he also had a good news sense. He was pure Jewish and his sufferings under the Hitler regime had left a profound scar. He told us that before 1933 his parents had been shopkeepers in a small Rhenish town. Their house was robbed and plundered by SS men during the so-called Crystal Night, and they themselves were sent to Buchenwald, where they perished in the gas chambers. After this event he was taken in charge by some half-Jewish relatives who had succeeded in hiding in Bavaria. When American troops reached the little village where he was living under a false name, he was immediately given privileged treatment. Before he left for Nuremberg, I instructed him as to his duties, and suggested that he write his first piece with the idea in mind that the war criminals he would see in court were the men responsible for his parents' martyrdom. His first article had the following lead:

"Today I saw twelve men in the Nuremberg Palace of Justice who are being tried for crimes that resulted in the death of millions and, in the case of the writer, in the death of his parents at Buchenwald." The story made the front page of all thirty-two of the German newspapers that had been licensed in the American zone by the Information Control Division of Military Government.

After a few months, having acquired an excellent nucleus of trained reporters, we sent others on the same assignment. One day Michel told me that the INS agency in Frankfurt had asked him to write a series of articles on his experience under the Nazis. I was delighted to see that he went at it like a veteran newspaperman. Meanwhile, he had made application for a visa to the United States.

"I hate it here," he told me. "I want to become an American and live over there." A short time later we saw him off for Bremen.

I myself went to Nuremberg every other week to inspect the work of DANA and attend court sessions. I listened to the American, British, French and Russian prosecutors, and watched the Nazi defendants trying to wriggle out of the juridical noose in the hope of escaping the hemp. Göring's effrontery struck me particularly, as he stood there before the judges mouthing Nazi platitudes in an effeminate voice. Newspapermen from all over the world were listening to the proceedings — a remarkable translating staff transmitted the testimony in the principal world languages — and for brief moments the atmosphere was one of an international congress. Then, inevitably, some new detail of horror would recall the gruesome origins of these unprecedented proceedings. I usually sat with the DANA correspondents and later stood by to help them with their copy. My last visit to the courtroom took place on the day when the criminals were brought in, one by one, to hear their sentence. A British judge spoke the fatal words with traditional phlegm and diamond-hard precision.

In October 1945, Information Control decided to convoke in Marburg the first German journalistic congress to take place in the American zone. Luther Conant, Lt. Col. Chesnutt and James Aronson organized the meeting and I was one of the men scheduled to address the Germans on the ideas behind the DANA news agency. Being in the midst of pressing editorial operations, I could not get away until the day after the congress had actually begun. On my way from Bad Nauheim to Marburg, I noticed brightly printed banners of welcome hanging across the Landstraße and I began to look forward to the meeting with growing interest.

After I had spoken my little piece, in German, explaining to my German listeners the modus operandi of American news-gathering and dissemination, there was stolid silence for a few moments. Then one of the new Munich licensees rose to answer my documentary report. He complained in typical pedantic style that the newly licensed newspapers were not interested in collecting too many facts, but that they must have an opportunity to "kommentieren" the news. He added that the news agency which the Americans were trying to foist on the unwilling Germans was not exactly what they wanted. A wrangling discussion developed, but fortunately there was a sufficient number of politically clean men to defend objective reporting methods. Among them was my friend Arno Rudert, a Frankfurt licensee, who had spent seven years in a Nazi concentration camp and who had no difficulty in getting his opinions accepted.

A glance at the newly founded papers of those early days sufficed to show that professional competence was lacking. With few exceptions—among them the *Rhein-Neckar Zeitung,* published in Heidelberg, and the *Frankfurter Rundschau*—they were more or less ignorantly organized sheets which, in any American city, would have been howled off the news stands. In spite of our admonitions, editorials continued to appear on the front page flanked by the ubiquitous feuilleton, and information was of lesser importance. Not without irritation I told the editors that the news agency in my charge would reject all compromise with feuilleton journalism and that the young German reporters under our direction would be trained in the American manner.

One of the speakers at that convention, whose address I relished, was

13. Germans buying their first democratic newspaper after World War II (photo: H. Lossen). Copyright Photo Lossen, Heidelberg. Used by permission.

Theodor Heuss, then co-editor of the Heidelberg paper. He did not at all belong in the same category as the other recent "licensees" who, although good democrats, were, for the most part, not particularly shining examples of modern journalism. Heuss, who spoke with a strong Swabian accent, swept the audience off their feet with the coruscating quality of his "punches" and the incisiveness of his arguments. He really spoke our technical language, in addition to which he had an inexhaustible stock of ideas.

"There is a man who'll go far in the new Germany," Col. Chesnutt whispered. As it turned out, Heuss, a few years later, was elected first president of the West German Republic.

On the final day of the convention the editors founded an Association of Newspaper Publishers in Hesse which was later used as model for similar groups set up in the other *Länder*, or states. At this last meeting there was a considerable give and take of ideas, and some of the younger men, in particular, made a very favorable impression.

DANA grew in size and efficiency as the months went by. In fact, it was certainly, at that time, the best of the four news agencies which Americans, Russians, British and French had organized almost simultaneously. The *Hellschreiber* — an ingenious German machine which transmitted our stories by radio into some thirty editorial rooms — worked with electric accuracy, while U.S. Army teletype machines, used by the German

14. DANA staff and Theodor Heuss (center), co-editor of the *Rhein-Neckar Zeitung* and future president of the German Federal Republic (photo: H. Lossen). Copyright Photo Lossen Heidelberg. Used by permission.

branch offices, flashed texts of official Military Government documents, new rulings of the Allied Control Council, developments in the war crimes trials, etc.

The first democratic elections in Land Hesse (to which Bad Nauheim belonged) furnished us with an opportunity to apply strictly American principles of reporting within our organization. I invited into my office the chief German editors — Haas-Haye, Fritze, and others of the "Inside Germany" news sections — and together we went over the operational details of presenting in news-fashion the election preparations that had been made in the vast region to be known as Land Hesse. This territory had just come under the jurisdiction of a unique governmental structure commanded by Col. James R. Newman, director for Military Government. Ours was a thorny task, for there was no precedent, but thanks to the energy and intelligence of these men, a staff of young men and women cub reporters was soon organized and sent through Hesse to collect preliminary news features, which were eagerly picked up by the papers. The various party programs — that of the Social Democrats (SPD), Christian Democrats (CDU), Liberal Democrats (LPD) and even the Communists (KPD) — were studied and presented in easily accessible form to the readers who seemed to be both bewildered by and perhaps a bit indifferent to the new democratic rulings. When the elections took place, on two successive Sundays, Haas-Haye was ready with a magnificent staff who rushed the news flashes through in the best manner of an American city-room. It was on this occasion that delegates were elected to the Constitutive Convention for the purpose of drawing up a new constitution, based on democratic principles. The enthusiasm of our city-room proved to be a great fillip to the reportorial efficiency of DANA, and showed the majority of German editors in the *Redaktionsstuben* that our system really did work.

Parallel with my activities at DANA I was given the task of launching the first "intellectual" review to appear in the American zone. An initial attempt to unearth suitable editorial personnel in the university town of Marburg gave no results, and the plan of editing the magazine from there was abandoned. Finally, after a thorough survey in various other cities, I came to the conclusion that the liberal ambiance of Heidelberg offered perhaps the best chances of success, so it was agreed that I should return there for a few weeks of intensive activity. In 1946 I settled again in the premises of the German-language newspaper, where I was working on VE Day, and began once more the wearisome process of interviewing editors, writers and publishers among the numerous academic candidates who poured into the office. Here I worked in close cooperation with Maj. Shepard Stone, who had been named chief intelligence officer for Wiesbaden, and who delegated my friend 1st Lt. Al Rosenberg to the Heidelberg information sub-section. With the help of these two men, I finally succeeded in assembling a brilliant publishing and editorial committee, composed of Dr. Lambert Schneider, Dr. Dolf Sternberger, Dr. Werner Krauss, Dr. Karl Jaspers and Dr. Alfred Weber. Arrangements for licensing were begun at once.

Dr. Sternberger had been cultural editor of the former *Frankfurter Zeitung* and in this capacity had succeeded for a long time in keeping the feuilleton pages free of Nazi propaganda by concentrating on abstract and purely literary themes. He had in fact fought the Nazi ideology with the weapons of indirectness and cunning and the vocabulary used in his own writings and in those of his contributors showed no trace of the distorted language of the Nazis. Finally, however, as the result of a frontal attack on the Nazi-sponsored "poet" Eckart, he was forbidden by Goebbels to engage in further publishing. When the Gestapo tried to arrest his Jewish wife he went underground with her, first in Frankfurt, then in Heidelberg, later in Baden-Baden, where they were living when French troops arrived. I felt that he was the ideal man for the difficult task of editing a review destined primarily for the re-education of German students. For he also had thorough academic training, and his philosophical work, *Death Understood,* published in 1936, constituted a forceful attack on the nihilistic viewpoint of the Existentialist philosopher Heidegger, who had taken a brief pro-Nazi stand in 1934.

At my request, Sternberger prepared a statement of his intentions. Following are some excerpts from this manifesto:

Although still faint with exhaustion, we are nevertheless trying to move our weakened limbs, to exercise them with simple, uninvolved gestures. But however hard we try, we find that we can do little more than watch our fingers and toes, to see if our joints can still be made to work.

Now the fog of the anesthetic is beginning to wear off and memory is returning. We are still shocked by the memory of fear and guilt, of the terrible, mute struggle in our tissues, of our sickness. But we must not doze off again, no matter how tempting that is. We must seize upon whatever floats to the surface and determine to endure! We must be accurate, patient and severe with ourselves!

We are alive. We feel the tingle of the fine elementary forces which, during the evil sickness, were relegated for so long to the most secret recesses of the tortured body. Now they have reappeared. But they have little room to grow in. If we give them free rein, they can spread and finally replace all the rotten tissue. They can rekindle everything that is lifeless, they can strengthen everything that is weak. They can rejuvenate old things and create new ones, new marrow and new bones. They can, in fact, transform the entire body.

The situation in which we find ourselves is only too evident. We can return neither to our former position nor to the manner of living to which we were once accustomed. We must take a deep breath, we must look about us!

Alien faces surround us, their eyes are upon us. At first we can recognize only faint silhouettes, for our sight is still weak. But we must keep looking, our gaze must continue to seek until it perceives something. Thus the world will become familiar.

Let us keep our feet firmly on the ground, however rough! Let us also seek to rise! We must lift one foot carefully after the other, in order to take a step, the very first step, which must neither falter nor stumble. Our eyes have come to recognize the abyss of danger, so that we shall not be swallowed up again.

All this is painful. But it is this step that matters, this test that matters.

For now that the gag has been taken out of our mouths, we must open them and try to speak again. We must listen to our own voices. Let us listen to them clearly and precisely. In that way, others too will listen. And answer us. For they are human beings like ourselves.

A delicate, transparent skin is forming over our wounds. It will grow firmer in the new air, but it must nevertheless remain delicate, it must feel quiveringly, it must not become crusty or tough.

Our first glance, our first breath, our first hand-grasp, our first step, our first utterance. Thus we shall move! May a new, sure spirit direct them all in order that they may be the right ones.

We are in process of transformation.

Dr. Werner Krauss was teaching in Marburg when he was arrested in 1942 by the Gestapo. From the beginning he had actively fought Nazi tyranny, and his arrest was based on a charge of participation in a plot against Hitler. With twenty others, he was sentenced to death by a so-called People's Court in Berlin. After Marburg University friends had succeeded in camouflaging his case as a psychiatric one, the sentence was reduced to several years' imprisonment, and he was among the many intellectuals liberated by American troops. My impression of him was of a man possessing an intelligent, brilliant mind. Although his special subject was Romance languages, he also had a genuine critical and creative interest in philosophy, literature and sociology, and I felt that he was destined to play a leading role in the evolution of a democratic Germany. Unfortunately, I was mistaken. After two years, he resigned from the editorial board of the new magazine, to take up residence in the Soviet zone.

Dr. Schneider, who acted as publisher, was another who had never wavered in his democratic, anti-militaristic convictions. As manager, not only of his own publishing house but also of the firm headed by Salomon Schocken, one of the most prominent Jews in pre-Nazi Germany and a well-known Zionist, Schneider had published, for nearly thirty years, books of great literary value, by such German Jewish writers as Martin Buber, the well-known philosopher and theologian, Rosenzweig, and others. After the Schocken Publishing Company had been dissolved by the Gestapo, Schneider published a magazine entitled *Die Kreatur,* under the joint editorship of Buber and a Protestant theologian, Victor von Weizsäcker. *Die Kreatur* lasted until 1936.

The world-famous philosopher Dr. Karl Jaspers, although an Existentialist, was the antipode of Martin Heidegger. From the beginning he had been a strong anti-Nazi and anti-militarist and he had never concealed this attitude in his writings or lectures. In 1937 the authorities became alarmed by the influence he wielded among his students, with the result that he was forbidden to teach at Heidelberg University. From that time until 1945, he lived in complete retirement with his Jewish wife. In 1939 publication of his books was prohibited, so that none of his writings appeared in Germany after that date. In 1941, on the grounds that he was "politically unreliable," he was refused permission to go to Switzerland, where he had been invited to give two lectures at Basel University. In a discussion of the anti-Semitic rioting that took place in 1938, he declared: "We stood aside while Jewish friends were being robbed, deported and assassinated, when what we should have done was to go down into the streets and shout until we too met with the same fate. What we are experiencing today is the result of our own guilt." I read all of Jaspers's works I could find and was deeply impressed by them. He received me several times in his book-cluttered study, where Sternberger usually joined us. These conversations were always stimulating, in addition to which I enjoyed listening to Jaspers's strong North German accent.

Dr. Alfred Weber, a brother of the famous sociologist, the late Dr. Max Weber, still possessed an extremely agile mind, despite his seventy-seven years. In 1920 he had been among the founders of the German Democratic Party, and he had consistently pursued a strongly democratic direction in the discussions that took place during the "sociological evenings" he organized at Heidelberg University. On these occasions he had constantly attacked the militaristic, totalitarian and fascist powers. During the war, at great risk, he continued to express his anti-Nazi attitude within the circle of his students. In his last book, which he gave me — *The Tragic Element and History* — he exposed a decidedly anti-fascist theory of the historic flux and its motivating forces. Nazism he considered to be the expression of "dark demonic powers."

After the choice of these men had been made, an editorial discussion was held at the home of Dr. Jaspers. Many titles were suggested, but all were rejected. I finally suggested *Die Wandlung* (Metamorphosis), which met with general approval. The first issue appeared a month later, with a number of interesting articles, somewhat heavy in tone, but well conceived. Since communication with the outside world was still impossible for Germans, I wrote to T. S. Eliot in London, asking permission for Dr. Sternberger to translate his *Four Quartets*. Eliot granted this with much grace. I suggested to Sternberger the serial publication of a new German lexicon which would replace the shoddy Nazi terms. He introduced this under the title: *Wörterbuch des Unmenschen* (Vocabulary of the monster). He sent me a copy of the first issue with personal dedications from each member of the editorial board. Major Waples, the ICD publications chief, reported to Gen. McClure that the review was "right on the beam."

I was pleased, yet I also felt somewhat disappointed, as the magazine got under way. It was a bit too academic, I felt, and because of a certain dry university spirit, failed to gain a wide circle of readers. It lasted for three years, however, under democratic conditions, and will one day, perhaps, have its place in the intellectual history of German defeat and American occupation.

Meanwhile, my friend 1st Lt. Rosenberg had undertaken a somewhat similar job in Frankfurt. He also believed that there were two categories of Germans: one, belonging to the great tradition of Goethe's "good Europeans" and of certain Romantics, like Novalis, the gentle, pacific, humanistic, somewhat *schwärmerisch* lovers of nature's infinite metamorphoses, and dreamers of a better world; the other, the German who understood only an authoritarian imperative and lived, according to the Prussian Junker's instinct, for force and militaristic trappings, with little taste for the real art of living, possessed of an envious rage with regard to the cultural achievements of France and the Anglo-Saxon countries. When I met Eugen Kogon, wl:om Rosenberg had chosen as editor of a review he called the *Frankfurter Hefte*, I felt immediately that here was the "good German," the "good European."

Kogon was essentially the cultivated writer. He was also an anti-Nazi whose convictions had been reinforced by seven years of incarceration in Hitler's notorious KZ in Buchenwald. From 1933 until his liberation by American troops in 1945, he had lived in that barbarous concentration camp, where millions were killed off by degraded representatives of the "other" Germany. His intelligent eyes looked out from behind thick glasses, and his high forehead was an impressive one. There was, too, something almost priestly about him, and indeed his rather puritanical Catholicism colored all his philosophical thinking. Rosenberg had already arranged for publication of Kogon's diary, *The SS State*, which is one of the great textbooks on Himmler's state sadism. What a joy it was to talk to this German humanist! Kogon considered his principal task to be the re-education of German youth, and this theme has remained the leitmotif of his powerful editorials in the *Frankfurter Hefte*. It is doubtless for this reason, in addition to the more dynamic personality of its editor, that the latter magazine has survived, while its more academic counterpart ceased publication.

After operating for nearly a year, Brig. Gen. McClure decided to fix a date for handing over the entire DENA operation to the Germans. On October 26, 1946, he came to Bad Nauheim with his staff and, at a ceremony in the news-room, announced that this service would henceforth be a German organization and that the only prerogative to be retained by the Americans would be the examination of the files *after* they had been written and put on the Hellschreiber. Kurt Frenzel, chairman of the German publishers' committee, answered this speech in a few short grateful phrases. When the meeting was over, ICD arranged a luncheon to which the German editors and their wives were invited. A certain mood of optimism prevailed that day.

It was during this period that I was awarded the Medal of Freedom by the United States Army for "exceptionally meritorious services" during the war.

In 1947 I took leave of absence to devote myself to literary work in Paris. When the moment came to sever my connections with the organization, I distributed the following memorandum to my fellow German editors:

> You are about to enter upon a new phase in the democratic reorganization of the German press, which the United States Army began over a year ago. With the licensing of DENA to the German editors, you will assume a new and heavy responsibility in the execution of your task.
>
> The year just ended has been a year of instruction and practice in modern journalism. All of you were part of the DENA School of Journalism, which did not devote precious time to study of Goethe, Schiller, or philosophy, or to the writing of feuilletons and editorials on eschatology, but to practical training in modern news-gathering and news dissemination. You know today that *hard facts* alone are the premise for discussion and analysis.
>
> You should never forget the basic rules with which we began this operation. You have learned the American idea of objective, impartial and accurate reporting which ICD introduced into Germany for the first time. This meant adopting a journalistic practice which has been developed in the United States over many years of intensive experimentation and which today is a routine adopted by the great international news agencies. You must always remember the technique of the news-story

as it has been practiced in DENA consistently from September 1945 till now: A story begins with the lead containing the main facts and answering the questions: who, when, where, why, how? . . . It concludes with a detailed chronological development of the events in the body of the story.

The Christian name and surname, the title, etc., should always be given in full. Attribution of source should be given in the lead or in the second paragraph, if necessary. The German translation must be accurate. Demilitarization and denazification of the German language are primary objectives and must be vigorously pursued. An anti-Nazi, anti-militaristic, anti-nationalistic attitude should animate DENA editors in their processing of news items.

You have been trained for over a year to give *facts* and nothing but *facts*. You must continue to separate fact from opinion, to avoid strictly all editorializing and to eschew all individualized commentaries.

I think you have done a grand job for the last year. You who were with DENA at the outset and you who came in the course of the year have all contributed to making the DENA file a model for other agencies. Without DENA the new licensed newspapers in Germany would have been unable to operate, and I stress this because the carping and pedantic critics of DENA always forget this simple fact. To be sure, you have made mistakes and I think you will continue to make mistakes — for DENA is a human institution. But serious mistakes have not occurred and I know you will try to avoid them. You should invite criticism, if it is serious and aims at improvement of the service.

Now that DENA is to be given into German hands, I hope all the members of the News Room, the Feature Section and the Economic Section will remember these fundamental principles. May I remind you also that the future of the German press is largely in your hands, for you have already created the crucible from which the new democratic journalism in Germany will emerge.

I want to thank every one of you for your diligence and your loyalty to the ideal of democratic journalism in Germany, and I wish you well under the new dispensation.

At a final gathering in my office, during which an atmosphere of something close to real friendliness prevailed, a spokesman for the thirty-odd young men and women present handed me the following slightly facetious, hand-painted document, signed by them all, in which they expressed in

English their appreciation—how sincere I should not attempt to say—of the American effort. The spelling and carefully corrected errors have been retained.

DENA Deutsche Nachrichten-Agentur

Flash
Service message

To: Mr. Eugene Jolas
From: Editorial Staff Dena

241200 The editorial staff of Dena wants to thank you very much for the work you have done to put Dena on its feet. You had much trouble with the first steps of your child, but we believe that the time of the BOBBY-soxers has past and we shall bear in mind your teaching and live up to your example.

Through your advise we got the real idea of modern journalism and the quick and objective handling of news. We shall never forget the flashes and rushes, the lead and the first names, and we shall think of your temperamental memos in which you branded our mistakes.

Wishing you the very best for your future, we hope that in the time coming you will stay in touch with Dena.

End

Bad Nauheim, 24.1.47

Some months later I was deeply gratified to receive the following letter from Gen. McClure, director of the Information Control Division of the American Military Government:

Office of Military Government for Germany (US)
Office of the Director of Information Control
APO 742
9 May 1947

Dear Gene:

Before I leave the European Theater I should like to express my appreciation of the work you did with PWD-SHAEF and with Press Control Branch of Information Control Division during 1944, 1945 and 1946. Your efforts both during and after the period of hostilities contributed greatly to the mission of PWD and ICD.

I would like to mention in particular your work in France, at Radio Luxembourg, Aachen, Heidelberg and Marburg, but above all, your work at Bad Nauheim, in setting up DENA. It is due in large measure to your work as Editor-in-Chief of the news agency and later as Chief Scrutiny Officer that the German DENA has become a real news agency with great possibilities for further development.

I believe that our efforts to build a free press in Germany have made considerable headway and I take this means of recognizing your share in this very important mission which we have all worked to further.

Sincerely yours

[signed] Robert McClure

Brigadier General, CSC

Director, Information Control Division

After a welcome year of absence, divided between Paris and New York, I returned to occupied Germany, where I remained until the summer of 1950. Some of this time I spent in Munich as news editor of the army's German-language newspaper, *Neue Zeitung*. From the first I had certain misgivings as to the success of this assignment, for I had expressed virulent criticism of the paper, which was, I knew, still in the grip of a few die-hard German nationalists who were frankly defiant of all attempts to democratize their methods of handling news. I recalled that already in 1945 my friend Lt. Edel had pointed out to Gen. McClure the fact that the paper was still following the traditional Nazi make-up, and orders had been given then, banishing all editorial and feuilleton items from the first page. Quite evidently, however, these orders had been ignored. After the pleasant, even friendly, experience of the DENA operation, working in this atmosphere of stubborn hostility proved tiring, and I grew pessimistically skeptical as to the efficacy of our reformatory work.

The *Neue Zeitung*, which was, and still is at this writing, the official newspaper published by the U.S. Army for the German population, was introduced in Germany in 1945 by Gen. Eisenhower, with a statement in which he expressed the hope that it would function according to democratic newspaper methods and become a model for the nascent post-Nazi press. It was unfortunate that the paper's management would have been, from its inception, more Austrian and German in character than American, also that some of the leading Germans engaged for editorial work had been actively associated with Nazi sheets until 1945. For this state of affairs created a psychological situation which gradually developed into real tension between members of the staff. Edited and printed in the fortress-like building of the former Nazi organ *Völkischer Beobachter*, the paper appeared three times a week, employing a staff of editors that would have sufficed to bring out a number of additional papers. I may add truthfully that I was never connected with any office in which intrigues were so numerous.

The newly appointed American editor-in-chief was my friend Jack Fleischer, a former UP news correspondent with a fine flair for American news traditions who, at the behest of his American colleagues, organized a copy-desk which Max Kraus and I were supposed to supervise. This arrangement was bitterly resented by almost the entire local staff, and everything was done to sabotage our efforts. A rumor even got around that the copy-desk was just a manifestation of American suspicion of German honesty and that the intention behind it was to introduce a direct, onerous censorship. We explained again and again at our staff conferences that there was no question whatever of censorship; that in American city-rooms all copy was obliged to flow across a central desk for grammatical or other technical criticism and that the functions of the copy-readers were vital to the smooth running of any newspaper. But the German editors continued to do everything in the their power to circumvent our intentions. Since the establishment did not contain a city-room, we played with the idea of having one built, but again there were murmurings of sullen protest. The editors, as a matter of fact, preferred working hermetically closed to the outside world, in little separate bureaus, a method I dubbed cubbyhole journalism. Here the *Herren Redakteure* would lock themselves in for abstruse meditation after scribbling a sign on the door to "Keep out—Editor at work."

Local reporting being practically unknown in Munich, we tried to do as we had done first in Aachen and then in DENA—that is, to stimulate reportorial skill. But whenever we attempted to give the younger men a lesson in the functions of a reporter, they would turn to their elders in protest against our intrusion. In addition, their dusty writing technique harked back to another century; not one of them could use a typewriter, which meant that each editor had to be furnished with a typist to whom he dictated his text. I sometimes took it upon myself to rewrite the awkward leads, or "mottos" as they called them, that were more the rule than the exception in their work. But this, of course, was considered an insult. The physical make-up of the paper, too, showed a defective news sense, and we gave instructions that headlines should not be written in their *Plakat*—or poster—style (a remnant of Nazi journalism), but in the modern manner demanding a verb as an integral, dynamic part of the head. The falterings were numerous and the scrutiny officers had to keep careful watch over each single item, whether emanating from *Innen-* or *Außenpolitik*.

The population of Munich, during the winter preceding the currency reform of June 1948, was living, like that of most German cities, in bleakness and dearth, and since the official ration was limited to 1,330 calories for the ordinary consumer, the American army helped the *NZ* staff by supplying extra rations and GI meals. The shop windows were empty and the faces one saw in the streets were pallid and drawn. Indeed most German houses were unheated and cheerless, except those inhabited by the well-paid editors of our paper. Black marketeers were prospering, especially in the district around the Hauptbahnhof, where fortunes were being made overnight. Prostitution too was rife, with the result that hundreds of women were sent for medical and police supervision to the venereal hospitals on the outskirts of the city. There was, of course, much grumbling and lamenting, and complaints against the "Amis"—the German sobriquet for the Americans—were distinctly audible. The ever-swelling population of DPs and expellees had increased the housing crisis, and it was rumored that communist agents were infiltrating into the zone. Then came the currency reform. As though by magic, the shops began to fill up with the choicest foods and manufactured articles, which the merchants had been hoarding in view of more advantageous prices. Now a new life began in the ruins, but curiously enough this was only the signal for greater discontent.

The autocratic attitude of our top German personnel had gradually prevailed, and the German's love of luxury soon took the form of ever-greater demands on the American material resources, accompanied by increasing criticism. In the new public institutions being organized by the American Military Government we noticed that the tradition of servile obedience to authority (*Kadavergehorsam* was what liberal Germans called it) was beginning to flourish once more. It was "Herr Doktor," or even Herr Doktor Doktor this, and Herr Oberregierungsrat that, all over the place. The old gang, with its mania for tyrannical bureaucracy, was back in the saddle, and there was evidence of this even in the newspaper plant, where the title-dementia and gratuitous vanity of certain individuals was paralleled only by their determination to undermine U.S. directives. I personally had great difficulty in getting along with these men.

For a few months I worked as slot man on the copy desk, coupled with the duties of make-up editor on the last shift, with a deadline at midnight. Around eleven o'clock, when I went down to the composing-room, I was usually followed by the remaining members of the German staff, who were eager, or so they claimed, to absorb "the American way." On these occasions they would gather around me, whisper frequently to one another, or make futile suggestions. Whenever I was obliged to change the headlines from their too-static word-arrangements to more kinetic ones, I would hear a murmur of disapproval behind me. Once, I lost my temper and asked them all to leave. The following morning, at staff conference, they condescendingly plucked our effort to pieces. During these discussions, which were frequent, the word *grundsätzlich* (basic) was tossed about with irritating monotony, while they heaped critical aspersions on our journalistic principles. Jack Fleischer would listen patiently and then make his decisions, which were inevitably those of a skilled American newsman.

Although we eventually succeeded in instituting a number of important reforms in this Munich operation, I believe few who participated in it would object to my saying that it represented the last redoubt of Nazi journalism, the most stubbornly resistant fortress of a spirit we were determined to extirpate.

We know that during the war there was hardly any literature of resistance inside Germany against Hitler and that, with the exception of Munich, there was no intellectual underground that expressed itself in creative work against Nazi sadism. Is it therefore to be wondered at that the theme of the age-old struggle for freedom is hardly noticeable in contemporary German letters? In talking to German writers, one found a pathological self-pity. They repeated threnodies about their economic plight and sputtered lyrical inanities about the *Dachböden* (attics) where they were compelled to live. This could also be discovered in reading their novels, short stories, essays or the feuilleton pages of the newspapers. Over six thousand books have been published since the end of the war by the 374 publishing houses licensed by ICD. To a large extent, these books represented translations from French and American, while only a few new German books could be considered major contributions to the new spiritual evolution of the country or of Europe. Of course, the paralysis began in 1933, but the observer continued to be astonished at the persistence of the malady.

The feuilleton of the *Neue Zeitung* launched a symposium to explore the state of mind of the young writers. Walter Kolbenhoff, the author of *Our Flesh and Blood,* a novel imitative of Ernest Hemingway, said, "Give us time!" He arrogantly rejected the "polished articles and stories of the older men, because they are sparkling pearls and the achievements of experienced littérateurs." "The new men," he asserted, "have no time for exercises in literary style. They speak the language of the age and will express what has not yet been expressed about the tortured, bewildered people to which we belong. . . . Our generation stands before zero." A lively discussion developed. Bruno E. Werner found that the young men spoke with too much pathos and bombast and needed greater serenity. Carl H. Ebbinghaus felt that there was "much ado about nothing" and proceeded to defend the "polished writers" against the onslaughts of the half-baked iconoclasts. Another young man wondered why his contemporaries were so certain they were writers, "for to be a writer is not a profession or calling like that of a stonemason. . . . It is simply a destiny." These vacant affirmations were characteristic of the post-Nazi generation's reasoning.

As for the new novelists, no first-class talent had emerged so far. A group of young story-tellers had recently banded themselves together under the banner of *magischer Realismus,* or as some call it, *blutiger Realismus* at a meeting in Bannwaldsee. About thirty of them read their stories and plays. They have published little for the most part — save Walter Kolbenhoff, whose *Our Flesh and Blood* has had a *succès d'estime* — and their stories are to appear in a review called *Der Skorpion.* One of their spokesmen, Hans Werner Richter, stated that the "bloody realism" they envisaged had a strongly anti-romantic orientation. "The young people have not yet recovered from the tremendous shock of the last years. . . . Some have withdrawn into an imaginary romantic world which can be seen in the steady growth of lyric poetry. . . . We want to depict the real world, and our language must be vigorous." What they really wanted, in effect, was a kind of amalgam of old-fashioned naturalism and modern existentialism, and a skeptical and cynical attitude was stressed. They took as their models American writers like John Steinbeck, Ernest Hemingway, William Saroyan and even Henry Miller. The influence of this Americanism could also be seen in a new magazine bearing the English name of *Story,* which was being issued by the publishing firm of Rowohlt.

A vague neo-Romanticism was also in the air among the prose writers. It was a synthesis of Expressionism and Surrealism, and emphasized the metamorphosis of the narrative into fables and magic tales of terror. The representatives were Elisabeth Langgässer, Gustav René Hocke and Hermann Kasack. A recent anthology, *End and Beginning,* presented the work of six young men and women, among whom Werner Illing, Susanne Kerkhoff and August Scholtis showed promise in creating a fantastic reality out of the experiences of their battered world. Wolfdietrich Schnurre used the dream and the nightmare as favorite motifs for depicting man's inner disarray. The most gifted of the visionary writers was Herman Kasack, whose *City Beyond the River,* with its powerful evocation of the nightside of existence, deserves to be known beyond the borders of Germany.

A good deal of poetry was being written and published, but the ferment and audacity of French, British and American poetic creation was obviously lacking. No outstanding original name had emerged. Classicism, neo-Romanticism and apocalypticism marked the tendencies which manifested themselves, and the influence of Rainer Maria Rilke was still overpowering. Rudolf Hagelstange (*Venezianisches Credo*), Marie Luise Kaschnitz ("Ode to Frankfurt"), Werner Bergengruen, Günter Eich, Hans Egon Holthusen, Manfred Hausmann, together with the older poets like Hans Carossa, Rudolf Alexander Schröder and Erich Kästner dominated the scene. Only Walter Heist tried to break the baroque aestheticism of these poets with prose-poems like "Chants for the Man in the Street," written in Whitmanesque form with Rilkean languor as an emotional substance.

The older generation who left the Germanic countries in 1933 — Thomas Mann, Franz Werfel, Alfred Döblin, Hermann Broch, Fritz von Unruh, Leonhard Frank and others — were then little read because their books were hard to obtain. But certain writers who claimed to belong to the "inner emigration" (although they continued to publish during the Hitler regime) were re-emerging. The sinister Existentialist philosopher Heidegger and the brilliant but confused novelist Ernst Jünger dominated the thinking of the younger generation. The recent death of Ricarda Huch at the age of seventy-eight years left a gap in German letters. She was in some ways a great writer (poet, novelist, historian) who left a bulky production behind, among which her story of German Romanticism, interpretations of the controversial movement, is one of the best. At the time of her death, she was preparing a book in honor of the few Germans in the Reich who resisted Hitler and lost their lives at the hands of the Gestapo.

Poetry and prose in the feuilleton pages attracted many readers, especially in the academic world. In the desolation of the mental wasteland which was Germany in 1947, one stumbled only occasionally over an esoteric plant amid the heaped-up masonry. When a writers' congress was announced, to be held in Frankfurt for the centennial celebration of the 1848 democratic revolution, the Munich Redaktion decided to send quite a contingent of editors to the Main city under my supervision to cover the event. I went up to Frankfurt with them, but the resultant work was quite meager.

Although there were novelists and poets from every part of Germany at the congress, they did not succeed in hiding the fact that there was a vacuum in German post-war literature. Listening to the speeches, I could only find that their utterances were pompous and hollow and often tinged with Nazi or communist ideas and words. I heard not a single admission of Germany's guilt. In the verbose and puerile discourses there was no international perspective, only a narrow self-sufficiency and insistence on a resurgent nationalism.

Two authors stood out, however: Fritz von Unruh and Elisabeth Langgässer. Von Unruh, the playwright who had just returned to his native Frankfurt after eight years of exile in the United States, spoke words out of a democratic consciousness and shook his listeners with a masterful exposé of Hitler's crimes against the spirit. Von Unruh, one of the great poets of the Expressionist movement, remained an interpreter of international humanism. Elisabeth Langgässer impressed me as a poet of creative force and mythological genius. Her sufferings under the Nazis gave her style a hard, lyrical quality, and as I began to read her prose and verse, I had the impression of hearing that other Germany which I had looked for all these years since Aachen.

The coverage of the congress by the German feuilletonistes was a dismal failure. I felt the long-winded, pseudo-philosophical meditations, which they cabled down to Munich, could not interest any reader, and that they had no instinct for writing under pressure. Their stories were not reports in the true sense of the word, and when you read their copy, you never knew what actually happened. I tried to explain again and again certain rudimentary rules, but to no avail. I tried to point out to them that literature which they claimed to love so much was, after all, based on the techniques of reporting, and mentioned Victor Hugo and even their great Romantic poet and story-teller, Heinrich von Kleist. But they argued, with that obtuse conservatism of the archaic mind, that they were attempting to give ideas, and not facts, about an intellectual event. I finally gave up.

Our Information Division got busy a short time later and cleaned house in the Munich news-shop. The correspondent of the *New York Herald* had gotten wind of the chaotic conditions prevailing in the Munich outfit and written a blistering exposé which rocked the organization. Several Nazis and nationalists had succeeded in worming their way into the new journalism we had tried to build after the war, and a few investigations brought their names out into the open. They were all summarily dismissed.

During this rather disturbed period, headquarters decided to send me on an official mission to Paris, where the General Assembly of the United Nations was in session. This constituted a welcome relief from the intrigues of the plant, and since I was able to live with my family, who occupied an apartment near the Chaillot Palace, a relatively normal life began for me. Working in a bilingual capacity, away from all bureaucratic difficulties, in this city that I loved almost as much as New York, was a new and exciting experience.

In addition to preparing a news file in English for the use of the American army, one of my duties was to write and deliver a daily radio commentary in the German language, on a program beamed directly to German listeners. In these broadcasts I tried to explain the complexities of UN proceedings and to encourage German and particularly Berlin resistance to the then extremely controversial communist blockade of the former German capital. A number of letters from listeners reached me at UN headquarters, and for a brief moment I enjoyed all the sensations of a radio star. I recall that on one occasion I read my piece in an insulated glass cabin built on one side of the very hall in which the Security Council was debating the Berlin issue. While I was speaking, it so happened that the Russian delegate, Mr. Vyshinsky himself, was also pronouncing, in Russian, one of his more vitriolic diatribes. As I pronounced my simultaneous counter-attack in the sound-proof booth, I had the eerie impression that I was having a private spat with the Moscow delegate.

The press section at UN headquarters was a beehive of activity, and I ran across many former colleagues now representing the newspapers, magazines and wire agencies of numerous capitals. Here was a true "internationale" of the printed word, a group of reporters, correspondents and commentators who were transmitting in every language, to the far corners of the earth, one of the greatest stories a modern newspaperman could wish for. It was a story of conflict on a high plane, the cold war of words, modern symbol of the curse of Babel.

All day long we listened through headphones to English, French, Russian, Chinese and Spanish syllables thundering over the loud-speakers, while a host of interpreters played deftly and vertiginously with running transliterations. Having some experience of the technical and psychological difficulties of translation, I watched the fabulous feats of these verbal mediators with admiration. As I walked through the corridors of the Chaillot Palace, which, before the war, I had known as the Musée de l'Homme, I meditated upon the linguistic and conceptual confusion that had resulted from totalitarian application of Marxist determinism; the luciferian pride of the rebels against the sacred word, the materialistic hubris that had sprung up in the minds of disciples. In listening to Vyshinsky, I was struck by the conscious cynicism with which he used the same terms the West has used to construct its ideal of a living democratic faith; I watched how he employed our words with diabolical semantic distortions; how he hollowed out the old words in order to give them a perverted and purely subversive texture. The Stalinists, I felt, were deliberately creating this philological entanglement in order to befuddle the peace-hungry masses, they were using the malady of language pragmatically for their own ends. Democratic newspapermen, I felt, needed to be aware of this fact; they needed the will to find new grammatical and lexical relationships in order to take up the cudgel against the enemy's desire for domination. They would have to be more daring.

Thanks to our official activities, we journalists had opportunities of seeing at close range the tremendous drama of these deliberations, on the success of which hung the decision of peace or war. We sat in at press conferences and briefings that revealed the mechanics of the conflict. We listened to Secretary of State Marshall answering questions with the frank, keen awareness of a mind steeped in the thinking processes of high military strategy. His personality radiated grandeur of character, and one sensed that here was a man who had already stepped into history. With what sharp precision he chose his words in answer to the frequently loaded questions of the international reporters, whose speech reflected origins in many different lands!

But the all-important problem of the Berlin blockade was not solved on this occasion. Stubborn resistance and casuistry on the part of the Russians who, with satanic cleverness, used the most far-fetched juridical loopholes in order to forestall the sincere efforts of reconciliation made by the neutral mediators, continued up to closing time, and by Christmas, weary and discouraged, the delegations were on their way east or west. My Berlin superiors sent me a final message with appreciative words for the work I had done, and after spending Christmas with my family, I left for Frankfurt, where a new assignment was waiting for me.

This UN meeting was followed several months later by the first conference of the "Big Four," which was held at the Rose Palace in Paris, and once again I was despatched by ISD to the French capital as their accredited correspondent. This time I wrote my features in both English and German. The atmosphere in Paris was sultry, and the task of gathering and processing the news demanded long, arduous hours of work and waiting, sometimes until late into the night. Press conferences and briefings by State Department officials succeeded each other at the Crilon, and I was obliged to scurry back and forth between the hotel, the embassy and the little U.S. Signals "blockhouse" near the Etoile, where our teletype machines were installed.

I saw the four foreign ministers — Acheson, Bevin, Schuman and Vyshinsky — arriving for their tempestuous gathering. Unfortunately, however, the press was excluded from the actual meetings, so that copy was for the most part based on "hand-outs." In consequence, my commentaries — destined for the *Amerikadienst* in Bad Nauheim and for the Munich, Frankfurt and Berlin editions of the *Neue Zeitung* — were not as interesting as I should have liked. Even so, our ears seemed to be filled with echoes of Vyshinsky's cunningly calculated caviling, and our nerves were finally a-jangle as a result of the continuous clashes provoked by communist Cold War thrusts. Acheson's vigorous forensic rebuttals and offensives had the desired effect in the end and the hoped-for lifting of the illegal Berlin blockade became a reality by the time the ministers were ready to separate.

After my return to Frankfurt I was assigned to help in an auxiliary capacity in organizing the Frankfurt edition of the *Neue Zeitung*. Although this necessitated a repetition of certain quite elementary gestures and frequent starts from zero, the experience was nevertheless a satisfying one, principally because Bob Lochner, the editor-in-chief, insisted from the first on the use of American techniques and enforced their application. There was a city-room in which reporters and editors worked together, and also a central copy-desk. Many of the young German employees were eager and intelligent, and the relationship between them and the Americans—Lochner, Freddie Jacobson, Joseph Franckenstein and myself—were friendly and cooperative. Here, for the first time in a year, I felt that we were actually getting somewhere.

This was a temporary assignment which I enjoyed, as earlier I had enjoyed the more independent ones in Aachen, Marburg, Heidelberg and Bad Nauheim. Here I was in close touch with young editors—men and women—and I felt that the best qualities of the Germans were being put to use. Here was evidence that the notion of there being "two Germanies" was not entirely false. I made friends with some of what we called the white Germans and often felt something akin to pity for these people who had watched their country fall from the high places of humanity under the whip of the Antichrist.

June 25, 1950, marked a tragic date in the already burdened history of the post-war world. News of the communist aggression in Korea came over the wires one night while we were reading copy, and a psychic tremor ran through the office as the implications of that bulletin came home to the Germans present. Everything seemed in flux again, the menace of the totalitarian myth was very near. The Kremlin's tactics were obvious: to test the strength of resistance in the West from Alaska to Murmansk, from Asia to Europe, as had been done with the Berlin blockade. This was to be the prelude to further plans for world conquest.

One felt now an existential fear in the office, where apprehension of possible atomic bombing hovered over anxiety-freighted dialogues. The specter of communism with its messianic distortions frightened many, and I thought, as I had thought in Hitler's time, that the diabolical forces had been given power over the earth in order that the logos should come again more quickly. We were living in a dislocated universe, man was stricken by the satanism of the State, by the power-hunger of subterranean forces.

During these first anxious months, I listened to the conversations of the young editors both inside and outside the city-room, and I found among them a collective emotion of fear, accompanied by a growing sense of religion. "The frontier between western and eastern Germany is not far away," they argued, and some predicted a Soviet attempt to create another Korea in western Germany. Unity in Europe—psychic and social unity—was the only answer, I felt, to their apprehensions.

Towards the turn of the half-century the military government of Gen. Clay was succeeded by a U.S. high commission, under the direction of John J. McCloy, representing the U.S. State Department. Our control of the German press had practically ceased, and all the new German papers were on their own. It seemed an opportune moment to hand in my resignation, which I did.

West Germany's slow and painful return to the traditions of the Occident (a process of such complexity that I shall not attempt to discuss it here) had undoubtedly begun. Having lived among these people since 1945, I could not help but see the pitfalls that lay ahead. There was no doubt in my mind, however, that in the struggle against the concept of a police state, most of the German people were determined to resist. Events in Korea had shown them that the firm attitude of the United Nations in the face of aggression was accompanied by the strength of Allied arms. The more clear-thinking among them seemed finally to have understood that they too, if they strove for it, might one day live and work in an atmosphere of freedom. As a native-born American of Franco-German stock, I crossed both the inner and outer frontiers with an almost mystic conviction that the last objective of war and peace must be a political entity to be known as the United States of Europe.

13

THE FRONTIERLESS WORLD

But what of Alsace-Lorraine during the apocalyptic years? How had the millenary frontier-mythos evolved since the Götterdämmerung of Hitler's regime flamed up in its last quivering phases?

In November 1944, while I was working for Radio Luxembourg, Col. Chesnutt, Grober and I decided to spend a short leave in Paris. Just as we were about to set out, however, the Metz garrison fell into Allied hands and we were ordered by PWD headquarters to make a quick preliminary survey of the printing situation in the newly captured city. It was on this occasion that I saw my native Lorraine again for the first time since 1939: a desert of ruins and misery, a wounded landscape, a symbol of world-end. Once more the ancient *fatum* had struck the frontier-land with its scourge of death and terror. It had been a time of Patmos, a collective malady that had held these unhappy people in ineluctable serfdom. Towns and villages had been macerated by shellfire and bombardment; bridges had been demolished, families disrupted, decimated, homeless.

As our jeep drove through the outskirts of the Gothic city, past familiar suburban villages with such quaint names as Woivry, Plappeville, or Mars-la-Tour, I felt deeply moved. At the sight of ruined peasant houses before which the former inhabitants stood in forlorn melancholy, I should have liked to stop and console them. Soon I realized that we were in the heart of the Moselle country, where I had spent my childhood only a few decades before. Anxious for news of my sister and brothers, I decided to make inquiries in the village of Budange, a short distance from Metz, where I knew relatives had been living before the war.

After dipping into Thionville, which was by then an American camp, we soon came to the Budange region, situated at the heart of the abandoned Maginot Line. Peasant girls were busy in the fields, as though war had never troubled the countryside, and they returned our vociferous greetings with broad smiles. This was all the more surprising since fighting had taken place in this region only four days before. An old man walking in a meadow beside our swiftly rolling jeep seemed possessed of a dream, and did not hear when we hailed him.

Budange itself, however, showed many signs of the recent passage of war. There were numerous interstices of shattered brick, the denuded church steeple looked sadly into the landscape, burnt-out tanks stood eerily in the nearby fields. As we passed through the spectral streets in which only the inevitable dung heaps marked the former location of certain houses, I recognized the ancient château. We stopped before a familiar farmhouse and I recalled a day before the war, when I had attended a hunting party there, after which we had been served a delectable meal of wild boar and venison. A little girl with pigtails was playing beside the door. Despite the fact that I had not seen her for four years, I realized that she must be my niece, Christiane. I embraced her and hurried into the house.

M. and Mme. Erminger, Christiane's aunt and uncle, received us with cries of pleasure. I introduced my American army friends, and soon we were seated around a large deal table before a bottle of *vin gris.* My sister was not at home, having left a few days before for Metz, where Christiane's older brother was to undergo an operation.

Erminger told us of the battle, as they had experienced it in Budange. "It lasted several weeks," he said. "We were hidden in the cellar when a shell smashed through the roof of our house. Fortunately, it landed in a meadow on the other side of the garden. The Boches tried to resist in the château, but the Americans blasted them out like rats. One morning we noticed that the shooting had stopped, and when we went to find out what had happened, the Americans were already masters of the situation."

Having a few hours free, we decided to make a tour of the village. Although most of the houses showed the sequelae of bitter conflict, the peasants were beginning to straggle back from the woods, and an old woman stood praying before a wayside shrine. We talked with the village priest, who had been in the little parish for twenty-five years. We listened to his account of Nazi tyranny, the first cannonade of the American liberating forces, their arrival in a bright dawn. When we returned, Mme. Erminger had prepared a simple luncheon, during which we heard further stories of the years that lay behind.

"One sultry day in June 1940," Erminger said, "the Germans arrived with a small detachment, and immediately let it be known that they intended to stay in Lorraine forever. The officers, who were overbearing and brutal, were billeted in the château, while the soldiers forced their presence upon the farmers, even driving them from their homes, on occasion." He added wearily, "And so we had the *schleus* here again."

Col. Chesnutt noted with surprise that our conversation was carried on half in German patois, half in French. I explained the bilingual character of Lorraine.

"Were you allowed to speak French at all during the occupation?" I asked Erminger, for I knew that the region had been contested ground from the linguistic standpoint.

"French was strictly *verboten*," Erminger said, "but we kept it up secretly at home and, as you see, Christiane still speaks well, in spite of strong German pressure."

We said good-bye, and an hour later arrived in Metz, where we went in search of my sister. We soon located her at the hospital and there was a happy, if tearful, reunion. Six years had gone by since our last meeting in Forbach. And what years they had been! I was relieved to hear that my young nephew's condition was satisfactory after his operation.

The hospital was a large structure, occupying an entire block, that had been requisitioned for civilian victims of the fighting. Throughout the long corridors there was a reek of drugs, and an acrid odor of wounded human bodies emanated from the wards which were crowded with mutilated and dying. One ward to which my sister led me was reserved for victims of the Forbach battle, and I found there old friends and acquaintances: several elderly women with ugly headwounds, a girl I had known and liked, as a boy. When I approached her bed she burst into tears; I glimpsed the outline of two stumps under the blanket. The older women stared at me with incredulous eyes, wonder-struck at the sight of the former Lorrainer wearing the American uniform. In the men's ward I saw other fellow-Forbachers with mangled bodies. Some of them hailed me by name and told me of their hardships.

"What of the town itself?" I asked my sister, as we walked through the corridors to my nephew's room.

"A mass of rubble," was her reply. "When the fighting started, people remained in the cellars and many were hit by shells. Then it was decided to shelter the four thousand survivors in a dugout underneath the Schloßberg. They stayed there during the entire three months that the battle lasted."

Of my brothers I learned that after the *exode* Emile and Charles had remained in the south of France, where they had been able to hide their identity so successfully that they were not troubled. Armand, however, had been arrested by the Gestapo in 1943, and liberated only when the American army arrived.

After visiting the newspaper plants, Col. Chesnutt, Grober and I sat down to write our report. It ended with the observation that the special patron saint of journalism had once more, apparently, watched over the temples dedicated to him. As we prepared to leave, I realized that in those few hours I had relived old cycles of my existence, the family link had re-asserted itself, an almost vanished religious emotion had overwhelmed me. The mere use of the local patois had served to heighten my sense of having returned to the very roots of my European ancestry. For a brief moment my heart had re-created a world that knew nothing of migration, or torture, or war. Unfortunately, Col. Chesnutt and I were obliged to move on. So I said goodbye to my sister and to Metz. We agreed to meet again in liberated Forbach on my next leave. Driving through the Rue Ambroise Thomas and across the esplanade, I recalled the visits to my grandfather before the First World War; I thought of his stories about the siege of the Lorraine capital in 1870.

Joyce's expression "the nightmare of history" had never seemed more apt.

For some months after the cessation of hostilities, my duties with Military Government in western Germany made a visit to Alsace-Lorraine impossible. I was, of course, in correspondence with my French relatives, and several times passed through Forbach in the Paris-bound train, but I was unable to stop off, even for a brief stay, although from the train window at night I could occasionally see the outlines of the debris-desolate town, lying in prodigal moonlight. It was not until Christmas Eve of 1945 that, having managed to get hold of a jeep, my friend Jack Stuart and I set off together from "Schloß Schrecklich" for the borderland, well supplied with bottles of Rhine wine and other delicacies. After passing through the almost vehicle-empty French zone of the Palatinate and the Saar, we crossed the Siegfried Line in the late afternoon.

As we cut across the dragons' teeth of tank traps—which, be it said in passing, had never succeeded in stopping a single American tank—we felt as though we had plunged into a landscape of death. The little town of Saarlouis was a complete shambles, the result of the RAF's virulent attacks, and Saarbrücken itself was unrecognizable. Soon we were over the frontier at the point known as Brème d'Or. On our left I pointed out to my American friend the site of the first battle in the war of 1870, the battle that had decided the fate of the frontier-land for forty-eight years. Compared with

15. Forbach in ruins.

what I was to see in Forbach a bit later, it might have been a medieval battlefield.

Winter dusk was settling over Lorraine as we entered French territory. The miners' cottages looked eviscerated, the coal-sooty plain was dotted with tents and rubble-strewn streets made a dolorous impression. By the time we arrived in Forbach it was growing dark, and in the half-light—for there were no street lamps— the town had a bleak, sickly look, while the pestilential odor of ashes lay over everything. We went directly to the house where I knew that Armand, Emile, Marie-Madeleine, her husband Celestin, and their children were expecting me.

For the first time I heard full details of the Forbach tragedy. During the *drôle de guerre,* or "phony war," after the evacuation of the civilian population, both the British and the French armies had participated in actions that took place in and near the town. Under Nazi occupation the reconstituted community had led a comparatively quiet, if painful, existence, marked mainly by Hitlerian attempts to Germanize the population and by Allied attacks on nearby industrial plants. Then, in 1944, the town had come under siege by Gen. Patch's army, and for three months American troops, who had captured the Schloßberg, poured lead into the town itself, the Nazis having turned it into a fortress. During this period, over four thousand persons vegetated in a huge bunker burrowed in one side of the hill, underneath the castle. Later, there was savage house-to-house fighting in every street, until the last enemy soldier was finally disposed of. Forbach was almost completely wrecked as a result. The house in which my relatives now lived was partially demolished, and the vista down what we had known before the war as the Nationale (and which the Nazis had rebaptized the Hermann-Göring-Straße) was a desolate one.

After supper it was with real emotion that I watched my sister prepare to carry on the family tradition that Mother and Father had always adhered to, of making a solemn festival out of Christmas Eve. A brightly decorated tree stood on a table in the living room, and soon the house was resounding with eager voices, as the first peace-time Christmas got under way. For a brief moment the ancient ritual allowed us to forget the misery and suffering that had lain like a blight on the lives and hearts of all Europe since 1939. With the opening of the wine bottles, we were soon in the gaiest of moods, until there came a pause and we left for midnight mass. There was no snow to hide the bleakness and dross as we walked through the silent, nocturnal streets of the decimated town, and the scarred church, in which the whole population seemed to have met together spontaneously, emerged like a haven from out of the gloom. As I stood in the entrance, I saw many old friends, who looked at me with astonishment when they finally recognized me in my American uniform.

Recalling other days, I decided to climb the winding staircase to the choir loft, where Bartels, the organist, was waiting to begin the service. The organ had been destroyed and there was only a small harmonium to accompany the large group of young people gathered about him. But the nave of the church was luminous with hundreds of candles, and the entry of the priests and altar boys was the prelude to a sacred rite. In this atmosphere of ruin and distress, the ancient forms and liturgy seemed once more to constitute an irreplaceable reflection of eternal things. "Peace on earth, goodwill towards men!" Well-trained voices chanted the antiphonal responses and Mozart's beautiful Mass was impeccably, movingly sung.

I spent the following morning walking about the melancholy town. The familiar streets were battered almost beyond recognition, and the walls of the old church were pock-marked with gun-fire. I heard stories of the bravery shown by American soldiers during the house-to-house fighting, especially in the hôtel-de-ville, which fronted on the large market-place (recently the Hermann-Göring-Platz), and where windows were little more than yawning shell holes. This was also true of the nearby grammar-school buildings, which were in a pitiable state. In a little side-street could be heard the tinkle of a piano coming from the half-ruined house of former neighbors. As I strolled through the Rue de la Chapelle, I noticed that the street sign the Nazis had put there in 1940 was still visible: Adolf-Hitler-Straße. With my bare hands I angrily tore it down and threw it into the gutter. An old monastery near the railroad station was scarred and blackened, and I was told that many of the men and women who lived there had been killed during the fighting. Strangely enough, our three-hundred-year-old house, which Mother had sold after Father's death, was hardly touched. It was now occupied by an elderly couple who had recently returned from their war-time exile in the Dordogne department and had just opened a grocery store. The acacia tree in front of the house was still standing.

Jack Stuart accompanied me on a walk to the Schloßberg, where reminders of the fighting during the terrible winter of 1944–45 could still be seen. American troops had moved up from the Oeting Valley, and after capturing the belvedere during a surprise night attack, dug in behind the medieval wall where we children used to play at Indians in the dim long-ago. A thick pine forest surrounding the castle had been completely annihilated during the futile frontal assaults made by the Nazis. Signs of the clash were everywhere to be seen: old, rain-washed copies of the U.S. Army paper *Stars and Stripes* (Paris edition), battered tin cans that once contained "K" rations for our troops, rusty tools and steel fragments lying about at random. Down below we visited the dugout where the four thousand Forbachers had hidden during the eventful days.

Before returning to Frankfurt, I paid a final visit, with my brothers, to the cemetery. Here war had once more left its destructive mark. Many tombstones had been battered by machine-gun fire, and graves and box-lined footpaths were strewn with stone fragments. Curiously enough, the monument to the French dead of the 1870 battle was untouched. As I stood before the graves of my own people, I thought of my mother who, three years before, had lain dying during an air attack on a nearby munitions factory. I thought of her immense faith and of how till the end she had retained indestructible confidence in the ultimate defeat of Hitler and his gang. Indestructible, too, was my memory of those far-off winter evenings when we children had sat enthralled at her knee in the warm kitchen, while she told us Grimm's fairy tales in her soft, Rhenish German: "Es war einmal . . ." Once upon a time . . . On the century-old family tombstone was carved bilingually: *Ci-gît . . . Hier liegt . . .* Beneath it my frontier parents had finally found peace.

In 1946, when trains were running regularly in Europe again, I occasionally stopped off for weekend visits to the little town, which was slowly lifting itself out of its prostration. As the months passed, one demolished house after another was rebuilt, and gradually the inhabitants seemed less sad, less desperate with regard to the future. By 1947 my brothers had resumed their various occupations and repaired the war damage in their homes.

The *comités d'épuration,* or purge committees, were very active throughout Alsace-Lorraine, and they uncovered a drama of pathological proportions. For although most of the inhabitants had resisted Germanization, and many had been sent to prisons or to concentration camps, there were some who had participated in racist or other political crimes. The border tragedy was brought home to me with force when I heard the story of how the youth of Alsace-Lorraine had been impounded into the Wehrmacht. Many who had worn the horizon-blue uniform of France during the "phony war" of 1939–40 were compelled after the French débâcle to wear the green uniform of Hitler's army, and sent to Russia; many lads of fifteen and sixteen were forced into the Nazi war machine. This was made possible by the fact that Alsace-Lorraine differed in status from occupied France, the Vichy government having signed a secret pact with the Nazis whereby they actually annexed the country and abolished its name, which was replaced by that of Gau Saar-Pfalz.

I visited the plant of the local newspaper where as a youth I had first smelled printer's ink. Nobody knew what had happened to the editorial staff, and since the Nazis had stolen the two principal linotype machines, Forbach was without a daily newspaper and depended for news on the weekly editions of bilingual papers from Metz. I had, of course, a professional interest in these, and was disappointed to see that they were once more being edited in an archaic style in which an awkward provincialism predominated. Politically, they were partisans of the Catholic clerical wing, which had just been reorganized as the Mouvement Républicain Populaire (MRP), under the leadership of M. Georges Bidault.

In Berner's half-ruined tavern I met old friends who were trickling back from the exiled homes to which they had been transferred after the outbreak of hostilities. I heard stories of berserk Teutonic nationalism, of the concentration camps in the Alsatian towns of Schirmeck and Nasswiller, of heroism in helping young men to escape service in the Nazi armies. I heard details of the persecution of the Jewish inhabitants of Forbach, most of whom had simply been wiped out by Hitler's anti-Semitic campaign. Their ancestors had lived here for centuries, and they had been honored members of the community until the Nazi conquest. Several of them had even served as mayor, and had been very popular. The Hermann family, with whose children I had gone to school, were sent to Auschwitz after the Gestapo, with Vichy help, had discovered their southern hideout. Only one member of the family, the brilliant and beautiful Sarah Hermann, had succeeded in escaping to Switzerland. To everybody's astonishment, Jules Simon had returned, and was carrying on the clothing business founded by his father, who had died in Dachau. A school friend of mine, Jacques Lévy, on the other hand, was never heard of after his arrest by the Gestapo in 1941.

When I talked with Lorrainers I had known before, I myself grew disquiet and was unable to shake off the old frontier anguish. The ancestral fear of death and mutilation that is innate with these border-people came over me again, and I felt somehow a close identity with the men and women of my generation who had once more been subjected to the horrors of a fratricidal war. I tried to understand their fate philosophically, but it seemed to lead only to repetition and return. I was unhappy among my people and I wanted to get away. They were tragically familiar, but they were also strangers. We seemed hardly to speak the same language; in fact, we seemed to have no language in common, due to the many years of migration that lay between us. Or was this only an illusion? I realized that throughout my wandering life I had been in constant flight from this land of restless frontier-shifting; that each time I had returned, it was only to flee. And yet in the

American world something had continued to live in me that was a part of this medieval night, something from this past lived on; wherever I went, I carried the burden of this earth with me. Was I never to escape it entirely?

I remembered strangely prophetic poems I had written in the twenties and published in *transition:*

> mongols will race down your valleys and shout
> they will play dice with your bones
> they will crash your gabled houses into cinders
> your gardens will lie trampled and sterile
> panic will sob like a whir of vultures
> horses will spew sacrilege in churches
> blood will trickle from wounds like wine
> all dogmas will shudder into ruins
> stars will fall into crackling ashes
> scattered moons will be christmas gifts
> when can whitsuntide be o sun
> jackals howl around corpses of silence

And there were new poems:

> ville de province o little town that has seen
> the mutilations of the violent war of steel
> o ravaged town that has heard the tread of marching
> robot feet the detonations of the shells
> and the sobs of the feartorn women
>
> wax and wane o the fearful metamorphosis
> the debris of life lies scattered here
> the ruins stare into the golden spring
> death and life and the deep mystery
> of the petaled rose and the white music
>
> the church bell tolls thunderously the hour
> the way it did in gothic days
> american soldiers ride in high trucks
> singing tender songs to the rhythm of swing
> a tin pan alley tune with false rhymes
>
> evening comes with a sunset elegy
> the street begins to nod a carousel cries sadly
> the nightmare is over and the malady of the wanderer has ceased

and there is a laughter in the eyes of a young girl
who forgets cruel fear in the riot of a dance

There came an autumn day in 1947 when the feast of the patron saint
was observed once more, and the big fair on the market-place revived the
saga of immemorial folkways. At first there was a sort of forced gaiety, as
old and young participated in the festivities, trying to forget the nightmare
years. The merry-go-round organ played an old tune I had never forgotten.
As I listened to a group of children accompanying it in a sort of Dionysian
incantation, it was with delight that I realized they were using the same
words we had used in another epoch. I thought of the age-old recurrence
of life's primal words and gestures, and I knew that nothing human is really
changed by wars; that the eternal rhythm of man's emotions goes on and
on across the Heraclitean flux of time. As I watched and listened, I wanted
to cry out affirmatively to life, as I had done when I was a liberty-hungry,
America-dreaming youngster.

EPILOGUE

In a few days I shall say good-bye to the military world, the tensions of the occupation, the German words and take a train for Paris. I shall leave behind the stark ruins of Frankfurt silhouetted against a violet sky of June, the dramas of the beaten nation, the optimism of the High Commission for a democratic reconstruction of this gifted, disturbed, fermenting nation. Now that spring has come over the Hessian land, with cascades of white and pink blossoms in parks and in the countryside, I ramble about in the plenitude of nostalgic emotion and cast myself into the rivers of my Western reveries. But when I am in New York, don't my reveries go eastward? My long wayfaring is not over, I feel again a wind from the Atlantic and I long to hear again the speech of my fellows on Broadway or on Main Street in the titanic workshop of the Columbias.

The year I passed in the nightmare city on the Main River has come to an end. The city-room of the *Neue Zeitung* with its German sounds and methods will become part of my memories of other city-rooms in American cities. What will I do with the German language which I now have conquered again as a newspaperman and a poet, the language of my childhood I have helped rid of the militaristic and autocratic bacteria that Nazi ideology had poured into its veins, the language of dead poets I admire? I can no longer write in it now that I leave German journalism, when I return to the Anglo-American area of thinking. I wonder how it will fit into my new life as an English-language newspaperman with the *New York Herald Tribune,* where I shall be reporting the European movements of ideas. As I walk through the wreck-jumble of the Frankfurt streets and stray through the leaf-tangle of greening nature, I sense the saga of a new language gleaming in my heart, a bright illumination of good hope for linguistic freedom in the oceanic night.

The Cold War is going on with threats and challenges, and the Hydrogen Age is enveloping us in a prodigious disquiet. The reporter takes a prominent part in this battle, and I for one know that the vision of a United Europe, a frontierless Europe, is the only answer to the communist blackguards. True, it is dark in Europe, and I have heard good Germans express to me their abysmal fear of a new war that would be unleashed from the East. There is a Spenglerian pessimism in the hearts of many Germans, a Weltuntergangsstimmung, as they call it, a feeling that the globe is approaching Judgment Day. Anguish, fear, apprehension is the basic emotion here. They are sick with the great anxiety over what might befall them when the "gray war" begins to ravage their country.

As I begin my Atlantic journey once more, I stand midway between Europe and America. My life and my fate are indissolubly linked with the existence and progress of these two continents. I was part of a century of migrations. In America as an immigrant journalist I always felt those gravid and fertile forces of the European archaic unconscious, from which demonic and celestial things will come. I became part of the titanic crucible of races and languages on the North-American continent, without ever losing my European heritage. The European myths and languages were always with me — for good or ill, they molded the synthesis of my character.

Often in my wearisome voyage through language I thought of Babel — the millennial curse — and I wondered why it was a mark of my own soul? I wondered if it would always go on gnawing my hopes and mocking my aspirations. I thought of Genesis: "Therefore is the name of it called Babel, because the Lord did there confound the language of all the earth . . ." I thought of the Whitsuntide message a few days ago, the apostles "were all filled with the Holy Spirit and began to speak in foreign tongues" and each of the multitude "heard them speaking in his own language." Here was the vision of the future language, I thought, for the enraptured apostles spoke the language of the spirit and thus exorcised the curse of Babel.

I felt: as man wanders anguished through this valley of crises and convulsions, his language and languages wander with him. Man's language is also sick today. This "malady of language" to which I repeatedly called attention in the Paris days before the war is today affecting the entire Western world. In pre-war years we were a handful of poets who sensed it perhaps more than others, who passed through the pathological experience of diverse tongues, who found a progressive sclerosis in all of them. Some of us tried to find radical solutions. We tried to create a poetic and prose medium in which words were invented, in which the miraculous philology was posited. We were passionately interested in inter-linguistic experiments, in sound poetry as a musical or prosodical ersatz for desiccated word sequences, in phantasmatic deformations for deformation's sake. In those days we were, as we are today, paralyzed by the increasing sterility of our vocabulary. We felt like von Hofmannsthal's young Lord Chandos, who said in his "Letter to Lord Bacon": "I cannot write anymore because the language in which it would perhaps be possible for me to write and to think is neither English nor French nor Latin nor Italian nor Spanish, but a language not a single word of which is known to me, a language in which mute things will speak to me and in which some day I shall be called to account by an unknown judge." And when we were not completely paralyzed by this disease, we tried to redefine basic words in a semantic revolution, we tried to go back to primitive etymons. We tried to give voice to the sufferings of man by applying a liturgical exorcism in a mad verbalism. We tried to discover a language of night for the expression of the fugitive states of mind which has never before been expressed in literature by invented vocables: the hypnogogic hallucination, the dream of deepsleep and the diurnal fantasies. We worked with James Joyce, whose titanic hero HCE, or the Universal Wanderer, had become our hero, whose journeys through languages illuminated our own personal peregrinations in the protean words of the night-mind.

Now that the greatest war in history is over and the nations are trying to construct a troubled peace in an atomic era, we realize that the international migrations which the apocalyptic decade has unleashed bring in their wake a metamorphosis of communication. The malady of language can be cured in the kinesis of our nomadic urges. We are going towards a glottological unity. We feel that men must go in search of new words to be incorporated in the structure of a basic language. I wondered: Why should not the new ecumenical language be the English language which today is being used all over the world by seven hundred million persons and which is already an international language *toute faite?* Is it possible to bring into this medium elements from all the other languages spoken today: languages native to the American soil and imported from other continents? This new language should not number several hundred thousand words, but millions of words. It will not be an artificial language, but one that has its roots in organic life itself. It does not mean that the great languages will be completely annihilated or absorbed into the "big language." These individual languages will continue their separate existence, but only their essence will flow into the thundering ocean of the language of the future.

Language is in a fevered state today. It wanders about like the ocean washing the shores of the nations, depositing verbal sediments here and there, nibbling at the soil in foaming surges. Why should language not be channeled into a universal idiom? Seven years ago I called this potential tongue Atlantica, because I felt that it might bridge the continents and neutralize the curse of Babel. It will not be invented by philologists—we have seen their inventions: Idiom Neutral, Ido, Esperanto, Novial, Interglossa.

16. Nathalie Sarraute and Maria Jolas in the 1970s. Used by permission.

These were pedantic, unimaginative creations without any life in them. Atlantica should be a challenge to the creative writers. It should force them
to think in supracontinental categories. This language of the future would
absorb Anglo-Saxon, Greco-Latin, Celtic, Indian, Spanish, French, Canadian French, German, Pennsylvania German, Dutch, Hebrew, the Slavic
and Slavonic languages, American slanguage and all the elements of language now active on the American soil. It is quite possible that this titanic
linguistic compound would facilitate intellectual communication and creative expression on a universal basis if the poets would stop writing imitations of desiccated lyrics and write in a more daring manner. It would be
the antithesis of Basic English, which destroys the creative impulse of language. Instead of having a paucity of words, it would have a multiplicity of
words. It would be a monolithic structure of infinite richness and imagery.
It would be the language of the New Occident.

Language, like man, is today engaged in a vast migration. We will have
to go through a period of corruption and suffering, but we shall face it
without fear. A new cycle in history is about to open. The huge urban col-
lectivities that are arising will forge the migratory and universal tongue in
an exaltation of sacred and communal vocables, in a voyage without end.

INTRODUCTION

1 B. J. Kospoth, "The Poems of a Reporter," *Chicago Tribune Sunday Magazine,* 16 November 1924, 3, 6.

2 Sherwood Anderson, "Introduction," in Eugene Jolas, *Cinema: Poems* (New York: Adelphi, 1926), 9–10; see also *Man from Babel* (henceforth abbreviated *MfB*), Chapter 5.

3 Jolas's poems are still represented in some anthologies of American verse published in the 1970s, one of which even took its title from *transition*'s proclamation of the "Revolution of the Word." Jerome Rothenberg ties Jolas's achievement to the success of *transition* in providing a "link with European modernism" and in maintaining a "consciously numinous & experimental tradition of American poetry between the wars." The editor of the volume discerns Jolas's intention of moving in the direction of a "total transformation of language & consciousness" by incorporating the insights of anthropology and psychology—and moreover recognizes the "germinal" significance of Jolas's emphasis on primitivism for the re-emergence of comparable interests in the poetry of the 1960s and 1970s. Yet Rothenberg judges his poetry to be "often spotty . . . naively one-dimensional." What seems to support Jolas's claim to be an American poet is the impact of his "energy." See Jerome Rothenberg, ed., *Revolution of the Word: A New Gathering of American Avant-Garde Poetry, 1914–1945* (New York: Seabury Press, 1974), 148.

4 See letter to Maria Jolas from "somewhere in Germany," 19 February 1945, Beinecke Rare Book and Manuscript Library, Yale Collection of General Literature, Gen. Mss. 108, box 2, folder 33. Manuscript material from this collection will henceforth be cited by box and folder numbers only: the box number is followed by a slash and the folder number: 2/33.

5 Three stories from Kafka's *Great Wall of China* were published in Jolas's translation in 1932 in *transition* 21; the serialization of *Metamorphosis* (translated by Maria Jolas in collaboration with her husband) was begun in 1936; "The House-Father's Care" was published in 1938; all these translations were completed well ahead of Edwin Muir's translations of Kafka. For details and a critical interpretation of Jolas's pioneering interest in Kafka and of *transition*'s other editorial and critical achievements, in relation to Expressionism, Dadaism, Surrealism, Gertrude Stein, and James Joyce, see Dougald McMillan's groundbreaking study *Transition: The History of a Literary Era, 1927–1938* (New York: George Braziller, 1976). McMillan's book is the only comprehensive study of Jolas and the journal's program and accomplishments in promoting the European and American avant-garde.

6 At times, even the language of journalism caused Jolas doubts: "Journalistic writing is flat and infertile. malediction of language continues. can the newspaperman dissolve this ancient curse?" At the same time, Jolas exhorted himself: "The reader must be shocked into seeing the whole!!! The newspaper method of the future must be consciously modern." Jolas, the American journalist who believed in reporting and communicating facts, deep down retained a strong aesthetic bent. He admitted that it was probably his newspaper work that made him aware of the "malady of language" to begin with. While emphasizing the democratic function of the journalist, he increasingly came to see newspapermen as modern myth-makers comparable to the literary avant-garde, whose task, according to Jolas, is to "reflect the logos" and "create myths." Thus his idea of the modern retains a spiritual dimension. Like the German Expressionists, Jolas could never overcome his "deep aversion to mechanical instruments," rather viewing them merely as a stimulating aesthetic phenonenon (a "mechanist euphoria" as he called them in his early "Reporter" poems). As a result, he refused to incorporate technology fully into his vision of modernity. See the fragments of his Paris Diary; 13/256, n.p.

7 Jolas, 12/233, n.p.

8 Eugene Jolas, "Notes on Reality," *transition* 18 (February 1929), 19.

9 We have borrowed the phrase "god of modernity" from Josep R. Llobera, *The God of Modernity: The Development of Nationalism in Western Europe* (Oxford, England: Berg, 1994).

10 Draft fragment in possession of Tina Jolas, folder 1, p. 6.

11 Advertisement in *La Révolution Surréaliste* 9–10 (1 October 1927).

12 Eugene Jolas and Elliot Paul, "A Review," *transition* 12 (March 1928), 144.

13 Eugene Jolas, "Notes," *transition* 14 (Fall 1928), 181–82.

14 Ibid., 183.

15 Eugene Jolas, "Surrealism: Ave atque Vale," *Fantasy* 7, no. 1 (1941), 24.

16 Eugene Jolas, "Surrealism and Romanticism," 5/128.

17 Dickran Tashijan argues in *A Boatload of Madmen: Surrealism and the American Avant-Garde* (London: Thames and Hudson, 1995) that during spring and summer 1925 Jolas "switched sides," but apart from the claim that Jolas was "mesmerized" by Breton he does not give any good reason why Jolas should have done so. On the whole, Tashijan identifies Surrealism squarely with Breton and ignores other groups and tendencies that Jolas was attracted to. Also, Tashijan repeatedly conflates events and positions that took place or evolved over several years; he ignores Jolas's European background, reducing it to his suitablity as "cultural broker" (12), and pays no attention to Jolas's universalist pan-romantic agenda, presenting that agenda as simply a synthesis of André Breton's and Matthew Josephson's ideas (33).

18 See Dougald McMillan, *Transition: The History of a Literary Era: 1927–1938,* 81.

19 Jolas, "Surrealism: Ave atque Vale," 29.

20 Ibid. It is illuminating to note that much of the material that Jolas translated for *transition* was taken from *Commerce,* which was edited by Paul Valéry, Léon-Paul Fargue, and Louis Aragon, and not only from Breton's magazine. In his "Rambles," Jolas reviewed each issue of *Commerce* with enthusiasm, eventually describing it as the "chief citadel" of Surrealism (8 February 1925).

21 Eugene Jolas, "On the Quest," *transition* 9 (December 1927), 196.

22 Jolas, "Surrealism: Ave atque Vale," 24.

23 Jolas, 9/194. Breton in turn rejected *transition*'s "Revolution of the Word" manifesto in his preface to the October 1929 Dali exhibition catalogue. A month later, by way of reply to Breton's "Introduction to the Discourse on the Dearth of Reality," Jolas published his "Notes on Reality," in which he credited Surrealism with "having crystallized a viewpoint in the modern spirit," but charged that the movement merely applied Freudian and Dadaist discoveries, without transcending them. For Jolas, Surrealism did not reconstruct a "synthetist reality" — a comprehensive experience that would reintegrate suppressed with conscious data, in short, a modern experience of "myth." In spite of later denials by Jolas, such as he made in "What Is the Revolution of Language" (*transition* 22, 1933), not only "such precursors as Arthur Rimbaud, James Joyce, the Futurists, the early Dadaists" but also Surrealism provided the inspiration for *transition*'s manifesto. Contrary to Tashijan's claim (in *A Boatload of Madmen*, 30), issue 16–17 (June 1929) did contain samples of Surrealist writing.

24 See Robert Sage's response, "Mr. Gold's Spring Model," *transition* 15 (February 1929), 184–86; also Gold's reply to Jolas's "Inquiry into the Spirit and Language of the Night," *transition* 27 (April–May 1938), 236–37.

25 Eugene Jolas, "Poetry Is Vertical," *transition* 21 (March 1932), 149.

26 Jolas, 9/194.

27 Ibid.

28 In *Man from Babel,* Jolas reveals that he was nevertheless prepared to start an American avant-garde review with Breton and Masson in 1941 in which Surrealism would have played a major part. It would have been exciting to see which political stance would have prevailed in such a journal at that juncture, one year after the fall of France and immediately before America's involvement in the world war. Before the project could get off the ground, however, Breton took exception to Jolas's negative view of Surrealism's future (as expressed in "Surrealism: Ave atque Vale") and began instead to cooperate with the American Surrealist reviews *VVV* and *View.* Jolas and Masson, who shared an interest in mythology and the occult, went on to collaborate on several projects.

29 G. A. Hutt in the *Left Review,* July 1935; cited in Valentine Cunningham, *British Writers of the Thirties* (Oxford: Oxford University Press, 1988), 5.

30 Jolas, "The Romantic Genesis," 14/273. Colin MacCabe, *James Joyce and the Revolution of the Word* (London: Macmillan, 1979), makes no mention of Jolas.

31 Eugene Jolas, "The Revolution of Language and James Joyce," *transition* 11 (28 February 1928), 109.

32 Eugene Jolas, "A Review," *transition* 12 (March 1928), 145.

33 See John Bishop, *Joyce's Book of the Dark: Finnegans Wake* (Madison: University of Wisconsin Press, 1986). In Joyce's linguistic exploration of the unconscious, Jolas, significantly, merits only one passing mention.

34 Jacques Mercanton, "The Hours of James Joyce," trans. Lloyd C. Parks, in *Portraits of the Artist in Exile: Recollections of James Joyce by Europeans,* ed. Willard Potts (Seattle: University of Washington Press, 1979), 207.

35 Richard Ellmann, *James Joyce* (New York: Oxford University Press, 1982), 69.

36 Eugene Jolas, "James Joyce und die Sprache der Nacht," 4/107, translated from the German.

37 Eugene Jolas, Fragments on Novalis, fragment 9, 22/405.

38 Eugene Jolas, "Novalis, the Mystic Visionary," 21/394, 8.

39 In assessing Jolas's vision of the avant-garde in theoretical terms, it is helpful to consult Renato Poggioli's *Theory of the Avant-Garde* (1962; trans. 1968), in which he argues for the continuity of Romantic assumptions within the avant-garde. By contrast, Peter Bürger, *Theory of the Avant-Garde* (1974, trans. 1984), sees in Dada and Surrealism an attempt to break with the institution of art.

40 Jolas, "Surrealism: Ave atque Vale," 29.

41 Greeting Card for Eugene Jolas, 23/425.

42 Dolf Sternberger, Gerhard Storz, Wilhelm E. Süskind, *Wörterbuch des Unmenschen* (Hamburg: Claassen, 1957).

43 See Eugene Jolas, "Some Notes on Existentialism, Heidegger and Poetry Sales," *New York Herald Tribune*, 1 November 1949 (newspaper clipping contained in 4/85). In the course of his debate with Breton over aesthetics, politics, and the role of language and "mythos," Jolas had gradually aligned himself with the growing trend in Germany toward existentialism. The existentialists' battle cry was "fear, anguish and despair," Jolas had claimed in 1927, after reading Scheler and Heidegger (Eugene Jolas, "Enter the Imagination," *transition* 7 (October 1927), 159; "On the Quest," *transition* 9, 194). Overcoming that "fear" by aesthetic means and defining "mythos" were to become his great projects over the next years, a move that further distanced him from Surrealism.

44 Dolf Sternberger's translations of T. S. Eliot's *East Coker* appeared in *Die Wandlung* 1, no. 1 (Heidelberg, 1945–46), 34–39. In his correspondence with Sternberger, Jolas expresses his appreciation for the high quality of the first issue and makes special mention of the translation. Wilhelm Hausenstein's translation of Arthur Rimbaud's *Bateau ivre* appeared in *Die Wandlung*, 1, no. 11 (1946), 975–80. Ulrich Bauer, "Eugene Jolas und *Die Wandlung*: Politische, journalistische und literarische Publizistik zwischen Kriegsende und Gründung der BRD" (graduate seminar paper for Dr. Klaus Kiefer, University of Bayreuth, May 1994), provides insight into Jolas's involvement in the founding of *Die Wandlung*.

45 Eugene Jolas, "Romanticism and Metapolitics," 5/125.

46 Ibid.

47 The most telling example of this problematic affinity is Jolas's essay "The Primal Personality" in *transition* 22 (February 1933), which to a considerable extent echoes Benn's essay "The Structure of the Personality," translated by Jolas for *transition*'s previous issue in March 1932. Benn's essay was a singular re-evaluation of the modern cogito of Western man, a rejection of the logocentric experience of the cortex as a late development within human evolution. It valorized the "bodily" experience of the glands, nerves, and ganglia, with their imprinted memory of the evolution from animal to man. Benn speculated on another great anthropological mutation, a retransition to the expression of that culturally suppressed archaic "brain kernel," the site of a collective unconscious. It is Jolas's great-hearted, wide-eyed idealism that allows him to concur on the one hand with Benn's assessment that "the new man's

chief characteristic will be a violent revolt against the intellect" (Jolas is apparently oblivious to the re-emerging threat from the physical realm) and on the other with Novalis's reintegration of unconscious into conscious experience.

48 Previously in the context of his "Inquiry Among European Writers into the Spirit of America" (1928) and "Metanthropological Crisis" (1932).

49 Eugene Jolas, "Super-Occident and the Atlantic Language," *Decision* 1, no. 6 (June 1941), 51–52.

50 Jolas, "Fragments on Novalis," 22/405, fragment 10.

51 Eugene Jolas, "German Letters in the Ruins: A Report from Frankfurt," *New York Times Book Review*, 4 July 1948, p. 7. See also Jolas, "German Literature Among the Ruins," 4/96.

52 Ibid.

53 Quoted from Chapter 12. Such writers were for Jolas, for example, Herman Kasack (*Die Stadt hinter dem Strom*), Elisabeth Langgässer, and Wolfdietrich Schnurre, who "uses the dream and the nightmare as favorite motifs for depicting man's inner disarray."

54 Jolas, Draft fragments, "DENA," 12/231. See Chapter 12 for more context.

55 "Souvenir de Gene Jolas," 26/499, translated from the French.

56 For a survey of such currents in Anglo-American modernism, see Robert Crawford, "Modernism as Provincialism," *Devolving English Literature* (Oxford: Clarendon Press, 1992), 216–70.

57 Jolas, 62/1456.

NOTE ON THE TEXT

1 12/244.

2 Charles Allen, "American Little Magazines: *Transition*," *American Prefaces* 4, no. 8, 115. The same phrase is included in a monograph by Charles Allen, Frederick J. Hoffmann, and Carolyn F. Ulrich, *The Little Magazine: A History and a Bibliography* (Princeton, N.J.: Princeton University Press, 1947).

3 Stanley Dehler Mayer, *Fantasy* 7, no. 1 (1941), 23.

4 Eugene Jolas, letter to Maria Jolas, London, 9 June 1944, 2/33.

5 E. Jolas, letter to Maria Jolas, "somewhere in France," 19 August 1944, 2/33.

6 E. Jolas, letter to Maria Jolas, 20 October 1944, 2/33.

7 E. Jolas, letter to Maria Jolas, 21 October 1944, 2/33.

8 E. Jolas, letter to Maria Jolas, undated ("Wednesday"), 2/33. The most detailed plan is the fragment "Long-Range Creative Planning" (5/134), in which Jolas speaks of books to be called "News Voyage" and "Atlantic Novels," which would comprise several volumes, and a series of "Fantastic Novels" and stories. In addition, detailed synopses in Eugene Jolas's papers indicate titles and contents for autobiographical projects, some of which overlap with what was to become *Man from Babel*. The titles include "Voyage Across Frontiers," with the alternative title "Columbiad" (5/134); "Columbiad: An Autobiographical Novel of Migrations" (62/1456); and "War" and "The War of Words in Germany" (14/260–64).

9 E. Jolas, letter to Maria Jolas, Marburg, Germany, 19 August 1945, 2/33. For details, see 5/139. Jolas also planned a book on the experience of a journalist in which impressions "From a Frankfurt Notebook" would alternate with the chronological

story of his journalistic experience in America and Europe; see draft table of contents, 10/200. "War" and "War of Words in Germany" (14/260–64) belong in the same category.

10 E. Jolas, letter to Maria Jolas, undated ("Sunday"), 2/33.

11 Maria Jolas, 7/169: "*Note.* This is the excerpted copy found among Gene's papers after his death in 1952. No indication of date, or by whom it was excerpted and typed, has been found. Also, although we (he and I) continued working on the mss. until shortly before his death (that is, from his return from Germany in 1950), he never referred to the existence of the excerpted version." See also 12/244, p. [2].

In order to facilitate smooth reading the editors have decided not to clutter the text with unsightly editorial markers. Notes are keyed to the main body of the text by page reference and a catch phrase. Explanatory, referential, and contextual notes are included. The number of references required was enormous, and the editors had to consider whether or not it was necessary to explain references that were perhaps readily understood by readers fifty years ago when Jolas wrote the text. Some references mention other writings or projects by Jolas, some of which are currently being edited for publication.

PROLOGUE

1 **Prologue:** the text of this fragment is said to belong to Draft E of *Man from Babel* and is taken from a folder entitled "Prologue" (Beinecke, Jolas papers, box 8, folder 190 henceforth 8/190).

Novalis (pseudonym of Friedrich Freiherr von Hardenberg, 1772–1801): German Romantic poet and novelist, author of *Hymnen an die Nacht* and two philosophical romances, *Heinrich von Ofterdingen* and *Die Lehrlinge zu Saïs.*

Brentano: Clemens Brentano (1778–1842), a German Romantic poet and novelist, who converted in 1817 to Catholicism; co-anthologist of collection of folk songs, *Des Knaben Wunderhorn.*

Tieck: Ludwig Tieck (1773–1853), a German Romantic writer, publicist, and translator.

Wackenroder: Wilhelm Wackenroder (1773–1798), an early Romantic writer, a friend of Tieck.

Görres: Joseph Görres (1776–1848), a Romantic-Catholic liberal publicist, writer, and politician.

Hoffmann: E. T. A. Hoffmann (1776–1822), a writer of grotesque and fantastic Romantic stories and novels.

Grimm: Jacob (1785–1863) and Wilhelm Grimm (1786–1859), German philologists and writers, best known for their collection of folk and fairy tales, *Kinder- und Hausmärchen* (first ed. 1812).

3 **byss:** Jolas's use of this obsolete English word links him with the mystic philosophy of Jakob Böhme (1575–1624), where "byss," being the opposite of "abyss," means "plenum," "substance," or "ground."

CHAPTER 1

4 **four decades ago:** An addition in Maria Jolas's handwriting reads "1910," but Jolas must have arrived in New York sometime in the fall of 1909, because his first surviving letter from New York to Forbach is dated 22 February 1910.

one of the ramshackle farmhouses: Jolas was born at 132 Union Hill Street, as he relates in *I Have Seen Monsters and Angels* (Paris: 1938), 76.

astrologers: Two horoscopes from the 1930s survive in the Jolas papers at the Beinecke Rare Book and Manuscript Library, Yale University. For Jolas's interest in astrology, see also the incident related in Henry Miller, *A Devil in Paradise* (New York: Grove Press, 1956), 8.

a third brother: Jean Jolas, who died at an early age.

5 **Forbach:** Throughout this version of the manuscript, Jolas used the fictitious place-name "Liring," probably to protect people still alive at the time. The name blends the word "lyre" and Stiring, a small village near Forbach. Maria Jolas altered "Liring" by hand to "Forbach."

Treaty of Frankfurt: Signed on 10 May 1871, this treaty ended the Franco-Prussia war of 1870–71 and confirmed that Alsace and Lorraine were part of the German Reich. These two regions were, however, not parts of the federation but "Reîchslande" subject directly to the Kaiser and his Prussian administration.

6 **débâcle of 1870:** Omitted here are a paragraph describing visits to his father's clerical clients and a paragraph describing the geography of Forbach and Lorraine.

centrist or conservative: The conservative Catholic Center Party (1870–1933), which held between ninety and a hundred seats in each national parliament from 1874 to 1914, was the dominant party in the rural and the non-Prussian areas of Germany, whereas the German Conservative Party (1876–1918) was the ruling political force in Prussia, the most powerful state in Germany.

9 **Voulez-vous vous wegschere', petits voyous** (Lorraine dialect): "Will you beat it, little rascals!"

10 **salle d'asile** (nineteenth century): Educational institution or classroom.

11 **coureur de femmes:** Woman-chaser.

12 **Morhange:** The battle at Morhange, 14 to 20 August 1914. Together with the battle at Sarrebourg, it came to be known as the Battle of Lorraine.

dullness of his gaze: A paragraph describing the German military presence in Forbach has been omitted.

Bechstein: Ludwig Bechstein (1801–60), late-Romantic poet and novelist best known for his collection of local folk and fairy tales.

Gerstäcker: Friedrich Gerstäcker (1816–72), a writer of adventure and travel books, traveled extensively in North and South America. His trilogy *Die Flußpiraten des Mississippi* was published in 1848.

Karl May (1842–1912): A prolific writer of adventure stories set mainly in North America and the Middle East. The protagonist of the Winnetou novels is a noble American Indian.

Adalbert Stifter (1805–68): Austrian novelist and story-teller famed for his poetic descriptions of scenery.

13 **Ernst Haeckel** (1834–1919): German zoologist, writer, and influential proponent of Darwin's theory and of the "biogenetic law," according to which each creature

passes in its embryonic stage through the same phases through which the species has passed as it evolved. His popular treatise *Die Welträtsel* (1899) reveals a pantheism which would have attracted Jolas.

Barrès: Maurice Barrès (1862–1923), a French novelist, publicist, and politician whose books are characterized by a mystical nationalism. His cycle of patriotic novels about his native Lorraine was extremely popular with readers in the early years of the twentieth century.

Hauptmann: Gerhart Hauptmann (1862–1946), a German Naturalist playwright and story-teller.

Holz: Arno Holz (1863–1929), a modernist German poet and playwright and chief theorist of naturalism. An extract from his long poem *Phantasus,* translated by Jolas, appeared in *transition* 2 (May 1927).

Liliencron: Detlev von Liliencron (1844–1909), a German writer best known for his impressionistic poetry.

Redaktion: Editorial office.

Dr. Bucher: Pierre Bucher (1869–1921), an Alsatian author and journalist, editor from 1902 to 1914 of the bilingual *Revue Alsacienne Illustrée / Illustrierte Elsässische Rundschau,* in which he promoted Alsatian nationalism and an eventual return of Alsace and Lorraine to France.

Schickele: René Schickele (1883–1940), an Alsatian of French and German parentage, was a journalist and author of novels, plays, and poems. He began his literary career as a member of the modernist group Jüngstes Elsaß (Young Alsace), which wanted to renew Alsatian literature and spoke out against French and German nationalism. His writings appeared in numerous little magazines, some of which he edited himself. He moved to Berlin in 1904.

Stadler: Ernst Stadler (1883–1914) was an Alsatian-born Expressionist poet and translator from the French. He began his literary career within the modernist Alsatian movement shortly after 1900.

14 **awed by their great age:** Four paragraphs that detail Jolas's childhood visits and school trips have been omitted here.

15 **Atlantic-hungry imagination:** A sentence has been omitted in which Jolas dates these thoughts to the summer of 1909.

Exerzierplatz: Drill ground.

Kermesse: Outdoor fair or festival on the anniversary of the dedication of the local church.

16 **images d'Epinal:** An early form of strip cartoon.

marchands forains: Fairground merchants or stall holders.

our Indian romancing: Three sentences describing details of the fair have been omitted.

CHAPTER 2

19 **Gen. Frossard:** Charles-August Frossard (1807–75), commander-in-chief of the Second Corps of the Army of the Rhine. In 1870 he fought at Saarbrücken and near Forbach.

living in parochial quietude: Two sentences have been omitted in which Jolas describes his efforts to befriend the younger family members.

Taft's conflict . . . Teddy Roosevelt's Bull Moose Party: Jolas refers to the 1912 presidential campaign between William Howard Taft (1857–1930) and Theodore Roosevelt (1858–1919); the bull moose was the emblem of Roosevelt's Progressive Party.

topers and dullards: Two paragraphs have been omitted in which Jolas describes more family gatherings.

21 *baragouin:* Gibberish, lingo.

conspirators, if rather innocent ones: Two paragraphs omitted in which Jolas describes his lodgings.

22 **Amsterdam Avenue:** Three paragraphs and three German poems by Jolas have been omitted.

to get a new job: Three sentences describing his job-search procedure have been omitted.

G. E. Stechert: Then located at 31–33 East 10th Street.

my brother Jacques came to join me: Jacques Jolas arrived in New York in late 1911.

24 **I had missed heretofore:** Three sentences have been omitted in which Jolas describes a Russian-Jewish classmate with literary ambitions.

25 **"Requiem for My Youth" . . . windows of sadness:** A poem, "Immigrant's Lament," has been omitted here, as well as two paragraphs in which Jolas describes how his brother temporarily lost his job.

27 *Vereine . . .* **had also to be covered:** Two paragraphs have been omitted in which Jolas describes his lodgings and the harsh Pittsburgh winter.

28 **expressed by any of them:** Four paragraphs have been omitted in which Jolas describes his colleagues at the time.

29 **moth-eaten immigrant generation:** Eleven paragraphs and one German poem have been omitted. In them, Jolas describes his days off, his poetic efforts, and his neighborhood.

William Ernest Henley (1849–1903): English religious poet, editor, and critic. "Margaritae sorori" was published in *A Book of Verses* (1888).

Francis Thompson (1859–1907): English religious poet who, after failing to become a priest, sank into opium addiction and poverty. His ornate, metaphorical poetry is typical of the 1890s. *The Hound of Heaven* and "The Poppy" appear in his first volume of poetry, *Poems* (1893); *Sister Songs* was published in 1895.

31 **American landlord's family:** Emended from "American family."

eulogistic word-pictures: A paragraph has been omitted in which Jolas describes one particular auto show and his ambitions to become more than just a reporter.

32 **filles de joie:** Prostitutes.

36 **Louis Untermeyer** (1885–1977): American writer, and editor of influential anthologies. Jolas wrote to Untermeyer on 8 March 1918, 4 February 1919, and 30 June 1921; the letters are held by the University of Delaware Library, Newark.

Oscar Williams (1900–64): American poet and editor who published Jolas's cycle of poems "Reporter" in his magazine *Rhythmus* 2, no. 2 (May–June 1924), 16–65.

Rhythmus: One untitled poem has been omitted. It begins with the line "In a delirious dusk I walked."

Lee Pape: Author of the play *The Bravest Thing in the World* (1917) and of *Little Benny's Book* (1926).

Mergenthaler: The linotype, named after its inventor, Ottmar Mergenthaler (1854–99).

37 **Joseph Kling:** American poet and editor. In May 1919, Kling published Jolas's poem "The Idiot" in his magazine *The Pagan,* and three further poems appeared in subsequent numbers (through spring 1920).

Hart Crane (1899–1932) had met Kling in 1917 and was associate editor of *The Pagan* from 1918 to 1919. Crane published his first poem in the magazine, in March 1917. Between 1927 and 1930, *transition* published numerous poems by Crane, who was then working on *The Bridge.* Jolas saw Crane as the creator of an American mythology and an influence on his own neo-Romantic poetics.

40 **those hitch-hikers and gypsies:** Maria Jolas deleted two sentences here in which Jolas described his fellow reporter John O'Rourke.

CHAPTER 3

42 **Capt. Joseph Patterson** (1879–1946): An American journalist and newspaper publisher, he began his career at the *Chicago Tribune,* whose co-editor and co-publisher he was from 1914 to 1925. In 1919, he founded the New York *Daily News,* which after a slow start attained the largest circulation of any U.S. newspaper.

Phil Payne (1899–1927): City and then managing editor for the *Daily News* from 1919 to 1925, when he went to work for the *Daily Mirror.*

43 **Schaedsche:** A professional Jewish marriage broker.

44 **Paul Gallico** (1897–1976) began to work for the *Daily News* in 1922 and in 1924 became a columnist and the sports editor for the paper. He also wrote novels and short stories, some of which were published in the Sunday magazine section of the *Chicago Tribune*'s Paris edition.

Vincent Sheehan (1899–1975) worked briefly for the *Daily News* in 1921–22, before going to Paris, where he joined the staff of the Paris *Chicago Tribune* and became a correspondent for several news syndicates, as described in his autobiography, *Personal History* (1936). He was also the author of numerous works of fiction and nonfiction.

Dick Clarke (1897–1971) was picture editor from 1919 to 1922 for the New York *Daily News,* where his father was managing editor. After working for other tabloids, Clarke returned to the *Daily News* in 1930 and eventually succeeded his father, serving as managing editor from 1939 to 1968.

Clifford Laube (1891–1974) worked for the *Daily News* from 1921 to 1929 and became the assistant city-editor and Brooklyn editor. He continued his career with the *New York Times.* He was also a poet and the editor of a Catholic poetry magazine, *Spirit.*

Lamar Middleton, Jr. (1902–69): American author, journalist, and press agent. Son of Lamar Middleton, a former chief European correspondent for the Chicago *Daily News,* he began his journalistic career in Chicago, worked for the New York *Daily News* from 1921 to 1923, and then went to Paris to join the Paris edition of the *New York Herald* and eventually the Paris edition of the *Chicago Tribune.* His articles appeared occasionally in the Paris *Chicago Tribune,* and in 1928 his book *Life Among Parisian Puppets of Fashion* was published.

Montgomery Belgion (1892–?): Author, biographer, and translator from the French, member of the *Daily News* drama staff from 1921 on.

45 **Hugo Gernsback** (1884–1967) edited *Science and Invention* from 1913 until 1931.

our nervous stamina: Six paragraphs have been omitted here in which Jolas describes Papa Charley's speakeasy in Manhattan.

Oppenheim: James Oppenheim (1882–1932), an American poet and novelist. Jolas's letters to Oppenheim are in the New York Public Library.

Scollard: Clinton Scollard (1860–1932), an American poet.

Underwood: Edna Worthley Underwood (1873–1961), an American poet, novelist, and translator.

stabilize my disturbed nerves: A sentence has been omitted here, along with the poems "Ink," "Paradox," and "On an Old Newspaper in the Street."

47 **appetite for the latest developments:** Two poems and nine paragraphs in which Jolas describes his colleagues and his work have been omitted.

white man had trod this ground: Two paragraphs have been omitted in which Jolas describes his Sundays in Waterbury.

the cataclysmic powers of poetry and art: A long dithyrambic poem, "Anti-Machine," has been omitted.

49 **devoted one issue to my *Ink* collection:** Two poems, "Reporters" and "The Lobster Shift," have been omitted.

Toller: Ernst Toller (1893–1939), a German Expressionist dramatist and poet, was imprisoned from 1919 to 1924 for his role in the Bavarian communist revolution. His plays include *Masse Mensch* (1920; translated as *Man and the Masses* in 1924) and *Die Maschinenstürmer* (1922; translated as *The Machine-Wrenchers* in 1923).

Werfel: Franz Werfel (1890–1945), an Austrian writer of poetry, plays, and novels, born in Prague. His Expressionistic plays include *Spiegelmensch* (1920), *Bocksgesang* (1921; translated as *Goat Song* in 1926), and *Schweiger* (1923). Werfel's plays were not performed in English until 1926, when the *Goat Song, Schweiger,* and his historical drama *Juarez and Maximilian* were staged in New York.

Kaiser: Georg Kaiser (1878–1945), a German Expressionist, author of more than seventy plays. *Von morgens bis Mitternacht* (1916; translated as *From Morn to Midnight* in 1920), *Die Koralle* (1918; translated as *The Coral* in 1929), and the two *Gas* dramas (1918; translated in 1924) were popular in the United States. Toller, Werfel, and Kaiser, despite their political differences, had in common their attack on the brutality and antihumanism of the machine age, which is also a major theme in Jolas's poetry of the time.

Rice: Elmer Rice (1892–1967), an American playwright. His most successful play, *The Adding Machine* (1923), satirizes, in Expressionistic fashion, the role of human beings in the machine age.

Čapek: Karel Čapek (1890–1938), a Czech playwright, novelist, and essayist, is best known as the author of *R.U.R. (Rossum's Universal Robots)* (1921), a critique of the excesses of technology that introduced the word *robot* into the English language.

Frank Harris (1856–1931): Irish-American writer, journalist, and literary editor, notorious for his difficult personality. He wrote an autobiography, *My Life and Loves,* in four volumes (1922–27).

50 **tournure:** Turn of phrase.

51 **Stirner:** Max Stirner, pseudonym of Johann Kaspar Schmidt (1806–56), was a German writer and journalist famous for his defense of individualism in *Der Einzige und sein Eigenthum* (The ego and its own, 1845), which influenced the anarchist movement and the Expressionist generation in Europe.

fostered my apolitical tendencies: A paragraph has been omitted in which Jolas describes his fellow reporters, as has a poem whose first line reads, "They lost the virginity of words."

CHAPTER 4

55 *Spezereiwarenhandlung . . . épicerie:* Grocery.

Weinhandlung . . . débit de vin: Wine store.

Wagnergässchen . . . Rue des Charretiers: Cartwrights' Lane. The paragraph following has been omitted. In it Jolas describes memories of the houses he lived in as a child.

56 **the decade whirled around me:** Here a paragraph has been omitted in which Jolas describes his school memories.

Huysmans: Joris-Karl Huysmans (1848–1907), a French novelist of Flemish background. Initially an exponent of naturalism, he became one of the most influential representatives of fin-de-siècle decadence (*A rebours,* 1884) and mysticism (*Là-bas,* 1891). His conversion to Roman Catholicism is reflected in *En route* (1892) and later writings.

Jean Paul: Pen-name of Johann Paul Friedrich Richter (1763–1825), German novelist and humorist. Some of his romantic descriptions of ascensions and dreams of flying (for example, "Walt's Dream," *transition* 23 [July 1935]) were translated by Jolas, who incorporated them into his verticalist agenda from the early 1930s on.

Trakl: Georg Trakl (1887–1914), an Austrian Expressionist poet, influenced by Hölderlin and French Symbolism. Jolas translated four poems by Trakl in numbers 1 and 3 of *transition* (April and June 1927).

translated from one language into the other: Several poems have been omitted here: "Tu ne m'attends plus sous l'arbre," "Release," "Pageant," "Regression," "Muttersprache," and "I Was Tired of the Clang of Hammers."

ruined villages . . . everywhere to be seen: Two poems have been omitted: "The Visit" and "The Egoists."

57 **comités de triage:** Selection committees.

Hans im Schnokeloch was also the title of an anti-war play by René Schickele (1914).

bilingualism of the border . . . , nevertheless: The following two pages in Draft D (108–9), in which Jolas describes Schickele and only briefly mentions Solveen and Betz, have been replaced by an edited insert from Draft B (7/162, 203–13). The insert ends with the phrase *an uncompromising attitude to which his lyrics offered a curious contrast.*

Weinstuben: Wine taverns.

Solveen: Henri Solveen (1891–1956), a Strasbourg-born artist and writer, in 1924 founded an Alsatian-Lorraine artists' and writers' group, l'Arc, whose anthology he edited the same year. He was also the editor of *Les Nouveaux Cahiers Alsaciens / Neue Elsässer Hefte* (1921–23) and *Elsässisch-Lothringischer Kunst- und Heimatkalender* (1926–33); in most of these periodicals he published poetry by Jolas, who in turn interviewed Solveen and mentioned the Strasbourg activities in his "Rambles Through Literary Paris" of 8 June 1924, translated a prose poem by Solveen for *transition* 7 (October 1927), and referred to him in a dream text in *I Have Seen Monsters and Angels* (1938), 56–57. Solveen also published a volume of poetry, *Die stille Stunde* (1952). Throughout Draft B, Jolas called him Albing, probably to protect Solveen, who in 1928 was charged with treason for his involvement in the Alsatian autonomist movement (see Chapter 6).

58 **Kurt Schwitters** (1887–1948): German artist and writer, the founder of Dadaist Merz art, his name for collage art made from everyday materials. *Transition* reproduced samples of Schwitters's collages, his visual and sound poetry, and photographs of some of his paintings and sculptures. Schwitters designed the cover for *transition* 18 (February 1929).

Hans Arp (1886–1966): A Strasbourg-born sculptor and poet, one of the founders of the Dada movement in Zurich, who went to Paris in late 1920.

Marcel Noll (born 1890): His writings appeared in Breton's *La Révolution Surréaliste.* Noll became director of the Surrealist Gallery, which opened in March 1926. Jolas translated two poems by Noll for the first issue of *transition.* According to Jolas, it was Noll who in 1923 introduced him to the nascent Surrealist movement, and to Breton and Eluard, who were visiting Strasbourg. See Jolas, "Surrealism: Ave atque Vale," *Fantasy* 7, no. 1 (1941), 23–24.

Louis Aragon (1897–1982): French writer and political activist, who in 1930 converted to communism. Co-founder with Breton of the magazine *Littérature* and member of the Surrealist group, Aragon during the 1920s wrote poetry (primarily) and a Surrealist novel, *Le paysan de Paris* (1926). An installment of that text, "Discours de la statue," appeared in *La revue européenne* 5, no. 27, on 1 May 1925 and was accompanied by a portrait of Noll by André Masson.

Morgenstern: Christian Morgenstern (1871–1914), a German poet, is best known for his nonsense poetry.

Jammes: Francis Jammes (1868–1918), a French author of religious and nature poetry.

Jacob: Max Jacob (1876–1944), a French Jewish poet, was an early proponent of the avant-garde and cubism; in 1914 he converted to Catholicism. He died in the Drancy concentration camp near Paris.

59 **Betz:** Maurice Betz (1898–1946), a poet, translator of Rilke and Sternheim, and Rilke scholar.

Albert Schweitzer (1875–1965): Medical missionary, theologian, and philosopher, who was born in Kaysersberg, Alsace.

61 **"l'Arc":** Jolas substituted "The Bridge" for "L'Arc" throughout this section of the manuscript.

Gottfried von Straßburg (circa 1200): Author of the epic poem *Tristan und Isolde.*

Geiler von Kaysersberg (1455–1510): German priest who preached in the Strasbourg cathedral, he was reputed to be one of the greatest pulpit orators of his age.

Fischart: Johann Fischart (1546–90) is considered one of the masters of the German language. In his writings the satirist and humorist attacked the corruption of society and the Church. His masterpiece, which came to be known as *Geschichtsklitterung* (1575), was a free adaptation of Rabelais's *Gargantua and Pantagruel.*

62 **Hölderlin:** Friedrich Hölderlin (1770–1843), a German poet, spent the second half of his life in isolation. His poetry was discovered by German modernists, and he was a favorite with the Surrealists. Jolas translated a selection by Hölderlin, under the heading "Poems of Madness," in *transition* 21 (1932).

Nerval: Gérard de Nerval (1808–55), a French Romantic poet who was a forerunner of the Symbolists.

Achim von Arnim (1781–1831): German Romantic writer. In 1931 Breton wrote the introduction to a French edition of Arnim's tales, *Contes bizarres.*

New elements: Two paragraphs have been inserted from a draft in possession of Tina Jolas, chapter 7, pp. 1–2.

Aubette: Arp and van Doesburg began work on the project in 1926.

63 **Sophie Taeuber** (1889–1943) was an artist, textile designer, and dancer. She designed the cover for *transition* 22 (1933) and, from 1937 to 1939, edited the magazine *Plastique,* to which Jolas contributed.

Jacques Maritain (1882–1973): French Catholic philosopher who was a supporter of the right-wing Action Française, he broke with the movement in 1926. He redefined the relationship between Catholicism and politics in his *Primauté du spirituel* (1927, Primacy of the spiritual). In his essay on modern poetry "Enter the Imagination" in *transition* 7 (October 1927), Jolas takes issue with Maritain's dogmatism and expresses sympathy with Lautréamont's (and the Surrealists') celebration of evil.

Ball . . . Swiss mountain village: Hugo Ball (1886–1927) spent the years after 1920 in Agnuzzo and Sorengo, near Lugano.

Yvan Goll (1891–1950): Born in Alsace, Goll was a bilingual poet, novelist, playwright, and translator. He lived in Zurich from 1915 to 1919 and then went to Paris, where in 1924 he launched his own short-lived *surréalisme* movement.

Claire Goll (1891–1971): German poet, novelist, and translator, the editor of an anthology of modern American poetry, *Die neue Welt* (1921). She and Yvan Goll emigrated in August 1939 via Cuba to New York. Jolas had known the Golls at least since 1924, when he frequently interviewed them and reviewed their work in his column "Rambles Through Literary Paris" (see the 1 June, 20 July, 31 August, 7 September, and 19 October 1924 issues of the European edition of the *Chicago Tribune*).

Maxime Alexandre (1901–64): A French poet, playwright, and essayist, he published his first collection of poetry, *Le corsage,* with Editions Surréalistes in 1931, followed by *Mythologie personnelle* in 1933 (with Editions des Cahiers Libres, which also published Jolas's *Mots-déluges* that year). He later wrote *Hölderlin le poète* (1942) and two autobiographies, *La sagesse de la folie* (1952) and *Mémoires d'un surréaliste* (published posthumously in 1968).

One of our lustiest insurgents: Two paragraphs from Draft B (7/162), 220, have been inserted here.

The second anthology: This paragraph has been inserted from the draft in the possession of Tina Jolas, chapter 7, p. 3. It is an edited version of a similar paragraph contained in Draft B.

64 **Meanwhile:** The manuscript read, "After a few months." These final paragraphs are once more taken from Draft D (109–10, 114).

Sorge: Reinhard Sorge (1892–1916), a German playwright. His *Der Bettler* (The beggar, 1912) is regarded as one of the earliest Expressionist dramas.

return to Forbach: The rest of this paragraph, the following six paragraphs, and the first sentence of the paragraph after that, as well as a poem, "Words for Europe," have been omitted. In these passages, Jolas describes his coverage for the *New York World* of the nuns' revolt in an Alsatian monastery near Hagenau.

David Darrah (1894–1976): An American journalist and editor, he worked for the Paris edition of the *Chicago Tribune,* beginning in 1919, and was its managing editor from 1923 to 1926.

CHAPTER 5

65 **I also suffered language:** Seven paragraphs have been omitted here in which Jolas describes the *Chicago Tribune* editorial offices, the Paris neighborhood, and some of his colleagues.

66 **Aristide Briand** (1862–1932): French political leader and prime minister (1909–11 and 1915–17). After World War I, he served as foreign minister and practiced a policy of rapprochement with Germany. He was chiefly responsible for the Treaty of Locarno, signed in 1925.

Edouard Herriot (1872–1957): French prime minister and foreign minister from June 1924 to April 1925.

Action Française: Influential right-wing political group in France. Founded in 1898 by the writer Charles Maurras, it ceased to exist after World War II.

Otto Kahn: Otto Hermann Kahn (1867–1934), a German-born New York banker and patron of the arts. "French Economic Situation Sound, Says Otto H. Kahn; Lauds Mussolini," Paris *Tribune,* 15 May 1925, covered Kahn's speech. In *Of Many Things, Being Reflections and Impressions on International Affairs, Domestic Topics and The Arts* (New York, 1926), Kahn quotes at length from a speech delivered in Paris (380–85) and goes on to describe meeting Mussolini (385) and to praise the achievements of Italian Fascism (389–95). Kahn was in Europe in summer 1924 and in May 1925, when he visited Paris and London.

Senator Capper: Arthur Capper (1865–1951), senator from Kansas beginning in 1919, visited Europe in September 1925.

Senator La Follette: Robert Marion La Follette (1855–1925), a senator from 1905 to 1924 who ran unsuccessfully for president in the 1924 campaign.

67 **the office of the *Chicago Tribune*:** 5 Rue Lamartine; the night entrance was at 61 Rue Lafayette.

voleur: Thief.

espèce de voyou: Hoodlum.

va sur le trottoir, toi: Out on the street, you!

68 **Bert McCormick:** Robert Rutherford McCormick (1880–1955), a newspaper publisher, took over the ownership and management of the *Chicago Tribune* in 1911. During World War I, he fought in France and was discharged a colonel. The Paris edition of the *Chicago Tribune,* whose first issue was published 4 July 1917, was originally intended for the American expeditionary force in Europe and only after the armistice was converted into the *Tribune*'s European edition. In 1919, McCormick founded the New York *Daily News,* which was run by his cousin Joseph M. Patterson. Jolas worked for it in 1921. The official name of the Paris paper was the *Chicago Tribune and the Daily News New York — Europe's American Newspaper.*

Eugène Rosetti: In spring 1924, he frequently reviewed French publications and wrote a column entitled "Little Tours of Paris." For an account of his political allegiances, see Al Laney, *Paris Herald: The Incredible Newspaper* (New York, 1947), 79.

Senator Caillaux: Joseph Caillaux (1863–1944), a French politician who served several times as finance minister and once as prime minister (1911). Arrested in 1918, he was convicted two years later of corresponding with Germans during the war. Reprieved in 1924, he was elected senator and once again became finance minister. He took part in the war debt negotiations with the United States.

headlines and news-stories: Four paragraphs have been omitted here in which Jolas describes visits to various Paris *faubourgs* on his days off, and his fascination with the *foires.*

69 **Paul Rosenstand:** Danish musician. Jolas mentions him in a dream text in *I Have Seen Monsters and Angels* (Paris, 1938), 47.

Dwight Fiske: American musician and poet (*Why Should Penguins Fly?* New York 1936).

Jacques Leclercq (1898–1972): French-American educator, prolific translator of French literature, and writer. He published three volumes of poetry in the United States — *Attitudes* (1922), *Sotto voce* (1923), and *A Sorbonne of the Hinterland* (1925) — and one volume of stories, *Show Cases* (1928).

Edmund Pendleton (born 1899): Composer of *Bid Adieu: Words and Air by James Joyce* (1949), among other works.

George Antheil (1900–59): American avant-garde composer; in the 1920s, an associate and collaborator of Pound's. He toured Europe as a professional pianist — just as Jacques Jolas did — before becoming known in 1925 for his *Jazz Symphony,* which was followed by *Ballet Mécanique* (1927) and the opera *Transatlantic* (1930).

71 **"triumph of American musicianship":** Four paragraphs have been omitted in which Jolas describes his move to the Left Bank in early 1925.

Ford Madox Ford (born Ford Madox Hueffer, 1873–1939): English novelist and editor. He wrote a series of twelve weekly articles entitled "Literary *Causeries*" for the Paris *Tribune,* which were published between 17 February and 4 May 1924. It is not clear why he resigned. From February 1924 onward, he also edited a monthly literary magazine *transatlantic review,* where he published e.e. cummings, Hemingway, Joyce, Stein, and Jean Rhys. For the "French pages" of the review, Ford was assisted by Cassou, Georges Pillemont, Ribemont-Dessaignes and Soupault, as he reports in one of his autobiographies, *It Was the Nightingale* (1934). Jolas's "Rambles Through Paris," at first entitled "Through Paris Bookland," appeared weekly beginning on 25 May 1924. Jolas interviewed Ford (27 July 1924) and discussed the *transatlantic review* (27 July, 12 October, 9 November, and 28 December 1924).

72 **Henri de Régnier** (1864–1936): French Symbolist poet and novelist who in his later writings turned toward classicism.

Stuart Merrill (1863–1915): Symbolist poet who published six volumes of French poetry and one volume of English writing between 1890 and 1909. Two posthumous volumes appeared in Paris in 1919 and 1925.

Saint-Pol-Roux-le-Magnifique: Saint-Pol-Roux, pseudonym of Paul Roux (1861–1940), a French Symbolist poet. He retreated to Brittany in 1898. The Surrealists praised him as a "master of the image" and "the sole authentic precursor of the modern movement."

Jules Laforgue (1860–87): French modernist writer and poet who had great influence on later poets, especially T. S. Eliot.

Jean Giraudoux (1882–1944): French diplomat and one of the best-known modern writers in France. He began as a novelist but later turned to drama. *Amica America,* an account of his travels in New England, appeared in 1918. For an account of Jolas's meeting with Giraudoux, see his "Rambles" of 12 October 1924.

Paul Morand (1888–1976): French diplomat, novelist, and travel writer. His books are for the most part impressionistic studies of the nightlife in Europe between the wars. The title remembered by Jolas, *L'Europe sentimentale,* is incorrect. Morand's *L'Europe galante* (1925), which depicted the decadence of the interwar years, went through many printings.

Francois Mauriac (1885–1970): French novelist, playwright, and critic. *Genitrix* appeared in 1923. See Jolas's "Rambles" of 11 January 1925.

Breton (1896–1966): André Breton, poet, founder and theorist of the Surrealist movement. Jolas first mentions Breton in his "Rambles" of 3 August 1924 and, beginning later that month, reported regularly on the development of Surrealism. For his interview with Breton, see his "Rambles" of 5 July 1925.

Philippe Soupault (1897–1987): Poet and novelist; a Surrealist in the 1920s, he was co-author with Breton of *Les champs magnétiques* (1920). Jolas's interview with Soupault appeared in his "Rambles" of 8 March 1925.

73 **Jacques Rivière** (1886–1925): Critic, essayist, and novelist, one of the literary personalities of his generation. He joined the *NRF* in 1910 and became its director in 1919. *Etudes* appeared first in 1911 and went through a number of reprints. For Jolas's first meeting with Rivière, see his article "Through Paris Bookland," 1 June 1924.

André Gide (1869–1951): The interview was arranged by Rivière; see Jolas's "Rambles" of 22 June 1924.

I was also presented: A paragraph break has been introduced by the editors.

Charles Du Bos (1882–1939): Man of letters and critic; born in Paris of partly American ancestry, he was especially committed to interpreting foreign thought and literature; in 1927 he converted to Catholicism. Jolas wrote about Du Bos in his "Rambles" of 22 June and 5 October 1924.

74 **Lafcadio:** The hero of Gide's *Les caves du Vatican* (1914).

Jean Prévost (1901–44): A French humanist novelist and critic.

Pierre Drieu la Rochelle (1893–1945): Novelist and political essayist of fascist tendencies; director of the *NRF*, 1940–44.

Jean-Richard Bloch (1884–1947): French Jewish novelist and critic. In his novel *... et Cie.* (1913) he describes the fate of an Alsatian industrial family after the Franco-Prussian War of 1870.

Pierre-Jean Jouve (1887–1976): French poet and novelist whose writings are characterized by erotic, psychoanalytical, and mystical elements; by the time Jolas met him, Jouve had converted to Catholicism.

Pierre MacOrlan (1883–1970): Pseudonym of Pierre Dumarchais, center figure of the Montmartre movement and author of humorous tales and adventure novels; his Paris novels of the 1920s express the disquiet of the interwar years.

Léon-Paul Fargue (1876–1947): Poet whose work spans several modernist styles, from Symbolism to cubism, and one of the editors of *Commerce*. *Poèmes, suivis de Pour la musique* appeared in 1919. Fargue exercised a major influence on younger poets after 1918. Jolas held his prose poems in high regard and translated them regularly for *transition*. On Fargue, see also Jolas's "Notes," *transition* 14 (Fall 1928), 184–85.

75 **the great review** *Commerce:* Edited from 1924 to 1932 by Valéry, Fargue, and Larbaud; see Jolas's review of the first issue, "Rambles," 31 August 1924. On 8 February 1925 he reported that Surrealism had "captured as its chief citadel" *Commerce*. In *Commerce*, Jolas found many items that were close to his agenda, from Aragon's "Une vague de rêves" (2; Autumn 1924) to Bernard Groethuysen's introduction of the German mystic Meister Eckhart (4; Spring 1925) and Hölderlin's poems of madness (5; Autumn 1925). A number of other texts, among them Breton's "Introduction au discours sur le peu de réalité" (3; Winter 1924) and the opening chapter of "Nadja" (13; Autumn 1927), Fargue's "La drogue" (12; Summer 1927) and "L'exil" (13; Autumn 1927), and Drieu La Rochelle's "Le jeune Européen" (9; Autumn 1926), appeared in translation in *transition*.

Vulturne: A volume of poetic prose that appeared in 1928.

D'après Paris appeared first in 1921. A second edition was published by the *NRF* in 1931, and then reprinted by Gallimard, in 1932.

Marcel Raval: For this interview, see Jolas's "Rambles," 3 August and 10 August 1924.

Tristan Tzara (1896–1963): Pseudonym of Samuel Rosenstock. He became known as the leader of the French Dadaists. In his "Rambles" of 28 September 1924, Jolas interviewed Tzara and reviewed his *7 manifestes dada* before its publication.

76 **the suburb of Meudon . . . ultra-modern house:** The Arps settled there in 1926; the house is constructed and decorated entirely from Sophie Taeuber-Arp's designs.

Valéry Larbaud (1881–1957): French novelist, poet, essayist, and translator. He was closely associated with the *NRF* and was the co-editor of *Commerce.*

77 **Stuart Gilbert** (1883–1969): British writer and prolific translator from the French (of Camus, Malraux, Sartre, Saint-Exupéry). With Jolas, he translated Artaud and Béguin for *transition,* and he assisted Auguste Morel and Valéry Larbaud in preparing the French translation of *Ulysses.* In 1930, his *James Joyce's Ulysses* was published.

recently written something about him: In his first "Rambles," 25 May 1924.

78 **Ernest Walsh** (1895–1926): See Jolas's obituary of him in the *Chicago Tribune* (Paris edition) of 26 October 1926.

79 **some new poems . . . to *This Quarter:*** Three "Cinema Poems" appeared in *This Quarter* 1 (2) in 1925, and two further poems, "Rhythms by Wireless" and "New York" in 1 (3) in 1927.

Hemingway published a violent poem in *Der Querschnitt:* "The Soul of Spain with McAlmon and Bird the Publishers," 2 (Summer 1924), 229–30. The poem mocks art movements, democracy, fellow writers, and literary magazines, mimics Gertrude Stein's repetitive style, and contains a number of four-letter words.

I wrote him an open letter: "Rambles," 16 November 1924. In this letter Jolas objects also to the other poem by Hemingway in the same issue of *Der Querschnitt,* "The Earnest Liberal's Lament," p. 231.

Sinclair Lewis (1885–1951). Possibly a mistake on Jolas's part: *Main Street* appeared in 1920. In 1926, Lewis was awarded the Pulitzer Prize for *Arrowsmith,* which had been published in 1925.

Woodward: William E. Woodward (1874–1950), whose novel *Bunk* was published in 1923.

80 **Paul Eluard** (1895–1952): Pseudonym of French poet Eugène Grindel.

the first issue of the *Révolution Surréaliste:* It was dated 1 December 1924.

with the fourth issue, Breton himself took over: The issue is dated 15 July 1925. The manuscript has "third issue."

81 **Raymond Queneau** (1903–76): French poet, novelist, and essayist who collaborated with the Surrealist group from 1924 until 1929.

82 **Michel Leiris** (1909–90): French writer whose Surrealist verbal experiments appeared in *La Révolution Surréaliste* and in book-form, *Glossaires j'y serre mes gloses* (1925).

Joseph Delteil (1894–1978): French writer who belonged to the Surrealist group but was expelled in 1925 for winning the Prix Fémina; he abandoned writing for reasons of ill health in 1930.

Roger Vitrac (1899–1952): French playwright and pioneer of Surrealist theater. When he and **Antonin Artaud** (1896–1948) were both expelled from the Surrealist group, they staged their plays at the Théâtre Alfred Jarry. Vitrac contributed two reviews, one article "Le langage à part," and poetry to *transition* in 1929 and 1930 (issues 16–17, 18, and 19–20).

Robert Desnos (1900–45): French Surrealist poet. His poetry and prose appeared in *transition* between 1927 and 1929 (issues 1, 6, 14, 15, and 18).

poems in what he called a *langage cuit*: These poems appeared first in *La Révolution Surréaliste* 11 (15 March 1928).

Max Morise (born 1903): A cartoonist and writer whose work appeared regularly in *La Révolution Surréaliste*. In 1926, Gallimard published *Le mouvement: Poèmes, 1920–1924*.

Marcel Duchamp (1887–1968): Avant-garde artist and writer (also on chess) whose ready-mades (bicycle wheel, 1913; bottle rack 1914) pioneered Paris Dada.

Maria McDonald (1893–1987) trained as a singer in New York, Berlin, and Paris. She and Eugene Jolas married on 12 January 1926.

83 **a French-language anthology of modern American poets . . . a little volume of Negro spirituals:** *Anthologie de la nouvelle poésie américaine* and *Le nègre qui chante* were published on 3 June 1928 and 15 June 1928, respectively, by Kra, one of the main publishers of Surrealist works.

Volstead Act: Passed in 1919 to enforce the Eighteenth Amendment, the act, named after the legislator Andrew John Volstead (1860–1947), prohibited the manufacture and sale of alcohol.

Buster proved to be almost mute: Maria Jolas added a note by hand: "His act!"

Edmund Wilson (1895–1972): American writer and journalist who like Jolas was born in New Jersey and during World War I served in the U.S. Army. He was associate editor of the *New Republic,* 1926–31, and a close friend of John Dos Passos and F. Scott Fitzgerald. His *Axel's Castle* (1931) was one of the first comprehensive studies of literary modernism in English and included discussions of Rimbaud, Stein, and Joyce, among others. He met the Jolases in New Orleans in March 1926; see his *The Twenties: From Notebooks and Diaries of the Period,* ed. Leon Edel (1975), 259–61.

84 **Julius Friend:** Julius Weis Friend, editor of the *Double Dealer* (1921–26); he was the co-author with James Feibleman of *Science and the Spirit of Man* (1933), *The Unlimited Community* (1936), and *What Science Really Means* (1937).

Hamilton Basso (1904–64): Editor, fiction writer, and historian who contributed to *transition* 16–17 (1929) and 22 (1933).

James Feibleman (born 1904): He wrote novels and poems as well as books on philosophy, religion, anthropology, and literature.

Lyle Saxon (1891–1946): Writer and historian. Among his published works were *Father Mississippi* (1927) and *Fabulous New Orleans* (1928).

Bill Spratling: William Philip Spratling (1900–67) painted portraits of Sherwood Anderson and William Faulkner and wrote architectural books on New Orleans and Louisiana.

Natalie Scott (born 1890) Scott wrote a play, *Zombi* (1929), and a number of cookbooks and gourmet guides to New Orleans.

Fred Oechsner: Frederick Cable Oechsner (born 1902) was a co-author of *This Is the Enemy* (1942). One of the other authors was Jack Fleischer (born 1914), later editor-in-chief at the Munich bureau of the *Neue Zeitung,* where he would meet Jolas again later (see Chapter 12).

new poems from his own *Testament*: Sherwood Anderson (1876–1941), primarily a novelist and short story writer, wrote some poems that were published in *Others* and *Poetry* in 1917, among them his "Song to Industrial America," which Jolas translated; "Chant de l'Amérique industrielle," *Revue Européenne* 46 (1 December 1926), 1–4.

86 **Sherwood was kind enough to write the following introduction:** The text given by Jolas differs slightly from the text published in *Cinema* (New York, 1926), 9–10, mainly in punctuation and the number of paragraphs. Anderson's statement: "He is an Alsatian" has been corrected here by Jolas to "Alsace-Lorrainer." Anderson's introduction is dated "June 1st, 1926." A year later, Jolas wrote the introduction to the French translation of Anderson's *Winesburg, Ohio* (*Un païen de l'Ohio,* trans. Marguerite Gay, Paris, 1927).

CHAPTER 6

87 **the Nazis' attempt to conquer the Occident:** Two paragraphs have been omitted in which Jolas defends Surrealism and irrationalism against "Midwestern" naturalism in literature.

Elliot Paul (1891–1958): American writer and journalist who came to Paris in 1925. He took over from Jolas the role of writing a literary column for the Paris *Chicago Tribune,* entitled "From a Littérateur's Notebook," which first appeared on 27 December 1925.

modest hotel: Hôtel de la Gare des Invalides, 40 rue Fabert, in the 7th arrondissement.

88 **Edwin Muir's collection of essays:** Muir (1887–1959) was an English poet, novelist, critic, and, beginning in 1930, translator with his wife Willa of the works of Kafka. As a poet he was interested in "mythological dreams" (see *First Poems,* 1925, and *Chorus of the Newly Dead,* 1926), which might have attracted Jolas's attention.

lowercase *t*: The title of Ford Maddox Ford's *transatlantic review* was in all lowercase letters. Ford explains in his autobiography, *It Was the Nightingale* (1934), 299–300, that he had seen a lowercase title in a shop window and liked the effect, and that he had read poems by e. e. cummings (whose poetry as it happened, appeared in the first issue of *transatlantic review*).

One day he arranged: Anderson stayed in Paris from early December 1926 until 4 March 1927. In an undated card written in December 1926, he invited Stein and Toklas to join him in calling on the Jolases and added that "Maria sings wonderful Negro songs" (Sherwood Anderson and Gertrude Stein, *Correspondence and Personal Essays,* ed. Ray Lewis White, 1972, letter number 46).

90 **Archibald MacLeish** (1892–1982): American poet who lived in Paris between 1923 and 1928. He published poetry in six issues of *transition* (1, 6, 13, 15, 19–20, and 27).

Raymond Larsson (born 1901): American poet whose works appeared in *transition* during its first year (issues 1 and 4) and fiction (issue 5).

Kay Boyle (1903–93): American novelist and poet. She published poetry, prose, and book reviews in *transition,* beginning with the first issue.

Malcolm Cowley (born 1898): His poetry was published in *transition* (issues 10 and 13). He compiled the anthology "New York: 1928" for the second of these.

He also responded to Jolas's inquiries into the "Malady of Language" (issue 23) and the "Spirit and Language of the Night" (issue 27).

Matthew Josephson (1899–1978): American writer and translator. From 1922–24 he translated French and German avant-garde writers (Apollinaire, Aragon, Arp, Cendrars, Eluard, Huelsenbeck, Péret, Reverdy, Soupault, and others) for little magazines such as *Broom* and *Secession*. Characteristically, Jolas makes no mention of this fact. Josephson contributed poetry to *transition* (issues 9 and 15), and an "American letter" and book reviews (issues 14 and 15). Josephson's allegiances shifted toward proletarianism and social realism. He condemned the Surrealist avant-garde in his autobiography, *Life Among the Surrealists* (1962).

Ludwig Lewisohn (1882–1955): American novelist and translator of Goethe, Thomas Mann, and Richard Beer-Hofmann. He published fiction in *transition* issues 1, 2, and 13.

Carl Sternheim (1878–1942): German Expressionist writer. Jolas's translation and adaptation of Sternheim's story "Busekow" appeared in *transition* 1 (April 1927), 36–56.

a short story by Gottfried Benn: Benn (1886–1956) was a German Expressionist poet and writer. Jolas translation of Benn's story "The Island" appeared in *transition* 2 (May 1927), 64–73. Jolas also translated "The Birthday" in *transition* 5 (August 1927), 32–44. The same number contained his essay "Gottfried Benn," pp. 146–49.

Ezra Pound . . . *Exile* . . . three numbers: Pound's magazine lasted for four issues, 1927–28.

91 **a letter from an American poet:** Archibald MacLeish.

93 **that I was violently opposed to the political aberrations of Surrealism:** Jolas, "On the Quest," *transition* 9 (December 1927), 196.

94 **Aragon . . . "A Wave of Dreams":** "Une vague de rêves" appeared in *Commerce* 2 (Autumn 1924). Jolas quotes from this text in his "Rambles" of 22 March 1925.

95 **in nearby Lorraine:** A paragraph has been omitted in which Jolas describes nature in Colombey.

Whit Burnett (born 1899): His stories were published in *transition* between 1928 and 1932 (issues 13, 14, 16–17, 19–20, and 21). He co-founded *Story* magazine in 1931. In 1939 Burnett's *Literary Life and to Hell with It* was published.

Martha Foley: Co-founder of *Story;* a story of hers appeared in *transition* 18 (November 1929).

Carl and Lyda Einstein: Carl Einstein (1885–1940) and Lyda Guevrekian met in early 1928.

Harry and Caresse Crosby: Harry Crosby (1898–1929) was a writer and publisher who contributed to *transition* throughout 1928 and 1929, became associate editor in 1929, and supported the magazine financially as well. In fall 1929, Crosby's Black Sun Press published Jolas's *Secession in Astropolis*.

96 **most of his political statements:** A paragraph has been omitted in which Jolas again describes the scenery around Colombey.

Raabe: Wilhelm Raabe (1831–1910), a German realist writer. Possibly an error on

Jolas's part: the Surrealists were attracted to the plays of Christian Friedrich Grabbe (1801–36).

Borel: Pétrus Borel, pseudonym of Joseph-Pierre Borel d'Hauterive (1809–59), writer of unconventional and shocking prose and poetry who is regarded as one of the forerunners of Surrealism.

Novalis . . . translated: Jolas translated "Hymns to the Night" in *transition* 18 (November 1929), prefaced by his "Homage to Novalis."

The Language of Night: Published by Servire Press, The Hague, in 1932.

97 **Stekel's studies in psychic criminology:** Wilhelm Stekel (1868–1940) wrote widely on the link between deviant sexuality and criminal behavior.

Wyndham Lewis (1882–1957): British modernist writer.

Time and Western Man: Published in September 1927, the book contained a revised version of Lewis's essay "The Revolutionary Simpleton," which first appeared in his one-man journal, *The Enemy* 1 (January 1927), and which sharply criticized Joyce, Stein, and Hemingway. In "Art and the Radical Doctrines," *The Enemy* 2 (September 1927), xxiii–xxviii, Lewis extended his attack to the whole *transition* group, which he saw as Dadaist and Surrealist.

The Diabolical Principle: Published in book form in 1931, first in *The Enemy* 3 (1929), which deals with Jolas, Paul, and Sage's "First Aid to the Enemy," Jolas's "Enter the Imagination," and Paul's "The New Nihilism." In it, Lewis presents *transition* as a Surrealist and communist organ.

debate with "the Enemy": "First Aid to the Enemy," signed by Jolas, Paul, and Sage, in *transition* 9 (December 1927), 161–76.

"Enter the Imagination": *Transition* 7 (October 1927), 157–60. Jolas plays Maritain's Catholic dogmatism in *Frontières de la poésie* (1926) off against the Lautréamont-inspired "conception of conscious revolt, the assertion of the negative — or as the theologians would say — the diabolical principle" (158).

98 **Kafka . . . "The Sentence":** *Transition* 11 (February 1928), 35–47.

99 **Padraic Colum** (1881–1972): Irish writer and editor. He contributed to *transition* 21 (March 1932) a poem celebrating Joyce's fiftieth birthday.

Thomas McGreevy: "A Note on Work in Progress" by McGreevy appeared in *transition* 14, some of his poetry in issue 18, and an article on Joyce in issue 21. In 1959, *Our Friend James Joyce,* by Thomas and Mary McGreevy, was published.

Paul wrote an interpretative article: "Mr. Joyce's Treatment of Plot," *transition* 9 (December 1927).

I followed with another: "The Revolution of Language and James Joyce," *transition* 11 (February 1928), 109–16.

100 **H. G. Wells:** In a letter to Joyce dated 23 November 1928.

101 **Ezra Pound . . . some venereal disease:** On 15 November 1926, Pound wrote to Joyce, who had sent him some chapters from "Work in Progress": "I make nothing of it whatever . . . nothing short of divine vision or a new cure for the clap could possibly be worth all the circumambient peripherization." And in a letter to Hilaire Hiler dated 10 March 1937, Pound, conflating that "*transition* crap or Jheezus in progress," wrote: "I am about thru with that diarrhoea of consciousness."

Pound . . . American poet named Dunning: Pound's review "Dunning" appeared in his magazine *Exile* 3 (Spring 1928), 53–60, followed by a choice of Dunning's poems (61–68). Verse by Ralph Cheever Dunning, a neo-Victorian poet, was published in Ford's *transatlantic review* (which Jolas mentions in his "Rambles" of 9 November 1924), in several issues of the Chicago-based *Poetry* during the mid-1920s, and in an earlier issue of Pound's *Exile* (2 [Autumn 1927], 31–34). In 1926, Dunning's collection *Rococo* was published.

103 **Breton's "Introduction to the Discourse on the Dearth of Reality":** *Transition* 5 (August 1927), 129–45.

we wrote a final joint editorial: "A Review," *transition* 12 (March 1928), 139–47.

Returning from Paris: The rest of this chapter is an edited version inserted from a draft in possession of Tina Jolas, chapters 5 and 6, pp. 1–7.

104 **Warrants . . . in the winter of 1927:** The first autonomists were arrested in late December 1927. Dr. Roos surrendered to the authorities in November 1928 and was tried in January 1929. The government of Prime Minister Raymond Poincaré (1860–1934), a Lorraine patriot who saw his homeland's future only within France, took a tough approach to the autonomists.

set for trial in Colmar: The trial was held in spring 1928 and the verdicts announced in July 1928.

105 **legislative elections were held throughout France:** Early October 1929. The Chamber of Deputies reconvened later that month. Eventually, a bill proposing amnesty for the autonomists was introduced in late 1929 and passed in early 1930.

106 **Liétard:** Possibly a fictitious name; the real person behind it may be Jean Fourmann, the editor of the Forbach-based *La Voix de Lorraine / Die Stimme Lothringens*.

CHAPTER 7

107 **paramyth:** Jolas used this term in his introduction to *transition* 23 (July 1935), 7.
"Revolution of the Word": *Transition* 16–17 (June 1929), 13.

109 **a New York "slanguage" dictionary:** Theodore D. Irwin, "Slanguage: 1929," *transition* 16–17 (June 1929), 32–34.

Walter Winchell (1897–1972): American journalist and broadcaster who joined the New York *Daily Mirror* in 1928. His column "On Broadway" was nationally syndicated. In his "Letter to Walter Winchell," *transition* 19–20 (June 1930), 166–67, Jolas explained the usefulness of newspaper slang in experimental writing.

Theo Rutra: Jolas began using this pseudonym in *transition* 8 (November 1927).

clock for dartalays: Several texts that follow in the manuscript have been omitted: "Storiette," "Rodeur," "Dusk," "Gulf," and "Story."

110 **ma milalla loo:** The poem "Astirolamistura!" has been omitted.

Benjamin Crémieux (1888–1944): French writer and critic known for his works on modern European literature. He died in Buchenwald concentration camp. For his assessment of the "Revolution of the Word," see his "Rule of Words," trans. Maria McDonald Jolas, *transition* 19–20 (June 1930), 189–93. The article first appeared in the French journal *Candide*.

Marcel Brion (born 1895): French novelist, critic, and art writer, reviewed *tran-*

sition 16–17 in the Marseille-based *Cahiers du Sud* 17, no. 4 (April 1930), 234–35. The review contains a French translation of the "Revolution of the Word" manifesto.

V. F. Calverton: Victor Francis Calverton (1900–40), American editor, lecturer, and author of numerous books on contemporary issues. See his "Revolution-in-the-Wordists," *Modern Quarterly* 5, no. 3 (Fall 1929), 276–83.

our *apologia pro verbo nostro:* Jolas, "Necessity for the New Word," *Modern Quarterly* 5 (3), pp. 273–75; Sage, "New Words for a New Age," pp. 289–91; Gilbert, "Why a Revolution of the Word?" *Modern Quarterly* 5 (3), pp. 284–85.

Harold Salemson: "James Joyce and the New Word," *Modern Quarterly* 5 (3), pp. 294–312.

Herbert Gorman (1893–1954): Writer and literary critic who was also the first biographer of James Joyce. He contributed the article "Experimentalism — and Experimentalists" to the forum in *Modern Quarterly* 5 (3), pp. 292–93.

S. D. Schmalhausen: Samuel Daniel Schmalhausen (born 1890), a writer and critic. He contributed the article "Gertrude Stein" to the discussion in *Modern Quarterly* 5 (3), pp. 313–23.

Pierre Loving (born 1893): American writer and critic, author of "The Confusion of Words," *Modern Quarterly* 5 (3), 286–88. His articles and poems appeared in *This Quarter* and the New Orleans magazine *The Double Dealer*. He also translated Hölderlin and Claire Goll into English.

111 **the language of the centuries to come:** A long quotation from Stuart Gilbert's contribution has been omitted.

Samuel Putnam (1892–1950): American poet, novelist, and translator from the Romance languages. He edited the *New Review* (five issues in 1930–32) and wrote *Paris Was Our Mistress: Memoirs of a Lost and Found Generation* (New York, 1947).

Putnam launched an assault: The manifesto "Direction" (1930), signed by Putnam, Harold Salemson, and Richard Thomas, called "for a contemporary expression, not an out-of-date modernity." For details, see Putnam's *Paris Was Our Mistress,* 227–29. Contradicting Jolas's assertion that the *New Review* ceased publication at the time (it did so only in 1932) and that Putnam returned to America, Putnam writes that he and Jolas had a friendly chat in the Café Flore.

too much under the influence of . . . Pound: Pound was associate editor of the *New Review* and contributed articles in which he discussed the merits of communism and fascism.

112 ***Mots-Déluge:*** Published 26 December 1933 by Editions des Cahiers Libres.

a *Comoedia* critic: Pierre Lagarde, in *Comoedia,* 12 March 1934.

Poètes à l'Ecart: This anthology was edited by Carola Giedion-Welcker in 1945, and included poetry by Arp, Ball, Huidobro, Kandinsky, Péret, Picabia, Picasso, Schwitters, Stramm, Tzara, and others.

Francis Vielé-Griffin (1864–1937): American-born French poet and translator.

113 **"Polyvocables":** *Transition* 23 (July 1935), 65–66.

114 **"The Grala":** This text, which is reminiscent of Kafka's *Metamorphosis,* was first published in *transition* 23 (July 1935), 22–23, and again in *I Have Seen Monsters and Angels* (Paris, 1938), pp. 21–22, the first literary text in the volume.

115 **"a curious word welder":** The title of Feeney's review in the Catholic weekly
    America, 11 February 1939, 451–52.
    "Subliminal subtleties," said the *Cincinnati Inquirer:* In a review by James John-
    son Sweeney, 8 January 1933.
    Stephen Spender . . . "an unfortunate development": Reviewing Jolas's col-
    lection *I Have Seen Monsters and Angels,* Spender (1909–96) wrote dryly:
    "Mr. Jolas is an American who spent his childhood in Europe and suffers from
    the misfortune of having to write in three languages." He went on: "He is un-
    fortunate, but he is not, as he seems to think, discovering a new language with
    James Joyce" ("Where Dons Delight," *New Statesman and Nation,* 30 Septem-
    ber 1939, p. 464).
    Mercure de France . . . a commendatory reception: In a review by Jean Catel;
    Mercure de France, 1 December 1939, pp. 439–40.
    James Laughlin . . . "New Words for Old": *Story* 9, no. 53 (December 1936), p. 109.
116 **"little household words" so dear to Sherwood Anderson:** In his introduction to
    Stein's collection *Geography and Plays* (Boston, 1922), Anderson had described
    Stein as a poet "uplifting our English speaking stage" and living among "the
    little housekeeping words, the swaggering bullying street-corner words, the
    honest working, money saving words" (8).
    the first to make a translation of her work into French: Jolas had translated
    Stein's "Captain Walter Arnold, a Play" for his *Anthologie de la nouvelle poésie
    américaine* (Paris, 1928), 217–18.
    Four Saints in Three Acts: The opera had its premiere in Hartford, Connecticut,
    on 8 February 1934 before it moved on to New York City the same month. The
    libretto was first published in *transition* 16–17 (June 1929).
117 **I published her latest work once more:** Stein's prose piece "She Bowed to Her
    Brother" and her typically solipsistic reply to Jolas's enquiry into the "Met-
    anthropological Crisis" appeared in *transition* 21 (March 1932). After Paul's
    departure as editor, and upon hearing rumors that a new series of *transition*
    was to be launched, Stein went to great lengths to persuade Jolas to include her
    work in it. In November 1931, she sent Jolas her book *How to Write* (1931), which
    he liked and from which he quoted in his pamphlet, *The Language of Night*
    (1932). Following the publication of Stein's *The Autobiography of Alice B. Toklas*
    (1933), the Jolases and others published a "Testimony Against Gertrude Stein,"
    transition 23 (July 1935), in which they responded to what they felt to be a per-
    sonal attack on them. Stein had stated that *transition* was run by Elliot Paul and
    implied a link between her absence from the journal and *transition*'s decline.
    "A Play Without Roses": Written in 1932 and published in *Portraits and Prayers*
    (New York, 1934), 200–202.
    open to young American writers and artists: The end of a poem from *Cinema*
    has been omitted.
118 **"Why do Americans live in Europe":** *Transition* 14 (Fall 1928).
    Hilaire Hiler (1898–1966): American-French writer on art, dance, and fashion.
    A. Lincoln Gillespie, Jr.: Philadelphia schoolteacher who went to Paris and be-
    came an expatriate writer.
    Paul Morand contributed a long essay: It is not clear to which essay Jolas refers.

The anonymous article "Paul Morand Knocks Exiles Who Like Paris Better Than America," which appeared in the Paris *Tribune* of 28 February 1930, reports on a talk given by Morand at a luncheon of the American Club on 27 February. A few weeks later, another anonymous article, "American Patrons," appeared in the Paris *Tribune* of 6 July 1930. It consisted almost entirely of quotes from an article by Morand in *Le Journal.* The bibliography of Morand's works, however, cites only one contribution to that journal, in 1928.

119 **"An International Quarterly for Creative Experiment":** First used in *transition* 13 (Summer 1928). For issues 21 (March 1932) and 22 (February 1933) the subtitle "An International Workshop for Orphic Creation" was used.

"An Intercontinental Workshop for Vertigralist Transmutation": Subtitle to *transition* 23 (July 1935).

St.-John Perse (pen-name of Alexis Saint-Léger Léger, 1889–1975), Symbolist poet and French diplomat.

120 **T. S. Eliot and I were the first to translate him into English:** His verse was simultaneously translated into English by Eliot (in his *Criterion*) and by Jolas (in *transition*) in the issues that appeared in February 1928.

even their hallucinations and nightmares: A lengthy paragraph about Stuart Gilbert's career and literary taste has been omitted.

121 **Georges Ribemont-Dessaignes** (1884–1972): French writer and contributor to *transition* associated with the Dada and Surrealist movements.

122 **the future of the machine civilization for my taste:** Two quotes by Cowley and Josephson have been omitted, as well as two paragraphs mentioning other international writers and artists who called at the *transition* offices.

Laura Riding (1901–91): American poet, short-story writer and critic. She and Gertrude Stein were friends, though only for a short time. Riding mentioned Stein favorably in her *Survey of Modernist Poetry* (London, 1927) and *Contemporaries and Snobs* (London, 1928). The book contained the essay "T. E. Hulme, the New Barbarism, and Gertrude Stein," part of which had appeared in *transition* 3 (June 1927). Graves and Riding founded the London-based Seizin Press, which in April 1929 published Stein's *An Acquaintance with Description.* But in Riding's *Four Unposted Letters to Catherine* (Paris, 1930), the prefatory letter beginning "Dear Gertrude" alludes to a quarrel between Stein and Riding which eventually estranged them from each other.

Richard Aldington (1892–1962): English writer, poet, and translator.

Locarno pact: After negotiations in Locarno from 5 to 16 October 1925, a treaty was signed in London on 1 December by Germany, Belgium, France, Great Britain, Italy, and Poland obliging the signatories to seek peaceful solutions to international conflicts. The treaty further stipulated the demilitarization of the occupied Rhineland.

August Stramm (1874–1915): German poet and playwright. Influenced by the futurists, he developed a condensed poetic language. Jolas published Stramm's poem "Verzweifelt" in German in the "Revolution of the Word" section of *transition* 16–17 (June 1929).

123 **Scheler:** Max Scheler (1874–1928), a German philosopher with a strong interest in phenomenology, anthropology, and sociology. A Catholic, he reflected on

man's religious consciousness, and his writings are characterized by a search for the spiritual. His concept of the "new man," formulated in his pantheistic *Die Stellung des Menschen im Kosmos* (1928), echoed Expressionist tendencies and influenced Jolas.

Husserl: Edmund Husserl (1859–1938), founder of phenomenology.

Heidegger: Martin Heidegger (1889–1976), a German philosopher. His *Sein und Zeit* (1927) is generally regarded as a break with his phenomonological beginnings and a shift toward Existentialism. In his lecture *Waṣ ist Metaphysik?* (1929), he stated that Western civilization was in steep decline, which resulted in alienation and angst. He proclaimed the necessity of searching for an authentic way of being. Jolas translated this pamphlet into English but could find no publisher for it (Draft E, 9/197, n.p.). For Jolas's assessment of Heidegger's impact on post-war German intellectual life, see Chapter 12.

Jaspers: Karl Jaspers (1883–1969), a German philosopher and friend of Heidegger during the 1920s. His *Die geistige Situation der Zeit* (1931) and three-volume *Philosophie* (1932) presented the Existentialist position. He believed in the role of prophetic vision in philosophy. In 1945 Jolas asked Jaspers to join the editorial board of the journal *Die Wandlung*.

my friend . . . Carl Einstein: Einstein had settled in Paris in 1928. The following five paragraphs have been taken from Draft E (9/197, pp. 4–5, n.p.) and replace pp. 209–10 of Draft D.

124 **Döblin** (1878–1957): Medical doctor and writer.

Georg Heym (1887–1912): Expressionist poet.

Alfred Mombert (1872–1942): Early Expressionist writer whose erratic visionary poetry must have attracted Jolas.

Ulysses . . . **in an excellent translation by Georg Goyert:** Published by Rhein Verlag, Zurich, in 1927.

125 **Döblin emigrated:** First to Zurich, then in September 1933 to Paris.

Carl Sternheim (1875–1942): German writer. His wedding to Pamela Wedekind (born 1906), daughter of the playwright Frank Wedekind (1864–1918) and his wife Tilly (1886–1970), took place on 17 April 1930. At the end of that month, the Sternheims moved to Brussels.

"Es ist und bleibt ein kulturloses Volk": They are and remain an uncultured people.

125 **Ullstein brothers:** The Ullstein publishing house, founded by Leopold Ullstein (1826–99) in 1877, was expanded by his sons Hans (1859–1935), Louis (1863–1933), Franz (1868–1945), Rudolf (1873–1964), and Hermann Ullstein (1875–1943). In 1934, the publishing house, and its newspapers and magazines as well, had to be sold to the Nazis.

Alfred Flechtheim (1878–1937): Art dealer, publisher, and editor. He emigrated in 1933 to London, where he died four years later.

126 **Carl Hofer** (1878–1955): German Expressionist artist.

Max Herrmann-Neisse (1886–1941): A German Expressionist writer, he came to Zurich on 2 March 1933 and went to England in September of that year.

Thomas and Heinrich Mann: Thomas Mann (1875–1955) came to the United States in 1938 via Switzerland, to which he had emigrated in 1933. His brother

(1871–1950) emigrated to France in 1933, and seven years later to the United States.

Walter Mehring (1896–1981): Writer, performer, and member of Berlin Dada, emigrated to Austria and France, and from there in 1941 to the United States.

Alfred Neumann (1895–1952): Writer who emigrated to France in 1938 and to the United States in 1941.

Theodor Plivier (after 1933, Plievier; 1892–1955): Writer of documentary novels. Jolas errs here: Plievier did not emigrate to the Americas; rather, he emigrated to France in 1933, and in the following year, via Sweden, to the USSR. In 1945, he returned to Germany and settled in the Soviet-occupied zone.

Erich Maria Remarque (pseudonym of Erich Paul Remark; 1898–1970): Author of *All Quiet on the Western Front*. He emigrated to Switzerland in 1931 and to the United States in 1939.

Ernst Toller (1893–1939): Expressionist playwright, communist. He emigrated to Switzerland in 1933, and after a brief stay in England came to the United States in 1936. He committed suicide in a New York hotel.

Berthold Viertel (1885–1953): Expressionist author and stage director. He came to the United States in 1933 but went on to England and returned in 1939. During his exile, he did mostly film and theater work.

Franz Werfel (1890–1945): A German writer who emigrated to France in 1938 and to the United States in 1940. He lived in New York and in 1942 moved to Beverly Hills, where he died three years later.

Paul Zech (1881–1946): An Expressionist writer who emigrated to Argentina in 1933 and died in Buenos Aires.

Stefan Zweig (1881–1942): Austrian writer. He emigrated to England in 1934, then to the United States in 1940. In 1941 he went to Brazil, where he committed suicide a year later.

Döblin told me to see his friend: The following eight paragraphs are from Draft C (7/166), pp. 346–49.

127 **Kretschmer:** Ernst Kretschmer (1888–1964), a German psychiatrist who developed a typology for the relation between body shape and character. His publications include *Körperbau und Charakter* (1921) and *Geniale Menschen* (1929).

Rosenberg: Alfred Rosenberg (1893–1946), an extreme right-wing writer and publicist and a fanatical supporter of National Socialism as early as the 1920s. The Nazis claimed that his *Mythus des 20. Jahrhunderts,* first published 1930, expressed their worldview.

Moeller van den Bruck: Arthur Moeller van den Bruck (1876–1925), a German writer and journalist whose early interest in Italian futurism gave way to adherence to Nazism.

128 **Grosz . . . still living in Berlin:** George Grosz (1893–1959) left Germany for America in May 1932.

he had found his ultima Thule: A brief paragraph about Benn has been omitted.

129 **After a few weeks:** This sentence is taken from Draft C (7/166), p. 357.

Cary Baynes (1883–1977): American psychologist and early member of the Jung circle. She and her husband, Helton Godwin Baynes (1882–1943), translated several of Jung's works into English. By the time the Jolases visited Jung and her, she had translated Jung's *Contributions to Analytical Psychology* (1928). In *transition* 21 (March 1932), Jolas, in the section "Metanthropological Crisis: Crisis of Man," published an excerpt from Baynes's translation of Richard Wilhelm and Jung's *The Secret of the Golden Flower*.

Jung was visited by the Jolases in early 1930. The Jung Archive in Zürich-Küsnacht has no record of that visit, but the Jolases addressed letters to Jung in 1935 and 1939.

"Poetry and Psychology": Published in *transition* 19-20 (June 1930), 23-45, the first text in the opening section, "Dream and Mythos." Jung declared that the secret of poetic creation was to delve once more into the primal state of *participation mystique*. This blend of Lévy-Bruhl and Jung was an integral part of Jolas's outlook from 1930 on.

The Jung "seminary": The following nine paragraphs are taken from Draft C (7/166), pp. 358-62.

130 **Siegfried Giedion** (1888-1968): Both Giedion, a Swiss art historian and architect, and **Carola Giedion-Welcker** (1893-1973), a Swiss art and literary critic, contributed to *transition*.

131 **Max Rychner** (1897-1965): Swiss critic, editor, and translator. A slightly revised version of Jolas's "On the Quest" (*transition* 9) appeared in *Neue Schweizer Rundschau* 21 (1928), 244-48, and Rychner's "Divagation" appeared in *transition* 19-20 (June 1930).

Shortly after New Year in 1933: Joyce and his family went to Zurich on 22 May 1933 and stayed there until September, except for a holiday in Evian in August. Jolas joined them in late spring or early summer 1933.

134 **with a cover by Arp:** *Transition* 21 (March 1932).

Erich Mühsam (1878-1933): German anarchist and revolutionary writer, killed in Oranienburg concentration camp on 11 July 1933.

Else Lasker-Schüler (1869-1945): A German poet who emigrated to Zurich in 1933 and traveled to Palestine in 1939, where she remained following the outbreak of the war.

CHAPTER 8

135 **roaming the earth:** A sentence and a poem, "Patmos," have been omitted.

William Bird (1889-1963): American journalist, author, co-founder of Consolidated Press Association and, since 1920, its European manager in Paris. In Paris, Bird, who was also a printer, had founded "Three Mountains Press," which published Hemingway's collection *In Our Time*.

Morris Gilbert (1894-1971): Journalist and novelist who worked for the Paris *Herald* (1921-25), the *New York Times* (1925-29), and as a freelance foreign correspondent in Paris for various American papers and a news syndicate. In 1937 he returned to New York, where he joined the *World Telegram*.

Lansing Warren: He contributed a literary column, "Dear Pard," to the *Chicago Tribune* (Paris) in 1924 and 1925.

Edgar Mowrer (1892-1977): Journalist and columnist, who was a war correspondent in World War I and later became chief of the *Chicago Daily News* bureau, first in Berlin and then in Paris.

Leland Stowe (born 1899): Journalist, author, and later professor of journalism. He worked for the *New York Herald* and was the *Herald Tribune's* Paris correspondent from 1926 to 1935. He wrote *Nazi Means War* (1934).

136 **After two months . . . Emile was released:** December 1935. The *Chicago Tribune* carried the following AP reports: "French Citizen Sentenced for Slur on Hitler. Metz, France, Oct. 22 — Emile Jolas, French merchant of Stiringwendel, France, was reported today to be in jail at Lerchesflur, near Saarbrücken, on a charge of insulting Reichsführer Hitler. French authorities' efforts to have him released have been futile. Jolas, who is understood to have brothers in Louisville, Ky., and Chicago, was said to have been sentenced to eighteen months in jail for making a remark about Hitler in a discussion with a Saarlander while standing near the frontier. The report had it that the Saarlander called the Nazi police, who crossed the frontier and seized Jolas" (23 October 1935). "France Urged to Try to Gain Release of Man Jailed by Nazis. Paris, Nov. 23 — The family of Emile Jolas, French merchant reported to be in jail at Saarbrücken, Germany, asked the French foreign office today to try to obtain his release. The family expressed fear for his health. Mrs. Eugene Jolas, sister-in-law of the imprisoned man, said previous official representations made by her husband, a writer, had apparently gone unheeded. She said her brother-in-law had been in jail since Oct. 11 and was in a 'nervous state.' Eugene Jolas asked the foreign office to secure his brother's release on Oct. 23. At that time he said Emile was on French territory when he was alleged to have made insulting remarks about Reichsführer Hitler and was carried over the frontier and placed in jail."

This frontier-terror haunted me: Several poems constituting pp. 225–28 of Draft D have been omitted: "Tremble-Fear," "All Souls' Day," and the poems beginning with the lines "Oh peaceful dead of the marches," "It was no longer a golden age," "Dusk-smilers we wandered into shadows," and "The old world town sighs."

137 **Earlier that year:** Transitional sentence introduced by the editors.

plebiscite: The plebiscite, a provision of the Versailles treaty of 1919, was held on 13 January 1935, with 90.8% of the population voting in favor of the region's "reintegration" into Germany. On 1 March 1935 the Saar was formally incorporated into the Reich.

Drawn by the impact: The following ten paragraphs are from Draft B (6/154), pp. 399–403.

Zurück zu Mutter!: Back to Mother!

Bill Shirer: William Lawrence Shirer (born 1904) worked at the copy-desk of the Paris *Chicago Tribune* from August 1925 until summer 1927 before becoming the paper's European correspondent. He describes his encounter with Jolas in Paris in his memoir *Twentieth-Century Journey* (Boston, 1976).

139 **the Lorraine land:** Two paragraphs have been omitted in which Jolas describes a pro-Nazi editorial in the Forbach paper following the plebiscite.

I settled in a skyscraper hotel: Jolas resided at the Hotel Winslow.

140 **Percy Winner** (1899–1974): Journalist and novelist. Having worked in Paris for the *Herald* and the *Chicago Tribune,* in London and Rome for Associated Press, and as news and foreign editor for the New York *Evening Post,* he became Havas's

chief correspondent for North America and also pursued a broadcasting career in the 1930s.

Leon Edel (1907–1997): Journalist, literary critic and biographer, best known for his biography of Henry James. He worked in Paris 1936–38, served in World War II, and in June 1945 was appointed director of the "German News Service" in Bad Nauheim. In September 1945, GNS became DANA, the German-American news agency which Edel headed until March 1946 when he returned to the United States.

141 **I intermingled words from several languages:** A long poem which begins with the line "Nightern clung to summer delirium the trees were stricken" has been omitted.

Drew Pearson (1897–1969): Publicist and columnist, worked as a freelance foreign correspondent in Europe, before joining the Baltimore *Sun* in 1929 and directing its Washington bureau.

Burns Mantle (1873–1948): He wrote a weekly column, "New York Theaters," in the Paris *Chicago Tribune* in 1924 and from September to December 1925.

142 **Gene McHugh** (1893–1962): Journalist with the New York *Daily News* from 1919 to 1961, serving as city editor, night managing editor.

that sensation-hungry organization again: A paragraph, two poems ("Tittle-tattle-Sheet Nocturne," and "Lobstershift"), and a French "word-mimicry" beginning with the sentence "Nous rêvassions dans la nuit fétide" have been omitted.

Richard Huelsenbeck (1892–1974): German writer and psychiatrist, co-founder of the Dada movement in Zurich 1916, traveled in the 1920s as ship's doctor and correspondent for German publishing houses to Africa, Asia, America. In 1936, he emigrated to the United States, where he called himself Charles R. Hulbeck. His autobiographical fragments have been published posthumously; he recounts his early years in exile in "Als Emigrant in New York," *Reise bis ans Ende der Freiheit: Autobiographische Fragmente*, ed. Ulrich Karthaus and Horst Krüger (Heidelberg, 1984), 254–66.

143 **James Johnson Sweeney** (1900–86): Writer, art critic, museum director. Before meeting Jolas in 1936, Sweeney had written art criticism, directed exhibitions on twentieth-century painting and sculpture at the University of Chicago (1934) and "African Negro Art" at the Museum of Modern Art, New York (1935), and embarked on a lectureship at New York University.

Wayne Andrews (1913–87): His fiction was published in *transition* 23 (July 1935) and 24 (June 1936).

144 **James Agee** (1909–55): Journalist and writer whose poems were published in *transition* 24 (June 1936) and 26 (1937). His first major collection of poetry, *Permit Me Voyage*, had appeared in 1934. At the time, Agee was film critic for *Fortune* and *Time* magazines.

Horace Gregory (born 1898): Reviewer for poetry magazines.

Muriel Rukeyser (born 1913): One of her poems was published in *transition* 26. The title of her volume *Theory of Flight* (1935) might have attracted Jolas's curiosity.

Oliver Wells (1907–70): A poem by Wells was published in *transition* 25.

the *New York Times* ... **transition movement:** Edward Alden Jewell, "In the Realm of Art: Along Paths that Summer Fields. Concerning the Revived 'Transition' and Various Thorny Problems of the Day," 12 July 1936, sect. 9, p. 7.

Time ... *News-Week* ... **two articles:** "Zululand," *Time* magazine, 13 July 1936, pp. 56–57; "Transition: In a New Dress It Renews Its Experimental Lease," *News-Week,* 11 July 1936, p. 40.

145 **Léger ... designed a special cover for *transition:*** *Transition* 24 (June 1936).

149 **as soon as vacation time should come around:** Four paragraphs have been omitted in which Jolas describes his stay in Montreal.

152 **marked interest in England's Elizabethan literature:** Jolas contributed an essay, "La révolution de langage chez les Elizabéthains," to *Cahiers du Sud* 154 (June–July 1933), 50–52, a special number devoted to Elizabethan literature.

Albert Béguin ... a remarkable study: *L'Âme romantique et le rêve* (Marseille, 1937). The excerpt entitled "The Night-Side of Life" was translated by Jolas and Gilbert, *transition* 27 (April–May 1938), 197–218.

Jean Ballard ... Romantic issue: Issue 194 (May–June 1937), "Le Romantisme allemand," comprised 444 pages.

155 **Ouspensky:** P. D. Ouspensky, a Russian mathematician and mystic. His reply to Jolas's "Inquiry about the Malady of Language" appeared in *transition* 23 (July 1935), 153–55. In *Tertium Organum* (1912) Jolas would have found two highly attractive ideas: the linguistic aspect — Ouspensky calls for "new parts of speech" and "an infinite number of words" (108–9, quoted in *transition* 23, p. 180) — and the "vertical" aspect, suggesting that the philosopher-artist is constantly moving to higher dimensions.

Richard Jefferies (1848–87): English naturalist, novelist, and essayist who in his work combined detailed observation of nature and mystical vision. His work was appreciated only after his death.

Saint John of the Cross (1542–91): Spanish mystic and founder, with St. Teresa, of the Carmelite order. His treatise *The Ascent of Mount Carmel — The Dark Night* begins as a commentary on the poem, "The Dark Night," and describes how to reach perfection through union with God.

Henry Vaughan (1621–95): Welsh poet, author of religious verse.

Paul Claudel (1868–1955): French poet and diplomat. In *Vertical: A Yearbook for Romantic-Mystical Ascensions* (New York, 1941), Jolas described Claudel as "the leading French Catholic poet of today" (p. 6).

O. V. de L. Milosz: Oscar Vladislas de L. Milosz (1877–1939), Lithuanian writer and diplomat. Jolas translated Milosz's "Canticle of Knowledge" in *Vertical,* pp. 50–59.

156 **"Revive our sense of wonder":** In his essay "Algernon Blackwood: Novelist and Mystic," *transition* 23 (July 1935), 89–96, Gilbert linked Blackwood's (1869–1951) fiction to *transition*'s anthropological discussion about the primal personality, and wrote: "To revive our sense of wonder is, perhaps, the highest function of imaginative art" (91).

"Far beyond the words": Quoted by Gilbert, p. 92. *The Centaur* has epigraphs by Novalis, William James, and Gustav Theodor Fechner, all of whom are crucial to Jolas's outlook. Jolas translated Fechner's *Life After Death* into English (New York, 1943); the introduction was by William James.

CHAPTER 9

160 **Ananke Strikes the Poet:** The title has been taken from one of the cover sheets for "Man from Babel," Draft B (6/150). This chapter, not included in Draft D, has also been taken from Draft B (6/155; pp. 580–609). Some of the passages are identical with Jolas's articles, "Homage to the Mythmaker," *transition* 27 (1938), and "My Friend James Joyce," *Partisan Review* March–April 1941, 82–93.

the sudden death of his father: John Stanislaus Joyce died on 29 December 1931.

162 **a trip we had planned to Feldkirch:** In summer 1932. The Joyces brought Lucia on 3 July to Feldkirch, where Maria Jolas had agreed to look after her, returned to Zurich, but came back to spend 10 August to 8 September 1932 in Feldkirch.

163 **"The Mime of Mick, Nick and the Maggies":** Published separately in June 1934 by the Servire Press, which also published *transition*.

165 **Bernhard Fehr** (1876–1938): Professor of English in Zurich from 1927 on.

Borach: Georges Borach (died 1934). His "Gespräche mit Joyce" was first published in the *Neue Zürcher Zeitung*, 3 May 1931, and reprinted by the Berlin magazine *Omnibus* in 1932.

166 **an article on *Ulysses* by Dr. Jung:** In 1930, Jung wrote the article as a preface to the German translation of Frank Budgen's book *The Making of 'Ulysses'*, but the publisher, Daniel Brody, did not include it in the book. A revised version of the essay was published as "Ulysses: Ein Monolog" in *Europäische Revue* 8 (9), 547–68, and included in Jung's book, *Wirklichkeit der Seele* (1933).

167 **Dunne's theory of serialism . . . *An Experiment with Time:*** John William Dunne's book was first published in London in 1927. Second and third editions came out in 1929 and 1936.

168 **Jousse . . . Paget:** Jolas's commentaries appeared as "The New Vocabulary," *transition* 15 (February 1929), 171–75, and "Marginalia to Work in Progress," *transition* 22 (July 1933), 101–5.

he even went so far as to consult Dr. Jung: Urged by Maria Jolas on 28 September 1934, Joyce had Lucia transferred to a Küsnacht sanatorium where Jung was on the staff.

the human types Yeats presents in "The Vision": See Richard Ellmann, *James Joyce* (rev. ed., New York, 1982), 596n.

169 **his life-long dream of seeing Copenhagen:** On 18 August 1936 the Joyces went via Liège and Hamburg to Copenhagen, where they stayed until 13 September.

171 **someone sent him an issue of the *Osservatore Romano:*** According to Ellmann, a friend of the Joyces, the French novelist and critic Jacques Mercanton (born 1910), read a positive review of *Finnegans Wake* from the Vatican paper to Joyce when they left unoccupied France for Zurich in December 1940. Jolas may be referring to an earlier review.

175 **One morning I knew it was "Finnegans Wake":** This happened some time in August 1938; see Joyce's letter to Maurice James Craig of 24 August 1938.

177 **Hermann Broch . . . able to escape as a result of his intercessions:** The Austrian

writer Broch (1886–1951) was arrested in March 1938 immediately following Austria's Anschluß to Nazi Germany. Friends, among them Joyce, obtained permission for him to emigrate, first to England, then to America. In 1932, Broch had written an important essay on Joyce's work, "James Joyce und die Gegenwart" (James Joyce and the present) which Eugene and Maria Jolas translated for the *James Joyce Yearbook* (Paris: Transition Press, 1949).

178 **sin-haunted HCE:** Two paragraphs have been omitted in which Jolas describes his motivation behind the final issue of *transition*. A slightly different version of these paragraphs has been included in Draft D and can be found in the previous chapter.

CHAPTER 10

179 **Maria and our two little girls:** The first eight pages of this chapter have been taken from Draft C (7/168), pp. 541–56. In telling these events, Jolas drew on his wife's account; Maria Jolas, "Joyce en France 1939–40," *Mercure de France* May–August 1950, pp. 45–58.

Georges and Marguerite Duthuit: The art critic Duthuit (born 1891) later edited the six issues of *Transition Forty-Eight* (1948–50), which was dedicated to presenting contemporary French thought and art in English translation.

180 **Sitzkrieg:** Static or nonaggressive warfare.

182 **Elle qui n'a été que dorlotée toute sa vie:** She who has been pampered all her life.

187 **his death in Zurich:** Joyce died 13 January 1941.

André Masson (1896–1986): French artist expelled from the Surrealist group in 1929. He moved to Marseilles in December 1940 and, after Maria Jolas acted as guarantor for him, in March 1941 embarked with Breton for the United States, where they arrived, via Martinique, in May. In October, he moved to New Preston, Connecticut, where the Jolases were then living. Jolas translated Masson's *Mythology of Being: A Poem* (New York, 1942).

188 **Many weekend guests:** This paragraph and the next have been inserted from Draft B (9/198).

189 **my mother had died:** Christine Jolas, née Ambach, died 10 October 1942, aged seventy-three.

Jean Wahl (1888–1974): French philosopher, author of influential books on Hegel and Kierkegaard in which he emphasized moral issues, and a supporter of Christian Existentialism. In 1948, he became advisory editor to *Transition Forty-Eight.*

Pierre Chareau (1883–1950): French architect and decorator. In 1942, Maria Jolas and Chareau organized an exhibition, "Free France," which was shown in Madison Square Garden and traveled under her direction to Boston and Quebec.

Antoine de Saint-Exupéry (1900–44): French aviator and author best known for his *Little Prince* (1943); declared missing after a flight mission in World War II.

Denis de Rougemont (1906–85): Swiss diplomat, writer, and cultural historian. He was interested in Surrealism and occultism before being won over by Protestant theology. He supported the Resistance from Switzerland and, in his diplomatic capacity, from the United States. In 1947, he founded in Geneva the Centre for European Culture in support of European federalism.

Yves Tanguy (1900–55): French Surrealist artist who came to the United States in 1939 and became a U.S. citizen nine years later.

Moïse Kisling (1891–1953): French artist of Polish descent.

Kurt Seligmann (1900–62): Swiss artist and book illustrator who came to the United States in 1939.

Max Ernst (1891–1976): German painter and sculptor, who joined the Dadaists and later the Surrealists. He settled in the United States in 1941 and returned to France twelve years later.

Darius Milhaud (1892–1974): French composer. He went to the United States in 1940 and subsequently taught at Mills College in California for seven years.

Henri Bernstein (1876–1953): French dramatist who came to America in 1940.

190 **The Gaullist canteen:** The canteen was in operation from 1943 until 1 March 1946 and served a total of more than 100,000 servicemen.

Robert Fitzgerald (born 1910): American poet.

Norman MacLeod (born 1906): Left-wing American writer and editor. In 1930 Jolas had contributed to MacLeod's little magazine *The Morada.*

192 **"Babel: 1940":** *New Directions* (5) (Norfolk, 1940), 319–24. Jolas's name was given as Eugène Jolás.

Dick Hottelet: Richard Curt Hottelet (born 1917): A foreign correspondent for United Press. He joined the OWI in 1942 and stayed there until 1944. After the war, he was a CBS correspondent in various European capitals.

193 **Ed Barrett** (1910–89): Journalist for and associate editor of *Newsweek* before joining OWI in 1942. In 1943, he was transferred to PWD in London, and a year later was made director of OWI's overseas branch.

Louis Atlas: American reporter, a regular columnist for the Paris *Chicago Tribune,* 1931–34. He returned to U.S. in 1935 to work for the Overseas Press Association.

Jack Iams (Samuel H. Iams, born 1910): Mystery novelist and journalist. He joined OWI in 1942, spent one year in French equatorial Africa, and was then assigned to Lisbon and Brussels, where he stayed until November 1945.

194 **Lévi-Strauss:** Claude Lévi-Strauss (born 1908): French social anthropologist and structuralist; lectured at São Paulo University from 1934 on and at the New School for Social Research in New York beginning in 1939. In 1950, he returned to France.

197 **SHAEF:** Supreme Headquarters, Allied Expeditionary Forces.

199 **Cyril Connolly** (1903–74): English novelist and literary journalist. *Horizon,* the magazine he founded with Stephen Spender, ran from 1940 to 1949. In *Horizon* 27 (March 1942), Connolly reprinted Jolas's translation of Kafka's "In the Penal Colony," which had appeared seriatim in *transition* 25 through 27.

Alex Comfort (born 1920): English poet, novelist, and critic who now lives in Los Angeles. He also pursued a distinguished medical career.

Nicholas Moore (1918–86): Son of philosopher G. E. Moore, prolific poet, anthologist, editor of the little magazine *Seven* (1938–40) and of *New Poetry* (1944–45). He was a central figure in the New Apocalypse movement in the 1940s.

Ruthven Todd (1914–78): Scottish poet, critic, and lecturer; became a U.S. citizen.

Dylan Thomas (1914–53): Popular Welsh poet, story writer, and broadcaster. A poem and a story by Thomas appeared in *transition* 25 (Fall 1936).

Francis Scarfe (1911–86): English novelist, literary critic, and translator of French poetry.

Anne Ridler (born 1912): English religious poet, librettist, and translator.

Henry Treece (1912–66): English poet and author of children's books; one of the founders of the New Apocalypse movement. In 1939 he reviewed one of Jolas's volumes of poetry for *Seven*.

La France Libre: This paper appeared between 15 November 1940 and 1947 in London, edited by André Labarthe.

201 **LST:** Landing ship, tank.

202 **Bravig Imbs** (1904–46): American poet and journalist, known to Jolas from Paris. Imbs worked for the *Chicago Tribune* during the 1920s; concerning this period of his life, see his autobiography, *Confessions of Another Young Man* (New York, 1936). He published poetry in *transition* (issues 2, 5, 6, 10, and 18) and translated for the magazine poetry by André Gaillard and Viteslav Nezval. During World War II, he was a radio correspondent and broadcaster for the OWI.

Le salaud: That swine.

Maquis: The French underground resistance movement.

203 **FFI:** *Forces Françaises de l'Intérieur* (French forces of the interior), soldiers fighting the Germans underground in occupied France during World War II.

204 **Wasser, Wasser:** Water, water.

Va demander à Hitler: Go ask Hitler.

mitraillette: Submachine gun.

206 **Robert A. McClure** (1897–1957): Chief of PWD at SHAEF, 1944–45, and director of the Information Control Division of the Military Government in Germany, 1945–47.

Luther Conant (born 1911): American journalist who worked for Boston and New York newspapers. In World War II he headed the Press and Information Department at SHAEF in London and Paris and, after May 1945, at Information Control Division in Berlin. He later became a correspondent for *Time* magazine, and public relations consultant.

sagesse: Wisdom, prudence, good behavior.

208 **Max Pol Fouchet** (1913–80): French writer and art critic with an interest in ethnology and anthropology. In 1939 he founded *Fontaine,* which then supported the Resistance movement and published international modernist writing. From 1948, he was, with Jolas, advisory editor to *Transition Forty-Eight.*

Breton's prolegomena to a "new Surrealist manifesto": "Prolégomènes à un troisième manifeste du surréalisme ou non" appeared first in the New York review *VVV* 1 (June 1942) in French and English. Fouchet's Editions Fontaine published in 1945 Breton's paper *Situation du surréalisme entre les deux guerres.* The edition that Jolas is here referring to might have been Breton's *Les manifestes du surréalisme suivis de Prolégomènes à un troisième manifeste du surréalisme ou non* (Paris, 1946).

211 **Battle of the Bulge:** Final German counteroffensive in the Ardennes area of southern Belgium, from 16 December 1944 until January 1945.

212 **ack-ack guns:** Anti-aircraft guns (from British signalmen's telephone pronunciation of "AA," short for "anti-aircraft").

213 **Hans Habe** (1911–77; until 1941, János Berkessy), Hungarian-born writer and journalist. He grew up in Vienna, worked in Geneva from 1935 to 1939, joined the French army in 1939, became a German prisoner of war in 1940, and escaped to America in 1941. He served until 1945 in the U.S. Army, training staff for psychological warfare. In 1944 he became director of the German Department at Radio Luxembourg; in 1945–46, chief of its American press; and in 1946, chief editor of the *Neue Zeitung*, Munich.

Bill Hale: William Harlan Hale (1910–74), American editor and writer. Beginning in 1941, he was editor in charge of radio broadcasts to Germany from OWI, New York; chief of the German Propaganda Division for OWI, London; and chief of Radio Luxembourg for PWD-SHAEF. After 1945 policy adviser for Information Control Division with U.S. forces in Europe.

CHAPTER 11

215 **Heinrich Hollands** (born 1876): A Social Democratic printer with no journalistic experience, he became the first German licensee of a democratic newspaper, the *Aachener Nachrichten,* which began appearing weekly on 24 January 1945 with a print run of forty thousand copies.

218 **Peter de Mendelssohn** (1908–82): A German writer and journalist who emigrated in 1935 to London, where he had been a correspondent until 1933. He worked in the Ministry of Information and in 1944 joined the Press and Information Department at SHAEF. In December 1944 he went to Allied headquarters in Paris, and in July 1945 he became American press officer in Berlin, where he founded *Der Tagesspiegel.*

219 **caught and sentenced:** Eight poems from Jolas's collection, "News from Germany," have been omitted.

When Cologne was captured: The city fell on 5 March 1945.

222 **von Arnim . . . had envisaged a "Christian Germanic Society":** Arnim founded the Berlin-based patriotic Christlich-Deutsche Tischgesellschaft in 1810, at a time when Germany was occupied by the French.

Fichte . . . "superiority of German greatness" . . . first to demand *Lebensraum:* Johann Gottlieb Fichte (1762–1814) wrote *Reden an die deutsche Nation* (Speeches to the German nation), 1807.

articles by Thomas Mann, Franz Werfel and other democratic German writers: Mann's radio broadcast "Über die deutsche Schuld" of 8 May 1945 "was received enthusiastically" by OWI London (letter from OWI, New York, to Mann, 10 May 1945), and published the same week in the Heidelberg *Mitteilungen.* Excerpts were also published in the New York *Aufbau* of 18 May 1945. Already while in Aachen, Jolas had had similar material published. Mann's "Eine Botschaft an das deutsche Volk" (A message to the German people), excerpted from his NBC broadcast of 14 January 1945, appeared on the front page of the second issue of *Aachener Nachrichten,* 31 January 1945. Werfel's speech "An das deutsche Volk" (To the German people) was disseminated by the OWI in spring 1945.

226 **Dick Crossman:** Richard Howard Stafford Crossman (1907–74), British left-wing intellectual politician. In 1932 he married Eva Landau, a German Jew. He taught philosophy at Oxford University (1930–37), joined the German Section of the BBC (1939), and became head of the German Section (PWD) and assistant chief of PWD-SHAEF (1944–45). From 1945 until his death, he was Labour MP for Coventry. He served in the late 1960s as minister for housing and secretary of state for social services.

ETO: European Theater of Operations.

CHAPTER 12

228 **Fred Jacobson:** He succeeded Jolas as DANA's chief scrutiny officer in January 1947 and served at DANA until it merged in August 1949 with Deutscher Presse-Dienst to become the Deutsche Presse-Agentur in August 1949.

229 **Eddie Glynn:** Robert E. Glynn was later to become deputy director of DANA.

Sylvia Weiss: Sylvia Weiss-Glynn, American press officer.

230 **Edel . . . left the army:** In March 1946.

Jack Stuart (1880–1975): Head of Press Control at DANA from March 1946 until summer 1948.

231 **Egon Jameson** (1895–1969; until 1933, Egon Jacobsohn): German-Jewish journalist and writer. He emigrated in 1934 to London, where he worked for the BBC and Soldatensender Calais. He joined the U.S. forces in 1945 and helped establish the DANA news archive in Bad Nauheim; he was later columnist for the *Neue Zeitung* and author of popular travel and how-to books in German. See his autobiography *Wenn ich mich recht erinnere . . .* (1963).

Franz Borkenau (1900–57): Austrian-born communist writer and political scientist, exiled in England and America; foreign news editor at DANA, 1945–46.

232 **Sternheim had died:** On 3 November 1942 in Brussels.

Alfred Flechtheim had succumbed: Jolas is wrong here; Flechtheim had died in London on 9 March 1937.

George Grosz was living in America: Grosz moved to the United States in June 1932. He died in 1959 while in East Berlin.

Pfemfert . . . in Mexico: Franz Pfemfert (1879–1954), a left-wing writer and critic, editor of the Expressionist periodical *Die Aktion.* He emigrated in 1933 and in 1940 arrived in Mexico City, where he died fourteen years later.

Benn . . . "double life": Benn's autobiography, *Doppelleben,* was published in March 1950; excerpts appeared in various magazines in 1949.

233 **Johannes Becher** (1891–1958): Expressionist writer. A communist since 1919, he returned to East Berlin from exile in Moscow to become a leading cultural organizer. In 1954 he was appointed first minister of culture of the GDR.

Elisabeth Langgässer (1899–1950): Catholic poet and novelist; her chef-d'oeuvre, *Das unauslöschliche Siegel,* was published in 1946.

Ernst Jünger's much discussed "peace" pamphlet: Jünger's brochure *Der Friede* was published in 1945.

235 **the first Nuremberg trials:** Held between 20 November 1945 and 1 October 1946.
   Suzanne Czapski (born 1923): She married von Paczensky. She and

236 **Ernst Michel** (born 1924), who had spent five years in a Nazi concentration camp, were among the first Germans to be employed by DANA as trainee journalists (in October 1945).

237 **James Aronson** (born 1915): Journalist in Boston and New York. In 1945–46 he was chief of press of the Western Military District, ICD, Germany.

238 **favorable impression:** A paragraph has been omitted in which Jolas describes a dinner banquet following the meeting.

239 **first democratic elections in Land Hesse:** The elections were held on 30 June 1946. The SPD gained 44.3% of the vote; the CDU, 37.3%; and the KPD, 9.7%. Along with Bavaria and Baden-Württemberg, which voted on the same day, Hesse was the first state to hold free elections after 1945.

240 **VE Day:** Victory in Europe Day (8 May 1945).
   Al Rosenberg: Albert G. Rosenberg (born 1918), a German Jew who in 1937 emigrated with his parents to America. An intelligence officer with PWD during and after the war, he screened prospective German staff at DANA for political and personal suitability. He and his team also assisted Kogon with his report on the Nazi concentration camps.
   Dolf Sternberger (1907–89): Journalist, political scientist, and author of numerous books on art and intellectual and social history.
   Werner Krauss (1900–76): Appointed professor of Romance studies in Marburg in 1933, he became critical of National Socialism and joined a communist resistance group in 1940. Arrested in 1942, he was sentenced to death. In 1944, thanks to the efforts of his friends, the sentence was commuted to lifelong imprisonment. Krauss later prepared a long statement of his experience under the Nazis, in which he described in detail his ouster from the university when he refused to spy on his colleague Erich Auerbach in exchange for being allowed to retain his professorial post, and his confinement and torture in a concentration camp for his communist activities (including the distribution of anti-Hitler pamphlets). In 1945, he was appointed director of the newly created Institute of Romance Studies in Marburg. He became a member of the German Communist Party. In 1947, he accepted a chair at the University of Leipzig in the Soviet-occupied zone.
   Alfred Weber (1868–1958): Social scientist who taught in Prague and Heidelberg. In 1945 he joined the newly reconstituted German Social Democratic Party.
   Sternberger . . . Nazi-sponsored "poet" Eckart: Dietrich Eckart (1868–1923), a nationalistic anti-Semitic writer, a member of NSDAP even before Hitler, and the originator of the Führerkult surrounding Hitler. Sternberger was banned by Goebbels from publishing on 5 May 1943.

241 **Sternberger prepared a statement:** Sternberger's first draft of a proposal for an intellectual magazine in occupied Germany is dated 3 August 1945, the day he first met Jolas. A later version of this proposal that differs in tone and substance from the excerpts quoted by Jolas is published in Sternberger's *Gesammelte Schriften*, vol. 11: *Sprache und Politik* (Frankfurt, 1991), 113–28.

244 **Eugen Kogon** (1903–87): Writer, publicist, and political scientist. Beginning in

1927, he was a journalist in Vienna. He spent 1939 to 1945 in Buchenwald concentration camp. He is the author of *Der SS-Staat* (1946), and co-editor of the liberal magazine *Frankfurter Hefte.* From 1951 to 1968 he was professor of politics in Darmstadt.

DENA: Draft D contains a footnote by Jolas: "A Danish news bureau having claimed priority for the name DANA, our organization changed its own to read DENA. It was later called by its German directors Deutsche Presse-Agentur (dpa), by which name it is still known at this writing (1951)."

245 **Kurt Frenzel** (1901–70): Licensee of the Augsburg *Schwäbische Landeszeitung,* whose detailed coverage of the Nuremberg trials and firm conviction that the Germans were collectively guilty of the Holocaust resulted in his appointment as deputy head of the DANA Board of Directors in March 1946.

248 **Director, Information Control Division:** The letter by Robert McClure was followed by a poem, beginning with the words "Unsere Worte waren wie Stahl," which has been omitted.

251 **We know that during the war:** The following two paragraphs are from Draft E (9/199), n.p.

    Dachböden: Allusion to Ernst Kreuder's (1903–72) best-selling novel, *Die Gesellschaft vom Dachboden* (Stuttgart, 1946).

    Walter Kolbenhoff: Pseudonym of Walter Hoffmann (1908–93), German writer and publicist; emigrated in 1933 to Denmark and Sweden; from 1947 to 1948 editor at the Munich *Neue Zeitung. Von unserm Fleisch und Blut* was published in 1947. "Laßt uns Zeit: Stimmen aus der jungen Schriftstellergeneration" was published in *Neue Zeitung* of 25 January 1948.

252 **As for the new novelists:** The following three paragraphs are from draft fragments (12/231), pp. 7–9.

    blutiger Realismus: Hans Werner Richter's phrase (1908–93), taken from a speech given in 1947. Richter's essay "Literatur im Interregnum," *Der Ruf* 15 (15 March 1947), and his editorial in the first issue of *Der Skorpion* express less anti-Romantic sentiments.

    Bannwaldsee: Emended from "Odenwald"—an error on Jolas's part. Odenwald is a region in southern Hesse; Bannwaldsee is a village near Füssen in Allgäu, where the meeting was held, 6–7 September 1947. It is considered to be the beginning of Gruppe 47, the most influential writers' group to have emerged in post-war Germany.

    Der Skorpion: Shortly before going to print, the first issue of this magazine, edited by Richter, was refused a license by the American military authorities on grounds of nihilism. Nonetheless, about two hundred copies were circulated among writers and journalists following the second Gruppe 47 meeting on 8–9 November 1947. Jolas's knowledge of the project suggests that he was kept well informed, probably by Walter Kolbenhoff. A reprint of the issue was published in 1991 by Wallstein Verlag, Göttingen. Three paragraphs that followed, in which Jolas quotes from Richter's editorial, have been omitted.

    Gustav René Hocke (born 1908): Writer and journalist who contributed to post-war newspapers and magazines and wrote extensively on art history and literature. His literary works today are little known; Jolas might have had in mind Hocke's stories in *Der Ruf* and his novel *Der tanzende Gott* (1948).

Hermann Kasack (1896–1966): Novelist and poet. His best-known work, *Die Stadt hinter dem Strom* (1947), combined realism and Symbolism and was one of the most widely discussed novels in the immediate post-war period.

End and Beginning: *Ende und Beginn: Sechs Erzählungen von Gegenwart und Zeit* (Berlin, 1946).

August Scholtis (born 1901): The only one of the three mentioned by Jolas who had not freshly emerged as a writer, he pursued a literary career in post-war Germany. After having had much of his work published under the Nazis, Scholtis went on to produce fantastic narratives such as *Die Zauberbrücke* (Berlin, 1948).

Wolfdietrich Schnurre (born 1920): Writer, journalist, and co-founder of Gruppe 47. His short stories were widely published in newspapers and magazines at the time. His first collection of stories did not appear until 1950.

deserves to be known beyond . . . Germany: Kasack's novel was translated into English by Peter de Mendelssohn (London, 1953).

253 **Rudolf Hagelstange** (1912–84): Religious poet and essayist. *Venezianisches Credo* was first published in Verona, Italy, in 1945 and then reprinted in Germany (Frankfurt, 1946).

Marie Luise Kaschnitz (1901–74): Poet and short-fiction writer, born into an Alsatian officer's family. She was a regular contributor to *Die Wandlung*. In her poems she combines classical form and a hermetic, elliptical language. "Ode to Frankfurt" is probably her "Rückkehr nach Frankfurt," first published in *Die Wandlung* 1 (10–11) in November 1946.

Werner Bergengruen (1892–1962): Religious poet and fiction writer who expressed a belief in a "heile Welt," an ideal world free of problems.

Günter Eich (1907–72): Modernist poet and author of numerous radio plays. He favored hermetic nature poetry. Jolas's translation of Eich's "Verses on Many Evenings" appeared in *transition* 14 (Fall 1928).

Hans Egon Holthusen (1913–97). Poet and essayist influenced by Rilke, Eliot, and Auden.

Manfred Hausmann (1898–1986): Journalist, poet, and fiction writer whose religious works are influenced by Romanticism and existentialism.

Hans Carossa (1878–1956): Classicist poet and short story writer.

Rudolf Alexander Schröder (1878–1962): Prolific religious Existentialist poet and translator.

Erich Kästner (1899–1974): German writer and journalist with left-wing sympathies. He is best remembered as the author of popular children's books. As a poet, he was the author initially of satirical poetry and later of moralistic light verse. From 1945 to 1948 he was arts editor at the Munich *Neue Zeitung*.

Walter Heist: Critic and poet. His "Gesänge an den Mann auf der Straße" would appear to in the first issue of *Der Skorpion*.

The older generation: The following six paragraphs are from Draft E (9/199).

Ricarda Huch (1867–1947): *Die Romantik* comprises two volumes first published in 1899 and 1902 and often reprinted since.

to cover the event: A sentence has been omitted. For Jolas's report to an American audience on the congress, held between 19 and 21 May 1948, see his "German Letters in Ruins: A Report from Frankfurt," *New York Times Book Review,* 4 July 1948, pp. 7 and 13.

Although there were: This sentence has been inserted from draft fragments (12/231), p. 17.

Fritz von Unruh (1885–1970): His "Rede an die Deutschen," a speech delivered at the congress, was published separately, with a preface by Eugen Kogon (Frankfurt, 1948).

Elisabeth Langgässer: Her address to the congress, "Die Sprache des Schriftstellers in Isolierung und dialogischer Begegnung," was published only in 1988, *Düsseldorfer Debatte* 6–7, pp. 32–36.

254 the General Assembly of the United Nations was in session: It took place in September 1948.

256 Berlin blockade: The blockade was in effect between March 1948 and 12 May 1949.
ISD: The Information Services Division, which succeeded ICD in August 1948.

EPILOGUE

270 In a few days: This epilogue has been taken from 14/260.

271 Hofmannsthal's . . . "Letter to Lord Bacon": The Austrian writer's "Brief des Lord Chandos" was first published in 1902. An essay in the form of a letter, it accounts for the fictitious author's silence after years of creative writing, concluding that words have lost their meaning and fail the writer. It is generally regarded as a milestone of the modernist crisis of language.

273 impulse: The word is the editors' conjecture: the torn manuscript page reads "im."

INDEX

Works listed are by Eugene Jolas unless otherwise indicated

Calder, Sandy, 144

Calverton, V. F., 110, 300

Campbell, Rosalie, 69

Carossa, Hans, xxix, 253, 317

Catholicism, xvii, 4, 5, 72, 155, 170

Césaire, Aimé, 187

Chaplin, Charlie, 168

Chapman, Jack, 44, 142

Chesnutt, James, 215, 216, 238, 261

Chicago, 36–37

Chicago Tribune Paris edition, 64–68; "Rambles Through Literary Paris," xv, 71–72, 75–77, 79–81

Cinema, xiv, 86, 117

Clarke, Dick, 44, 142, 285

Claudel, Paul, 73, 155, 191

Collective unconscious, xix–xxii, 129

Comfort, Alex, 199, 311

Commerce (review), xix, 75, 94, 293

Conant, Luther, 228, 312

Connecticut, 46–47, 187

Connolly, Cyril, 199, 311

Cooper, James Fenimore, xii, 12

Cowley, Malcolm, xx, 73, 90, 296–97

Crane, Hart, 37, 90, 111–12, 120, 122

Crémieux, Benjamin, 110, 299

Crevel, René, 121

Crosby, Henry, 95, 120–21, 297

Cummings, e. e., 48

Czapski, Suzanne, 235–36

Dada, xxii, 58, 63–64, 74, 76, 82, 123, 128; Zurich origins of, 130–31, 142

Daily News (New York), 41–45, 109, 142

DANA (Deutsche Allgemeine Nachrichten-Agentur), xxiii, xxiv, 228–31, 234–35, 314; Berlin office of, 231–33; elections coverage by, 238–40; at the Nuremberg trials, xxv, 235–36; turned over to Germany, 245–47

Darrah, David, 64, 65, 71, 290

De Chirico, Giorgio, 81

De Gaulle, Charles, 95, 211

Delteil, Joseph, 82, 294

Desnos, Robert, xix, 82, 96, 294–95

DeWitt Clinton High School, xiii, 23–24, 196

Döblin, Alfred, xvi, 124–26, 253, 303

Documents (review), 115

Double Dealer (review), 84, 85

Dreams, 23, 113–15, 167

Drieu La Rochelle, Pierre, 74

Du Bos, Charles, 73, 293

Duchamp, Marcel, 82, 295

Dunne, John William, 167, 309

Duthuit, Georges, 188, 189, 191, 310

Ebbinghaus, Carl H., 251–52

Eberhart, Richard, 191

Edel, Leon, 140–41, 228, 230, 235, 248

Eich, Günter, 253

Einstein, Carl, xxvii, 95, 123–24, 128, 143, 208, 297, 303

Eisenhower, Dwight D., 218, 248

Eliot, T. S., xxv, 120, 122, 154, 178, 243, 302

Eluard, Paul, xix, xx, 80–82, 94, 96

English language: Americanization of, 111; Jolas's education in, 15, 19, 21, 22–25, 28, 47–50; Jolas's poems in, 24–25, 46, 48, 49–50; in New York's melting pot, 147–48

Ernst, Max, 81, 90, 189, 311

Expressionism, xxii–xxiii, 49, 56, 58, 64, 90, 122–24, 126, 232–33

Fanning, Ray, 48

Fargue, Léon-Paul, 74–75, 110, 191, 293

"Faula and Flona," 109

Fichte, Johann Gottlieb, xxvi, 222, 313

Fiske, Dwight, 69, 70–71, 291

Fitzgerald, Scott, 67–68

Flechtheim, Alfred, 125–26, 232, 303

Fleischer, Jack, 249, 251

Forbach, xii, 282; autonomist agitation in, 103; Jolas's childhood in, xxxvii, 5–10, 14–16; Jolas's interwar visits to, 53–56, 64, 136; ruin of, 261–69; Uncle John's remembrances of, 18–19

Ford, Ford Madox, xv, 71, 100, 291–92

Fort Sheridan (Illinois), xiii, 36–37
Fouchet, Max Pol, 208, 312
France: Allied liberation of, 200–201, 203; Nazi invasion of, 179–85; PWD-SHAEF tour of, 202–6
Frankfurt, 257–58, 270
French language, 7–10
Frenzel, Kurt, 245, 316
Freud, Sigmund, xxi, 96, 124, 129–30, 141, 166

Galantière, Lewis, 193–94
German language, 10, 18, 41, 225, 270; denazification of, xxiii, xxv, 228, 244, 246; and Expressionism, 122–24; in the Lorraine patois, 7–10; provincialism of in Pittsburgh, 28
Germany: democratization in, 227–31; *feuilleton* style of journalism in, 64, 213–14, 237, 251; Jolas's interwar trips to, 64, 123–28; postwar literature of, xxix, xxxviii, 251–54; reformation of journalism in, xvi, xxiii–xxix, 214, 215, 218, 222, 224–25, 227–31, 237–38, 245–46, 249
Gernsback, Hugo, 45, 286
Gide, André, 73, 74, 292
Giedion, Siegfried, 130, 131–32, 134
Giedion-Welcker, Carola, 130, 131–32
Gilbert, Don, 230
Gilbert, Morris, 135, 190, 201, 206–7
Gilbert, Stuart, 76, 95, 99, 100, 110, 156, 173, 174, 294
Gillespie, A. Lincoln, Jr., 118, 301
Giraudoux, Jean, 72, 292
Glynn, Robert E., 235, 314
Goebbels, Joseph, 202, 233
Goethe, 1, 59, 123, 124, 164, 222
Goll, Yvan, xix, 63, 64, 112, 189, 289
Gorman, Herbert, 110, 174, 300
Görres, Joseph von, xxv, 1
Grober, Abraham, 209–11
Gronauer, Hans, 231
Grosz, George, 126, 128, 142, 232, 304

Habe, Hans, 213, 313
Hale, William Harlan, 213, 220, 313
Harris, Frank, xiv, 49–50, 287
Hart, Jim, 198
Hauss, Charles, 104
Havas News Agency, 140–42, 148
Heidegger, Martin, xxv, 123, 155, 156, 240, 243, 253, 303
Heidelberg, 220–26, 237–38, 240–44
Heist, Walter, 253, 317
Hemingway, Ernest, 74, 78, 90, 119, 169–70, 294
Herrmann-Neisse, Max, 126, 134, 303
Heuss, Theodor, xxiv, 238
Hiler, Hilaire, 118, 301
Hitler, Adolf, 125, 128, 138–39, 158, 199, 221, 233, 306
Hölderlin, Friedrich, 62, 96, 289
Hollands, Heinrich, 215, 219, 313
Holocaust, xxv, xxviii, 220–23
Holthusen, Egon, 253
Horizon (review), 199
Hottelet, Richard, 192, 311
Huch, Ricarda, xii, 253, 317
Huelsenbeck, Richard, 63, 142–43, 307
"Hymn for the Lonely," 30

I Have Seen Monsters and Angels, 94
ICD (Information Control Division), 227–28, 245, 318
Illing, Werner, 252
Ink, xiv, 48–49

Jackson, Joe, 39
Jacobson, Fred, 228, 314
James, Henry, 117, 141, 146
Jameson, Egon, 231, 314
Jarry, Alfred, 75
Jaspers, Karl, 123, 222, 240, 242–43
Jean Paul, xix, 56, 71, 287
Jefferies, Richard, 155, 308
John, Uncle, xii, 15, 18–19, 26
Johnson, Ed, 193
Jolas, Armand (brother), 137, 262, 264
Jolas, Betsy (daughter), xv, 149–50

Lewis, Wyndham, xx, 97, 298
Lind, Ralph, 25–26
Lindsay, Vachel, 151
London, 196–200
Lorraine, xii, xxxvii–xxxviii; autonomist agitation in, 103, 106; interwar climate of, 57, 59; journalism in, 13–14; Jolas's childhood in, 5–16; Kaiser Wilhelm's visits to, 11–12; linguistic turmoil in, xvi–xvii, 6–10; ruins of, 259–66
Loving, Pierre, 110, 118, 300
Luxembourg, 211–13

McAlmon, Robert, 74, 76, 78, 79, 100, 118, 121
McClure, Robert A., 206, 228, 245, 248
McCormick, Robert R., 68, 291
McDonald, Maria. *See* Jolas, Maria
McGreevy, Thomas, 99, 100, 161, 298
McKee, Chester, 69, 70–71
MacLeish, Archibald, 90, 121, 296, 297
Madeleine, Cousin, 15, 19, 32
Mann, Thomas, 61, 123, 126, 222, 253
Marburg journalistic congress, 237–38
Masson, André, 187–88, 189, 310
Masson, Paul, 80, 81
Matisse, Henri, 116
Mauriac, François, 72, 292
Mauthner, Fritz, 166
Mayenne, 91–92, 97
Medal of Freedom, 245
Merrill, Stuart, 72, 112, 292
"Metamorphosis," 49
Metz, 12, 14, 210, 259, 261
Michel, Ernst, 235, 236, 315
Miller, Henry, 111, 155, 208
Milosz, Oscar V. de L., 155–56, 191
Miró, Joan, 90
Modern Quarterly, 110
Monnier, Adrienne, 74–75, 76, 89
Monologues sur les Boulevards, 71
Monroe, Harriet, 37
Montigny seminary, 14, 210–11
Morand, Paul, 72, 76, 118, 292, 301–2
Morise, Max, 82, 295
Mots-Déluge, 112

Mühsam, Erich, 134, 305
Muir, Edwin, 88
Munich, 248–51

Nancy, 209–11
Nazism, xxiii, 123, 125, 127–28, 134, 136–39, 155
Nerval, Gérard de, 62, 71, 80, 289
Neue Zeitung (newspaper), 248–51, 257
Neumann, Heinrich, 13
New Directions (anthology), 192
New Jersey, 4–5
New Orleans, 83–86
New Review, 111
New York, xii–xiv, 1–2; Columbus Avenue grocery store, 20–22; *Daily News,* xv, 41–45, 109, 142; Havas News Agency, 140–42, 148; Jolas emigrates to, 1–2, 15–17, 18; Jolas's English education in, 22–25; Jolas family in, 149–50, 179, 186; Jolas returns to, 135, 141–42; Jolas's wedding in, 82–83; as linguistic melting pot, 145–48; Office of War Information in, 192; refugees in, 142, 189–90; Stechert bookshop, 22, 26; tenement-house on 100th Street in, 19–22; Uncle John's apartment in, 18–19
New York Herald Paris edition, 66
New York Herald Tribune, 270
News-Week magazine, 144–45
Nietzsche, Friedrich, xvi, 28, 51, 73
Noll, Marcel, xix, 58, 63, 90, 288
"Note to Another Civilization," 51–52
Nouvelle Revue Française, 73–74
Novalis, xii, xx, xxii, xxvi, xxvii, 1, 56, 71, 96, 281
Nuremberg trials, 235–36

Ouspensky, P. D., 155, 308
OWI (Office of War Information), 192–96, 213, 218, 222, 313

Paris, 2; Allied liberation of, 206, 208; American literary colony in, 79–80, 87, 117–19; *Chicago Tribune* office in, 64–68, 71–72; on the eve of World War II,

Stricker, Bill, 235
Stuart, Jack, 230, 262, 265, 314
"Suggestions for a New Magic," 93
Sullivan, John, 162, 169
Sullivan, Thomas, 24
Surrealism, xix–xxiii, xxviii, 74, 76, 82,
    208; in America, 143; Jolas's break with,
    xx, 188; neo-Romanticist, 93–94, 96
Surrealists, xvi, 80–83, 94, 96; in *transi-
    tion*, 90, 93
Swanson, Gloria, 66
Sweeney, James Johnson, 143, 307

Tanguy, Yves, 90, 129, 189, 311
Theresa, Aunt, xii, 15, 19
This Quarter (review), 78–79, 121
Thompson, Francis, 29, 155, 284
Thomson, Virgil, 117
Thoreau, Henry David, 47
Tibbett, Lawrence, 169
Tieck, Ludwig, 1, 13, 56, 281
Time magazine, 144
"To My Mother Engulfed in the War,"
    xxiii, 191–92
"To the Tremendum," 109–10
Toklas, Alice, 78, 88, 116
Toller, Ernst, 49, 126, 286, 304
Trakl, Georg, 56, 58, 122, 124, 287
transition, xi, xiv–xvi, xxii, 77; American
    issues of, 143–45; American writing
    in, 90, 121–22; Boyle-Riding debate in,
    122; at Colombey-les-deux-Eglises, 88–
    89, 91, 110; dream transcriptions in,
    115; Elliot Paul's contribution to, 102–
    3; European writers translated in, 98;
    experimental writings in, 98, 119; first
    issue of, 87–93; Gertrude Stein's works
    in, 116; Harry Crosby's contribution to,
    120–21; as higher journalism, 93; Joyce
    homage in, 160–61; Jung's work in, 129;
    New York "slanguage" dictionary in,
    109; "Revolution of the Word," xvi,
    xviii–xx, xxxviii, 107–8, 110–12; at St.-
    Dizier, 98; St.-John Perse's works in,
    119–20; Surrealist works in, xix, 90, 93;

tenth anniversary issue of, 151–54; ver-
    ticalism in, 156–57; "Work in Progress"
    by Joyce in, 89, 97–101, 108, 131, 154, 172;
    Wyndham Lewis's denunciation of, 97
Tull, Clyde, 191
Tzara, Tristan, 60, 63, 75–76, 112, 131,
    142–43, 293

Underwood, Edna Worthley, 45, 286
Union City (New Jersey), xii, 4
Unruh, Fritz von, xxix, 253–54, 318
Untermeyer, Louis, xiv, 36, 284

Valéry, Paul, 74, 75
Vaughan, Henry, 155, 308
Verlaine, Paul 75
Vertical, 191
Verticalism, xx, 121, 156–59
Vico, Giambattista, 164
Vitrac, Roger, 82, 110, 294
Vix, Geneviève, 70–71
Volksblatt (Pittsburgh), xiii, 26–31
Vyshinsky, Andrei, 255–56

Wahl, Jean, 155, 189, 310
Walsh, Ernest, 78–79, 121, 294
Wandlung, Die (periodical), xxiv–xxv,
    240–44
War of 1870, 5, 9, 14
Waterbury *Republican*, xv, 46–47
Weber, Alfred, 240, 243, 315
Wedekind-Sternheim, Pamela, 125, 303
Weiss, Sylvia, 229, 314
Wells, H. G., 100–101
Werfel, Franz, 49, 126, 222, 253, 286
Whitman, Walt, xiv, 29, 45, 48, 146
William II (Kaiser Wilhelm), 11–12
Williams, Oscar, 36, 49, 190, 284
Williams, William Carlos, 190
Wilson, Edmund, 83–84, 173, 295
Winchell, Walter, 109, 299
Winner, Percy, 140, 306–7
World War I, xiii, 31–36, 56–57, 128
World War II, xiii, xxxv–xxxvi; Allied
    invasion of France, 200–201, 203; Battle

World War II (*continued*)
of the Bulge, 211–12, 215; and German guilt, 220–24; Nazi invasion of France, 179–85; SHAEF Psychological Warfare Division, xxiii, 197–206, 209–26; United States Office of War Information (OWI), 192–96, 213

Zenner, Jacques, 210
Zurich, 129–34, 142–43, 162, 165–66